UNNEUTRAL IRELAND

UNNEUTRAL IRELAND

An Ambivalent and Unique Security Policy

TREVOR C. SALMON

CLARENDON PRESS · OXFORD
1989

Oxford University Press, Walton Street, Oxford OX2 6DP
Oxford New York Toronto
Delhi Bombay Calcutta Madras Karachi
Petaling Jaya Singapore Hong Kong Tokyo
Nairobi Dar es Salaam Cape Town
Melbourne Auckland
and associated companies in
Berlin Ibadan

Oxford is a trade mark of Oxford University Press

Published in the United States
by Oxford University Press (USA)

British Library Cataloguing in Publication Data
Salmon, Trevor C.
Unneutral Ireland: an ambivalent and unique security policy.
1. Ireland (Republic). Foreign relations. Neutrality
I. Title
327.417
ISBN 0-19-827290-1

Library of Congress Cataloging in Publication Data
Salmon, Trevor C.
Unneutral Ireland, an ambivalent and unique security policy / Trevor C. Salmon.
Bibliography: p. Includes index.
1. Ireland—National security. 2. Ireland—Neutrality.
3. Ireland—Non-Alignment. I. Title.
UA829.I7S25 1987 341.6'4'09417—dc 19 89-3113
ISBN 0-19-827290-1

Set in 11/12 pt Bembo
by Colset Pte Ltd., Singapore
Printed in Great Britain
by Biddles Ltd.
Guildford and King's Lynn

In gratitude to my late parents, and in love to my wife June and daughter Jenny, particularly for bearing with my obsession over many years

PREFACE

IN any work such as this a great debt is owed to many people. I am especially grateful to those current and retired members of the Irish Department of Foreign Affairs, Department of Defence, and Permanent Defence Force who assisted me in the research for this study. Similarly, I must thank those Irish politicians of all parties, especially those familiar with the burdens of office, who gave of their time, experience, and insight. In accordance with their wishes, the specific contributions of those interviewed remain anonymous. I am also aware that by no means all of them agree with either the central hypotheses of the work or its conclusions.

I am also indebted to the library staff of the National Institute for Higher Education, Limerick, and of the University of St Andrews, especially Ken Fraser and Miss S. Rowe. I am grateful for the copyright permissions and the help received from the Public Records Office, Kew, and the State Paper Office, Dublin. I also owe a debt to Mrs Rodger and Mrs Reed for their efficiency in producing the typescript, and to my St Andrews colleagues for bearing with me, especially Mark Imber.

My biggest debt is to Mr John Main, Fellow of St Leonard's College, University of St Andrews, for his innumerable suggestions regarding earlier drafts and for his general advice and support. I am also indebted to Dr Clive Archer of Aberdeen University for a series of helpful comments on earlier drafts. Both will know cases where their advice was and was not followed, and will know the final responsibility for the book is mine.

Finally, it is important to record that, despite what some may feel, this study was conducted and pursued over many years because of my great affection for Ireland and the Irish people. I believe they deserve better than the shibboleths with which they have been, and are, so often presented.

T.C.S.

CONTENTS

LIST OF TABLES

ABBREVIATIONS

Bibliographical:

Assembly Debates	*Official Report of Debates: Consultative Assembly, Council of Europe 1949–1963* (Strasburg; Council of Europe, 1949–63) [sessionally].
Commons Debates	*Parliamentary Debates: House of Commons: Official Report.*
Dáil Debates	*Parliamentary Debates: Dáil Éireann: Official Report.*
Developments	*Developments in the European Communities,* 1–29 (Dublin; Stationery Office, 1973–87) [annually].
DGFP	*Documents on German Foreign Policy 1918–1945,* ser. D (1937–1945), 1–13 (London; HMSO, 1949–73).
DSFP 1951 etc.	*Documents on Swedish Foreign Policy* (Stockholm; Royal Ministry for Foreign Affairs, 1951–81) [annually].
EEC Treaty	'Treaty Establishing the European Economic Community, Rome, 25 March 1957', in *Treaties Establishing the European Communities* (Brussels; Office for Official Publications, 1978).
Ireland/UN 1957 etc.	*Ireland at the United Nations* (Dublin; Department of External Affairs, 1957–70; Department of Foreign Affairs, 1971) [annually].
Kelsen–Tucker	Kelsen, Hans, rev. Tucker, Robert W., *Principles of International Law,* 2nd edn. (New York; Holt, Rinehart, & Winston, 1967).

Lauterpacht–Oppenheim	Lauterpacht, H., and Oppenheim, L., *International Law*, 7th edn. (London, Longman, 1952).
NAB	National Archives Building
OJ	*Official Journal of the European Communities* (Luxemburg; Office for Official Publications of the European Communities) [daily].
Seanad Debates	*Parliamentary Debates: Seanad Éireann: Official Report.*
1962 Struye Report	'Memorandum on the Legal Aspects of Neutrality', presented by Mr Struye, Chairman of the Political Committee, Consultative Assembly of the Council of Europe, 9 May 1962 (Consultative Assembly of the Council of Europe, doc. 1420, for 1962).
1963 Struye Report	'Memorandum on the Political Aspects of Neutrality', presented by Mr Struye, Chairman of the Political Committee, Consultative Assembly of the Council of Europe, 29 April 1963 (Consultative Assembly of the Council of Europe, doc. 1581, for 1963).
Supreme Court	*The Supreme Court: Crotty* v. *An Taoiseach and Others* (9 April 1987).
Texts re NAT	*Texts Concerning Ireland's Position in Relation to the North Atlantic Treaty* (P. 9934; Dublin, Stationery Office, 1950) [presented to both Houses of the Oireachtas by the Minister for External Affairs on 26 April 1950].
TL	Truman Library
WNRC	Washington National Records Center

Political:

CAP	Common Agricultural Policy
CCP	Common Commercial Policy
CET	Common External Tariff
CSCE	Conference on Security and Co-operation in Europe
ECSC	European Coal and Steel Community
EDC	European Defence Community
EFTA	European Free Trade Association
EMS	European Monetary System
EPC	European Political Co-operation
LSF	Local Security Force
NAM	Non-Aligned Movement
NNA	Neutral and Non-Aligned
NSC	National Security Council
OAU	Organization for African Unity
OEEC	Organization for European Economic Co-operation
OECD	Organization for Economic Co-operation and Development
ONUC	Opération des Nations Unies au Congo
PDF	Permanent Defence Force
UNEF	United Nations Emergency Force
UNFICYP	United Nations Force in Cyprus
UNTSO	United Nations Truce Supervision Organisation
WEU	Western European Union

1

Introduction

SOME states have a great deal written about them, others little or
nothing, except in so far as their own nationals delve into their history.
These states remain largely forgotten by the world at large, or merely
footnoted. While Ireland does not fall quite into this category, crucial
aspects of Irish history and policy have been glossed over or simply
ignored by Irish, British, and other authorities. Indeed, Ireland is in
some respects a forgotten state, if not a forgotten nation.

Geography and history help to explain this circumstance. Ireland is on
the periphery of a continent, a position compounded by being sheltered
and obscured as 'une île derrière une île'.[1] Its large neighbour not only
influences the Irish, it also insulates them or at least has done so in the
past.[2] Moreover, given the relative position and importance of the two
islands, political 'independence did not automatically bring economic
independence or cultural autonomy'.[3] Indeed, the ability of the Irish to
pursue any independent policy had been thwarted for centuries by the
political subsumption of the small island by the larger. Nevertheless, the
Irish have played a rather more significant role as a people and nation in
international relations than is sometimes credited. The aspects of
isolationism and insulation can be exaggerated.[4]

The political literature on Ireland deals predominantly with Irish
history, the seven hundred years of British domination and the Irish
freedom struggle. Traditionally the works on its external relations have
been similarly orientated, focusing on the independence question,
Anglo-Irish relations, and the British Empire's evolution into Commonwealth and the Irish role in that process.[5]

Little or no attention has been given specifically to the self-
proclaimed basis of Irish security policy. While rhetoric and practice

---

[1] Jean Blanchard, *Le Droit ecclésiastique contemporain d'Irlande* (Paris, 1958), 11, quoted in
Basil Chubb, *The Government and Politics of Ireland* (OUP, 1974), 46.

[2] Chubb, loc. cit.

[3] Ibid.

[4] See Patrick Keatinge, *A Place Among the Nations: Issues of Irish Foreign Policy* (Dublin, 1978),
for a detailed analysis of the Irish involvement in 'international relations as a people' (p. 17).

[5] See Maria Maguire, *A Bibliography of Published Works on Irish Foreign Relations 1921–1978*
(Dublin, 1981).

have varied somewhat with circumstances, for over half a century that
policy has been predicated upon an attempt to pursue a variant of
neutrality, in addition to a periodic aspiration to non-alignment, in both
official statements and doctrine. No comprehensive attempt has been
made to assess whether these claims are valid, whether the Irish interpretation and understanding of these concepts is legitimate, or whether
the practice has matched the rhetoric. This work attempts to fill the
vacuum.[6]

This examination of Irish statements and practice is based upon a
conceptual analysis aimed at identifying the true nature of neutrality and
the meaning of non-alignment. In addition, the practice of three well-
established European neutrals, Austria, Sweden, and Switzerland, is
examined to determine the extent to which the Irish meet the requirements of the European model. This analysis allows the extrapolation of
two sets of variables against which the Irish claims can be tested: two are
needed because of the crucial distinction between policies *of* and *for*
neutrality.[7] Neutrality *per se*, as will be seen, is only applicable in wartime, and the first set of variables will be confined to the Second World
War period. These variables are: (1) the rights and duties which neutrality entails, particularly in regard to due diligence in defending and
upholding those rights and duties; (2) the recognition of that neutral

[6] The only comprehensive work on Irish foreign and security policy is that by Patrick Keatinge,
particularly *The Formulation of Irish Foreign Policy* (Dublin, 1973) and *A Place Among the Nations*.
These works, however, do not focus upon neutrality. In *A Singular Stance: Irish Neutrality in the
1980s* (Dublin, 1984) he does examine some of the central issues but the focus is largely contemporary. Other works on Irish neutrality have generally focused on a specific period or aspect of the
policy. See Joseph T. Carroll, *Ireland in the War Years 1939-1945* (Newton Abbot, 1975); Carolle J.
Carter, *The Shamrock and the Swastika: German Espionage in Ireland in World War II* (Palo Alto,
1977); Patrick Comerford, *Do You Want to Die for NATO?* (Cork, 1984); Sean Cronin, *Washington's Irish Policy 1916-1986: Independence, Partition and Neutrality* (Dublin, 1987); John P. Duggan,
Neutral Ireland and the Third Reich (Dublin, 1985); T. Ryle Dwyer, *Irish Neutrality and the USA
1939-47* (Dublin, 1977); Robert Fisk, *In Time of War: Ireland, Ulster and the Price of Neutrality
1939-45* (London, 1983); William FitzGerald, *Irish Unification and NATO* (Dublin, 1982);
Henry Harrison, *The Neutrality of Ireland: Why it was Inevitable* (London, 1942); V. P. Hogan, 'The
Neutrality of Ireland in World War II' (University of Notre Dame, thesis, 1953); Norman
MacQueen, 'Irish Neutrality: The United Nations and the Peacekeeping Experience 1945-1969'
(New University of Ulster, D.Phil. diss., 1981); Bill McSweeney, *Ireland and the Threat of Nuclear
War* (Dublin, 1985); Paul F. O'Malley, 'The Origins of Irish Neutrality in World War II
1932-1938' (University of Boston, Ph.D. 1980); Raymond J. Raymond, 'The Economics of
Neutrality: The United States, Great Britain and Ireland's War Economy 1937-1945', 2 vols.
(University of Kansas, Ph.D. diss., 1980); Bernard Share, *The Emergency: Neutral Ireland 1939-45*
(Dublin, 1978).

[7] Adam Roberts, writing of Swedish policy, makes this crucial distinction: 'the foreign policy
. . . is one *for* neutrality rather than one *of* neutrality' (emphasis in original), Adam Roberts,
Nations in Arms: The Theory and Practice of Territorial Defence (London, 1976), 69.

status by belligerents and others; (3) the disavowal of external help, which might compromise neutral status; and (4) the retention of freedom of decision and action.

The second set of variables acknowledges the periodic post-war concern with non-alignment but more importantly reflects the absence of European war since 1945. The test thus becomes the requirements necessary to pursue a policy *for neutrality*, namely the peacetime policy most likely to enable a state to pursue the legal status *of* neutrality in the event of war. To render them appropriate for the post-war period the variables applied to the Second World War experience need to be extended and modified. The second set of variables are: (1) due diligence in maintaining the inviolability of territory and sovereignty, and the taking of active measures to maintain the current status; (2) the recognition and acceptance of that status by other states; (3) the disavowal of external help in any future conflict; (4) the degree to which freedom of action and decision are maintained; (5) the lack of isolationism in attitudes and policy, and the presence both of a willingness to contribute to the amelioration of world problems and of an attitude of impartiality with respect to superpower rivalry; and (6) the attitude to national identity, nation-building, unity, stability, and self-determination.

The conceptual framework provides a basis for an examination of five distinct phases in the evolution of Irish policy and the changing circumstances of the external environment, although in the first period, from the beginning of the present century to the outbreak of war in 1939, neither the first nor the second set of variables can be strictly applied. This is because of the complications engendered by the Irish constitutional position, Commonwealth membership, and the 'ports' issue. The period is nevertheless critical in that it provides an understanding of the basic ethos of the Irish people and policy-makers, and illustrates a fundamental feature of Irish discussion and practice regarding security policy, namely the existence of at least two alternative traditions in this area, the one stressing (albeit not exclusively) the pursuit of an aspiration for neutrality, and the other stressing an acceptance of practical and current realities. The pre-war background also helps to explain why the notions of neutrality and non-alignment have appealed so strongly to the Irish.

The Second World War provided a good test for the Irish policy of neutrality, and the rhetoric and policy of the Irish government during this period are examined in the light of the first set of variables. Subsequently, the modified and enlarged second set of variables are applied to three distinct phases of post-war Irish policy. In the period between the ending of the war and entry into the United Nations in December 1955 the Irish, freed from Commonwealth and wartime constraints, struggled to establish the basis of their policy in a largely indifferent world. Most significantly, in 1949 it was decided not to adhere to the North Atlantic Treaty, a decision which in conjunction with the legacy of the wartime years set the framework for subsequent policy.

Entry into the United Nations transformed the external environment for Irish policy-makers and the scope and depth of Irish involvement in world affairs. Within five years came the further challenge posed by the question of whether Ireland should join the European Economic Community. In the period 1956–72, therefore, the Irish had to wrestle with their equivocation between what might be termed two foreign policies, the one reflecting the aspiration for 'neutrality' and 'non-alignment', and the other pragmatic and aimed at promoting material prosperity. The Irish were confronted anew with the question of whether it was 'possible to meet both the imperatives of political nationalism (for an independent economy) and the demands of the populace for the modern high-consumption life. Eamon de Valera . . . said "no"—and that it was better to be independent than well-off. Since then, southern Irish politicians have been tacitly admitting that the two goals were indeed incompatible, but that it is better to be comfortable than independent.'[8]

In the post-1973 period the previous equivocations have generated confusion both in Ireland itself and among other states as to the real nature and foundations of Irish policy. In particular, questions have been raised about the extent to which the Irish are committed to solidarity with their European Community partners, or alternatively, because of their past, to the pursuit of an independent foreign policy. Is Irish *neutrality* absolute or conditional?—conditional, moreover, not only upon the prospect of relative material prosperity and Community membership, but also upon Partition, the Ulster situation, and some arrangement with the British over these questions.

The application of the conceptual framework to Irish policy leads to a direct challenge to Irish conventional political orthodoxy, and raises the question of whether the notion of neutrality is applicable to Ireland at all. The orthodoxy has been built upon the general tenor of the language used by Irish political leaders, and facts such as the non-participation in the Second World War and the non-adherence to the North Atlantic Treaty. It has thus become axiomatic for many in Ireland and elsewhere

[8] Donald Harman Akenson, *The United States and Ireland* (Cambridge, Mass., 1973), 129.

to assume that Ireland has a tradition either *of* or *for* neutrality. On 2 May 1982, for example, during the Falklands conflict the Irish government itself issued a statement referring to 'Ireland's traditional role of neutrality'[9]. Five years later, when the Irish deposited the instrument of ratification for the Single European Act of the European Community, in June 1987, they simultaneously deposited a 'Declaration by the Government of Ireland' which referred to 'Ireland's long established policy of military neutrality'.[10]

The orthodoxy has been given added currency by an endorsement, if not an unqualified one, by prominent contemporary Irish scholars, such as Keatinge and Fanning. Although both acknowledge that Ireland has not fulfilled the requirements of the legal status of neutrality, and Keatinge admits that 'the use of neutrality is best qualified in the Irish context',[11] the belief remains that in the 'broader sense', as Fanning puts it, Ireland has pursued a 'traditional policy' of neutrality 'since independence'.[12]

The application of the variables, however, suggests that such orthodoxy must be questioned. At best, the evidence in support of it is equivocal and, at worst, it is equally possible to posit an alternative tradition. The so-called policy of traditional neutrality turns out on examination to be not so much principled neutrality as unprincipled *non-belligerency*, the determination to stay out of war at any cost without regard for the upholding of neutral rights or the fulfilling of neutral duties. Those with government responsibility in Ireland have always taken a more pragmatic view than the orthodox school generally admits of, and such pragmatism was even displayed by Éamon de Valera, the alleged architect and apostle of the neutral tradition.

The misunderstandings and misconceptions have endured because of a lack of rigour in the application of concepts and language by the Irish themselves. This has been exacerbated by Irish politicians using neutrality as a shibboleth behind which to hide and by changes in the environment since 1907, when classical neutrality reached its zenith at the Second Hague Conference. These changes led Ogley to predict that in future the 'neutrality that we are likely to see will . . . be a somewhat

---

[9] For this statement *Ireland Today* (Bulletin of the Dept. of Foreign Affairs), 988 (May 1982).
[10] Ibid. 1037 (May–June 1987).
[11] Keatinge, *A Singular Stance*, 56. He also refers to the 'limited nature of Irish neutrality' (ibid.).
[12] Ronan Fanning,'Irish Neutrality: An Historical Review', *Irish Studies in International Affairs* 1/3 (1982), 27.

messy neutrality'.[13] This raises the questions of whether neutrality in general and Irish policy in particular can be so 'messy' as no longer to meet the requirements either *of* or *for* neutrality as properly understood, and whether the Irish position is not rather *sui generis*.

These questions are particularly apposite now, given that in the 1980s the nature and implications of Irish neutrality have become important issues in Irish politics. In the early summer of 1982, for example, the Irish government was required to determine its position *vis-à-vis* the British, the European Community, and the Falklands conflict in the context of its wish to adhere to its perception of Irish political orthodoxy and the apparent tradition of neutrality. The 1980s also saw the protracted discussions with Britain which culminated in the Anglo-Irish Agreement of 15 November 1985.[14] While the agreement itself did not touch on the question of neutrality, at various times in the discussions suspicions had been raised as to whether a deal on the ending of neutrality would be part of the arrangement. Equally troublesome were the protracted negotiations on the future of the European Community, European Union, and European Political Co-operation, and their respective scope, negotiations which led to the Single European Act of 1987.[15]

A re-examination of Irish policy is also necessary because the Irish have claimed on several occasions that their position is of relevance as an example to others. In particular, they have argued that there is no inherent incompatibility between their apparent neutrality and full membership of the European Community. This, of course, places Ireland in a very different position from the other self-confessed neutrals and non-aligned in Europe, who, as will be seen below, explicitly rejected the argument that the two conditions were compatible.[16] The Irish, on the other hand, have continued to advance the view that their own position and experience can serve as a model for these doubters, demonstrating that there is a distinction between NATO and the Community, and that membership of the Community need not involve a military commitment.[17]

[13] Roderick Ogley, *The Theory and Practice of Neutrality in the Twentieth Century* (London, 1970), 205.

[14] See *Ireland Today* special issue (Nov. 1985), and Anthony Kenny, *The Road to Hillsborough: The Shaping of the Anglo-Irish Agreement* (Oxford,1986).

[15] See Roy Pryce (ed.), *The Dynamics of European Union* (London, 1987), and *Single European Act* (*Bulletin of the European Communities*, suppl. 2/86; Brussels, 1986).

[16] See below, pp. 59–79.

[17] See e.g. the speeches of Mr Richie Ryan, as reported in e.g. the *Irish Times*, 24 Oct. 1978, and 24 Oct. 1981. Mr Ryan was Fine Gael spokesman on foreign affairs and Minister of Finance 1973–7.

The Irish case is also interesting because Irish policy for long periods has not been constrained by international treaty or by a constitutional commitment to neutrality, but rather has been the result of a 'free', albeit constrained, choice. There is always the question of how 'free' any decision by a small, weak state really is in an interdependent world, and particularly for a state like Ireland with a very heavy trading dependency upon the United Kingdom.[18] But it was 'free' in the sense that Ireland has faced no legal constraint *vis-à-vis* its neutrality for many years— unlike Switzerland, which is constrained by the 1815 Treaty of Paris, whereby Swiss 'perpetual' neutrality was both recognized and guaranteed, or Austria, which is constrained by the Constitution of 1955, which by Austria's own volition decreed its perpetual neutrality, [19] or Finland, which has been self-constrained by the ambivalent and ambiguous nature of the 1948 Treaty of Friendship, Co-operation, and Mutual Assistance with the Soviet Union.[20] In this sense, the Irish position has been much more analogous to that of Sweden, similarly unconstrained by constitution or treaty.[21] Indeed, on occasion Irish officials and politicians have wanted to model Irish policy upon the Swedish example, even to test the Irish position against the Swedish touchstone.[22] However, the critical difference has been that in looking at the same European treaties, commitments, and obligations in the 1960s and 1970s, the Swedish and Irish governments came to diametrically opposed conclusions concerning Community membership and neutrality.

It may be that their relative economic strength and interdependence *vis-à-vis* other nations critically affected their evaluations. Ireland's

---

18 See Marshall R. Singer, *Weak States in a World of Powers: The Dynamics of International Relationships* (New York, 1972).

19 Albeit that, in practice, this was implicit in the negotiations over the Austrian State Treaty of 1955, although not explicitly stated in the treaty. See Michael Cullis, 'The Austrian Treaty Settlement', *Review of International Studies*, 7/3 (July 1981).

20 See Brian Faloon, 'Aspects of Finnish Neutrality', *Irish Studies in International Affairs* 1/3 (1982); G. Maude, *The Finnish Dilemma* (OUP, 1976); M. Jakobson, *Finnish Neutrality* (London, 1968); Raimo Vayrynen, 'The Evolution of Finland's Foreign Policy since the End of the Second World War', and Aimo Pajunen, 'Some Aspects of Finnish Security Policy', in Karl E. Birnbaum and Hanspeter Neuhold (eds.), *Neutrality and Non-alignment in Europe* (Austrian Institute for International Affairs: Vienna, 1981), 132–65; and R. Allison, *Finland's Relations with the Soviet Union, 1944–1984* (Oxford, 1985).

21 In 1956 the Swedish parliament 'rejected the idea that Sweden should bind its foreign policy . . . in an unforeseeable future under the guarantee of foreign powers': Nils Andren, *Power-Balance and Non-Alignment: A Perspective on Swedish Foreign Policy* (Stockholm, 1967), 191.

22 A prominent example is Conor Cruise O'Brien, sometime foreign affairs official and politician. See e.g. his *To Katanga and Back* (London, 1965) 25. Michael O'Leary, ex-Leader of the Labour Party, thought similarly.

constrained choice with regard to the Community is typical of the dilemmas faced by it since 1921–2. While Ireland may have retained some element of choice, economic factors, especially trade dependency upon other countries, particularly the United Kingdom, have always impinged heavily upon Irish policy and the extent to which successive Irish governments have been able to follow a policy of neutrality.

A central hypothesis of this work is that the socio-economic and political environment of Ireland, both domestically and internationally, has in the practice of Irish foreign and security policies necessarily led to the aspirational pursuit of neutrality being overshadowed by more pressing and immediate concerns of an economic and social-welfare nature. The Irish cannot claim like the Swedes that their 'neutrality is determined by fundamental evaluation relating to security policy, not by economics interest'.[23]

Furthermore, the Irish cannot properly claim to be neutral at all, either in the sense of neutrality *per se* or in the sense of successfully meeting the requirements of aiming at neutrality in the event of war, that is, a policy *for* neutrality. The Irish have deviated so much from the essential characteristics of both of these concepts that even the appellations 'messy', 'qualified', and 'limited' neutrality are inappropriate. It will also be argued in what follows that Ireland lacks the necessary inherent prerequisites to be genuinely non-aligned. There is no currently accepted concept which fits the Irish case. Ireland differs from Austria, Sweden, and Switzerland, and is unique within the European Community. It has had its aspirations, such as they were, to neutrality compromised by Community membership. Irish security policy in the twentieth century is therefore best regarded as *sui generis*.

---

[23] Broadcast by Swedish Foreign Minister, 1 Nov. 1971, reproduced in *Documents on Swedish Foreign Policy 1971* (Royal Ministry for Foreign Affairs, N S 1: C21; Stockholm, 1971), 81.

2

Neutrality and Non-Alignment

ALTHOUGH most writers are agreed that '1648 marks the beginning of neutrality as a formally recognized principle',[1] there had always been states which sought to take no part in the quarrels of others, with relations between belligerents and non-belligerents being 'governed by variable customs and rudimentary rules'.[2] However, it was after 1648, with the embryonic emergence and recognition of both sovereign states and international law, 'that neutrality as a legal concept was born'.[3] At that time the concept appeared to mean merely not participating fully in wars. As sovereignty became more firmly entrenched, and with it the apparent absolute and unconditional right of war, the no less logical consequence of 'the equally absolute and unconditional right of neutrality' also became established. As Politis points out, 'sovereignty, wars and neutrality have been closely allied ideas'.[4] However, the emphasis upon sovereignty, coupled with the development of international economic relations, had to contend on the one hand with the belligerents' desire to cut off all trade with their opponent, and on the other with the neutrals' desire to maintain their own trade with belligerents. As a consequence it was 'natural for governments to seek precision in written undertakings, and it was in this way that the law of neutrality was formed and became explicit'.[5]

Despite this evolution there remained no general international agreement codifying neutral rights and duties, and as war became more absolute with the Napoleonic struggles, increasingly including economic warfare and blockade, so neutrality came under strain. Yet ironically it was just at this time that the real foundations were laid for 'that strange and important political creation of the nineteenth century, impartial and passive neutrality or neutrality built on law'.[6]

---

[1] Nils Ørvik, *The Decline of Neutrality*, 2nd edn. (London 1971), 11.

[2] Nicholas Politis, *Neutrality and Peace* (Washington, D C, 1935), 11.

[3] Peter Lyon, 'Neutrality and the Emergence of the Concept of Neutralism', *Review of Politics*, 22 (Apr. 1960), 258, *passim*.

[4] Politis, 6.

[5] Lyon, 'Neutrality', 257.

[6] Ørvik, *Decline of Neutrality*, 17.

All writers stress the seminal importance of the American attitude during the period 1793–1818.[7] Of particular significance was the 'Proclamation of Neutrality' in April 1793, which stressed for the first time impartiality as one of the principal duties of a neutral power.[8] Another key principle was that belligerents were not to be allowed to engage in hostilities within neutral territory, and Ørvik correctly asserts that 'Respect for neutral territory has ever since been the corner-stone of all neutral policy, since it involves the related question of sovereignty.'[9] The Americans also emphasized abstention.

Before long many European countries, especially the weak who desired to stay out of war, followed the United States model, and an increasingly strict view was taken of the requirements of neutrality. 'Wanting to be left alone, they adopted the principles of impartiality and non-participation . . . From that time on, Europe spoke of traditional neutrals.'[10] This process was aided by the return to limited wars and a readiness on the part of the major Powers to see war regulated, codified, and thereby to some extent limited. Lyon has described the nineteenth century as 'like a golden age for the theory and practice of neutrality' and has argued that this reflected 'the coincidence of a multiple balance of power, a general respect for international law and the absence of any widespread and prolonged international conflict. This period found its apogee in the Hague Conference of 1899 and 1907.'[11]

As Ørvik argues, for the 'first time, the whole system of neutral rights and duties, on sea and on land, was defined and officially incorporated in international law to its fullest extent. What had for centuries been the shifting usages and interpretations of the "law of nations" were now put into an international code which had the official approval of all nations.'[12] The codification was, however, incomplete, and it largely involved codifying existing customary law.[13] Moreover, because of insufficient international ratification, the Convention did not become an international obligation in a strictly legal sense. None the less, the

---

[7] e.g. H. Lauterpacht and L. Oppenheim, *International Law*, ii, 7th edn. (London, 1952); Ørvik, *Decline of Neutrality*, 17–25; Lyon, 'Neutrality', 259–60; Politis, 15 ff.

[8] Ørvik, *Decline of Neutrality*, 18, quotes from the Proclamation 'The duty and interest of the Unites States require that they should, with sincerity and good faith, adopt and pursue a conduct friendly and impartial toward the belligerent powers.'

[9] Ibid. 20.

[10] Ibid. 28.

[11] Lyon, 'Neutrality', 260.

[12] Ørvik, *Decline of Neutrality*, 33.

[13] Politis, 27.

system was approved, if not ratified, by all. Refinements were added subsequently by the Declaration of London in 1909, which again, although not ratified, served as a model for neutral conduct.[14] But it was the Fifth and Thirteenth Conventions of 1907 which were of most significance.[15] Of general significance in the Conventions were the following: (1) 'The territory of neutral Powers is inviolable';[16] (2) 'The fact of a neutral Power resisting, even by force, attempts to violate its neutrality can not be regarded as a hostile act';[17] and (3) 'it is, for neutral Powers, an admitted duty to apply these rules impartially to the several belligerents'.[18]

What had emerged as the essence of neutrality was abstention, the inviolability of neutral territory, and impartiality. Each of these aspects had associated with it a number of rights and duties.[19] Since 1907 there has been virtual unanimity among writers on international law as to the essence of neutrality in this classical sense.

NEUTRALITY: ITS CORE, CHARACTERISTICS, REQUIREMENTS AND DEFINITION

Several definitions of neutrality equate it simply with non-participation in or abstention from war(s). For example, Ogley suggests that the 'idea of neutrality is simple enough. It means, obviously, not taking part in others' quarrels; that is, for states keeping out of other states' wars.'[20] Lyon comes to a similar conclusion; after arguing that today 'the law on the rights and duties of neutrals is neither undisputed nor unchanging', he goes on to suggest that 'given a hot war, every state which stays out of it is "*eo ipso*" neutral'.[21] Other authorities have sought to impart

[14] See Lauterpacht–Oppenheim, ii. 663. The Declaration dealt with the law of blockade, contraband, unneutral service, destruction of neutral prizes, transfer to neutral flag, enemy character, convoy, resistance of search, and compensation. See also L. Oppenheim, *International Law: A Treatise*, 3rd edn., ed., R. F. Roxburgh (London, 1921), 396–9.

[15] Details concerning these Conventions may be found in James Brown Scott (ed.), *The Hague Conventions and the Declarations of 1899 and 1907* (New York, 1915), 133–9 and 209–19. See also his *Reports to the Hague Conference of 1899 and 1907* (New York, 1917).

[16] Article 1 of Convention V.

[17] Article 10 of Convention V.

[18] Preamble to Convention XIII.

[19] Lauterpacht–Oppenheim contains a detailed and generally accepted analysis of these rights and duties (ii. 652 ff., 673 ff., 684 ff., *passim*). In addition to the texts on neutrality cited there is the standard work by P. Jessup and F. Deak, *Neutrality: Its History, Economics and Law* (New York, 1935). See e.g. vol. i, *The Origins*.

[20] Roderick Ogley, *The Theory and Practice of Neutrality in the Twentieth Century* (London, 1970), 1.

[21] Peter Lyon, *Neutralism* (Leicester, 1963), 18.

more content to the concept of neutrality by making inherent within it not just non-participation, but also the concept of rights and duties, especially the obligation of impartiality, and the concept that neutrality is a legal status. For example, Jessup, in his authoritative definition, sees neutrality as 'a legal status arising from the abstention of a state from all participation in a war between other states, and the recognition by the latter of its abstention and impartiality'.[22] Ørvik argues that a 'status of neutrality is dependent upon strict impartiality and absolute non-participation and passivity'.[23] Perhaps the most authoritative definition, found in Lauterpacht–Oppenheim, takes a similar view, seeing neutrality 'as the attitude of impartiality adopted by third states towards belligerents and recognized by belligerents, such attitude creating rights and duties between the impartial States and the belligerents . . . Since neutrality is an attitude during a state of war only, it calls into existence special rights and duties which do not generally obtain . . . they expire *ipso facto* with the termination of the war, or with the outbreak of war between neutrals and a belligerent.'[24]

Kelsen–Tucker, rather than seeing these elements as integral to neutrality, prefers to draw a distinction between neutrality 'as the status of non-participation in war' and 'the specific consequences that are attached to the status of non-participation according to the traditional law'. It is accepted that the legal significance of non-participation is that it brings 'into operation rules for the regulation of neutral–belligerent relations', that these rules impose duties and confer rights upon both belligerents and neutrals, and indeed that 'the law of neutrality comprises the totality of the duties imposed and the rights conferred upon participants and non-participants'. None the less, Kelsen–Tucker is firmly of the view that while

Not infrequently . . . these rules—the consequence of non-participation—have been identified with neutrality and particularly with the neutral's duty of impartiality . . . this identification of neutrality with the duties imposed by international law upon non-participants is nevertheless incorrect. Instead, neutrality should be considered simply as the status of states which refrain from participation in hostilities; the only essential condition for neutral states being that of non-participation in hostilities.[25]

[22] P. Jessup, 'Neutrality', *Encyclopaedia Britannica*, xi. 363.

[23] Ørvik, *Decline of Neutrality*, 37.

[24] Lauterpacht–Oppenheim, ii. 653.

[25] Hans Kelsen, *Principles of International Law*, rev. and ed. Robert W. Tucker (New York, 1967), 154 (cf. 155, 170).

The distinction between non-participation and the consequential rights and duties, especially impartiality, does pose fundamental problems, not least because of the emergence of the notion of 'non-belligerency'. It can be argued that the term 'neutrality' 'should be abandoned, . . . where the object is not impartiality, but keeping the country out of war'. According to Wright, the mere object or even the fact of staying out of war at any price is not sufficient to enable a state to use the term 'neutrality'.[26] Supporting this argument, Ørvik draws particular attention to the neutrality of the late 1930s, which, he argues, 'boiled down to one single object, namely, to stay out of the war that was to come. Not conditionally, by insistence on rights and duties, but almost at any cost and by all means . . . Unbound by rules and obligations, they prepared to steer their course, through discrimination and compromise, in order to stay out of war. It was no longer neutrality, it was non-belligerency.'[27] Kelsen–Tucker itself notes that 'the pursuit of discriminatory policies', coupled with 'the abandonment of the impartiality required by the traditional law', led to the emergence of so-called 'non-belligerency'—non-belligerency being regarded as indicating 'the position of states that refrained from active participation in hostilities while at the same time abandoning the duties imposed upon non-participants . . . it involved the abandonment by non-participants of the impartiality required by customary law'.[28] In fact, these non-belligerent states were seeking to assert and establish that 'there could be an intermediate position between impartial neutrality and belligerency'.[29] In practice the relationship between belligerents and non-belligerents was governed by political and military factors, so that the degree of partiality shown varied considerably and was not governed by legal formulas.

Given these problems, a more satisfactory approach is that of Lauterpacht–Oppenheim, with its equation of neutrality with 'an attitude of impartiality'. Indeed, so strong is that identification that it is argued that 'the rights and duties arising from neutrality come into existence, and remain in existence, through the *mere* fact of a state taking up an attitude of impartiality, and not being drawn into the war by the belligerents'.[30] Neutrality has to be seen as involving both

26 Quoted by Ørvik, *Decline of Neutrality*, 155.
27 Ibid. 189–90.
28 Kelsen–Tucker, 166.
29 Lyon, 'Neutrality', 265.
30 Lauterpacht–Oppenheim, ii. 654 (emphasis added).

non-participation in military conflict and the rules regulating this non-participation:[31] the two must be taken together. Building upon Lauterpacht–Oppenheim,

neutrality . . . supposes a state of war in the formal or factual sense of the word. It describes the situation of a state which remains outside armed conflicts involving other states. When a state decides to adopt this attitude, its decision takes the form of a *conditional* act which involves the application, for a time, of rules predetermined and pre-arranged in international law. These rules involve a balance of rights and obligations and make up what is called the law of neutrality.[32]

This attitude must also be recognized and accepted by the belligerents.

A further difficulty with the simple criterion of non-participation is what might be termed the 'far-off country' phenomenon. Can a state thousands of miles away aptly be termed neutral in a local or regional conflict simply upon the basis of its non-participation? Involving rights and duties in neutrality does at least imply a *consciousness* on the part of the state concerned, rather than neutrality by default.[33] This way of looking at neutrality leads to an appreciation that a state is neutral towards specific wars involving specific belligerents and that a distinction is therefore to be made, since that state could be neutral towards one war and one set of belligerents, but not necessarily so regarding another war with a different set of belligerents.

Certain other aspects of neutrality are worth looking at briefly in view of common misconceptions. For example, neutrality is *not a unilateral* action. It requires to be recognized by the belligerents. As Lauterpacht–Oppenheim suggests, a 'belligerent who, at the outbreak of war, refuses to recognize a third state as a neutral does not indeed violate neutrality, because neutrality does not come into existence in fact and in law until both belligerents have, expressly or by implication, acquiesced in the attitude of impartiality taken up by third States'.[34]

---

[31] Gerald Stourzh, 'Some Reflections on Permanent Neutrality', in A. Schou and A. O. Brundtland, *Small States in International Relations* (Uppsala, 1971), 93. See also George Schwarzenberger, 'The Scope for Neutralism', *The Yearbook of World Affairs*, xv (London, 1961), 234.

[32] 'Memorandum on the Legal Aspects of Neutrality' presented by Mr Struye, Chairman of the Political Committee, of the Consultative Assembly of the Council of Europe (doc. 1420; 9 May 1962) (hereafter 1962 Struye Report), 37 (emphasis added).

[33] See Francis Low-Beer, 'The Concept of Neutralism', *American Political Science Review*, 58/2 (June 1964), 384.

[34] Lauterpacht–Oppenheim, ii. 661. Kelsen–Tucker disagrees with this view, partly because of the key distinction relating to consequences discussed earlier. It argues that 'the decision

Secondly, the 'Rights and duties derived from neutrality do not exist *before* the outbreak of war, however imminent it may be.'[35] Thus, legally there cannot be any such thing as 'peacetime neutrality': it is a contradiction in terms.

Thirdly, given impartiality, there is no duty to break off all intercourse or economic exchange with the belligerents.[36] Indeed, it can be argued that the very *raison d'être* of the 'rules of neutrality is to ensure the maintenance of the normal economic relations of neutral States'.[37] Impartiality necessitates that trade cannot be totally free, but rather that exchange takes place as before.

Fourthly, 'International law does not recognize ideological, political or economic neutrality.'[38] In international law there is no question of 'military neutrality', which in some way might be regarded as distinct from other forms of neutrality. While in the past 'qualified neutrality' was occasionally allowable, the majority of modern writers have maintained 'that a State was either neutral or not, and that it violated its neutrality if it rendered *any* assistance whatever to a belligerent from any motive whatever'.[39]

Fifthly, legally speaking, a 'special assertion of intention to remain neutral is not . . . necessary on the part of neutral states, although they often expressly and formally proclaim their neutrality'.[40] It is clearly in the self-interest of the states concerned that a special declaration of neutrality be issued, given the need for that neutrality to be recognized by others.[41]

Sixthly, as has been argued above, certain correlative rights and duties are inherent in the concept of neutrality, and non-participation is not

whether or not to recognise the existence of a state of war, and thereby to bring into force the law of neutrality, must rest principally with third states. The attitude of the parties engaged in armed conflict need not prove decisive' (p. 55). Another difficult question is 'What is a "war"?'. See Kelsen–Tucker, 23–4, 28, 91, 155 ff.; Lauterpacht–Oppenheim, ii. 293 ff. Peter Lyon has summed up the problem by reference to 'the present fuzzy *status mixtus* of war and peace', in 'Neutrality', 257. See also his *Neutralism*, 18–19.

[35] Lauterpacht–Oppenheim, ii. 655 (emphasis added).

[36] Ibid. 659.

[37] 1962 Struye Report, 40.

[38] Ibid. This point is particularly significant given the looseness with which the term 'neutrality' is often used and the German concept of 'integral neutrality', i.e. the neutrality of both State and population. See Joachim Joesten, 'Phases in Swedish Neutrality', *Foreign Affairs*, 23/2 (Jan. 1945), esp. pp. 327–8.

[39] Lauterpacht–Oppenheim, ii. 663–4 (emphasis added).

[40] Ibid. 654. Thus, at the beginning of the Second World War a number of members of the League of Nations informed the Secretary-General of their intention to remain neutral.

[41] Kelsen–Tucker, 155.

enough. Neutrality can only be carried out if both neutrals and belligerents follow a certain agreed code of conduct in their relations with one another.[42]

In essence both the rights and duties of neutrals can be simply expressed in two sets of ideas. As to rights, these are the inviolability of their territory and freedom in the commercial relations between them and with each of the belligerents,[43] whereas the 'duties incumbent upon neutral states in time of war can be expressed with the two words: abstention and impartiality'.[44] Certainly, the duty of impartiality is universally regarded as essential. In addition to that duty, Kelsen–Tucker identify others: 'the duty to abstain from furnishing belligerents any material assistance, whether goods or services, for the prosecution of war; the duty to prevent the commission of hostile acts within neutral jurisdiction as well as to prevent the use of neutral jurisdiction as a base for belligerent operations; and . . . the duty to acquiesce in certain repressive measures taken by belligerents against private neutral commerce on the high seas'. Under these four general duties, which also establish correlative rights for belligerents, 'may be grouped almost all the specific obligations regulating the conduct of neutral states'.[45]

Finally (and also, incidentally, another reason why neutrality cannot be simply equated with non-participation), neutrality requires '*active* measures from neutral States'. Neutrals must prevent belligerents, even by means of physical resistance and fighting, from making use of their territory or their resources for military purposes during the war. Similarly, they must seek to prevent any interference by one belligerent with their legitimate intercourse with the other belligerent in commerce.[46] While they are not obliged to prevent such acts under all circumstances and conditions, to escape the charge of neglect of duty if such acts are nevertheless performed, 'due diligence' must have been exercised 'for the purpose of preventing such acts'.[47] What is clear is that a simple pious declaration of neutrality is *not* enough. The neutral state must exhibit a willingness to uphold that condition. For example, neutral states have not only the right to prevent misuse of their waters 'but also a

---

[42] Lauterpacht–Oppenheim, ii. 673.
[43] Ibid., and 1962 Struye Report, 37–8.
[44] 1962 Struye Report, 38.
[45] Kelsen–Tucker, 156.
[46] Lauterpacht–Oppenheim, ii. 654.
[47] Ibid., 757–8, 'due diligence' being understood as 'such diligence as can reasonably be expected when all the circumstances and conditions of the case are taken into consideration'.

duty to take adequate measures of prevention'. Thus, a neutral may need to convince belligerents that it will seek to stop encroachments and has some reasonable prospect of so doing. Even if it is militarily weak, some effort is necessary, as the neutral is 'obliged to use the means at its disposal'.[48]

This, then, is the classical legal meaning of neutrality, but neutrality has a 'general diplomatic or political connotation' as well, and this can cause confusion when it comes to understanding and applying the term.[49] It must be emphasized, however, that the real essence of neutrality remains that outlined above.

NEUTRALITY: TWENTIETH-CENTURY CHALLENGES

(a) Legal Problems

The legalistic view of war, and thus of neutrality, has always faced challenges. Historically, one significant challenge has rested on the 'just war' doctrine, with the implication that abstention from such a war was either illegal or immoral, or both. A modern-day variant of it has arisen from changes in the legal position of war. Of particular significance have been the provisions of the Covenant of the League of Nations, the Treaty for the Renunciation of War (the Kellogg–Briand Pact), and the Charter of the United Nations, which have led to doubts 'whether it is correct to assume the continued validity of the law that has traditionally served to regulate the conduct of war'.[50]

The Covenant did not at first sight give a clear-cut answer, there being particular debate about Articles 10, 15, and 16. In practice neutrality had not been abolished, and the League Covenant did not abolish war under all circumstances.[51] The collective-security system established was almost completely decentralized, since the 'decisive question whether a member had resorted to war in disregard of the Covenant was to be answered by each of the members *for itself*'.[52] Moreover, the League was

---

[48] Kelsen–Tucker, 160.   [49] Lyon, *Neutralism*, 17.
[50] Kelsen–Tucker, 87.
[51] Kelsen–Tucker, 34–5, Lauterpacht–Oppenheim, ii. 645 ff., and Politis, 44 ff., all agree on this point.
[52] Kelsen–Tucker, 36 (emphasis added). See also Ørvik, *Decline of Neutrality*, 119 ff., esp. p. 125, where the report of the International Blockade Committee of August 1921 is quoted, particularly its opinion that 'It appears difficult indeed, to make it obligatory for a free and independent nation to accept the opinion either of the Council or the majority of the members of the League, when the issue is the adaptation of measures of such importance as those prescribed in case of violation of the Convenant.'

not universal. In addition, Switzerland was accepted for membership while at the same time insisting upon maintaining its position of permanent neutrality.[53] Finally, there was the constant stream of statements from governments qualifying their commitment, their understanding of their obligations, and the Covenant itself.[54]

While clearly not abolishing neutrality, the Covenant and the League did modify some of its classic tenets, particularly impartiality. Measures such as economic sanctions 'would normally constitute an abandonment of absolute impartiality', and thereby represent a violation of neutrality. Yet, ingeniously, the concept was arguably saved since 'the Covenant-breaking belligerent was deemed, by signing the Covenant, to have consented in advance to measures of discrimination being applied against him by those Members of the League who did not elect to declare war upon him'.[55]

Under the Kellogg–Briand Pact it remained lawful to be neutral since a degree of discrimination against an aggressor appears to have been acceptable, without violation of the duties imposed upon neutrals by the traditional law of neutrality. Certainly the Pact was not as radical an attack upon neutrality as is sometimes suggested.[56] Apparently much more genuinely radical were the innovations introduced by the UN Charter.

At the San Francisco Conference which drew up the Charter it was clearly thought that a status of permanent neutrality was incompatible with membership in the new organization. The issue was raised directly by the French, who wished this to be stated explicitly in the Charter.[57] This was not done and the term 'peace-loving' was retained, but it was

[53] Not only the Swiss worried about the incompatibility between neutrality and membership; the League Council recognized their unique position, while at the same time emphasizing that 'neutrality in everything, economic or military, is clearly inconsistent with the position of a member of the League': Ørvik, *Decline of Neutrality*, 122. The League Council exempted Switzerland from the military obligations contained in the Covenant in their resolution of 13 Feb. 1920: Lyon, *Neutralism*, 153.

[54] A typical example was a joint declaration in July 1936 by seven small 'neutral' states complaining about the changed conditions since they signed the Covenant and the inconsistent application of Covenant articles and undertakings. Given this, they would reserve their position regarding the application of Article 16: League of Nations, *Official Journal* (special suppl. 154; 1936), 19. In 1938, most members of the League denounced their obligation to participate in economic sanctions: *Official Journal* (1983), 385.

[55] Lauterpacht–Oppenheim, ii. 646.

[56] Kelsen–Tucker, 168–9.

[57] Lauterpacht–Oppenheim, ii. 647. For details see Leland M. Goodrich and Edvard Hambro, *Charter of the United Nations: Commentary and Documents*, 2nd edn. (London, 1949), 132 ff., and Ørvik, *Decline of Neutrality*, 247–9.

agreed that any applicant for membership would have to be ready and able to accept and fulfil the obligations of the Charter. For the Swiss these provisions were enough to deter Switzerland from applying, especially since there was to be no special treatment for it, as had happened vis-à-vis the League. Other 'neutrals' also had doubts: prominent Swedes, for example, believed that membership involved writing off the traditional policy of neutrality. Although prepared to do this in support of 'international solidarity', they also anticipated that the likely absence of Great Power unanimity meant that certain obligations were not likely to be imposed upon them. Sweden joined the United Nations in 1946.[58]

Austria was admitted to membership in 1955. This was despite its announced intention to pursue permanent neutrality and its request to all states to recognize its position and status. Most did, including (it should be noted) the permanent members of the Security Council. Austria was apparently to be allowed to refrain from involvement in war and to uphold the traditional law requirements.[59] This did not lead to a change in the Swiss position.

Perhaps the main innovation of the Charter was the greatly enhanced centralization with respect to the legitimate use of force and the bringing into operation of the new international security system. Under the Charter the Security Council has the authority to determine, with an effect binding upon all the member-states, whether there has been aggression, who is responsible, and what action shall be taken to remedy the situation. It can make obligatory even the collective use of force.[60]

Articles 43, 44, 45, 46, and 47, which relate to the obligation 'to make available to the Security Council, on its call and in accordance with a special agreement or agreements, armed forces, assistance, and facilities, including rights of passage, necessary for the purpose of maintaining international peace and security' and the establishment of a Military Staff Committee, also theoretically pose problems for

---

[58] See Nils Andren on the Swedish Govt.'s message to Parliament on 22 Oct. 1945, in his *Power-Balance and Non-Alignment: A Perspective on Swedish Foreign Policy* (Stockholm, 1967), 41–6. As well as commentary, this volume contains extracts from a number of central documents on post-war Swedish foreign policy.

[59] Kelsen–Tucker, 171.

[60] Lauterpacht–Oppenheim, ii. 647. This volume and Kelsen–Tucker have excellent discussions of the impact of the Charter upon neutrality. See further the Charter of the United Nations (1945), Chapter VII, 'Action with Respect to Threats to the Peace, Breaches of the Peace, and Acts of Aggression', esp. Articles 39, 41, and 42. Also relevant are Article 2, para. 5, in which members undertake to assist the U N in action taken in accordance with the Charter, and Article 25, whereby they agree to accept and comply with Security Council decisions.

neutrals.[61] Some have argued that there is no obligation to conclude any such agreement and that the absence of an agreement negates any Security Council competence to oblige member-states to undertake military action.[62] This interpretation, however, so undermines the letter and spirit of Chapter VII of the Charter as to appear perverse.

However, the notion of neutrality is not completely undermined in the Charter. For example, the Charter 'contains no direct obligation to outlaw "aggressors" or to take sanctions against them',[63] nor does it lay down 'that the determination of a State as an aggressor shall automatically be followed by a general war against it'.[64] Moreover, one must not lose sight of the fact that action requires unanimity on the part of the permanent members of the Security Council, and that has been lacking. It should perhaps also be noted that if, in the event of Security Council inaction, the General Assembly decides to seek to take action, it can only make a recommendation, not a mandatory decision.[65]

In summary, the position is confused. Under certain circumstances neutrality has been abolished by the Security Council's power to call upon members to declare war or take warlike actions. But there are other cases where the situation is not so clear-cut and the maintenance of neutrality may depend upon whether a member-state's general obligation under Article 2 (5) undermines impartiality.[66] Certainly neutrality, as classically understood, has been circumscribed by the Charter, although the actual practice and experience of the UN have meant that those constraints have not been as wounding as was perhaps imagined in 1945.

In addition to these specific legal problems for neutrality, there is a more general and profound challenge to the continuing vitality of the concept. So far the discussion has presumed the existence of an international community 'where all the members could agree to abide by certain rules of conduct recognized by them as binding in peace and in war', whereas what has occurred has been the break-up of the inter-

---

[61] Ibid., Article 43, para. 1; cf. Articles 46, 47.

[62] Kelsen–Tucker, 46–7, n. 36, 170.

[63] Ogley, 21.

[64] Lauterpacht–Oppenheim, ii. 650; see also ibid. 648–9, and Kelsen–Tucker, 172, discuss the significance of this.

[65] Of particular relevance here is the Uniting for Peace Resolution of 3 Nov. 1950 (General Assembly Resolution 377A(V)). Inis Claude, *Swords into Plowshares*, 3rd edn. (London, 1965), 245–7, discusses this, and is emphatic that the operative organ for Uniting for Peace 'has only recommendatory authority' (p. 246).

[66] Lauterpacht–Oppenheim, ii. 222–3; Kelsen–Tucker, 170–1.

national law community and a growing reluctance to accept predominantly Western legal concepts and philosophy.[67] A significant example is that Communists have a view of neutrality which is not in accordance with traditional Western thinking.[68] This is of great relevance to states contemplating neutrality in any future war involving Western and Communist states. What one demands of a 'neutral' may well not be regarded as neutrality by the other side. The 1962 Struye Report puts this issue very pertinently in relation to the issue of whether neutrality is compatible with participation in the European Community: 'the communist theory must reply "No"', as such participation does not serve the Communist cause'.[69] Yet these states need to acquiesce in the neutrality of Ireland and other states in a European war or a global war involving European states, since neutrality does not come into existence until recognized by both belligerents.

(b) Political Difficulties

A number of conditions underlay the classical period of neutrality, including the nature of war and the international system. Wars were limited in scope, method, and objective, and while war remained an instrument of policy, it was becoming regulated and codified. Furthermore, there was a growing acceptance of international law, and the need to regulate trade, even during periods of conflict. Despite the challenges produced by trade and technological innovation, faith in sovereignty remained.

A number of developments after 1907 undermined several of these conditions. In particular, the industrial revolution with the concomitant mass-production of weapons of ever greater destructive power, coupled with growing economic interdependence, the evolution of democracy, and the growing assertiveness of nationalism, led to changes in the attitude to and the nature of war, making total victory more appealing and restraint more difficult.[70] These developments, moreover, placed strain

---

[67] 1962 Struye Report, 34. Struye focuses only upon the Communist–Western divide and 'two entirely different and perhaps irreconcilable concepts of neutrality: the Communist concept and what can perhaps be called the Western concept'. There is also the example of the question of diplomatic immunity etc. during the Iranian hostage crisis, when some sought to justify the action by reference to the inadequacy or inapplicability of Western concepts.

[68] See P. H. Vigor, *The Soviet View of War, Peace and Neutrality* (London, 1975), and Harto Hakovirta, 'The Soviet Union and the Varieties of Neutrality in Western Europe', *World Politics*, 35/4 (July 1983).

[69] 1962 Struye Report, 37.

[70] See R. Osgood and R. W. Tucker, *Force, Order and Justice* (Baltimore, 1967), *passim*, for a general review of these issues.

upon a vital ingredient which allowed states to be neutral, namely that a state should be 'absolutely sovereign and absolutely independent of other states in all matters',[71] since the status of neutrality is 'inseparably connected with and dependent upon the amount of sovereignty which a country enjoys'.[72] To be neutral a state requires a reasonable degree of self-sufficiency, and at least sufficient military strength to deter violation of its territory and rights. Ørvik has argued, however, that in the 'realistic, interrelated world of today, a true, impartial and legal neutrality is impossible', since neutral rights, duties, and sovereignty are threatened.[73]

Politis felt that 1914–18 'dealt the death-blow to neutrality' because the determination of the belligerents to engage the entire resources of the other side meant that, since the economic situation of each belligerent was regarded as crucial, the economic rights of neutrals were overridden—by blockades, for example.[74] Thus, the conditions prevailing in the two world wars could hardly be reconciled 'with the conditions that are plainly assumed by the traditional law'.[75] In addition, since those wars the further geographical expansion of the international system has contributed, as has been seen, to the general undermining of the sense of comity of nations.

These trends have clearly had a profound effect upon the possibility of genuine neutrality. Moreover, the interdependence literature of recent years has tended to give the impression that no country has total independence, and even that 'dependence in one area tends to correlate highly with dependence in other areas . . . If a country is highly dependent economically upon another country, the likelihood is that it will also have a high perceptual, communication, military and political dependence as well.'[76] None the less, this trend towards determinism may be misleading, since states can break the links of interdependence, albeit at

[71] Ørvik, *Decline of Neutrality*, 268.

[72] Ibid. 73.

[73] Ibid. 277.

[74] Politis, 39.

[75] Lauterpacht–Oppenheim, ii. 796, and Kelsen–Tucker, 158.

[76] See the superb analysis of Marshall R. Singer in *Weak States in a World of Powers: the Dynamics of International Relationships* (New York, 1972), 48–50, *passim*. (The quotation is from p. 49.) On interdependence see e.g. Robert D. Keohane and Joseph S. Nye, *Power and Interdependence: World Politics in Transition* (Boston, 1977); Richard N. Cooper, 'Economic Interdependence and Foreign Policy in the Seventies', *World Politics*, 24/2 (Jan. 1972); Edward C. Morse, *Modernization and the Transformation of International Relations* (New York, 1976). For an excellent analysis of the concept and much of the associated literature see David A. Baldwin, 'Interdependence and Power: A Conceptual Analysis', *International Organization*, 34/4 (Autumn 1980).

cost to themselves. States do not always choose to do what is of economic advantage to their citizenry, and there may be other values which,
on occasion, are considered higher than the economic.[77]

The trend towards absolutism in war can also be overstated since it is
self-evident that not all wars since 1945 have exhibited that character.
Scores of conflicts have remained limited. Moreover, the economic
weapons of sanctions, blockades, and boycotts have not enjoyed total
success.[78]

While they have been challenged by a number of developments in this
century, the necessary conditions for the existence of neutrality have not
definitely been destroyed, although there should be no illusion as to the
difficulties involved. Neutrality has always been problematic, however,
in that it depended more upon power than upon law, and upon the good
pleasure of the belligerent(s), who were always liable to disregard it
whenever they perceived it to be in their interest to do so.[79]

Neutrality relates as much, if not more, to factors such as location,
strength, and the balance of power as to aspiration and law. According
to Bjøl, the crucial importance of 'security geography' must be recognized:[80] for example, the 'situation of each country on the operational
map makes its neutrality improbable or probable in advance'.[81] Neutrals
may be attacked not because of their own intrinsic value, but rather
because of their strategic position.

The relative strength of a neutral is also crucial. This is somewhat
paradoxical in that many neutrals, particularly in Europe, have tended to
possess only a limited capacity for military action. None the less, as will
be seen, some of the leading 'neutrals' in contemporary Europe do take
their own defence seriously, in addition to relying upon the dictum
'Marginal Resource Attack, Marginal Cost Deterrence'.[82] In the battle

---

[77] As events in Iran in the last decade perhaps illustrate.

[78] There is an extensive literature on these issues, e.g. Morton H. Halperin, *Limited War in the Nuclear Age* (New York, 1963); Robert R. Osgood, *Limited War Revisited* (Boulder, Colo., 1979); Robin Renwick, *Economic Sanctions* (Cambridge, Mass., 1981); Gary C. Hufbauer, Jeffrey J. Schott, with Kimberley A. Elliott *Economic Sanctions Reconsidered: History and Current Policy* (Washington, DC, 1984).

[79] Politis, 31; Samir N. Anabtawi, 'Neutralists and Neutralism', *Journal of Politics*, 27/2 (1965), 355.

[80] Erling Bjøl, 'The Power of the Weak', *Cooperation and Conflict*, 4/3 (1968), 158. He makes a similar point in 'The Small State in International Politics', in Schou and Brundtland, 32.

[81] Raymond Aron, *The Century of Total War*, quoted by Lyon, *Neutralism*, 89. See also Roberts, *Nations in Arms: The Theory and Practice of Territorial Defence* (London, 1976), 41, and Ogley, 8.

[82] Roberts, 90 ff.

between David and Goliath, Goliath may only have one arm free and will probably be looking elsewhere also. Neutrals do, however, need the ability to deter by making the cost of attack too high, relatively, for the belligerent.

A further complication is what has been termed 'defence against help' or 'the protective umbrella'.[83] A neutral may need defence against potential allies as much as against potential adversaries. A neutral needs to be able to resist the idea of 'friendly' intervention, whereby one belligerent will protect it against another by direct action, and it will be placed by a major power under its protection whether the neutral requests it or not. A major power may let it be known that 'it would consider penetration by another power as a hostile act and would respond militarily' to it.[84]

In meeting these difficulties a neutral may be helped by the existence of a 'balance of power' system. Indeed, Haggloff and Hopper both argue that a basic condition of neutrality is the existence of a balance of power.[85] Today, it has been argued that this condition is met, since the independence of small European states 'is protected not by their policy of neutrality but by the existence, thanks to the defensive measures adopted by the Western committed nations, of a balance of power which compels the Soviet Union to respect the neutrals'.[86] Clearly, however, this position may degenerate into a protective umbrella.

These issues are relevant to the critical issue of credibility since a 'neutral must . . . convince each belligerent that, if left alone, it will not go over to the enemy, nor help the enemy in any unneutral way . . . [and] that it can and will stop encroachments and attack from the other'.[87] Also relevant in this context are the predisposition and behaviour of the neutral state before the commencement of hostilities, and whether it has given any putative belligerent cause to believe that it will not remain neutral. Such cause may emanate from its ideological stance, its socio-economic and political system, or from the pattern of its trade, which may appear to make abstention or impartiality difficult. The

[83] See Nils Ørvik, 'Defence Against Help: A Strategy for Small States', *Survival* (Sept.–Oct. 1973), 228–31, and Singer, 285.

[84] Singer, loc. cit.

[85] See H. Gunnar Haggloff, 'A Test of Neutrality: Sweden in the Second World War', in Ogley, and Bruce Hopper, 'Sweden: A Case Study in Neutrality', *Foreign Affairs*, 23/3 (Apr. 1945).

[86] Jacques Freymond, 'The European Neutrals and the Atlantic Community', in F. O. Wilcox and H. F. Haviland jun. (eds.), *The Atlantic Community: Progress and Prospects* (New York, 1963).

[87] Ogley, 14–15.

difficulties are compounded in that neutrality lies in the eye of the beholder.[88]

A neutral needs 'to make clear the unequivocal and determined character of its foreign policy; and in Europe those states which have turned the legal status of neutrality into a great national dogma have in fact generally been the more successful neutrals—simply because their neutrality is widely understood and accepted'.[89] In some cases the 'tendency to transform neutrality into an ideology' may be so pronounced as to raise it beyond the everyday level of political debate, and to lead to it being accepted internally as axiomatic.[90] Similarly, it may be transformed into an unquestioned tradition, whereby, rather than there being any contemporary compelling rationale for the position, it is the case that 'We are neutral because we have always been neutral.'[91] Neutrality may 'surreptitiously', or deliberately, be allowed to creep 'to a much higher station in the hierarchy of policy aims' than its logical status entitles it to. It is a means, not an end.[92]

A neutral may also seek to establish its position by a formal declaration of intent, and, while not legally required, such a declaration is normal practice. Another method is by way of international treaty or guarantee, or by joint affirmation of neutrality by a group of countries, such as the agreement among Scandinavian countries in 1938.[93] States may also seek to have their status recognized by having it written into communiqués after bilateral meetings with putative belligerents.[94]

The problem of credibility remains, however, since 'Formal arrangements did not solve the core problem of credibility. A declaration of traditional, legal neutrality would hardly be credible when a state's

[88] Manfred Scheich, 'The European Neutrals after Enlargement of the Communities: The Austrian Perspective', *Journal of Common Market Studies*, 12/3 (1973–4), 336–7, argues that 'it lies primarily with the neutral to create this credibility' but also notes that there 'has to be international confidence' in the position.

[89] Roberts, 44.

[90] D. Frei, 'Switzerland and the EEC: Facts and Trends', *Journal of Common Market Studies*, 12/3 (1973–4), 260.

[91] Ibid. 259.

[92] The quotations are taken from an excellent article by Low-Beer (cited above, n. 33), which focuses upon the contextual aspect (esp. p. 390). See also Scheich, 236, and Stourzh, in Schou and Brundtland, 96–7.

[93] See the *Declaration between Denmark, Finland, Iceland, Norway and Sweden for the Purpose of Establishing Similar Rules of Neutrality, Signed at Stockholm, May 27th, 1938* (League of Nations Treaty Series, 188, doc. 4365; [Geneva, 1938/9]), 294–331 (Ørvik, *Decline of Neutrality*, 217, wrongly refers to Ireland instead of Iceland as participating).

[94] The Swedes have been particularly assiduous in this regard: see the *Documents on Swedish Foreign Policy*, issued annually from Stockholm in 1951–82, for a number of such communiqués.

economic and perhaps also military capabilities depended upon continued massive exchange and cooperation with the states that would be involved in a major conflict . . . the ties of organised interaction could not be undone overnight.'[95]

This, and other difficulties mentioned above, have not been ameliorated by the high degree of flexibility shown by so-called neutral states in the twentieth century. Writing in the winter of 1944/5, Joesten asked which of the 'few surviving neutral countries can claim to have maintained the same status throughout the war? . . . All of them have passed through various stages of affiliation with one or the other of the belligerents, ranging from unavowed collaboration to non-belligerent alliance, or even "moral belligerency".'[96]

A related issue is whether abstention and impartiality are to be regarded as 'equivalent to complete disinterestedness', whatever the cause or character of the war.[97] Given a concern with self-preservation, can any state be uninterested in the course and outcome of a war between third parties? The classical view has been that the ambience, and indeed definition, of neutrality 'cannot be given without invoking the concept of the negative',[98] and that 'political passivity was the main characteristic' of neutrality.[99] Indeed, Frei has argued that 'it is legitimate in the Swiss case to interpret neutrality in terms of isolationism',[100] while Andren has noted the 'traditional idea of Sweden's attitude to international events—long prevailing, not least in Sweden itself—as one of not having any foreign policy at all'.[101]

Most neutrals, however, no longer wish to identify with passivity and disinterestedness; this is 'definitely and absolutely obsolete'.[102] Petitpierre has challenged the isolationist view of Swiss neutrality,[103] while Vukadinović, amongst others, has done the same for Finland and Sweden, arguing that on European soil 'the conception of neutrality has essentially changed', since only an 'active international policy can satisfy the interests of small countries'.[104] One consequence has been the activity of neutrals in mediation and UN peace-keeping. UN member-

[95] Ørvik, Decline of Neutrality, 282.

[96] Joesten, 'Phases', 324. See also Hopper, 'Sweden'.

[97] Politis, 28.

[98] Low-Beer, 384–5.

[99] Max Petitpierre, 'Is Swiss Neutrality still Justified', from Switzerland, Present and Future, (n. p., 1963), cited in Ogley, 176.   [100] Frei, 259.

[101] Andren, Power Balance and Non-Alignment, 9.   [102] Ibid.

[103] Petitpierre, op. cit.

[104] R. Vukadinović, 'Small States and the Policy of Non-Alignment', in Schou and Brundtland, 106.

ship in itself, with the concomitant need to take a view and to vote, has been a factor in this transformation, although it is salutary to recall the Soviet argument that 'there are no neutral men'.[105]

Because of the foregoing difficulties, Roberts argues that neutrality 'should not . . . be regarded as a totally fixed quantity' but rather as 'a rudimentary framework' of foreign policy, within which changes of style and substance may occur.[106] Somewhat similarly, Ogley, while suggesting that neutrality is 'far from being an anachronism', since it is 'a condition that states are likely to find themselves in . . . with increasing frequency', goes on to argue that this 'will not . . . be a status governed very meticulously by the international law of neutrality', since the rules will be 'improvised' and may be disregarded by the powerful. None the less, he argues, there will persist 'a reluctance of third parties to involve themselves in others' conflicts'.[107] But this is no longer neutrality, although it may be non-belligerency, there being 'a clear distinction' between the two.[108]

For neutrality *per se*, as demonstrated earlier, certain conditions must be met; and by utilizing them one can give content to the concept. The fact that the concept is often wrongly applied, or that the conditions may be difficult to attain in the contemporary world, is not a ground for abandoning it, especially since the term is still widely used, not least by states themselves, and does provide a useful yardstick against which to analyse the policies of such states. *The essence of neutrality is a deliberate, conscious policy of impartial absention during a war or armed conflict with concomitant rights and duties, together with an intention to resist violations of those rights and duties by armed resistance if necessary.* In view of this, a number of 'types of neutrality' are in reality nothing of the kind, whether they be termed 'integral', 'qualified', 'benevolent', 'spiritual', 'ideological', 'military', 'neo-', 'peacetime', or indeed 'non-belligerent'.[109]

---

[105] Khrushchev said this in a famous interview with Walter Lippman, *New York Herald Tribune* (17 Apr. 1961), although he prefaced it by acknowledging that 'there are neutral countries'.

[106] Roberts, 79.

[107] Ogley, 204–5. In a somewhat similar vein is Harto Hakovirta, 'Effects of Non-Alignment on Neutrality in Europe: An Analysis and Appraisal', *Cooperation and Conflict, 18* (1983). He looks at neutrality in terms of the 'positions and policies' of five European states (p. 57), claiming that neutrality has been 'largely disconnected' from its legal basis (p. 60). However, 'neutrality' is perhaps not the appropriate term in such circumstances.

[108] Ørvik, *Decline of Neutrality*, 278; he also comments upon how the two concepts became somewhat intertwined (p. 183). See also Robert L. Rothstein, *Alliances and Small Powers* (New York, 1968), 31.

[109] See Stourzh, in Schou and Brundtland, 93–4.

Within 'genuine neutrality', however, it is worth noting an important distinction, namely that in some cases neutrality may be imposed by international treaty, while in others it is voluntarily adopted by the state concerned. This distinction is important because it vitally affects the freedom of action of the states concerned: in the first case, the state is governed by the specific requirements of the treaty by which it is bound, while in the latter, it has no obligation save to itself and the policy is a matter of choice, to be continued or abandoned as it sees fit. Occasionally a certain confusion arises because some authorities wish to term the former 'perpetual' or 'permanent' and the latter 'occasional' or 'temporary' neutrality.[110] It can be argued, however, that perpetual neutrality need not be neutralization, while in practice 'occasional' or 'temporary' neutrality may well be exceedingly long-lasting, elevated indeed into a 'traditional' neutrality.

Voluntary neutrality may indeed by subdivided between 'traditional', by which is usually meant 'general', and *ad hoc*, by which is usually meant 'particular'. With respect to the former, the state concerned has the objective of keeping out of all and any war, while with respect to the latter, the state merely wishes to be neutral in a particular conflict at a particular time. A succession of such *ad hoc* decisions may transform the state into a traditional neutral, as has occurred in the Swedish case. The credibility of a general and traditional neutral is likely to be higher than that of an *ad hoc* neutral, since in the latter case no state can be sure in advance what the putative neutral will actually do.

The issue of types of, or variants of, neutrality is of particular relevance to the European context, because of the conventional wisdom (often supported by internal rhetoric from the states concerned) regarding Austria, Finland, Sweden, Switzerland, and the focus of this study, Ireland. If they are not pursuing a policy of neutrality, are they pursuing what Roberts terms a policy '*for* neutrality', by which he means a policy aiming at neutrality in the event of war?[111] They themselves have wished to see their policies in this light, and may therefore be used as a model to identify the key requirements of such a position in as far as it differs from neutrality *per se*.

Before I turn to examine their position in Chapter 3, however, the essence of non-alignment will be identified.

[110] Thus Lauterpacht–Oppenheim, 661, suggests that 'Perpetual or permanent neutrality is the neutrality of States which are neutralised by special treaties'; and the 1962 Struye Report refers to 'Occasional or temporary neutrality—often called simply neutrality . . .' (p. 37).

[111] Roberts, 69, writing of Sweden, suggests that 'The foreign policy, in other words, is one *for* neutrality rather than one *of* neutrality' (emphasis in original).

NON-ALIGNMENT: PROBLEMS OF DEFINITION

There is some dispute about dating the origins of non-alignment, depending upon whether non-alignment is regarded principally as a movement, with its origins in Belgrade in 1961, or as a more amorphous development of ideas and tendencies.[112] There is also the difficulty that the main policy concerns of the non-aligned have changed in the last twenty-five years, so that some, notably Rothstein, now emphasize the declining importance of the old core-issues such as cold war tensions and colonialism, and the ever-increasing importance of internal problems relating to development. Rothstein argues that non-alignment has been 'transformed into something quite different' from what it was, and has coined the aphorism 'from non-alignment to class war' to sum this up.[113] Indeed, at the seventh summit of the Non-Aligned Movement in Delhi in 1983 the unifying message was non-alignment as 'the voice of the poor', with the gap between rich and poor countries being regarded as 'the most serious problem threatening world peace'.[114]

Not surprisingly, there is almost unanimous agreement that the term non-alignment has been used 'so often by so many people in such different circumstances and with such different intentions, that its meaning seems to change, chameleon like, depending on the context in which it appears'.[115] This diversity has increased because of the exponential rise in the number of adherents, each influenced by its own interests, values, and backgrounds. The amorphous character of non-alignment also reflects the fact that it did not come into being as a fully fledged idea but evolved in a series of *ad hoc* reactions to contemporary stimuli. Only later were there attempts to construct a legitimizing conceptual framework.[116] Lyon and Jansen both emphasize that non-alignment was

112 Cf. Peter Willetts, *The Nonaligned Movement: The Origins of a Third World Alliance* (London, 1978) 3, 14; Leo Mates, *Nonalignment: Theory and Current Policy* (Belgrade and New York, 1972), 44–53, 58–74, 227–8; G. H. Jansen, *Afro-Asia and Nonalignment* (London, 1966), *passim*.

113 Robert L. Rothstein, 'Foreign Policy and Development Policy: From Nonalignment to International Class War, *International Affairs*, 52/4 (Autumn 1976). See also Carol Geldart and Peter Lyon, 'The Group of 77: A Perspective View', *International Affairs*, 57/1 (Winter 1980/1).

114 *The Economist*, 286: 7281 (19 Mar. 1983), 55. For further details of the Delhi meeting see *Keesing's Contemporary Archives*, xxxix (London, 1983), 32349–55.

115 Lyon, *Neutralism*, 15. See also Cecil V. Crabb, jun., *The Elephants and the Grass* (New York, 1965), 16, quoting an *Indian Express* editorial of 7 Mar. 1963.

116 See Mates, 75 and III; N. Choucri, 'The Non-alignment of Afro-Asian States: Policy, Perception and Behaviour', *Canadian Journal of Political Science*, 2/1 (Mar. 1969) 15; and Cecil V. Crabb, jun., 'The United States and the Neutralists', in his *Nonalignment in Foreign Affairs* (Annals of the American Academy of Political and Social Science, 362; Nov. 1965), 93.

'pragmatic' and 'a policy, not a creed; a tactic, even a weapon, but not a gospel; for whatever else gospels may do, they do not establish or preserve the national self-interest of newly and fiercely independent states'.[117] For these reasons non-alignment is eclectic, lacking both 'canonical works' and a 'corpus of knowledge . . . [an] integrated body of theory', and is 'rather a constellation of concepts . . . shrouded in a confusing medley of supporting arguments'.[118] To add to the problem, the 'constellation of concepts' is not static, so that 'non-aligned states, except in the most general terms, do not agree among themselves' about the nature of non-alignment. As a result, generalizations are 'dangerous and largely erroneous'.[119]

As a consequence, both Crabb and Lyon argue that the term means 'little in abstract'[120] and needs to be applied to policies and viewpoints of particular countries in particular cases, the first question being 'whose neutralism is referred to and what forms does it take, [and] how general or particular are these forms?'[121] Indeed, Lyon believes it is 'a mistake and a distraction of political enquiry from its proper concerns to seek for a quintessential neutralism'.[122] None the less, it is worth while to pursue the search for the essence of non-alignment, since, if a concept is to be used, it should have a clearly understood content.

In establishing that content there are difficulties, although Willetts suggests that 'there is an easy way out', since the summit communiqués should 'be relied upon as the most authoritative statements of the principles of non-alignment'.[123] While Willetts is right to emphasize such communiqués and other important declarations, such as the principles enunciated at the Cairo preparatory meeting for the Belgrade summit in 1961, as a guide to what the participants understood non-alignment to be[124] and thus vital sources in the endeavour to understand non-alignment, there are dangers in relying too heavily upon

---

[117] Lyon, *Neutralism*, 87; Jansen, 402.

[118] Ibid., 59–62.

[119] Theodore L. Shay, 'Nonalignment Si, Neutralism No', *Review of Politics*, 30/2 (Apr. 1968), 230. See also Mates, 78, and Crabb's Introduction, in *Nonalignment in Foreign Affairs*, 8.

[120] e.g. Crabb, *Elephants and the Grass*, 212.

[121] e.g. Lyon, *Neutralism*, 196.

[122] Ibid.

[123] Willetts, *Nonaligned Movement*, 18–19.

[124] The Cairo principles were: an independent policy based on peaceful co-existence; support for liberation movements; avoidance of military pacts or bilateral treaties which involved entanglement in East–West dispute; and avoidance of agreements for the establishment of foreign military bases on their territory. See Jansen, 278–90, and Odette Jankowitsch and Karl P. Sauvant, *The Third World without Superpowers: The Collected Documents of the Non-Aligned Countries*, i (Dobbs Ferry, 1978), 1–42.

such pronouncements. For example, even the Cairo principles were not strictly applied in all the invitations to Belgrade,[125] while Willetts himself had earlier warned that it is 'too facile to accept the judgement of the Non-Aligned politicians'.[126] Moreover, communiqués are the result of bargaining rather than of pursuit of an ideal, while using such pronouncements tends to confine the phenomenon of non-alignment to members of the Non-Aligned Movement (NAM). In addition, many states professing non-alignment and belonging to the movement may in practice 'be more fettered than some aligned states'.[127] Singer demonstrates this vividly, showing that formal treaties or alliances are not necessary to create 'Ties that Bind'.[128] Thus, the behaviour of a non-aligned state may not accord with the pronouncements of the movement. This is evident in the way that such states tend to ignore pronouncements on peaceful co-existence, military pacts, and the use of force in international relations, when it comes to localized, regional disputes.[129]

The first response to the questions raised in the foregoing discussion is that non-alignment is not a foreign policy. Rather it is 'an approach to policy-making . . . [defined] not in terms of what . . . [a] government's policy will be on the problems . . . but in the spirit in which the government would approach the decision . . . That non-alignment is an approach is a point seldom grasped.'[130] Thus, non-aligned countries are to be 'identified more according to their position in the international community than according to their concrete and specific foreign policies'.[131] Indeed, non-alignment is to be seen as 'a "frame of mind" that sharpened and emphasised the distinction between "we" and "they" '.[132] After all, 'The new countries became non-aligned first in the *consciousness* of their political leaders and statesmen.'[133]

---

[125] Jansen, loc. cit.

[126] Willetts, 2.

[127] Lyon. *Neutralism*, 89. See also the discussion in Rothstein, *Alliances and Small Powers*, 52, 247, *passim*; Low-Beer, 389–90; Crabb, *Elephants and the Grass*, 72–6; and Willetts, *Nonaligned Movement*, 223–34.

[128] Singer, 87 ff.

[129] See Anabtawi, 354.

[130] This view of Keita of Mali is reported by M. Legum, 'Africa and Nonalignment', in J. W. Burton (ed.), *Nonalignment* (London, 1966), 56. See also Crabb's 'Introduction', in *Nonalignment in Foreign Affairs*, 4.

[131] Mates, 362.

[132] Quoted by Rothstein, 'Foreign Policy and Development Policy', 607, from Fayez A. Sayegh (ed.), *The Dynamics of Neutralism in the Arab World: A Symposium* (San Francisco, 1964), 93.

[133] Mates, 75 (emphasis added).

THE 'KEY' TO NON-ALIGNMENT

While one cannot discount the idiosyncratic and national variations shaping the consciousness and position of each society and leader, 'most of the leading neutralist "ideologues" share a wide range of strikingly similar national and personal problems' which tend to give them 'something of a common character'.[134]

At the very least there is something of 'a racial and cultural aspect' of non-alignment. Non-aligned countries are those 'which have been made to feel that they live in a world apart from Europe . . . [and] which have been exploited economically and dominated politically by others'. It is not just a question of colour; the 'fact that non-aligned nations are predominantly non-white is . . . incidental. There are other peoples who have equally been exploited and dominated.' The key is that they have 'natural reactions against being made use of by major Powers . . . The common "cultural" tie in non-alignment is probably far more related to traditional relations with major Powers than it is to race.'[135]

More fundamentally, a number of factors have contributed to the perception of a 'common identity' whereby individuals perceive 'some aspect of the external world more or less similarly, [and] communicate their similarity of perception among themselves, thus forming an identity group'. Singer argues that for this to happen there need to be channels of communication, and that, most importantly, 'the members of the group must understand the common language or "code" '.[136] Even though individuals or states may use the same phraseology and pursue similar policies, this is not the same as belonging.

Moreover, 'the very ties binding individuals from one state to individuals and groups in another are often the barriers separating them from other states', so that membership 'in one group implies membership or non-membership in certain others'. In a useful analogy, Singer argues that, while a man may act and think 'as do women', this does 'not make him a member of the perceptual/identity group called "women" '.[137] This argument is of seminal importance in understanding why Sweden, Finland, Austria, Switzerland, and Ireland are not non-aligned. The inner consciousness of these societies is different and cannot be trans-

[134] Lyon, *Neutralism*, 60.

[135] J. W. Burton, *International Relations: A General Theory* (Cambridge, 1965), 194. Cf. Singer, 129.

[136] Singer, 71.

[137] Ibid. 89.

mogrified into something which it is not. Non-alignment is not a rigid formula but rather a feeling of belonging 'to a world which is different from the developed part of the world, whether East or West', so that the North–South divide is not merely economic but 'embraces all aspects of life as well as the form, substance and structure of society'.[138] In creating this common identity three 'pillars' are crucial.

(a) The Political Pillar

The overwhelming majority of the non-aligned have experienced colonial rule. That experience, together with the struggle against such rule, was enough to engender a sympathy towards non-alignment.[139] As products of this struggle, most countries concerned accorded it priority in their foreign policies, once they were independent. Non-alignment served a dual function in this regard: on the one hand, it was 'both a visible symbol of a nation's dedication to anti-colonialism and a method of inhibiting new colonialist tendencies',[140] while, on the other, it seemed to epitomize all that the struggles had been about, non-alignment being an 'assertion of state sovereignty'.[141] It implied an 'ideological and philosophical emancipation', promoting the 'quest for ideological and spiritual "identity" '.[142]

Willetts argues, indeed, that while the East–West issue did not provide a 'common identity' for the the non-aligned, 'anti-colonialism did provide a bond between them', and he sees this as an important distinguishing characteristic between the European neutrals and the non-aligned. His statistical analysis of voting behaviour in the United Nations purports to back up this view, enabling him to claim that the 'pro-colonial record of the European neutrals makes it completely explicable that these states remained so distant from non-alignment'.[143] If, says Willetts, 'anti-colonialism is a stronger identifying characteristic of the Non-Aligned than is abstention from East–West alignment, then it is not surprising that the European neutrals have not joined the Non-Aligned'.[144]

---

[138] Mates, 230.
[139] Edward W. Blyden III, 'The Idea of African "Neutralism" and "Nonalignment"': An Exploratory Survey', in K. London (ed.), New Nations in a Divided World (New York, 1963), 147.
[140] Crabb, Elephants and the Grass, 41–2.
[141] Willetts, Nonaligned Movement, 29.
[142] Crabb, Elephants and the Grass, 50.
[143] Willetts, Nonaligned Movement, 191–2.
[144] Ibid. 167; and see pp. 89–113, on 'Voting in the General Assembly'.

The Europeans concerned are not, in fact, pro-colonial. However, they have flinched at some of the vigorous means encompassed in UN resolutions concerned with eliminating colonialism. Their experience of foreign rule was not generally by different ethnic groups, nor by geographically remote and alien socio-political systems and cultures.[145] There was not the same degree of alienness, and perhaps as a consequence these states have been more restrained than non-aligned states in their attitude to the means to be employed in ending colonialism, although they do share the same objective. Experiencing foreign rule is not a sufficient condition in itself to form that common identity underlying non-alignment.

The experience of colonialism left a number of other legacies relevant to an understanding of non-alignment. One was the need for nation-building, a concern for national unity, since the new states were often not conterminous with pre-existing nations or tribal grouping, but were superimposed upon ethnic and economic diversity by the colonial power. As a result, the search for a cohesive force, for national unity, was usually an 'overriding and unavoidable concern' for the new leaders of these states.[146] Non-alignment proved to be a mechanism helpful in achieving political stability and unity, since it served as a 'broad national front behind which extremely divergent sections of the population are able to come together';[147] it helped to secure support, moreover, 'by reinforcing the goal of independence in foreign policy'.[148]

Inextricably related was the pursuit of independence in foreign policy. According to Mates, 'non-alignment can be defined as a policy strictly based on independence'.[149] Non-alignment was regarded as an ideal vehicle for demonstrating the new states' independence since it implied 'diplomatic freedom of action and choice'.[150] It conformed to the need 'to discover, to articulate, and to safeguard and strengthen one's own national interest in the world',[151] while also serving to emphasize that

---

[145] See David Thornley, 'Historical Introduction', in Basil Chubb. *The Government and Politics of Ireland* (London, 1974), 2, and Hakovirta, 'Effects of Non-Alignment on Neutrality in Europe'.

[146] Lyon, *Neutralism*, 108.

[147] N. P. Nayar, 'Nonalignment in World Affairs', *India Quarterly* (1962), 51, quoted by Crabb, *Elephants and the Grass*, 58.

[148] Fred L. Hadsel, 'Africa and the World: Nonalignment Reconsidered', in J. C. Charlesworth (ed.), *Realignment in the Communist and Western Worlds* (Annals of the American Academy of Political and Social Science, 372; July 1967), 96.

[149] Mates, 108. See also Crabb, *Elephants and the Grass*, 12, and Lyon, *Neutralism, 72.*

[150] Crabb, *Elephants and the Grass*, 11.

[151] Lyon, *Neutralism*, 73.

the new states were concerned with their own interpretations of their national interest rather than somebody else's interpretations or interests.

This insistence upon independence in foreign policy is one reason for their attitudes to alliance; but equally significant is the connection with the non-aligned ' "penchant" for deciding each issue on its merits'.[152] Whether this *penchant* is put into operation is the subject of some controversy, but, at least theoretically, the non-aligned proclaimed that they had 'the right to think for ourselves and to speak for ourselves. Our voice is not an echo.'[153] This attitude forms the heart of Jansen's definition of non-alignment, although perhaps it should be regarded as a necessary but not sufficient criterion. Jansen suggests that non-alignment is simply 'the desire and ability of an independent country . . . to follow an independent policy in foreign affairs; it is the desire and ability to make up its own mind, to take its own decisions or not to take them, after judging each issue separately and honestly on its merits'.[154] The combination of national interest and judgement helps to explain why divergences exist among the non-aligned, and why, while exercising independent judgement, the non-aligned are not impartial. It is an independent yet partial judgement. A further complication is that informed judgement requires both information and expertise, which many of these states may lack the resources to attain.

The foregoing helps to explain the attitude of the non-aligned to alliances and foreign military bases. The non-aligned believe that 'membership in an alliance would involve at least some compromise in the interests of coalition diplomacy, and may even involve subordination to the stronger power'.[155] They fear the possible inferior position within such an arrangement, and the likelihood that bloc leaders would seek to control the foreign policy of alliance members and even 'the internal development of weaker nations'.[156] There is a certain air of disapproval of alliances, but this usually means the alliance of others rather than oneself. There is also a belief that a relationship remains between alliances and colonialism, and a vague concern that perhaps alliances (particularly

---

152 Ibid. 68 (emphasis in original).

153 Indian Prime Minister Shastri in 1964, cited in Crabb's Introduction, in *Nonalignment in Foreign Affairs*, 17.

154 Jansen, 115; cf. 116–17, 404.

155 Lyon, *Neutralism*, 108.

156 M. Nikezic, 'Why Uncommitted Countries hold that they are not "Neutral" ', in J. C. Charlesworth (ed.), *Is International Communism Winning?* (Annals of the American Academy of Political and Social Science, 336 (July 1961), 78.

involving Great Powers) are a cause of tension and war, and certainly not in conformity with the principles of peaceful coexistence.

Despite this scepticism, the non-aligned are clearly not opposed to all alliances, most of them being heavily involved in alliances of one sort or another themselves.[157] The key distinction to be drawn was reaffirmed at the Havana summit of 1979 as opposition to participation in military pacts and alliances arising from Great Power or bloc rivalries and influences.[158] It is the link with out-of-area Great Powers which leads to opposition, not the mere fact that alliances exist.[159] Non-alignment was never simply a question of opposition to alliances and alignment. This partly explains why non-alignment has outlived many of the alliances current at the time of its gestation: it has had much more to do with the pursuit of an independent foreign policy.

The attitude to alliances has not been related to pacifism but rather to a feeling of outrage at being dragged into the quarrels of others.[160] Gupta, indeed, argues that the desire for 'non-involvement in irrelevant political contexts paved the way for the subsequent emergence of the doctrine of non-alignment'.[161] The cold war was regarded as a conflict between countries in a different part of the world, whose philosophy, culture, interests, and levels of economic development were very different.

Yet distaste is not to be equated with isolationism, since distance and water are not enough to ensure safety. Therefore, while they sought to avoid involvement in the cold war, the non-aligned were determined to do their 'utmost to prevent the next war which we believe will only result in the extinction of human civilization'.[162] Indeed, one of the key aspects of non-alignment, its lack of passivity, partly stems from 'an underlying conviction . . . that nonaligned countries are in a peculiarly advantageous position to ameliorate cold war conflicts and to make "peaceful coexistence" a reality'.[163]

---

[157] See Willetts, *Nonaligned Movement*, 127 ff.

[158] This appears several times in the Political Declaration agreed at Havana: see Peter Willetts, *The Non-Aligned in Havana: Documents of the Sixth Summit Conference and an Analysis of their Significance for the Globul Political System* (London, 1981), 77–137.

[159] Nehru e.g. is quoted on this in Jansen, 138.

[160] See Nehru on this as quoted by Mates, 240.

[161] S. K. Gupta, 'Asian Nonalignment', in Crabb, *Nonalignment in Foreign Affairs*, 45. See also Mates, 120–1.

[162] Indonesian views cited by Crabb, *Elephants and the Grass*, 8.

[163] Ibid.

(b) The Economic Pillar

In considering common experiences which have touched the non-aligned, it is necessary to heed the warning of Geldart and Lyon with respect to a closely related area of concern. They point to the fact that by the early 1980s it had increasingly been 'recognised that it is grossly misleading to equate North and South with rich and poor, industrialised and non-industrialised, developed and underdeveloped countries, because each grouping brings together states of considerable diversities by any economic measures'.[164] Similarly, one must be wary of any simple developed/aligned–underdeveloped/non-aligned division.

Notwithstanding this important truth, it is also true that many of the non-aligned have experienced certain similarities of economic circumstance.[165] A number of related economic experiences in the economic sphere which have directly or indirectly influenced the non-aligned can be identified, including poverty, dependency, underdevelopment and lack of industrialization, unfavourable terms of trade on the world market, a desire to attain economic independence in order to make a reality of political freedom, and a low economic status.

Of the poverty and relative underdevelopment, even now, of most of the non-aligned, there can be little doubt. When a number of indices of development and industrialization are examined, there emerges a clear correlation between lower income per capita (as a basic, if simple, measure of a lower stage of economic development), and involvement in the NAM.

Using World Bank classifications, it emerges that 34 out of 36 states classified as 'low-income' had full membership of the NAM, and attended the Havana summit in 1979 (with China and Haiti being the exceptions). In the 'middle-income' group over half were full members of the movement in 1979 and a further quarter fell into the categories of 'Observers' and 'Guests'. By contrast, of 18 'industrial market economies', it is striking that none attended as full members or even appeared in the next most significant category of Observers. Similarly, none of the 'non-market industrial economies' were involved. In summary, of 96 'low-/middle-income' states, 68 were full members and 11 attended in some other capacity. This compares with 4 states as Guests from the 24 industrial market and non-market economies.[166]

---

164 Geldart and Lyon, 101.
165 Lyon, Neutralism, 82.
166 World Bank, World Development Report 1981 (Oxford, 1981), 113 ff., categories and figures

Although figures for many countries are not available, an examination of 'gross manufacturing output per capita'[167] as a measure of industrialization tends to confirm the pattern of per capita income, as do measures of 'adult literacy rate'[168] and energy consumption per capita (although in this latter case Romania and Trinidad and Tobago break the pattern).[169] Although one should be cautious in accepting this evidence as definitive, there is an element of commonality in the circumstances of the countries under review.

One of the most striking things to emerge is that in the World Bank figures Austria, Finland, Sweden, Switzerland, and Ireland are in a completely different economic league from virtually all of the 'non-aligned'. For example, in GNP per capita they rank 14th, 16th, 3rd, 2nd, and 24th respectively, and even the Irish figure is at least double that of any of the poorest 85 states.[170] There is an economic aspect to the 'identity' dimension of the non-aligned, even if diverse interests do lead them to pursue widely differing economic policies.

While they are not definitive, figures on trade dependency are similarly suggestive. Singer examined 116 states and found that over 40 had more than one-third of their trade with just one state. He drew two conclusions from his material: firstly, that the 'weaker could legitimately be considered economically dependent upon the stronger'; and secondly, that it is 'a generalization that seems to hold with remarkable consistency that the more economically developed the country, the less likely it is to be dependent upon one major trading partner'.[171] The less developed tend to be most dependent.

Dependence and lack of development have led these states to seek greater economic independence and to escape their predicaments by seeking aid, preferably without strings and from multilateral sources,

---

for 'World Development Indicators'. Not all attenders at Havana have figures in these tables. See also Willetts, *The Non-Aligned in Havana*, 77, 248–54: he uses categories based on UNCTAD groups, but the broad pattern is similar.

[167] World Bank, table 6, pp. 144–5.

[168] Ibid., table 1, pp. 134–5.

[169] Ibid., table 7, pp. 146–7, esp. 'Energy consumption per capita', which is an indicator of industrialization.

[170] Ibid., table 1, pp. 134–5. Excluding capital-surplus oil-exporters, no full member of the NAM came higher than Ireland in the rankings, and of members' Guests' or Observers at Havana, only Spain, a Guest (23rd in ranking), marginally does. A similar pattern emerges from energy consumption figures, where only Singapore and Trinidad and Tobago of the full members rank higher than Ireland, and only Romania of the Guests, Ireland being the lowest of relevant Europeans.

[171] Singer, 238–9; but see also tables 6.1 and 6.2, and the associated commentary, pp. 227–46.

and also by developing and diversifying trade.[172] However, it does not appear that the old cliché about non-alignment as a tactic to maximize aid (either by obtaining help from both sides or by attempting to play each side off against the other) is true.

All these problems are compounded for these states, since they are confronted with an unfavourable situation in the world market, which has been 'dominated by countries that had gone far ahead in labor productivity and generally in technical progress'.[173] It is thus not surprising that increasingly they have turned their attention to the structural weaknesses of the international economic system and demanded a 'New International Economic Order', in order to overcome the inequalities which exist. The 'compartmentalization of foreign policy and domestic development . . . could not survive', and 'the economics of development and the diplomacy of development have become increasingly difficult to separate'.[174] It is also true that the 'economic factor constituted one of the main motive forces and later became the strongest motive which impelled the non-aligned countries to cooperation and joint-action', although it may be going too far to suggest that 'actions in the economic domain brought most of the countries together under the banner of non-alignment'.[175]

Certainly, the non-aligned themselves now appear to be fully aware that political and economic questions are inextricably linked. Thus, while the Group of 77 and the NAM 'maintained their separate identities until the mid-1970s despite some degree of overlapping membership',[176] increasingly they have been complementary to each other, with a certain division of labour but with 'each taking up, developing and using the proposals and decisions of the other'.[177]

Given this strong concern with the economic pillar, there is truth in the argument that non-alignment was 'not simply a by-product of the conflict between the two protagonists in the cold war' but that it was rather 'inspired by . . . desires stemming from their low level of development, their internal problems and from the awareness of the gap separating them from the developed countries, and from the fear which is generated by all these disadvantages'. There is perhaps even some truth

---

172 Hadsel, 97–100.
173 Mates, 150.
174 Rothstein, 'Foreign Policy and Development Policy', 615–16.
175 Mates, 112.
176 Geldart and Lyon, 80.
177 Ibid. 95.

in the view that they would have found themselves essentially 'in a similar position even if there had been no cold war', and would in any case have constituted themselves as a 'separate part of the international community'.[178]

(c) The Social Pillar

As Burton points out,'types of domestic institutions are not considered by the non-aligned nations to be a test for non-alignment'.[179] None the less, there is a degree of congruity among the non-aligned in their domestic circumstances in the social sphere. The social pillar, like the other pillars, reflects the colonial experience and legacy, particularly the consequent need for social integration and national political unity. Integration has been a major post-colonial problem, as the political institutions left by colonial regimes have proved to be largely unable to cope with the lack of socio-political homogeneity. The new states often lacked the bonds usually associated with nationalism. These societies were thus often fragmented, lacking socio-economic development, and not yet transformed or integrated by the impact of industrialization. While they have experienced a social transformation during the last generation, this has often exacerbated rather than ameliorated the problems.

One important consequence of these factors is the differentiation they reflect between European and non-European societies; whereas 'the internal problems of the industrially advanced world were due to different social and political systems based on modern economies and social structures, the underdeveloped countries faced completely different problems which resulted from their backwardness', and clearly their social structures and problems were different also.[180] The social origins, experience, and orientations of their societies resulted in many of the non-aligned lacking 'any identification with, or attachment to, the traditions of the Western state system . . . They tend, that is, to think differently than their Western counterparts . . . most significantly, perhaps, they do not have the *same* sense of what being a Small Power implies in terms of a range of acceptable behaviour.'[181]

The urgency accorded to development appears to have influenced the type of regime these countries have adopted, or submitted to, and both

---

178 Mates, 173–4.
179 Burton, *Nonalignment*, 198.
180 Mates, 42.
181 Rothstein, *Alliances and Small Powers*, 243–4 (emphasis in original).

regime-type and attitude to development tend clearly to distinguish non-European from European states.[182]

CONCLUSION

(a) The Europeans are not Non-Aligned

In general, the European countries under discussion are different in the following ways from the non-aligned:

1. Most importantly, they differ in 'identity', 'consciousness', and empathy of perceptions.
2. They have different experiences of alien rule, and consequently differing legacies from it.
3. They are different with respect to socio-economic levels of income, development, and modernization.
4. They are part of a system of society, economies, philosophy, and politics which is alien to most of the non-aligned.
5. Their geographic/strategic location compounds their alien nature.
6. The European states have a concern with issues which differ from the inescapable concerns of the non-aligned.

(b) Neutrality and Non-Alignment

'Neutrality' and 'non-alignment' are often used as generic terms for each other, as if they were synonymous or one was a derivation from the other.[183] However, from the foregoing discussion it is evident that there is *no* inherent relationship between non-alignment and neutrality. On the contrary, it can be argued that the specific demands of neutrality run counter to the ethos of non-alignment. Moreover, non-alignment is 'not a policy of seeking for a neutral position in the case of war':[184] indeed, in the 'event of open warfare between the main power blocs, non-aligned countries would be obliged, as all countries are, to declare themselves either as neutral or at war',[185] since non-alignment does not involve any declaration or decision in advance 'of a fixed position to be taken in case

---

[182] See e.g. R. W. Cox and H. K. Jacobsen, *The Anatomy of Influence* (New Haven, 1974), 463, table C.3, and pp. 457–64.

[183] Thus, Hamilton Fish Armstrong, 'Neutrality: Varying Tunes', *Foreign Affairs*, 35/1 (Oct. 1956), discusses both, while Ogley, 4 and 33, sees non-alignment as a category of neutrality. See also Crabb, *Elephants and the Grass*, 7.

[184] Choucri, op. cit. 6.

[185] Burton, *International Relations*, 220.

of war'.[186] Moreover, the non-aligned 'admit no binding obligations to remain indifferent and impartial':[187] indeed, the very motivation of non-alignment is to be not an idle bystander but an active participant in the unfolding of events. As early as 1961 this positivism was integral to non-alignment: there was a profound belief that it was 'essential that the non-aligned countries should participate in solving outstanding international issues concerning peace and security in the world as none of them can remain unaffected by or indifferent to these issues'.[188]

Nevertheless, a degree of confusion persists and the concepts are often loosely applied simultaneously to the same countries. In part this is simply a problem of the distinction being slurred in popular usage, and that slur being deeply entrenched.[189] Politicians also slur the distinction, whether deliberately or unconsciously. The problem is compounded in that superficially the two have certain characteristics in common, especially when they are translated into the actual foreign policies of states, such as the stress on independence in foreign policy, sovereignty and freedom of decision, freedom from entanglements, and non-membership in confrontational alliance systems of the superpowers. There is more confusion in the use of the word 'neutrality', which is not an appropriate description for a peacetime policy, but is widely used as if it were. Such problems are extenuated when one is seeking to classify states whose official policy is non-participation in alliances in peacetime, aiming at neutrality in the event of war.

The confusion over these terms is rife with respect to Austria, Finland, Sweden, Switzerland, and Ireland, who often claim to be neutral or non-aligned or both. Before we examine the Irish case in depth, attention will be turned to the 'European neutrals'.

---

[186] Armstrong, 61.
[187] Burton, *Nonalignment*, 22.
[188] See Jankowitsch and Sauvant, i. 1–42.
[189] Lyon, *Neutralism*, 20.

3

A European Model

FIVE European states, Austria, Sweden, Switzerland, Finland and Yugoslavia, are commonly identified as neutral or non-aligned in the literature.[1] While Austria, Sweden, and Switzerland are always included in any such identification, Finland and Yugoslavia are sometimes not. In the case of Finland this is because of its lack of full participation in mainstream West European developments, and more particularly because of the ambivalent nature of its position, stemming from the 1948 Treaty of Friendship, Co-operation and Mutual Assistance with the Soviet Union. Especially problematic are those provisions concerning the agreement for 'assistance, in case of need' from the Soviet Union.[2] Moreover, whatever the arguments concerning that treaty, the Soviet Union has always considered the essence of Finnish policy to be 'benevolent relations' with the USSR.[3] Despite its position in the NAM, Yugoslavia is more often excluded, given its radically different ideological, political, and economic systems and its even more pronounced lack of involvement in West European institutions.[4]

This chapter focuses upon 'the three neutral countries'[5] universally regarded as such, and particularly upon Sweden, since it is unfettered by

[1] See Karl E. Birnbaum and Hanspeter Neuhold (eds.), *Neutrality and Nonalignment in Europe* (Vienna, 1981); Hanspeter Neuhold, 'Permanent Neutrality in Contemporary International Relations: A Comparative Perspective', *Irish Studies in International Affairs*, 1/3 (1982); and Harto Hakovirta, 'The Soviet Union and the Varieties of Neutrality in Western Europe', *World Politics*, 35/4 (July 1983).

[2] 'Treaty of Friendship, Co-operation and Mutual Assistance between the Soviet Union and the Finnish Republic, Moscow, 6 April 1948', in J. A. S. Grenville, *The Major International Treaties 1914–1973: A History and a Guide with Texts* (London, 1974).

[3] Brian Faloon, 'Aspects of Finnish Neutrality: An Historical Review', *Irish Studies in International Affairs*, 1/3 (1982), 10. For aspects of the debate on the Finnish position see G. Maude, *The Finnish Dilemma* (OUP, 1976); M. Jakobson, *Finnish Neutrality* (London, 1968); Bengt Sundelius (ed.), *Foreign Policies of Northern Europe* (Boulder, Colo., 1982); Raimo Vayrynen, 'The Evolution of Finland's Foreign Policy since the End of the Second World War', in Birnbaum and Neuhold; and Aimo Pajunen, 'Some Aspects of Finnish Security Policy', ibid.; Karen E. Örvik, 'The Limits of Security: Defence and Foreign Trade in Finland', *Survey*, 24/2 (Spring 1979); and R. Allison, *Finland's Relations with the Soviet Union 1944–1984* (Oxford, 1985).

[4] For a Yugoslav view see Leo Mates, *Nonalignment: Theory and Current Policy* (Belgrade and New York, 1972).

[5] The phrase is from the EEC Commission, 'Report to the European Parliament on the State of the Negotiations with the United Kingdom' (Brussels, 1963), 97.

constitutional or international treaty obligations regarding its position
and because some Irish politicians have regarded Sweden as a possible
model for Ireland.[6] The analysis of these states' policies and attitudes
leads to an extrapolation of their essential position, which, taken together with the key characteristics of neutrality and non-alignment
identified in the previous chapter, forms the basis of a model against
which the Irish case is examined in subsequent chapters.

THE THREE NEUTRAL COUNTRIES

Austria, Sweden, and Switzerland each 'arrived at their neutrality under
rather different conditions', this being 'reflected in the diversity of their
ideas and policies'.[7] However, despite this diversity, significant similarities in their positions have been perceived both by third parties and by
the states themselves. For example, they engaged in a joint exercise in
negotiating with the European Community,[8] and joint activity has also
been evident in the membership of the Neutral and Non-aligned (NNA)
caucus at the review meetings of the Conference on Security and Co-
operation in Europe (CSCE). They have all had the status of Guests at
NAM summits,[9] and have shared a common perception of how they
differ from NAM members, recognizing the latter as 'the political
expression' of the poor, while they themselves are rich. Indeed, they do
not wish 'to be politically identified with such states'.[10] As the Swedes
have acknowledged, 'many of the decisions made by this group diverge
from Swedish views',[11] as do the 'origin' and 'form' of non-aligned

[6] One prominent example is Conor Cruise O'Brien, one-time Foreign Affairs Department
official and politician. See e.g. his *To Katanga and Back* (London, 1965), 25.

[7] Jacques Freymond, 'The European Neutrals and the Atlantic Community', in F. O. Wilcox
and H. F. Haviland, jun. (eds.), *The Atlantic Community: Progress and Prospects* (New York, 1963),
86.

[8] Manfred Scheich, 'The European Neutrals after Enlargement of the Communities: The
Austrian Perspective', *Journal of Common Market Studies*, 12/3 (1973-4), 240. See also Struye's
'Memorandum on the Political Aspects of Neutrality', presented to the Consultative Assembly of
the Council of Europe (doc 1581; 29 Apr. 1963) (hereafter 1963 Struye Report).

[9] Harto Hakovirta, 'Effects of Non-Alignment on Neutrality in Europe: An Analysis and
Appraisal', *Conflict and Cooperation*, 18 (1983). The category of Guest was introduced at the Lusaka
summit in 1970 primarily for liberation movements, but on Austrian initiative it was extended to
European states not aspiring to full membership. Finland attended the 1964 Cairo meeting as an
Observer.

[10] Swedish Foreign Minister Wickman in 'Afrique–Asie' Sept. 1973, reproduced in *Documents on Swedish Foreign Policy 1973* (NS 1: C: 23; Stockholm, 1976), 65 (hereafter *DSFP*). See
also Hakovirta, *'Effects'*, 61.

[11] Govt. dec. to Riksdag, 31 Mar. 1976, in *DSFP 1976*, 23.

policies, even if the 'foreign policy objectives are similar'.[12] The Irish have attended neither NAM summits nor NNA caucus meetings.

The three neutral countries also took a common position on the International Energy Programme and the International Energy Agency. They joined once a special clause guaranteeing their neutral status had been inserted in their agreements, despite the provisions these still contained for weighted majority voting and the possibility of automatic oil-sharing.[13] Ireland, incidentally, did not insist on a similar clause.

More generally, Austria, Sweden, and Switzerland have adopted broadly similar positions regarding West European institutions. But, before turning specifically to those positions, the attitudes of the three states towards alliances, trade, Western values, and independence will be examined, as will their rejection of passive isolationalism as a basis for foreign policy.

The three states are not signatories to any military treaties with other powers,[14] nor indeed are they members of any military alliances. Austria and Switzerland have both consistently maintained that a 'neutral country cannot join a military alliance in time of peace because in so doing it would destroy its ability to remain neutral in time of war'.[15] The Swedes have also taken this attitude on most occasions, arguing that they 'do not wish, by advance commitments, to deprive [themselves] of the right and opportunity to remain outside a new war',[16] and that 'neutrality is not only a legal concept but indeed also a matter of policy. It implies a conduct, even in peacetime, which maintains confidence in the determination as well as the ability to remain neutral in war or crisis.'[17] Treaties, alliances, and organizations which prejudice that ability are to be avoided.

[12] Swedish Prime Minister Erlander in a speech to Swedish Steel and Metalworkers' Union, 22 Aug. 1961, *DSFP 1961*, 119.

[13] See *Agreement on an International Energy Program, 18 November 1974* (Cmnd. 5826; London, 1975). See also Maude, p 128; and for Swedish view and position see 'Press release', 18 Nov. 1974, in *DSFP 1974*, 251–2, and Parliamentary reply by Foreign Minister Andersson, 16 Jan. 1975, in *DSFP 1975*, 251–2.

[14] This does not apply to their commercial military activities, i.e. the buying and selling of equipment. See e.g. *DSFP 1961*, 93, *DSFP 1971*, 244, and *DSFP 1975*, 10. See also Nils Andren, *Power-Balance and Non-Alignment: A Perspective on Swedish Foreign Policy* (Stockholm, 1967), 174, and Adam Roberts, *Nations in Arms: The Theory and Practice of Territorial Defence* (London, 1976), 57–8, 109.

[15] Bruno Kreisky, 'Austria Draws the Balance', *Foreign Affairs*, 37/2 (Jan. 1959).

[16] Govt. message to Parliament, 4 Feb. 1948, in Andren, *Power-Balance and Non-Alignment*, 51.

[17] The quotation is from the Swedish Minister of Commerce, 28 July 1962, in *DSFP 1962*, 148; cf. Swedish Foreign Minister, Nov. 1971, in *DSFP 1971*, 77.

The Swedes have wavered when the issue of a Nordic or Scandinavian defence pact has arisen. Andren has characterized Swedish initiative on this issue as 'remarkable' given that their 'traditional policy of neutrality had meant not only freedom from engagements with the great powers but on the whole a stubborn refusal to undertake any military commitments in relation to any other state'. In fact, the Swedish initiative represented 'an attempt to increase the possibilities to attain the first goal by giving up the second'.[18]

In 1948 the Swedes spoke out clearly against joining 'any bloc of the great powers' on their own part.[19] But, a year later, it was emphasized that this did not exclude the possibility of 'blocs of equal, smaller countries', and clearly a 'Scandinavian defence alliance is not a great power bloc'.[20] The Swedes were not against participation in alliance *per se*, but they would not participate in any alliance 'if the aim would be that this alliance should form part of a major security system with the character of a great power alliance'. Hence a Scandinavian defence alliance was only acceptable if 'free of outside alliances'.

Moreover, it was to be 'directed towards neutrality in case of a conflict', and, if not directly involved in the war, the signatories were to consult on both the rules and the maintenance of their neutrality. In fact, while directed to 'strengthening . . . the power of resistance of the participating countries in the event of an attack against any one of them', this stipulation was linked to strengthening their neutrality, and to helping them 'keep . . . outside a general conflict, and in time of peace to stay outside other groups of powers'. While acknowledging that the plans represented 'a departure and an important one from [a] policy of neutrality', the Swedes felt that, given the conditions they had laid down, 'this Scandinavian alliance would, looked at as a whole, mean an extension to all those countries of a zone not bound by any alliances to any third power. And so the main idea of Sweden's foreign policy would still be maintained.'

If agreed, the Scandinavian arrangement (involving Sweden, Denmark, and Norway) would have been a throughgoing alliance, since the Scandinavian countries 'would consider themselves, from the point of view of defence, as one unit'. There were to be plans for a joint

---

[18] Andren, *Power-Balance and Non-Alignment*, 60. He has an interesting commentary on these developments, pp. 53 ff.

[19] Govt. message to Parliament, 4 Feb. 1948, ibid. 48–52.

[20] Minister of Foreign Affairs to Riksdag, 9 Feb. 1949, ibid. 62–72. The quotations in the next three paragraphs are from the same speech.

defence council and joint defence, in addition to close collaboration in foreign policy. Crucially and fundamentally, an attack on any one of the three signatories was to be considered an attack on all, and the others 'would be obliged immediately to render military aid'. Also considered for a time was 'a partial defensive cooperation in peacetime without an alliance', although this seems to have been discarded since 'the cooperation could not be pursued as far as possible within a defensive alliance, neither could it in war be set in motion as quickly and become effective'.

As Roberts has noted, 'Sweden does not base her arguments for neutrality on any sweeping condemnations of alliances as such; indeed, there is a tendency to go to the opposite extreme and argue that neutrality is a function of the balance of power and can only exist in circumstances of such a balance.'[21] Although by the late 1960s and 1970s many felt that this basic condition of Swedish neutrality was 'in a process of dissolution', an alliance balance has been crucial to Swedish policy.[22] It has been given a particular twist and importance by the concept of the 'Nordic balance' and the position of Finland.[23]

All three states have also given a number of general reasons for hostility to alliances. A basic factor has been 'a stubborn, almost instinctive distrust of being entangled in great-Power alliances and military blocs',[24] a feeling 'that the rest of the world is something dismal and threatening: hence, the best policy is to keep away from foreign entanglements'.[25] More specifically, there is a fear that they would be drawn into a war by an allied Great Power, and that membership 'increases the risk that local conflicts of various kinds will be magnified into becoming major political issues'.[26] The real objection to alliances is the link between neutrality and independence of mind and action. There is a profound belief that neutrality is 'the condition precedent for a free and independent attitude. Our deeply rooted resolve to define our own policy makes it impossible for us to consider joining alliances where decisions must nevertheless make allowances for the interests of all

21 Roberts, 80.

22 Andren, *Power-Balance and Non-Alignment*, 192.

23 See J. J. Holst (ed.), *Five Roads to Nordic Security* (Oslo, 1973); Nils Andren (ed.), *The Future of the Nordic Balance* (Stockholm, 1977); id., 'Prospects for the Nordic Security Pattern', *Cooperation and Conflict*, 13/4 (1978); A. O. Brundtland, 'The Nordic Balance', and Erik Moberg, 'The "Nordic Balance" Concept: A Critical Commentary', both in *Cooperation and Conflict*, 2 (1966).

24 Swedish Foreign Minister, 13 Mar. 1964, in *DSFP 1964*, 9.

25 D. Frei, 'Switzerland and the EEC: Facts and Trends', *Journal of Common Market Studies*, 12/3 (1973–4), 260.

26 Prime Minister Erlander, 24 Jan. 1961, in *DSFP 1961*, 12.

members.'[27] The governments have regarded it as inherently inimical to their basic policy that, on various international questions, their attitudes should be determined beforehand by any group, so that a fundamental line of their foreign policy 'of neutrality is that we shall be free to take our own stand and to rely on our own independent judgement'.[28] To pursue 'a credible policy of neutrality, the neutral country has as a matter of principle to maintain its freedom of decision and action in all spheres of national policy'.[29] Of course, the policy they have pursued is regarded as being 'firmly anchored in our own interests',[30] and is of their 'own choosing'.[31] However, the problem of choosing is exacerbated by the trade patterns and linkages of the economies concerned.

The foreign-trade distribution of Austria, Sweden, and Switzerland over a twenty-year period is shown in Table 3.1. Their foreign trade has been decisively with the West, particularly with West European markets. The three countries have themselves been conscious of this economic dependence and have not hidden their concern about it.[32] The figures also help to explain why there has been significant debate over political and economic priorities in these countries, in the form of the question 'Should the country be allowed to stagnate by not participating in an essential political-economic alliance?—or, equally difficult, should the reasoned principle of neutrality be abandoned in order to continue the economic well-being of the nation?'[33] Even setting aside this dilemma, Austria, Sweden, and Switzerland have had 'to come to terms with a politically loaded economic situation which threatens the very premise of neutrality, i.e. independence of action'.[34] None the less, there has not been any significant trade diversification between economic blocs; rather, they have preferred a free-trade policy as a way of enhancing independence. However, it is clear that, while officially the Swedes have maintained that 'neutrality is determined by fundamental evaluations relating to security policy, not by economic interests', it has not always been quite so distinct in practice.[35]

[27] Swedish Foreign Minister, 13 Mar. 1964, in DSFP 1964, 11.

[28] Govt. statement, 31 Mar. 1971, in DSFP 1971, 31.

[29] Scheich, 237, referring to the Austrian position.

[30] Govt. statement, 19 Apr. 1961, in DSFP 1961, 15.

[31] Swedish Foreign Minister, 11 Mar. 1965, in DSFP 1965, 17.

[32] Although on 22 Aug. 1961 Prime Minister Erlander attempted to argue that Swedish trade was not predominantly in one commodity or product, which allowed 'a certain amount of freedom of action': DSFP 1961, 116–17.

[33] James L. Waite, 'The Swedish Paradox: EEC and Neutrality', Journal of Common Market Studies, 12/3 (1973–4), 335.   [34] Ibid. 319.

[35] Swedish Foreign Minister, 1 Nov. 1971, in DSFP 1971, 81.

Table 3.1. Foreign Trade, by Area (%)

	1961		1971		1981	
	Imp.	Exp.	Imp.	Exp.	Imp.	Exp.
AUSTRIA						
OECD	78.7	69.7	81.7	74.8	74.7	70.4
OECD Europe	*72.8*	*65.8*	*75.5*	*66.8*	*66.5*	*64.9*
Comecon	3.1	14.6	9.1	12.2	11.9	11.4
SWEDEN						
OECD	79.6	78.3	84.2	85.2	79.5	78.0
OECD Europe	*68.2*	*73.8*	*73.0*	*74.8*	*66.6*	*68.4*
Comecon	4.4	4.2	4.8	4.3	4.5	3.9
SWITZERLAND						
OECD	85.5	68.5	90.2	77.4	86.0	72.9
OECD Europe	*75.2*	*59.2*	*78.2*	*59.9*	*72.7*	*57.6*
Comecon	2.3	3.2	2.2	4.0	4.0	3.3

Note: Over the years the figures for various countries and groups are not always calculated on an identical basis, but the margin of error is small.

Sources: *OECD Economic Surveys* (Paris): SWEDEN—(July 1982), 64, (Mar. 1967), 36–7; AUSTRIA—(Feb. 1983), 72, (July 1976), 54, (Mar. 1967), 33; SWITZERLAND—(May 1983), 54, (Mar. 1976), 56, (Feb. 1972), 76; *OECD Statistic Bulletin*, Ser. A (Paris, monthly).

These problems are exacerbated by the close identification which these countries have with West European developments and civilization. Even the careful Swiss have acknowledged that 'We are not placed . . . between the Communist world and the Western world; *we are part of the latter. Its civilization is ours*',[36] and that the bonds create 'a moral solidarity'.[37] Austrians have spoken in a similar vein,[38] while the Swedes have regarded themselves as linked to Western Europe 'by many links deriving from a common civilization and a common history no less than

[36] Max Petitpierre, 'Is Swiss Neutrality Still Justified?', in *Switzerland: Present and Future* (n.p., 1963), cited in Roderick Ogley, *The Theory and Practice of Neutrality in the Twentieth Century* (London, 1970), 176 (emphasis added).

[37] Quoted by Freymond, from Swiss presentation to Council of Ministers, 1962, in Wilcox and Haviland, 77.

[38] Ibid. 76.

from geographical affinity'.[39] In fact, the three states are faced with the problem that on the one hand 'a strong emphasis on the fact that . . . foreign policy is conducted without ideological ties would undermine the feeling of solidarity with the democracies',[40] while on the other hand too great an emphasis upon that solidarity, leading perhaps to 'neutrality with a Western flavour',[41] would undermine the credibility of their independence, a credibility essential for neutrality.

One way in which these states have attempted to overcome this problem has been the pursuit of active and independent foreign policies, with the concomitant affirmation of the belief that the 'policy of neutrality is not an isolationist policy'.[42] This has been most marked in the Swedish case, and the current Swedish position is centred around a belief that they have a positive contribution to make, and that neutrality does not require silence. Indeed, this is regarded as strengthening their own position, since as 'long as these standpoints are independent standpoints on matters of principle, there is no reason to suppose that they detract from the credibility of our policy of neutrality. On the contrary, . . . our independent opinions . . . can if anything help to make our neutrality more convincing.'[43] Somewhat hesitantly, even the Swiss have now acknowledged that isolationalism 'is not only a crime but a political blunder'.[44] The Austrians under Chancellor Kreisky also moved to a more active role.

However, the essence of the three neutrals' policies has been the need to be *seen* to be independent, since neutrality is to some extent in the eye of the beholder, with the concomitant need to retain as much sovereignty and freedom of action as is possible.

(a) The Need to be Seen to be Independent

For the Swedes

an essential condition determining whether a policy of neutrality can be maintained when put to the test is of course that the rest of the world must have

---

[39] Swedish Minister of Commerce, 28 July 1962, in *DSFP 1962*, 146.

[40] Andren, *Power-Balance and Non-Alignment*, 54.

[41] Howard Turner, 'Sweden and European Integration: The Significance of the Neutrality Component in Swedish Foreign Policy' (Leicester University, M. A. diss., June 1975), p. iv.

[42] Swedish Foreign Minister, 6 Oct. 1972, in *DSFP 1972*, 71.

[43] The quotation is from the Swedish Foreign Minister, 5 Nov. 1975, in *DSFP 1975*, 81; cf. Govt. dec., 31 Mar. 1976, in *DSFP 1976*, 19.

[44] Jacques Freymond, 'How the Small Countries Can Contribute to Peace', in A. Schou and A. O. Brundtland (eds.), *Small States in International Relations* (Stockholm, 1971), 182.

confidence in the will of the neutral state to uphold without faltering its chosen line of foreign policy . . . We must make it clear by words and deeds that it is our intention in the event of war to use the freedom of action we have possessed in peacetime to assert our neutrality. We must not give the Great Powers any grounds for suspecting that Swedish territory may be placed at the disposal of another Power and form a base from which an attack could be launched. Our foreign policy must not be drawn up so as to give rise to suspicions in the country of one Great Power or expectations in the country of another.[45]

Indeed, the Swedes have tried to emphasize that even if 'a war between the Great Powers breaks out, *we cannot choose*, even in a critical situation and under heavy external pressure, to enter the war on the side of one of the belligerents'.[46] Of course, the problem is that all states retain the ultimate right to choose.[47] To try and demonstrate that the state has no choice, with any great credibility, the policy must be pursued with consistency and steadfastness: 'it must not be made dependent on transitory factors but must be an expression of a lasting programme. The world must be able to rely on our assurances.'[48] Periodically, the government has argued that a high degree of domestic unity on the issue is the strongest guarantee for the policy's success and credibility.[49] The neutral must be particularly aware that in 'an acute and tense situation it is particularly important . . . not to give the rest of the world the impression that . . . actions are dependent upon consultations with a certain group of states'.[50] Even more fundamentally, it must recognize that to renounce its right to defend itself would also be to renounce its chances of upholding neutrality in a future war. A neutral must recognize that 'defence effort is an instrument of . . . foreign policy. It makes . . . foreign policy more credible.' Yet, if not taken seriously, 'it immediately affects the question of confidence in . . . [one's] tenacity to uphold . . . [the] chosen line of policy', giving rise to suspicions and distrust. At worst, it might be contended 'that we were trying to ensure that we should be able to co-ordinate our policy with

---

[45] Swedish Foreign Minister, 11 Mar. 1965, in *DSFP 1965*, 17. Cf. Govt. dec., 23 Mar. 1972, in *DSFP 1972*, 22.

[46] Swedish Prime Minister, 2 Feb. 1970, in *DSFP 1970*, 14–15 (emphasis added).

[47] It is worth stressing that the Swedish position is not immutable, because of its lack of legal foundation, especially since the Swedish parliament in 1956 'rejected the idea that Sweden should bind its foreign policy . . . in an unforeseeable future under the guarantee of foreign powers': Andren, *Power-Balance and Non-Alignment*, 191.

[48] Govt. statement, 21 Mar. 1968, in *DSFP 1968*, 13.

[49] Swedish Prime Minister, 9 Nov. 1961, in *DSFP 1961*, 80–1; Foreign Minister, 6 Oct. 1972, in *DSFP 1972*, 72–3.

[50] Swedish Govt. statement, 31 Mar. 1971, in *DSFP 1971*, 31.

that of a Great Power in the event of armed conflict'.[51] In fact, the credibility and viability of neutrality presuppose a strong, independent defence,[52] as an essential precondition of the policy *for* neutrality.

(b) The Need to Retain as much Sovereignty and Freedom of Decision and Action as Possible

This dimension may be divided into political, economic, and military elements, which interrelate and overlap. The political element is apparent from the repeated stress upon the link between independence, national interest, and neutrality, and also in the attitude to alliances. It will be examined in more detail in the discussion of attitudes to European co-operation.[53]

Many of the same concerns are apparent in the economic element, since the need to 'maintain . . . freedom of decision and action . . . includes economic and trade policy',[54] and 'undoubted viability in economic life' is a crucial condition of neutrality.[55] Strictly speaking, such economic viability and independence require self-sufficiency and reliance upon one's own resources. Any diminution in this area involves the potential loss of economic sovereignty, which in turn has repercussions for political sovereignty by undermining independence of action.[56] The three neutrals are aware of these requirements, but they are also aware that in a world of growing interdependence they 'must frame their policies in such a way that it is possible for them to reap the benefits of cooperation without giving up their independence and national identity. On occasion this can be a difficult tight-rope act'.[57]

One solution has been a stress upon 'total defence', whereby an economic defence programme becomes an indispensable component of defence, since if 'economic defence or . . . civil defence arrangements are not sufficiently strong, there is less likelihood that other nations will have confidence in our ability to defend our neutrality . . . We must be able to hold out in the case of a blockade.'[58] Special efforts have therefore

---

[51] Swedish Prime Minister, 2 Feb. 1970, in *DSFP 1970*, 16.

[52] See below, pp. 54–7.

[53] See below, p. 57 ff.

[54] Scheich, 237.

[55] Peter Lyon, *Neutralism* (Leicester, 1963), 175.

[56] Waite, 319–36.

[57] The quotation is from the Swedish Foreign Minister, 1 Nov. 1971, in *DSFP 1971*, 81; cf. Roberts, 74.

[58] Swedish Prime Minister, 2 Feb. 1970, in *DSFP 1970*, 16. See also *Sweden's Total Defence 1982–1987* (Ds Fo 1981: 5; Stockholm, 1981).

been made in regard to economic preparedness, seeking 'to ensure necessary supplies in the event of war and in situations where war or conflicts outside Sweden threaten our independence and disrupt international trade'.[59] Such action was also to apply to peacetime crises.

The problem with this programme is that the countries are part of the international division of labour, as Roberts points out, and, because their trading patterns are committed in a particular way, it is difficult to see how 'suddenly in a crisis' they would be able 'to reverse the dependence on international trade'.[60] All the states concerned are so committed to international trade that they find it difficult to meet the requirements of self-sufficiency, despite efforts at strategic stock-piling.[61] On the other hand, the central question in a crisis would not necessarily be maintaining the current (or recent) standard of living, but avoiding involvement in a war, whatever the economic consequences may be. It is clearly a matter of judgement, what minimum requirements are necessary 'to safeguard the survival of the people and the maintenance of the most essential functions of society'.[62] It is worth noting that states do not necessarily have a certain level of economic development as their foremost value, and all three states have, in their peacetime policy, been prepared to make some economic sacrifices for neutrality.[63]

While economic independence and political freedom of action are indispensable props to neutrality, even more crucial, although not entirely separate, is the question of defence.[64] It is essential to credibility and independence that a state has the physical ability to defend its territory (including, if appropriate, its territorial waters), its interests, and its neutral rights.

Few in the countries concerned have any illusions that neutrality offers complete security, but there is a sense, in those neutrals with long experience of neutrality (Sweden and Switzerland), that on the whole armed neutrality has served them well in the past. However, it is also appreciated that 'no solution exists which in the present situation is completely satisfactory' with regard to defence and security.[65] The

[59] *Sweden's Total Defence 1982–1987*, 15.

[60] Roberts, 103, 73.

[61] *Sweden's Total Defence 1982–1987*, 16; *Sweden in Brief* (Stockholm, 1982), 32–4.

[62] *Sweden's Total Defence 1982–1987*, 15.

[63] Swedish Prime Minister, 5 Aug. 1971, in *DSFP 1971*, 46; Foreign Minister, 1 May 1972, in *DSFP 1972*, 32–6.

[64] For basic facts about the respective forces and equipment of Austria, Sweden, and Switzerland see *The Military Balance 1985–1986* (London, 1985), 62–3, 65–7, and 170.

[65] Cf. Swedish Minister of Defence, 21 May 1963, in *DSFP 1963*, 151, and Foreign Minister, 9 Feb. 1949 (quoted in full in Andren, *Power-Balance and Non-Alignment*, 62–72).

fundamental solution has been neutrality with the concomitant attitude
to alliances. It leads to a disavowal of help, an emphasis upon own
resources, and a belief in a significant defence effort with a willingness to
pay the price.

The explicit disavowal of help is vital, and applies to both formal and
informal arrangements, since 'only by making it clear that it will not be
forced into an alliance, nor tolerate a "friendly" intervention, can a
neutral convince its adversary that it really is neutral, and not a wavering
and potentially hostile power'.[66] There must be a lack of preparation for,
or expectation of, military assistance from other states. The neutral must
act independently, relying upon its own resources and stressing self-
help, and 'cannot let others assume responsibility for . . . [its] security'.
Moreover, neutrality is regarded as 'a policy that would have little
substance if it were not secured by a well-equipped defence'.[67] Furthermore, given the feeling that it is necessary to avoid being dependent
upon imported arms and supplies, it is also necessary, as far as practicable, to supply one's own weapons and equipment.[68]

If defence and self-sufficiency are taken seriously then there must also
be a willingness to accept the consequences in terms of expenditure. This
appears to have been the case in Sweden, with an acceptance that they
could not 'create the society we want, nor carry out the foreign policy
we want, unless we are prepared to pay the price'.[69] Thus, by the 1970s
the Swedes could boast that their defence expenditure per capita 'is by far
the highest in Europe'. Clearly this was not the case for either Austria or
Switzerland; and, even so, by the end of the decade Sweden had fallen
back behind others.[70] Indeed, the much-vaunted Swedish defence effort
came under strain in the late 1970s, experiencing 'a period of retrench-
ment and contraction', caused by 'new and more pessimistic evaluations
than before of Sweden's economic and technological potential'. Inside
Sweden this development has been 'accompanied by gloomy predictions

---

66 Roberts, 42.

67 Swedish Foreign Minister, 25 Feb. 1964, in *DSFP 1964*, 10.

68 *The Times*, 10 May 1983, reported that '70% of the armed forces' equipment is made in
Sweden', albeit at 'a very much higher cost than the equivalent bought elsewhere'. See also
Roberts, 57–8, 108–9; Andren, *Power-Balance and Non-Alignment* 174; *DSFP 1961*, 93; *DSFP
1969*, 9–11; *DSFP 1971*, 244; *DSFP 1975*, 10.

69 The quotation is from the Foreign Minister, 25 Feb. 1964, in *DSFP 1964*, 10;
cf. Foreign Minister, 9 Feb. 1949 (quoted in Andren, *Power-Balance and Non-Alignment*,
62–72).

70 The quotation is from the Swedish Foreign Minister, 1 Nov. 1971, in *DSFP 1971*, 81; see
The Military Balance 1985–1986, 170, for the statistics.

. . . on the future capability of the defence organization'.[71] Nevertheless, in comparison with other European states Sweden still ranked sixth
in the early 1980s in terms of expenditure per capita on defence, and
tenth in terms of percentage of GNP spent on defence (3.6%).[72] In
comparison with other European non-members of alliances, Sweden
also emerges relatively high, as shown in Table 3.2. Sweden takes
defence seriously, although the same is perhaps less true of Austria
and Switzerland. This may reflect the differing foundations of their
position.

Table 3.2. Comparative Defence Effort of European Non-Alliance States, 1982

	$ per head	% of GNP	Nos. in armed forces (000s)
Austria	112	1.3	49.4
Eire	101	2.0	16.4
Finland	179	1.8	36.9
Sweden	379	3.6	64.5
Switzerland	314	2.1	20.0
Yugoslavia	132	5.2[a]	252.5

[a] Derived from Gross Material Product.

Sources: The Military Balance 1982-3 (London, 1982), table 5, p. 124; *The Military Balance 1984-5* (London, 1984), table 4, p. 140.

Of course, statistics alone cannot answer the question of whether
these efforts are 'enough'[73]—indeed it is almost impossible to answer.
The Swedes have admitted that 'no defence of our making would have
sufficient scope to meet every eventuality. The degree of security our
defence arrangements can give us must always be limited.' None the less,
they do believe that 'our defence efforts do show that we take our
neutrality seriously',[74] and that it 'prevents the emergence of a military
vacuum in northern Europe. It should also enable Sweden to repulse

---

[71] Andren, 'Prospects', 189–90. See also Swedish Foreign Minister, 21 Jan. 1967, in *DSFP 1967*, 10.

[72] *The Military Balance 1984–1985* (London, 1984), 140. *The Times*, 7 Apr. 1981, reported that 'Sweden . . . possesses as many inceptor fighters—432 Viggen and Saab aircraft—as Nato has in the whole of northern Europe.'

[73] Defence comparisons involve a number of difficulties, e.g. whether there is conscription, and whether reservists are included in the count.

[74] Both quotations are from the Swedish Foreign Minister, 25 Feb. 1964, in *DSFP 1964*, 10.

even far-reaching attempts to violate Swedish neutrality during hostilities.'[75]

Also significant is the Swedish conception of the circumstances of the likely attack. The Swedes believe that Sweden would not be liable

to be attacked except in conjunction with a major conflict. There is no reason for an isolated attack on Sweden and we do not therefore take such an attack much into account. In a major conflict . . . even the Great Powers must plan the use of their resources . . . and they cannot therefore afford to throw in overwhelming troop concentrations against a minor secondary objective. Accordingly we are building up a defence which has naturally not much of a chance of surviving against a concentrated attack by a Great Power but which, nevertheless, may be rather troublesome to overcome if Sweden is a secondary objective.[76]

Similarly, the Swiss do not expect to be involved in an isolated war, and they therefore aim to provide a 'deterrent to the spread of any conflict to Swiss territory' by 'raising the price of entry'.[77] In the last hundred years belligerents have been 'deterred when they contemplated the difficulties the Swiss forces would place in their way', difficulties exacerbated by geography.[78] Moreover, while not enthusiastic about the devolution of responsibility inherent in guerrilla warfare, the Swiss are emphatic that if any parts of their territory were occupied, they would pursue 'the struggle with the remaining armed forces everywhere where conditions for a protracted resistance are favourable'.[79]

As Roberts notes, it is not so much that any attack could not succeed but rather that it 'would be unpleasant and costly for the attacker'.[80] The Swedish position is reinforced by a belief that there are 'no areas of primary strategic interest to the great power blocs within our borders'.[81] Sweden would therefore hope 'to refuse to be at the beck and call of any Great Power' and 'to defend ourselves against violations of our integrity and threats of attack'.[82] However, it is noticeable that, to some extent,

[75] Swedish Foreign Minister, 1 Nov. 1971, in *DSFP 1971*, 80–1.

[76] Swedish Prime Minister, 7 June 1962, in *DSFP 1962*, 30. See also Minister of Defence, 21 May 1963, in *DSFP 1963*, 150–1.

[77] Quoted by Roberts, 50–4.

[78] M. R. D. Foot, *Men in Uniform: Military Manpower in Modern Industrial Societies* (London, 1961), 63.

[79] Roberts, 54, citing official Swiss documents.

[80] Ibid. 94.

[81] *Sweden's Security Policy and Total Defence: A Summary of the First Report by the 1978 Parliamentary Committee on Defence, June 1979* (Ds Fo 1979: 3; Stockholm, 1979), 12–15.

[82] Swedish Prime Minister, 22 June 1961, in *DSFP 1961*, 104.

the defensive ambitions of the countries concerned are inherently limited. There is much stress on the defensive aspects of their policies; what appears to be worthy of only slight mention (at the most) is a more positive defence, in the sense of defence of a neutral's rights, such as trade.

Although periodically the appropriate strategy has been called into question,[83] the countries concerned have been consistent in the basic principles they have espoused, which are non-participation in Great Power alliances, with a concomitant insistence upon their own resources and a disavowal of outside help, coupled with an attempt to have a deterrent strategy based upon a reasonably strong defensive effort.

ATTITUDE TO EUROPEAN INSTITUTIONS

Austria, Sweden, and Switzerland have become full members of the Council of Europe, despite Soviet hostility to the Council.[84] It is important that the Council of Europe can only make recommendations, while Article 1 (d) of the Statute states that 'Matters relating to national defence do not fall within the scope of the Council of Europe.'[85] This question, of vital importance to the neutrals, was the subject of early constitutional difficulties within the Council, as a result of the call for a European Army in the Consultative Assembly of the Council of Europe in 1950. After dispute between the Assembly, which wished to delete Article 1 (d), and the Committee of Ministers, the latter finally accepted that the Assembly might discuss 'the political aspects of European peace and security', though it could not address recommendations to the Committee on this issue.[86] In fact, the Assembly has taken as a guide the suggestion that 'it can properly discuss questions which, in a national parliament, would be dealt with by the minister for foreign affairs, but not those that would be handled by the minister of defence'.[87] It has avoided military questions in the technical sense, but proposals for the European Defence Community (EDC) and the Western European Union (WEU) have been discussed by the Assembly. However,

---

[83] Minister of Defence, 21 May 1963, in *DSFP 1963*, 149; Prime Minister, 2 Feb. 1970, in *DSFP 1970*, 18.

[84] Sweden as a founding member, Austria almost immediately upon regaining its independence, and Switzerland in 1963. Both Austrian and Swiss observers had previously contributed to debates.

[85] Article 20 (a) of the Statute of Council of Europe, 5 May 1949, and Article 1(d). See A. H. Robertson, *The Council of Europe*, 2nd edn. (London, 1961), at pp. 257–69, for the Statute.

[86] Ibid. 46–7, citing Resolution (51) 31 of the Committee of Ministers.

[87] Ibid. This formula originated with Harold Macmillan.

Sweden's main initial problem was the federalist desire on the part of others to use the Assembly as, at best, a constituent assembly for a new Europe, or, at least, to delete Article 1 (*d*) and allow discussion of 'political' questions. A further difficulty emerged with the Eden Plan of 1952, which envisaged remodelling the Council of Europe so that it could also serve as the institutional framework of the European Coal and Steel Community (ECSC), the proposed EDC, and other subsequent developments.[88] The Swedish reaction was vehement, with Foreign Minister Unden pointing out that 'Sweden would not be able to engage herself in any way in an international organisation for joint defence, seeing that we have chosen our line of no alliances.' Joining the EDC would be the same as joining NATO, but even 'a looser form of adhesion as would result from the EDC forming, so to say, an element of the Council of Europe would naturally have as a consequence that we were forced to reconsider our entire position within the Council'. He was emphatic that an essential condition of Swedish entry to the Council had been the existence of Article 1 (*d*), and that, while Sweden could not veto revision of the Statute, he felt that Sweden would leave rather than prevent what other members desired. Interestingly, as of May 1952, he felt that 'probably all members of the Council of Europe except Sweden are in favour of the British proposal . . . and it is to be expected that it will be proceeded with in a positive direction'.[89] In fact this was not the outcome, and the issue died after a few other proposals.[90]

Although not full members of the Council of Europe at that time, the Swiss were also unhappy about such discussions, which they regarded as going beyond the terms of the Statute of the Council. They subsequently acknowledged that 'some of the actions of the Council of Europe in the first years of its existence' had caused them 'misgivings' from the point of view of their neutrality.[91] When they transferred from Observer status to full membership of the Council in 1963, the first Swiss speech in the Assembly mentioned neutrality on four occasions and alluded to it on three others.[92]

[88] Full text in *Documents of the Consultative Assembly, Council of Europe, 1952* (doc. 11; Strasburg, 1952). For a discussion of the proposals and reaction see Robertson, 94–9.

[89] 27 May 1952, extracts reproduced in Andren, *Power-Balance and Non-Alignment*, 122–4. It is worth noting that this view, if valid, says much concerning Ireland's position.

[90] Robertson, 102–8. Neither the Swiss nor Austrians were members at this time.

[91] Mr Wahlen, Head of the Political Dept. of the Swiss Confederation, in *Official Report of Debates: Consultative Assembly, Council of Europe* hereafter *Assembly Debates* (15th Ordinary Session; 7 May 1963), 44.

[92] Mr Duft, ibid. (6 May 1963), 7–9.

It was the lack of centralized decision-making power which allowed these states to become founding members of the Organizations for European Economic Co-operation and for Economic Co-operation and Development (OEEC/OECD) and the European Free Trade Association (EFTA). Most importantly, there was a lack of supra-national decision-making and any common external tariff in EFTA. It was felt that, while the obligations of a customs union would pose difficulties for neutrality, a free-trade agreement did not, especially given certain escape-clauses in the Stockholm Convention.[93] The membership of EFTA was different (it was less close to NATO), and it did not have political objectives similar to those of the EEC.

AUSTRIA, SWEDEN, AND SWITZERLAND AND THE EUROPEAN COMMUNITY

In attempting to determine their appropriate relationship with the European Community, the three neutrals have been faced with a fundamental conundrum, the nature of the Community. No one has been entirely sure what was involved in membership in or association with the Community, given that 'no one today can know what sort of EEC there will be . . . Will it be an EEC without supranational elements and without a political content other than of economic affairs and trade cooperation, or will it be an EEC according to the terms of the Treaty of Rome?'[94]

Given this conundrum, and changes in the policies and attitudes not only of the members but also of important non-members (e.g. the United Kingdom, formerly), the neutrals have had to live with unpredictable factors that they could not 'directly influence but that pose[d] considerable problems of policy adjustment'.[95] It is thus perhaps not surprising that their own policies and attitudes have not been entirely consistent over the past twenty-five years. Moreover, since states are not monolithic actors, the neutrals have also been affected by internal political debate.[96] Yet, notwithstanding these difficulties, it is

[93] EFTA Secretariat, *Convention of Stockholm Establishing The European Free Trade Association, 4 January 1960* (Geneva, 1967).

[94] The quotation is from the Minister of Commerce, 23 Mar. 1966, in *DSFP 1966*, 122; cf. id., 23 and 30 Nov. 1970, *DSFP 1970*, 153–4; Govt. message, 25 Oct. 1961, in *DSFP 1961*, 133; Foreign Minister, 23 Oct. 1967, in *DSFP 1967*, 54.

[95] Carl-Einar Stalvant, 'Neutrality and European Integration: A Comparison of Finland's and Sweden's EEC Policies', *Scandinavian Studies*, 46/4 (Fall 1974), 406. See also Swedish Prime Minister, 6 Aug. 1971, in *DSFP 1971*, 48.

[96] See e.g. Bengt A. W. Johanson, 'Sweden and the EEC: An Approach to the Study of the Political Process', *Cooperation and Conflict*, 1/4 (1970), which is a review of Mats Bergquist, *Sverige och EEC* (Lund Political Studies, 2; Stockholm, 1970).

possible to identify a relatively consistent strand of principles and issues which have concerned the neutrals in their relationship with the Community, and which may serve as a bench-mark for comparative purposes, although some of these points have waxed and waned in importance over the years.

A real difficulty was an awareness that the decisive question of 'whether membership in the EEC is compatible with or conflicts with a consistent policy of neutrality . . . cannot be answered by a formal study of the provisions of the Treaty of Rome alone',[97] and that one must study in addition 'the history of the founding and development and the economic and political aims of the signatory powers'.[98] The general and political aims were regarded as *integral* to the Treaty of Rome: 'whether they have been directly expressed in the Treaty or not, there can be no misunderstanding on that point. The signatory Powers . . . declare . . . that its political content is one of the main points of the Treaty',[99] and 'the Swedish Government have taken the distinctly political purposes of the members of the Community quite seriously and not merely as empty words', assuming that 'the Community will energetically strive not only for economic integration but for political unification'.[100] The Swiss also believed that signature 'of the Treaty of Rome involves acceptance of the Spirit in which it was devised'.[101]

While it can be argued that by the spring of 1970 the Swedish Prime Minister, Palme, believed that 'at least some of the discussion about political goals within the EEC appeared to be empty rhetoric',[102] none the less, the neutrals thought that the goal of political integration was inherent in the situation. Moreover, their view of the Community was reinforced at a critical moment by the Hague communiqué of December 1969, which 'agreed to instruct the Ministers for Foreign Affairs to study the best way of achieving progress in the matter of political unification, within the context of enlargement'.[103] Those ministers, in their own reports issued in the summer of 1970, emphasized 'the corre-

---

[97] Swedish Prime Minister, 6 Aug. 1971, in *DSFP 1971*, 48.

[98] Govt. Message to Riksdag, 25 Oct. 1961, in *DSFP 1961*, 132.

[99] Ibid. see also Swedish Prime Minister, 22 Aug. 1961, in *DSFP 1961*, 120.

[100] The quotations are from the Minister of Commerce, 15 May 1962, in *DSFP 1962*, 133; cf. Foreign Minister, 25 Aug. 1970, in *DSFP 1970*, 45.

[101] Freymond, in Schou and Brundtland, 184.

[102] Stalvant, 415.

[103] 'Communiqué of the Conference of the Heads of State and Government of the European Community's Member States of 2 December 1969, in The Hague', in *Bulletin of the European Communities*, 3/1 (1970).

lation between membership of the European Communities and participation in activities making for progress towards political unification'.
They also laid down that applicant-states 'will have to adhere' to the
'objectives and machinery described in the present report . . . when they
join the Communities', and would have to accept that 'in line with the
spirit of the Preambles to the Treaties of Paris and Rome, tangible form
should be given to the will for a political union'.[104] Thus, it is perhaps
not surprising that the Swedish government concluded that it is 'obvious that the Davignon co-operation is regarded as an important stage in
the realisation of the political aims of the Treaty of Rome, the acceptance
of these aims being laid down as a pre-requisite for membership'.[105]
Indeed, the Hague communiqué itself had stressed that applicants must
accept the treaties and their political finality.[106] The neutrals sincerely
believed that there was a basic incompatibility between the goal of a
federal united Europe, or even of some confederal arrangement, and the
desire to be neutral. Inherent in conceptions of federalism and political
unification was the notion that the Community should progressively act
'as a single entity', so that a 'genuinely European foreign policy' and a
'European identity' could evolve.[107] Discussions had repeatedly taken
place on these questions, some dating from proposals for the EDC and
an associated European Political Community.[108] A decade later there
were the Fouchet negotiations following the Bonn summit of 1961.[109]
However, added significance was given to these matters at the very
moment when enlargement of the Community became a real possibility,
since, as well as envisaging enlargement, the Hague summit also saw
agreement to reaffirm the intention to pave 'the way for a united Europe
capable of . . . making a contribution' to the world.[110] Moreover, when
the Foreign Ministers reported later on how to achieve political union, as

[104] 'Report by the Foreign Ministers of the Member States on the Problems of Political
Unification', *Bulletin of the European Communities*, 3/11 (1970).

[105] Govt. statement, 31 Mar. 1971, in *DSFP 1971*, 30 (see also p. 228). 'Davignon' was the
name given to the new system.

[106] The Swedish Prime Minister visited Bonn, Paris, and London in the spring of 1970 in an
endeavour to discover what this implied.

[107] Following the Paris summit of 1972, the Nine agreed in July 1973 to define the European
identity in a Declaration. The text was approved by the Foreign Ministers in Nov. 1973, and was
published during the Dec. 1973 Copenhagen summit. The text is in *Bulletin of the European
Communities*, 6/12 (1973), 118–22.

[108] See Edward Fursdon, *The European Defence Community: A History* (London, 1980).

[109] See A. Silj, *Europe's Political Puzzle: A Study of the Fouchet Negotiations and the 1963 Veto*
(Occasional Papers in International Affairs, 17; Cambridge, Mass., 1967).

[110] 'Communiqué', in *Bulletin of the European Communities*, 3/1 (1970).

instructed by the summit, they argued that 'foreign policy concertation should be the object of the first practical endeavours' in this area. Solidarity was to be enhanced 'by working for a harmonization of views, concertation of attitudes and joint action where it appears feasible and desirable'[111] This prospect worried the neutrals, who were adamant that they could not involve themselves with 'co-operation in matters of foreign policy which is *binding* and which aims at the working out of common policies'.[112] Furthermore, they understood that East–West relations, and possibly defence, would be discussed in this framework, and that such discussions would not be confined to routine matters only, since the 'nature and intensity' of co-operation were to be 'directly dependent upon whether there was an increase in tension and unrest in the world'.[113] The proposals, for example, did include provision for meetings of heads of state or government in 'the event of a serious crisis'.[114] The neutrals felt that it was precisely at such times that they should not appear to be bound by consultations with others.[115] It may be that the neutrals took the proposals too much at face value, but clearly it was legitimate to believe that the Foreign Ministers meant what they said.

A further difficulty was the often-assumed trinity of union, foreign policy, and defence, arising from the belief that it was difficult to conceive of a union which would not be responsible for the defence of its citizens, or a common foreign policy that did not on the one hand guide that defence, and on the other require a military instrument to sustain it. This perception was strengthened by the fact that the union was not going to be neutral, non-aligned, or even alliance-free. This had been made clear at Bonn in the declaration that 'only a united Europe, allied to the United States of America and other free peoples, is in a position to face the dangers which menace the existence of Europe and of the whole free world'. Indeed, co-ordinated action was to come about partly for the purpose of 'strengthening the Atlantic alliance'.[116]

This declaration was a determining factor in the preparation of the seminal speech by the Swedish Prime Minister, Erlander, to the Swedish Steel and Metalworkers' Union on 22 August 1961. He noted that 'the

---

[111] 'Report', in *Bulletin of the European Communities*, 3/11 (1970).
[112] Swedish Minister of Commerce, 10 Nov. 1970, in *DSFP 1970*, 60 (emphasis added).
[113] Swedish Govt. Statement, 31 Mar. 1971, in *DSFP 1971*, 31.
[114] 'Report', in *Bulletin of the European Communities*, 3/11 (1970).
[115] Swedish Govt. Statement, 31 Mar. 1971 in *DSFP 1971*, 30–1.
[116] See Silj, pp. 133–5, for text.

political aim of strengthening the Atlantic Alliance is no inducement for us to participate in European cooperation. On the contrary, in view of the fundamental line of our foreign policy, a political aim of this kind gives us very definite cause for restraint.' He went on to stress all the reasons why this was so, particularly the need to 'avoid commitments restricting our chances of enlisting confidence in our policy of neutrality and of carrying it out'. An application for membership of the Community might do that since it '*might* be interpreted as a political move signifying that we were prepared to depart from our policy of neutrality and to seek membership of the Atlantic Pact'.[117] If this was true for Sweden, the danger was even more acute for Austria, because of the circumstances surrounding the Austrian State Treaty and the Soviet attitude to the Community.[118]

The problem arose because of the initial overlap in membership between the Community and NATO, which generated fears that it would not be possible 'to distinguish clearly political solidarity within a group of states from military solidarity'.[119] However, it was not just a question of virtual identity of membership but also the fact that many outside observers saw the Treaty of Rome as 'supplementary to the Atlantic Pact' as well as 'strengthening it'.[120] Paul-Henri Spaak saw 'economic co-operation within the Community' as a 'complement to the military co-operation of NATO', so that in his view they 'belonged together'. [121] Moreover, apart from the Bonn Declaration, there was the evidence of the call from the Monnet Action Committee for the United States of Europe for a 'partnership between a united Europe and the United States'.[122] In other words, while the neutrals could see that co-operation of a military nature was likely to continue 'in bodies other than the EEC . . . the intention to achieve political, economic and defence integration has been voiced so often and so explicitly' that they felt they had 'no choice but to pay regard to their declarations'.[123] The neutrals could point to numerous statements by politicians from the Community, and indeed from the applicant, Britain, concerning the

[117] Swedish Prime Minister, 22 Aug. 1961, in *DSFP 1961*, 111–25.

[118] See Michael Cullis, 'The Austrian Treaty Settlement', *Review of International Studies*, 7/3 (July 1981).

[119] Swedish Foreign Minister, Nov. 1971, in *DSFP 1971*, 78.

[120] Swedish Prime Minister, 22 Aug. 1961, in *DSFP 1961*, 120–1.

[121] Swedish Prime Minister, 5 Aug. 1971, in *DSFP 1971*, 48.

[122] Quoted in M. Palmer and J. Lambert *et al.*, *European Unity* (London, 1968), 142–3. This was a precursor to the famous Philadelphia speech by President Kennedy on 4 July 1962.

[123] Swedish Foreign Minister, Nov. 1971, in *DSFP 1971*, 78.

possibility of military co-operation being taken up within the framework of the Community.[124] It seemed 'unavoidable that progress towards a common foreign policy will be followed by a greater degree of co-operation in respect of defence'.[125] However, the real problem was not so much any particular proposals as the general orientation which they revealed, so that, while the neutrals did 'not know how soon a common foreign policy will be worked out, [and] neither do we know how soon such a common foreign policy will be linked with a common defence policy',[126] they had legitimate grounds for believing that the member-states of the Community were committed to such possibilities and that Europe might well evolve in such a manner.

The neutrals did not regard it as realistic to suppose that they 'could systematically co-ordinate . . . [a] course in foreign affairs with that of the Western Powers while at the same time maintaining international confidence in . . . [a] policy of neutrality'.[127] Sweden, for example, felt that its policy could not 'be combined with *declared or implied* pledges that we will enter into systematic cooperation in foreign policy or consultations with a certain Power bloc'.[128] The precise legal text and obligation, the distinction between voluntary and obligatory co-operation, was not regarded as being so important as the impression created in the minds of others. Moreover, the neutrals felt that, morally, they could not reserve their position on matters of foreign policy and security which before entry they knew the Community members felt to be important.[129]

There were also other political problems, some of which related directly to the treaties, such as the issue of whether or not to hand over the right to make decisions to the institutions of the Community.[130] Indeed, Scheich, writing from an Austrian perspective, felt that 'We have arrived at the point where the two spheres—neutrality and European integration—meet, or rather where they do not meet. *Integration in the real sense of the word and with its institutional requirements is not compatible*

---

[124] Swedish Prime Minister, 5 Aug. 1971, in *DSFP 1971*, 49; and see e.g. Edward Heath, *Old World, New Horizons: Britain, The Common Market and the Atlantic Alliance* (Godkin Lectures, Harvard University, 1967; OUP, 1970), 59–84, esp. pp. 72–4.

[125] Swedish Prime Minister, 2 Feb. 1971, in *DSFP 1971*, 228.

[126] Swedish Foreign Minister, 1 Jan. 1972, in *DSFP 1972*, 33.

[127] Swedish Govt. dec., 23 Mar. 1972, in *DSFP 1972*, 26.   [128] Ibid. (emphasis added).

[129] Swedish Prime Minister, 5 Aug. 1971, in *DSFP 1971*, 49; Swedish Foreign Minister, Nov. 1971, in *DSFP 1971*, 78.

[130] Govt. message to Riksdag, 25 Oct. 1961, in *DSFP 1961*, 134; Minister of Commerce, 10 Nov. 1970, in *DSFP 1970*, 60.

with the status of permanent neutrality. The neutral country is condemned to independence, condemned to staying alone.'[131] Even if by the 1970s there was a realization that over time the 'efforts to institute supranational ties to determine the actions of the EEC states have become less intense',[132] there was still unwillingness 'to give up . . . national sovereignty by transferring [the] right of decision-making on important economic and political questions to supranational organs'.[133]

It should be remembered that, despite the 1965–6 crisis and the Luxemburg agreement of 1966, the EEC treaty did still contain provision for the use of majority voting on a wide range of issues after the end of the transitional period. The *de jure* position remained that established by the treaty. Thus, for the neutrals, the fundamental problem remained unaltered. Indeed, if anything they became more concerned about this when the proposals for economic and monetary union were published, since they feared the possibility of centralized decision-making on crucial economic matters.[134] Moreover, the neutrals did not take a sanguine view regarding the possibilities of using the veto, since 'for a small, neutral country . . . It must be assumed that in practice the chances of using the right of veto will be very limited in cases where the neutral country stands alone.'[135] In addition, it was felt that they 'should accede to international co-operation only when . . . convinced that [they will themselves] be able to make a constructive contribution . . . not . . . on the understanding that [they] must limit . . . participation by having recourse, if necessary, to the right of veto'.[136]

The insistence upon sovereignty was closely related to the desire to pursue a policy *for* neutrality, but there was a somewhat wider concern about the issue of sovereignty; for example, at least some in Sweden thought that close ties with the EEC reduced Sweden's capacity to decide its own policies and that it was 'to purchase free trade with an . . . expanded Community at the cost of limited sovereignty',[137]

131 Scheich, 237 (emphasis in original).
132 Swedish Foreign Minister, 23 Oct. 1967, in *DSFP 1967*, 54; but it was a concern: see Swedish Prime Minister, 22 Aug. 1961, in *DSFP 1961*, 122.
133 Swedish Minister of Commerce, 23–30 Nov. 1970, in *DSFP 1970*, 150.
134 The 'Werner Report'—'Report to the Council and the Commission on the Realisation by Stages of Economic and Monetary Union in the Community' (Bulletin of the European Communities, Suppl. 11-1970; Brussels, 1970).
135 Swedish Govt. Statement, 31 Mar. 1971, in *DSFP 1971*, 29. Of course, in May 1982 even a British veto was overridden. 136 Ibid.
137 Tord Ekström, Gunnar Myrdal, and Roland Palsson, *Vi och Västeuropa: Andra ronden* (Stockholm, 1971), 106, cited by M. Donald Hancock, 'Sweden, Scandinavia and the EEC', *International Affairs*, 48/3 (July 1972), 434.

especially with the risk of a threat to egalitarian policies within Sweden.[138] Such arguments and pressures were 'apparently a major secondary consideration (after neutrality) in the government's final decision against full membership'.[139]

The issue of sovereignty is crucial *vis-à-vis* the Community: Mitchell has cogently argued that 'already by 1973, the Treaty of Rome had become a constitution having its effects within the internal law of the whole Community and having consequentially effects, even then sufficiently clear, on the constitutional situation and internal law of each of the original Member States'. In addition, the EEC Treaty itself claims that certain decisions (e.g. in Article 189) may be 'directly applicable'. Therefore, Mitchell argues that Community law does enjoy primacy, citing in addition the *Van Gend en Loos* and *Simmenthal* cases. The original treaties had become by 1973 a constitution which overrode national constitutions.[140]

Crucial is the question of whether a state can turn over its sovereignty, or a portion of it, to an international organization for a period of time; or whether, if it has only 'devolved' that sovereignty, it still actually retains ultimate sovereignty, because it can either reclaim the sovereignty which it has devolved or simply withdraw. In 1973 some of the arguments within the new member-states contained the implicit assumption that, despite the lack both of a definitive clause within the treaties themselves concerning withdrawal and a mechanism for withdrawal, it was evident that any state could at any time use its powers— physical and democratic—to reassert its sovereignty, that withdrawal from treaties was always possible, and that in reality the Community lacked any effective instruments for prohibiting or physically stopping secession. While this debate perhaps lacks clear resolution, the neutrals

---

[138] Tord Ekström, 'Sverige, EEC och jämlikhetspolitiken', *Tiden*, 63/7 (1971), 409, cited in Hancock loc. cit. See also Swedish Prime Minister, 22 Aug. 1961, in *DSFP 1961*, 122–4.

[139] Hancock, 435.

[140] The quotations are taken from J. D. B. Mitchell, ' The Sovereignty of Parliament and Community Law: The Stumbling-Block that isn't there', *International Affairs*, 55/1 (Jan. 1979), 34–5. This article produced a rejoinder by Stephen A. George, 'Letter to the Editor: The Sovereignty of Parliament and Community Law', *International Affairs*, 56/1 (Jan. 1980), which concluded that there was no definitive proof that Mitchell was correct. On the sovereignty question see Charles Burton Marshall, *The Exercise of Sovereignty* (Baltimore, 1965); M. Wight, *Systems of States*, ed. H. Bull (Leicester, 1977); J. E. S. Fawcett, *Law and Power in International Relations* (London, 1982); H. Bull, *The Anarchical Society* (London, 1977); and two interesting articles, P. A. Reynolds, 'International Studies: Retrospect and Prospect', *British Journal of International Studies*, 1/1 (Apr. 1975), and Alan James, 'Sovereignty: Ground Rule or Gibberish?', *Review of International Studies*, 10/1 (Jan. 1984).

were insistent that the formal and explicit right of denunciation should be in any agreement with the Community, and did not wish to rely upon unilateral denunciation, which might have left their status unclear in law.

To some extent the letter of the treaties and prosaic legal argument were secondary considerations: what mattered were the perceptions of the neutrals and others. In addition, these arguments took place both in the context of discussion on union, steps towards political co-operation (and, latterly, economic and monetary union) and in relation to the specific treaty articles and policies on such questions as the Common Commercial Policy (CCP).

However, the Swedes were emphatic that even if the process of political integration

was left out of account, it being maintained that the Treaty of Rome in actual fact only had a bearing on economic matters, we would nevertheless be compelled to point out that there are provisions in the Treaty which cannot be reconciled with our policy of neutrality in that certain cardinal points, few in number though they may be, affect our ability to implement it in practice.[141]

Articles 223–5 of the EEC Treaty were—and are—a case in point, with the Swedes believing that, on some interpretations, 'in wartime all the institutions of the Common Market would continue to function more or less in the same way as in peacetime. If this interpretation is correct a neutral state would not be entitled in wartime to renounce its obligations'; they felt, then, that there was a legal incompatibility between membership and continuing neutrality.[142] More generally, even as late as 1984, a Chatham House study argued that 'Article 224, which recognized that the operation of the common market depended on security factors, could be generously interpreted to permit Community concern with defence in cases in which the market's operations might be under threat as a result of civil and international disorder', and further suggested that defence was not formally excluded

from the Community agenda in the Treaty of Rome. Instead it was largely ignored . . . Unless the narrow view is taken that anything not specifically allowed is illegal, it would seem that the EC could expand into defence without actually violating the Treaty of Rome if its members so chose.

[141] Swedish Minister of Commerce, 26 Nov. 1962, in *DSFP 1962*, 161.
[142] Swedish Prime Minister, 22 Aug. 1961, in *DSFP 1961*, 120; and 'Treaty Establishing the European Economic Community, Rome, 25 March 1957' (hereafter, *EEC Treaty*, in *Treaties Establishing the European Communities* (Brussels, 1978).

Evidence favouring a wide interpretation of the Treaty can be found in the Preamble, which notes members' determination to "strengthen the safeguards of peace and liberty", and in Article 235 . . . [143]

Clearly the three neutral countries took a similar view in the earlier period.

Other problems arose with the EEC Treaty in respect of its internal provisions *per se*, its internal provisions with external effects, and its specifically external provisions. While it may be true that in the external area as a whole the Community's responsibility for laws and treaties is relatively limited in scope, in that the 'Rome Treaty . . . did not dwell at length or in detail on the external relations of the Community, apart from the provisions for association and trade agreements and a common commercial policy',[144] in these areas Community organs can play a significant role in shaping the economic and trade relations both with the Community and with non-members.[145]

Most important in this respect is Article 113, establishing the CCP, based upon 'uniform principles, particularly in regard to changes in tariff roles, the conclusion of tariff and trade agreements, the achievements of uniformity in measures of liberalisation, export policy and measures to protect trade'. The article also gives the Commission a specific negotiating role, albeit 'within the framework of such directives as the Council may issue to it'.[146] In 1970 a common foreign trade policy came into being, and since 1 January 1973 the member-states of the Community have not been free to conclude independent bilateral trade agreements. They were to be replaced by multilateral agreements negotiated by the Commission under the terms of Article 113, and the Community was henceforth to act as a collective entity in such matters. Indeed, in 1974 'the Commission began to insist that all negotiations for trade agreements with East European countries be conducted exclusively by the Community'.[147] This made the policy of interest to neutrals, who were also aware that all the countries of the Community, bar Ireland, were members of NATO, and that NATO had sought to operate an embargo on strategic goods against Eastern Europe.

[143] Trevor Taylor, *European Defence Co-operation* (RIIA, Chatham House Papers, 24; London, 1984), 17–18.

[144] Geoffrey Goodwin, 'The External Relations of the European Community: Shadow and Substance', *British Journal of International Studies*, 3/1 (Apr. 1973), 39.

[145] Werner J. Feld, *The European Community in World Affairs: Economic Power and Influence* (Sherman Oaks, 1976), 11.

[146] EEC Treaty, Article 113.

[147] Feld, *European Community*, 219.

In fact, the customs union and Common External Tariff (CET) are also important foundations of the external policy of the Community, since the CET is the basic instrument of the Community's trade policy and has been responsible for the Community states negotiating collectively in both the General Agreement on Tariffs and Trade and other international forums. Moreover, the Community has begun on occasion to be represented by the Council Presidency, or the Commission, or some combination thereof, on trade and commercial matters.[148] The neutrals were also aware that, especially on economic matters, other countries were more conscious of the unity and strength of the Community than they were of the centrifugal pressures and divisions within it.

While the apparently severe restrictions upon members in concluding trade agreements did not come into effect, the neutrals made their judgement upon the basis of the relevant Treaty articles, their understanding of the motivations and principles behind the CCP and Community trade policy, and the declared policy of the member-states, and they therefore had reason to suspect the possibility of supranational intervention, or worse, in their commercial policies. Indeed, they considered that the 'rules on trade with outside countries are . . . most characteristic of the political restrictions imposed upon its members by the Treaty of Rome'.[149] In fact, the formal transfer of responsibility for external relations has been heavily constrained by the increasing use that has been made of so-called economic co-operation agreements between individual member-states and non-members, which have been developed as a means of bypassing Treaty requirements and obligations under the CCP.[150] However, the significant point remains the genuineness of the neutrals' belief before 1973 and the general cause for that belief. Moreover, since then it has been clear that foreign economic policy cannot always be separated neatly from foreign policy, or even security, and that the economic external relations of the Community have on occasion been given a 'political' flavour.[151]

Another area of the Rome Treaty which has an external dimension is Part IV, 'Association of the Overseas Countries and Territories' (Articles 131-6), whereby the dependent territories of the member-states

---

[148] Based on the provisions of EEC Treaty, Articles 116, 229, 230, and 231.

[149] Swedish Prime Minister, 22 Aug. 1961, in *DSFP 1961*, 119-20.

[150] Feld, *European Community*, 219 cites e.g. the ten-year accord between the Federal Republic of Germany and Romania of 29 June 1973.

[151] See e.g. Jean Siotis, 'The European Economic Community and its Emerging Mediterranean Policy', in Frans A. M. Alting von Gesau, *The External Relations of the European Community* (Farnborough, 1974), 69-70.

were to be linked with the EEC. This further contributed to a certain image of the Community as capitalist or imperialist.[152] Whatever one's view of this, the capability of Community institutions to negotiate agreements for association with these dependent territories and other countries is a significant aspect of the international trade relations of the Community, particularly given the ever-spiralling numbers involved. Another form or category of association is provided for by Article 238, which allows for 'agreements establishing an association involving reciprocal rights and obligations, common action and special procedures'. It is necessary under this Article for the Council to act with unanimity.[153] Countries treated in this manner have included Turkey, Cyprus, Malta, and (before membership) Greece.

However, as noted earlier the role of the Community in the world is not to be seen as simply the outcome of specific articles on external trade policy. One of the most important internal policies, the Common Agricultural Policy (CAP), has been another important element of the Community's external relations and persona. The establishment of the CAP also imposed specific restraints on certain areas of member-states' trading policy.[154] For a while, because of the commitment to economic and monetary union, it appeared that the Community would also have this as a basis for common external activity. However, this development has been hampered by fundamental differences over policy.[155]

A somewhat similarly disjointed picture emerges in another area where there is an overlap between the treaties and non-treaty areas, namely energy.[156] While the EEC Treaty itself does not specify the development of an energy policy, energy has been central to the Community's development, in view of the very remit of Euratom and of the ECSC. It also true that these treaties involve direct interaction with the international environment. The Community itself could not avoid involvement either, particularly because of the events of 1973, with the Arab embargo of oil exports to certain European states and reductions in

---

[152] See e.g. Johan Galtung, *The European Community: A Superpower in the Making* (London, 1973). [153] EEC Treaty, Article 238.

[154] For a review of the CAP see John S. Marsh and Pamela J. Swanney, 'The Common Agricultural Policy', in Juliet Lodge (ed.), *Institutions and Policies of the European Community* (London, 1983).

[155] See Dennis Swann, *The Economics of the Common Market*, 5th edn. (Harmondsworth, 1984), esp. pp. 175–205.

[156] See Robert A. Black, jun., 'Plus ça change, plus c'est la même chose: Nine Governments in Search of a Common Energy Policy', in Helen Wallace, William Wallace, and Carole Webb (eds.), *Policy-Making in the European Communities* (London, 1977).

production. Although most would judge that the Community failed to rise to the challenge, this is an area where united common action could have important international consequences.

There are several areas where the linkage between the political objectives, the economic means as embodied in the treaties, and that undefined grey area of overspill between treaty and non-treaty concerns and activities can be demonstrated. One such is the attempt to evolve a global Mediterranean policy;[157] another is the signing of the Lomé Agreements by both Community and national authorities under the system of *mixtes accords*;[158] and a third occurs in a topic assumed to be of low political interest, access to Icelandic waters. Rosemarie Allen has suggested that the 'small lever in the Community's hands to prise open access to these rich fishing grounds was the wish on the part of the Icelandic Government to increase its tiny share of industrial exports to the EEC. This lever was not, however, used because strategic considerations about Iceland's position in NATO restrained the Nine from exerting such pressure.'[159]

Most of the foregoing discussion has centred upon the EEC Treaty, but it should be noted that problems exist under the Euratom Treaty also. In the 'external' area, for example, Articles 103 and 106 curtail the freedom of member-states to conclude agreements with third parties. Article 2 has implications for sovereignty and the external relations of the member-states, and does represent some curtailment of a member-state's independence.[160] For Sweden, with its own uranium, the possibility of part or all of the responsibility for its use being transferred to Euratom and possibly onwards to the programmes of other states was particularly worrying, if not publicly referred to by the Government. This latter observation is also true of the ECSC Treaty, which gave the High Authority (now the merged Commission) direct control over certain aspects of the activities of firms within states, and a role in prohibiting 'unfair competitive practices' or 'discriminatory practices' by states.[161]

---

[157] See Roy Howard Ginsberg, 'The European Community and the Mediterranean', in Lodge.

[158] See e.g. Carol Cosgrove Twitchett, *Europe and Africa: From Association to Partnership* (Farnborough, 1978), and *A Framework for Development: The EEC and ACP* (London, 1981).

[159] Rosemarie Allen, 'Fishing for a Common Policy', *Journal of Common Market Studies*, 19/2 (Dec. 1980), esp. p. 129.

[160] 'Treaty Establishing the European Atomic Energy Community, Rome, 25 March 1957', Articles 2, 103, and 106, in *Treaties Establishing the European Communities*.

[161] 'Treaty Establishing the European Coal and Steel Community, Paris, 18 April 1951', Articles 47 and 60, in *Treaties Establishing the European Communities*.

This concern with the issues of political freedom of action and, specifically, of neutrality led directly to the so-called 'neutrality reservation', entered by all the neutrals in their approaches to the Community as early as 1961. In essence the reservation was the same for each country, although each year saw slightly different formulations. As outlined by the Swedish Minister of Commerce before the EEC Council of Ministers on 28 July 1962, there were essentially three requirements for neutrality:[162]

The first of the neutrality points relates to trade policy towards third countries . . . As a neutral country, we would have to keep a certain liberty of action and to reserve the competence to negotiate and sign agreements with third countries in our own name. On the other hand we are prepared, within institutional arrangements for consultation, to coordinate our tariff and trade policy closely with that of the Community . . .

The second neutrality point relates to the safeguarding of certain supplies vital in wartime . . .

The third point has to do with a neutral country's need to be able to take or abstain from measures according to the requirements of neutrality. It may, for instance in cases of war and grave international crisis, have to introduce controls on trade or to refrain from taking part in sequestration of property directed against a belligerent. The derogation from any common action in an integrated market, which this need might imply, would be of varying importance according to the circumstance. But it is not excluded that it might go as far as the suspension of parts of, or the whole of, the agreement . . . or withdrawal from the agreement . . .

The minister referred to the provisions of Article 224, which allowed the possibility of certain derogations to member-states in some circumstances. The neutrals were adamant that, if the international situation warranted it, they must be free to 'take, or omit to take, certain steps, even if necessary' terminating the agreement.[163]

While these were the main reservations, on occasions other elements were added, or the above were embellished. One such additional requirement was the insistence upon the principle of unanimity in any joint institutions involving the neutrals and the Community.[164] In summing up the reservations expressed in 1961–2, and indeed subsequently, the Swedish Minister of Commerce was anxious to emphasize that 'the three neutrality requirements . . . have the common feature of implying

[162] Swedish Minister of Commerce, 28 July 1962, in *DSFP 1962*, 152–3.
[163] Swedish Minister of Commerce, 23–30 Nov. 1970, in *DSFP 1970*, 150.
[164] Partly as a safeguard against new obligations being created: Scheich, 240.

a certain liberty of action or right of derogation for the neutral country . . . A basic feature of the liberty of action to be reserved is to make it possible for the neutral country not to take part in measures which, although of an economic nature, are actuated by political considerations alone and directed against third countries'.[165] In view of the later debate in the Community about sanctions, these reservations revealed a certain prescience on the part of the neutrals; they also demonstrated that the neutrals did see the Community as more than a narrow economic arrangement.

What the neutrals really wanted was 'to retain the right to determine their policies unilaterally and independently', and to arrive at the same result as the Community, but in their own way.[166] Any convergence of policy was to be by their own decision and not imposed by a third party, and certainly not to flow automatically from a majority decision in a supranational body.

The decision about the relationship between Austria, Sweden, and Switzerland and the Community was not solely in their hands, since it also depended upon the attitude of the Community. While there was no consistent exposition by the members of their attitude to neutrality, it is clear that the most ardent Europeans were hostile to the very notion of neutrality. Indeed, in November 1961 President Hallstein of the EEC Commission attacked neutrality, arguing that European neutrality had its origins in European conflicts, but that the aim of European unification was to make war, in Schuman's phrase, 'not merely unthinkable, but materially impossible'.[167] It aimed to abolish the very state of affairs which created neutrality and occasioned its existence, and all effort should therefore go into this attempt to make war impossible.

Another prominent European, Paul-Henri Spaak, had said at the beginning of 1963 that he did not believe that the Community should open its doors to countries which did not share its political ideal and philosophy, especially the philosophy underlying the Treaty of Rome.[168] Moreover, many felt that there was not necessarily any inherent incompatibility between membership and neutrality, and that as a result the neutrals were trying to gain advantages without reciprocal obligations.

[165] Swedish Minister of Commerce, 28 July 1962, in *DSFP 1962*, 153.

[166] Miriam Camps, *Britain and the European Community 1955–1963* (OUP, 1965), 497–8.

[167] For Schuman's speech see *Keesing's Contemporary Archives*, 13–20 May 1950 (Keynsham, 1950), 10701, while Hallstein's arguments are reproduced in the 'Macmillan Report' of May 1962 to Consultative Assembly of the Council of Europe (doc. 1420), 21. This report—to which the 1962 Struye Report is appended—gives a revealing insight into a number of attitudes.

[168] The 'Macmillan Report', 23.

This problem of attitude towards the neutrals was further complicated by the fact that within each member-state various pressure-groups held their own views.[169] The predominant view of the pro-Europeans was that there was a need to preserve their own aspirations and the integrity of the Community. If non-members were prepared to accept these, then the Community (France permitting) would welcome them. If not, then perhaps no arrangement would be possible. The Community was anxious that no special arrangement should weaken its own cohesion, or lead to an impression that some form of loose arrangement without any acceptance of far-reaching objectives was possible. In this latter respect, there was a fear of creating precedents.

One of the most considered responses to the neutrals' arguments came in the 1962 Struye Report, and it must be recognized that it came to conclusions diametrically opposed to those of the neutrals concerning the arguments over sovereignty and decisions by majority voting. Struye argued that one could no longer regard sovereignty as one and indivisible, and therefore that states could, and often did, voluntarily limit their own powers or delegate them to others. If sovereignty simply meant 'the powers belonging to the State', permanent neutrality only affected them 'in a field which is strictly limited by rules of law', and, apart from that area (in any case a very narrow one in peacetime), 'the powers of the State and consequently its sovereignty are not subjected to any restrictions'. The State could therefore exercise these powers in complete freedom, even delegating them to supranational authorities, except where 'such limitations or delegations are concerned with fields which are affected by neutrality'. The conclusion was that such limitations or delegations would be incompatible with neutrality as a goal 'if they prevent the State from deciding freely whether to take part or not in a war, or threaten the very existence of the State concerned. This is not so of the limitations of sovereignty contained in the Treaty of Rome.' Perpetually neutral states 'can, at least in time of peace, submit to the majority decisions of the Treaty of Rome, as these do not concern fields affected by the law of neutrality'. Similarly, in time of peace 'participation in a joint commercial policy as laid down in the Treaty of Rome raises no legal objection' for the neutral. But there was a very significant, if somewhat grudging, admission that 'such participation by neutrals in a joint commercial policy might be considered as incompatible with the duties of neutral States in time of war if one follows the extensive interpreta-

169 Camps, 498.

tion of the duty of impartiality', with the result that the neutral might have to leave the Community, in order to avoid participation in potentially discriminatory commercial decisions. But this conclusion was weakened by a reference to neutrals being allowed to maintain 'normal intercourse' and trade. Notwithstanding the problems caused by the CCP, Struye concluded, 'in our opinion neither the independence nor the neutrality of the States we have been dealing with would be threatened by their participation in the European Economic Community'.[170] Impressive though these arguments are, they underestimate the constraints on freedom of decision and action imposed by Community membership, which were discussed earlier, and the key issue of the perceptions of third parties.

Before examining the detailed arrangements agreed in 1972 between the neutrals and the Community, it is necessary to discuss briefly the attitude of the Soviet Union to the European Community. Although this does not appear to have been a decisive factor in either Swedish or Swiss discussions (the case of Austria was different because of the events, undertakings, and treaty of 1955), it remains important in the sense that, if these states were concerned about the damage membership might do to their image and credibility, the attitude of the Soviets would have been an important guide for them. The opinion of the other superpower regarding the Community was clear; indeed, support by the United States for the European idea had on a number of occasions been crucial and an important stimulus to European action.

In the Soviet mind there seems to have been a clear linkage between the economic, political, and military moves towards integration. They were regarded as tools of United States capitalism, cold-war instruments, and an economic underpinning of NATO. In 1957 the Soviet Union gave its considered view on the Common Market in the form of seventeen theses, which argued that 'under cover of the "unification" of Europe, the imperialist promoters of integration have divided Europe into economic, political and military groups opposed to one another; they have created an aggressive military bloc of Western European powers aimed against the Soviet Union and popular democracies'.[171] In 1962, thirty-two theses echoed the earlier seventeen. However, one significant difference by that time was the recognition that the

---

[170] 1962 Struye Report, 49–51.

[171] An English version of 'The Seventeen Theses on the Common Market', issued by the Institute of World Economics and International Relations, Moscow 1957, is to be found in Richard Vaughan, *Post-War Integration in Europe* (London, 1976), 156–8.

Community was an economic and political reality which had to be countered and contained and whose expansion had to be prevented. This attitude was combined with a refusal to extend diplomatic recognition to the Community or to treat it as an entity in diplomatic relations.[172]

This basic hostility has remained the fundamental Soviet position, although they have had to come to terms with the Community's continuing existence and enlargement and the change of atmosphere in the 1970s, with *détente* and *Ostpolitik*. Moreover, in the early 1970s the movement towards the CCP was also significant, as it affected state-trading countries. In the face of these developments, there was a certain moderation of rhetoric, and by 1972 Brezhnev was contemplating the possibility of business relations between Comecon and the Community.[173] What is clear is that in the critical years 1961–72 Austria, Sweden, and Switzerland could have been in no doubt concerning the Soviet attitude.

Certainly, the Austrians must have been fully aware of Russian views: for example, Khrushchev had warned them in 1960 that the Soviet Union would not tolerate any violation of Austrian neutrality or of the provision of the 1955 State Treaty prohibiting 'all agreements having the effect, either directly or indirectly, of promoting political and economic union with Germany' (the Soviets inclined to interpret a relationship with the Community in that vein);[174] the Soviets reiterated their concern in 1972. In fact, they did not make a major issue of this, and the Austrians did not heed the Soviet warnings, although these may well have reinforced Austrian conclusions or stiffened their attitude.[175]

At the end of 1972 Austria, Sweden, and Switzerland came to virtually identical arrangements with the Community, comprising preferential trade-agreements establishing a free-trade area in industrial products, but excluding agriculture. Significantly, the agreements were concluded under Article 113 (i.e. CCP arrangements) and not Article 238 (association agreements). The neutrals themselves made much of

---

[172] See David F. P. Forte, 'The Response of Soviet Foreign Policy to the Common Market, 1957–63', *Soviet Studies*, 19/3 (1967–8); John Pinder, 'The Community and the State-Trading Countries', in K. J. Twitchett, *Europe and The World: The External Relations of The Common Market* (London, 1976); I. John (ed.), *EEC Policy towards Eastern Europe* (Farnborough, 1975); A. Shlaim and G. Yannopoulos, *The EEC and Eastern Europe* (CUP, 1978); C. Ransom, *The European Community and Eastern Europe* (London, 1973).

[173] I. John, 'The Soviet Response to Western European Integration', in John, 47.

[174] Austrian State Treaty, Article 4. See Michael Cullis, 'The Austrian Treaty Settlement', *Review of International Studies*, 7/3 (July 1981), for background on the 1955 negotiations.

[175] Scheich, 245.

Article 21 (in all three agreements), which allowed them to take any measures they considered essential to their 'own security in time of war or serious international tension', and Article 34 (in all three agreements), which gave each side the right to renounce the agreement, albeit that it would remain formally in force for a further twelve-month period. The institutional arrangements were minimal (Articles 27–31), with the creation of a Joint Committee composed of representatives from both the Community and the state concerned. There was a requirement for unanimity and an avoidance of supranationalism. The Joint Committee was to supervise the proper functioning of the agreement and to act as a clearing-house for information. More importantly, it was also the custodian of the so-called 'evolutionary' (or 'amplification') clause, namely Article 32 (in all three agreements), which allowed for potential entry by mutual agreement into fields not covered by the original agreements.[176]

This clause, which appears to have been a particular Swedish initiative, was a way for the neutrals to reconcile their original aspirations with the restricted agreement finally reached. It has also proved to be one of the most contentious articles of the agreements. The official view was that the partnership between Community and neutrals would be dynamic—that it would naturally spill over into other fields, such as general economic and monetary policies.[177] It was precisely this that critics feared. In response, the Swedish government asserted that 'this clause is not something forced on us by the EEC' but was rather a Swedish idea. Moreover, at any time mutual agreement determined whether anything happened, there being no 'automatic implications'.[178]

Another area of relevance to the argument about neutrality was agriculture. Firstly, the Swiss in particular were reluctant to have it included, for reasons of neutrality, since according to official Swiss views 'maintaining a certain level of Swiss agricultural production is necessary for economic self-reliance (or at least partial self-reliance) in case of

---

[176] 'Agreement between the European Economic Community and the Republic of Austria: Regulation (EEC) No. 2836/72 of the Council of 19 December 1972', in *Official Journal of the European Communities* (hereafter O J) (L300; 31 Dec. 1972); 'Agreement between the European Economic Community and the Kingdom of Sweden: Regulation (EEC) No. 2838/72 of the Council of 19 December 1972', ibid.; 'Agreement between the European Economic Community and the Swiss Confederation: Regulation (EEC) No. 2840/72 of the Council of 19 December 1972', ibid.

[177] Swedish Minister of Commerce, 18 Oct. 1972, in *DSFP 1972*, 275. The Commission of the European Community had a rather more cautious view: see *Bulletin of the European Communities*, 9-1972 (Brussels, 1972), 19.

[178] Swedish Minister of Commerce, 5 Oct. 1972, in *DSFP 1972*, 66–7. This speech touched on a number of relevant questions.

war'.[179] Secondly, apart from French worries over particular items, the Community (and especially the Commission) was reluctant to see any tampering with the institutional system behind the CAP, given its insistence upon Community autonomy. It was thus difficult to see how non-members could be accommodated. Agriculture was therefore excluded.

The governments concerned, particularly the Swedish, who perhaps had had the highest expectations, were ready to admit that 'No settlement comes entirely up to expectations',[180] but argued that the disadvantages were the price of neutrality, since the 'limited nature of the agreement is an outcome of the fact that . . . [the states] refrained from seeking membership'.[181] The governments were emphatic that the agreements signed contained 'no undertakings, either formal ones or in practice, which might restrict our freedom to pursue an independent foreign policy and to preserve our neutrality'.[182] Given the governments' self-proclaimed concern over this issue, this perhaps remains the real test.

The issue of neutrality is not closed, since the real problem is not *formal* agreements but whether, with economies increasingly tied to those of the Community, the governments of Austria, Sweden, and Switzerland would be prepared to sever economic links with their major trading-partners. It is this interdependence which undermines neutrality.

Writing from a Swiss perspective, Frei concluded that 'there will most definitely be no whirling process of rapid spill-over', since the items on the agenda 'are quite remote from the sensitive political areas . . . when it comes to . . . central questions, there are myriad difficulties and a host of diverging interests'. But on the other hand he was also aware that what happens 'will take the form of *action* by the EEC and of *reflex action* by Switzerland', since 'Swiss integration policy is, in most fields, a function of EEC policy.'[183]

Thus, the kernel of the matter remains the pace and depth of development within the European Community, with the additional problem that the increasing economic interdependence may eventually subvert

---

[179] Frei, 253; although according to Scheich, 243, the Austrians would have been prepared to include it. The Swedish position varied: see Swedish Minister of Commerce, 10 Nov. 1970, in *DSFP 1970*, 57–62, and id., 23 and 30 Nov. 1970, in *DSFP 1970*, 151.

[180] Swedish Minister of Commerce, 5 Oct. 1972 in *DSFP 1972*, 63–4.

[181] Swedish Minister of Commerce, 15 June 1972, ibid. 262.

[182] Swedish Minister of Commerce, 5 Oct. 1972, ibid. 63.

[183] Frei, 256–8 (emphasis in original). See also Scheich, p. 244, and Waite, pp. 331–5, for views on the Austrian and Swedish cases.

the possibility of neutrality *de facto* by tying the neutrals irrevocably to the Community and perhaps ultimately causing them to join. If the Community had developed as expected after 1972, the problems for the neutrals would have multiplied, given their exclusion from Community decision-making and the Community movement towards economic and monetary union, etc. As it happens, that has not occurred. Moreover, there is perhaps one great advantage in the 1972 agreements, compared especially with membership and perhaps with association, in that the world does tend to perceive the Community externally as a single unit in many areas of activity. Austria, Sweden, and Switzerland have a somewhat amorphous relationship with the Community in the public's perception, and it can be argued that this relationship is much more obscure than would have been the case, had they joined. They are not identified with the Twelve to the same extent that Ireland is (by virtue of membership), and their distinctive persona is evident, for example, in many international forums. In view of the significance attached to the need to be seen to be independent, to credibility and expectations, this may be very important.

However, the critical point is that, if such agreements under Article 113 can lead to continuing doubts over the status of Austria, Sweden, and Switzerland, the doubts must be more serious when they concern a putative neutral which actually chose to become a full member of the Community, and tried for over a decade to join.

SUMMARY

The discussion in this and the preceding chapter makes it possible to identify the most significant variables associated with neutrality, non-alignment, and the European model of 'Neutral and/or Non-Aligned', albeit in a somewhat compendious and integrated form. With regard to neutrality, the key variables are:

1. the *rights and duties* of neutrality, including impartiality; abstention from war; inviolability of territory and sovereignty; active measures and due diligence with regard to upholding rights and fulfilling duties; and normal trade;
2. the *recognition of neutral status* by belligerents and others, since neutrality is not a unilateral act but rather requires to be credible, to have the confidence of others, and to give no ground of suspicion to one side or hope to the other;
3. the *disavowal of external help* which might compromise neutral

status, including the lack of preparation for and expectation of help, as well as 'defence against help', and action against having a 'protective umbrella'; and

4. the *freedom of decision and action*, in the political, economic, and military spheres, with the avoidance of entangling commitments, alliances, or dependence, and the pursuit of independence.

In Chapter 5 these variables will be applied specifically to Ireland in the years of its great test, namely the period of the Second World War.

It has already been established that non-alignment *per se* derives from experiences and reflects attitudes which are not directly relevant to the European and Irish cases. None the less, certain aspects of both non-alignment and the European model can usefully be related to the variables already established, which in any case need to be modified to take account of the post-war move to peace, and thus to the requirements 'for neutrality' rather than 'of neutrality'. For example, the quest for independence and the question of attitudes to alliance can be discussed under a modification to the variable 'freedom of decision and action'. However, it is necessary to add two new variables, not only to reflect the non-alignment dimension but also to distinguish it from neutrality *per se*. Therefore, the modified and extended variables for the period 1945–82 are:

1. *due diligence*, with respect to maintaining inviolability of territory and sovereignty, and the related question of taking active measures to maintain the current status (the strict requirements of neutral rights and duties will not be applied, given the absence of war, although the crucial issue of impartiality will be discussed under Nos. 2 and 5);

2. the *recognition* and acceptance *of neutral status* by other states, with regard to the credibility of the Irish position, the confidence of others in it, and the lack of grounds for suspicion on the part of one side or hope on the part of the other;

3. the *disavowal of external help* in any future conflict, including the lack of preparation for or expectation of help, as well as 'defence against help' or action against having a 'protective umbrella';

4. the degree to which *freedom of decision and action* are maintained, in the political, economic, and military spheres, with the avoidance of entangling commitments, alliances, dependence, or 'ties that bind', and the pursuit of independence;

5. the *lack of isolationism* in attitudes and policy and the presence both

of a willingness to contribute to the amelioration of world problems and of an attitude of impartiality with respect to superpower
rivalry; and

6. the *attitude to national identity*, nation-building, unity, stability, and
self-determination.

However, before either set of variables can be applied, it is necessary
to examine the pre-war foundations of Irish policy. In the pre-war
period, the complications engendered by the Irish constitutional
position, its Commonwealth membership, and the 'ports' issue are so
severe as to make inappropriate the strict application of the variables
identified, although, as will be seen in the following chapter, the
themes represented by the variables permeate the discussion.

4

A Neutral Tradition or a 'Certain Consideration'?

THE PRE-INDEPENDENCE PERIOD

The post-war confusions that have arisen over the nature and status of Irish neutrality (and, in particular, the question of whether it is *the* national tradition) owe something of their origin to a confusion over the historic role of Ireland, or, more accurately, the Irish, in the international political system—not only since independence in 1922 but even before then. Ronan Fanning, for example, observes that the Irish 'predisposition towards non-involvement in international relations has earlier origins in the nineteenth century and beyond', and suggests that by the turn of this century the nationalist movement had become 'increasingly introverted and isolationist as the very name "Sinn Féin" with its emphasis on self-reliance testifies'[1] A case can be made for the view that for most of its history Ireland was cut off from the mainstream of world events, with Britain acting as an effective screen between it and the world. Ireland was an integral part of the British political and economic system, and for many countries it was 'almost out of the world'.[2]

None the less, this view of Irish experience before independence can be exaggerated. Ireland, or at least Irish people, made a significant contribution to the international community even before 1922. Particularly significant was the Irish diaspora—the contribution the *émigré* Irish made to their new homelands, and the influence of the Irish religious, who spread not only Christianity but also something of Ireland.[3]

Clearly, sections of the population were preoccupied with the struggle for freedom against the British, but this led to an awareness of the potential help that the Irish abroad or sympathetic nations might give to

---

[1] Ronan Fanning, 'Irish Neutrality: An Historical Review', *Irish Studies in International Affairs*, 1/3 (1982), 28. See also Donald Harman Akenson, *The United States and Ireland* (Cambridge, Mass., 1973), 192.

[2] Patrick Keatinge, *The Formulation of Irish Foreign Policy* (Dublin, 1973), 2: cf. 3–4.

[3] Patrick Keatinge, *A Place Among the Nations: Issues of Irish Foreign Policy* (Dublin, 1978), 10.

their cause.[4] Moreover, de Valera was adamant that 'Sinn Féin' did not mean, as was usually suggested 'Ourselves Alone', but rather 'We Ourselves', a motto of self-reliance, not selfish isolation. Indeed, Ireland wanted independence so that 'she might freely give of her gifts to, and receive in return of their gifts from, her sister nations of the world over'.[5] Yet, before 1922 (and even thereafter) the central problem was lack of independence and freedom; as Michael Collins put it, the 'Irish struggle has always been for freedom—freedom from English occupation, from English domination'.[6] This obsession was manifest not only in the physical struggle against the British but also in the opposition to involuntary (or even voluntary) Irish participation in *British* wars, and in a willingness to engage in alliances with Britain's enemies.

The former trait was perhaps most sharply revealed by the widespread opposition to the very idea of conscription in Ireland during the First World War, although opposition to recruitment into the British army to fight British wars had been manifest earlier, e.g. during the Boer War. Indeed, Patrick Keatinge observes that the 'objection to participation in what were seen as Britain's rather than Ireland's wars was widespread, a forerunner of an instinctive Irish predilection for neutrality',[7] and furthermore, that the trauma produced by the British decision in 1918 to impose conscription in Ireland (although this was never implemented) 'was to establish significant restrictions on future Irish political leaders faced with the issue of some form of military participation in international politics; the popular basis of Irish neutrality was enshrined in 1918'.[8]

This profound antipathy to participation in British wars found expression in the anti-conscription campaign. It was in 1918 that the issue of conscription really came alive, and the cause became 'almost overnight, the most massive demonstration of nationalist solidarity that had been seen since the beginning of the war'.[9] It is important to appreciate that at this time the support for the campaign came from disparate

[4] Perhaps one of the most famous examples was the protracted visit to the United States by de Valera between 1917 and 1920.

[5] Quoted in Lord Longford and Thomas P. O'Neill, *Eamon de Valera* (London, 1970), 90, from the *Daily Herald*, 2 Apr. 1919.

[6] Michael Collins, *The Path to Freedom* (Cork, 1968 edn.), 32.

[7] Patrick Keatinge, *A Place*, 38.

[8] Ibid. 47.

[9] F. S. L. Lyons, *Ireland Since the Famine* 2nd edn. (London, 1973), 393; but see also 360–1. For a nationalist view see Dorothy Macardle, *The Irish Republic* (London, 1968), 109 ff., 242; and for details of the Mansion House pledge and declaration of 10 Apr. 1918 see Éamon de Valera, *Speeches and Statements by Éamon de Valera 1917–1973*, ed. Maurice Moynihan (Dublin, 1980), 12–18.

parliamentarians and parties, trade unions, and the Roman Catholic Church. The impact of the campaign was to help Sinn Féin in its triumph at the polls in December 1918.

The sentiment against both conscription and British wars was reflected in the formation of the Irish Neutrality League. It appears to have evolved out of a series of meetings of progressive nationalists in September 1914, when the possibility of a rising was discussed. The circulars announcing an inaugural public meeting were issued on 5 October 1914, and the first (some suggest the only) public meeting took place seven days later, although Greaves is adamant that 'there were several others' and that the 'main decision of the meeting was to start a campaign against recruiting'.[10] Apart from its title, there is no evidence that the League as such had any particular conception of neutrality, beyond the basic opposition to participation in British wars, or indeed any very clear idea of what neutrality involved.

At least in the initial period of the war Irish opinion was more genuinely reflected by the leader of the Irish Parliamentary Party, John Redmond, for 'in the autumn of 1914 there had been quite considerable enthusiasm for the war'.[11] It is interesting that Redmond took an increasingly strong line, moving from a pledge to defend Ireland and to allow the British to withdraw troops from Ireland,[12] to the claim that 'Ireland would be false to her history, and to every consideration of honour, good faith, and self-interest, did she not willingly bear her share in [the war's] burdens and its sacrifices'.[13] The culmination of his gradual evolution towards full commitment came in his famous Woodenbridge speech of Sunday, 20 September 1914. Having noted that the duty of Ireland was 'to defend the shores of Ireland against foreign invasion' and that the 'interests of Ireland . . . are at stake in this war', he urged his audience to 'account yourselves as men, not only in Ireland itself, but wherever the firing-line extends, in defence of right, of freedom, and of religion in this war'.[14]

---

[10] C. Desmond Greaves, *The Life and Times of James Connolly* (London, 1961), 293. For other accounts of the League see Lyons, 339; Fanning 'Neutrality', 28; Keatinge, *A Place*, 45; and Samuel Levenson, *James Connolly: A Biography* (London, 1973), 263–4.

[11] Lyons, 360.

[12] See Redmond's speech to the House of Commons on the outbreak of war: *Parliamentary Debates: House of Commons: Official Report* (hereafter *Commons Debates*), 5th ser., 65/8 (1914), col. 1828–9.

[13] Redmond's official declaration to the people of Ireland, reproduced in Denis Gwynn, *The Life of John Redmond* (London, 1932), 385.

[14] Reproduced ibid. 391–2.

It was this speech which split the Volunteers, although, from a membership of about 180,000, nearly 170,000 supported Redmond.[15] 'The vast majority of Irish nationalist opinion—those whose nationalism found expression in the idea of Home Rule—remained as nationalist and active as before, behind Redmond's policy of support for the Imperial war effort.'[16] In late 1914 to early 1915 Redmond was in the ascendancy, and antipathy to Britain and British wars was not nearly as widespread, at least at that time, as is often subsequently suggested by reference to the anti-conscription campaign and the Irish Neutrality League. Even after the Rising of 1916, the emotional backlash it produced, the disillusionment with the offer of Home Rule, and the rise of Sinn Féin, 'the British Army, without any particular campaign at all, had managed to secure 14,013 voluntary recruits from Ireland'.[17] At the very least it may be asked whether this accords with Keatinge's description of 'an instinctive Irish predilection for neutrality'.[18]

Even so, aspects of the minority point of view did prevail, becoming transformed into a majority point of view between 1916 and 1918, and gaining a degree of *ex post facto* legitimacy in the election of 1918. None the less, it is as well to remember that, before the First World War, 'Irish nationalism pursued almost as many foreign policies . . . as it contained different groups, objectives and strategies',[19] and that all 'of this did not add up to a very consistent foreign policy image . . . When asked what Sinn Féin's foreign policy was, Griffith is alleged to have said: 'In any issue I find out where England stands. Ireland will be found on the other side.'[20]

When contemplating Irish attitudes to Britain and alliances, advocates of the 'tradition' of Irish neutrality often point to the writings of Sir Roger Casement. Casement was keen to show that a defeat for Great Britain might in fact be to Ireland's advantage. He suggested that a German victory and subsequent German dominance in Europe would lead to a situation in which an 'Ireland, already covered by a sea held by German warships, and temporarily occupied by a German Army, might well be permanently and irrevocably severed from Great Britain, and

---

[15] See Macardle, 112–15; Lyons, 330; and Robert Kee, *The Green Flag: A History of Irish Nationalism* (London, 1972), 520.

[16] Kee, 521–3.

[17] Ibid. 525, 623. By Oct. 1915 there were 132,454 Irishmen in the British Army, over 80,000 having volunteered since the outbreak of war.

[18] Keatinge, *A Place*, 38.

[19] Ibid. 24.

[20] Ibid. 38.

with common assent *erected into a neutralised independent European State under international guarantees*.[21]

That some arrangement with Germany might last even after war and independence was also hinted at during the crucial time of the Rising, when apparently both Pearse and Plunkett, in conversations with Desmond FitzGerald, talked of the possibility of a German prince ruling an independent Ireland after a German victory.[22] In the Proclamation of Easter Monday, 1916, the IRA, the Irish Volunteers, and the Irish Citizens' Army made reference not only to Ireland's own strength, to the support of 'her exiled children in America', but also to the support 'by gallant allies in Europe'.[23] As Lyons notes, this last claim 'was more fantasy than fact, though it was fantasy based on fact'.[24] Despite problems at a very late stage, there had been expectations of German support in the form of ammunition and other war equipment.

By the end of 1914 Casement had entered into a formal agreement with the Germans on the question of support for Ireland, an agreement which he, incidentally, regarded as a treaty. It is necessary to stress that this alliance did leave crucial decisions to the Irish, but while there is an implication that the fighting would be performed by the Irish, it is not clear from the agreement itself that the Germans were to be prohibited from direct participation on Irish soil.[25]

Fanning claims that the German episode 'in itself was hardly the stuff of a diplomatic tradition, especially as the attractions of a German alliance vanished overnight once the United States entered the war in 1917', and he also makes a general point that independence would transform the environment, making it inappropriate for alliances with British enemies.[26] While the point is generally true, it does, perhaps, tend to gloss over an important feature of this period, namely the clear demonstration of a strand of pragmatism. The real concern was, and has remained, independence, not the questions of alliance or neutrality, and this was epitomized by the pronouncements of the Dáil at its first

[21] Writing under pseudonym 'Shan Van Vocht', 'Ireland, Germany and the Next War', *Irish Review* 3 (July 1913), 217–27, esp. 224–5 (emphasis added), reproduced in Denis Gwynn, *The Life and Work of Roger Casement* (London, 1930), 195–204 (quotation from p. 202).

[22] Desmond FitzGerald, *Memoirs of Desmond FitzGerald, 1913–1916* (London, 1968), 140–1.

[23] ' "Poblacht na hÉireann": The Provisional Government of the Irish Republic to the People of Ireland', fac. in Macardle, 157.

[24] Lyons, 371.

[25] It was signed by Casement as the 'Irish Envoy' and Von Zimmermann as 'Staat-sekretar, Deutsche Regierung', and is reproduced in Gwynn, *Casement*, 329–31.

[26] Fanning, 'Neutrality', 28.

meeting on 21 January 1919—the Declaration of Independence, the Message to the Free Nations of the World, and the Democratic Programme of Dáil Éireann.[27] In all three there was a preoccupation with sovereignty, yet no mention of neutrality.

As well as being willing during the war to ally with Britain's enemies, Irish leaders seemed to be ready after it to envisage some arrangement with, or guarantee to, Britain regarding British security after Irish independence. De Valera put it this way in February 1920: 'Mutual self-interest would make the peoples of these two islands, if both independent, the closest possible allies in a moment of real national danger to either.'[28] Other possibilities for British security were also touched upon at the same time. The most famous was the reference to the Monroe Doctrine and the Cuban analogy, in which de Valera suggested that Ireland's relationship with Britain should be analogous to Cuba's with the USA. The third suggestion is occasionally identified as the proposal, namely: 'An international instrument could easily be framed, as in the case of Belgium.' The fourth envisaged Irish participation in a League of Nations, in which all would agree to respect and defend each other's integrity and independence.

However, the most important point is that de Valera identified four possible ways of preserving British security, establishing a working Anglo-Irish relationship, and securing Irish independence, and that there was no question of neutrality being the only option, or necessarily the preferred one. The Irish were prepared to take cognizance of British needs, and indeed even saw, to paraphrase de Valera, that they should 'see fear in the downfall of Britain and fear, not hope, in every attack upon Britain'. This gave rise to the idea of Irish guarantees not to let Irish territory be used as the base for foreign invasion or attacks upon Britain.

The Irish were not isolationist, even on the eve of independence. In April 1919, for example, the Dáil debated the motion that 'We are eager and ready to enter a World League of Nations based on equality of right . . . We are willing to accept all the duties, responsibilities and burdens which inclusion in such a League implies.'[29] Unfortunately, the

---

[27] All reproduced in Macardle, 252–3, 850–1, 254–5.

[28] De Valera handed the draft of a speech outlining alternative strategies to a journalist from the *Westminster Gazette* who selected passages and edited it as an 'interview'. It is reproduced in *Speeches and Statements*, 32–4: the quotations which follow are taken from it.

[29] 'Report of the First Dáil, 11 April 1919', as reported by the *Irish Independent*, 12 Apr. 1919.

League that was created appeared to the Irish simply to perpetuate the power of those who had it. They were also unhappy about Article X of the Covenant, which with its emphasis upon 'territorial integrity' appeared to cement the status quo.[30] These events left a mark on subsequent Irish thinking.[31]

On all of these questions the central preoccupation, the litmus-paper indicating attitudes, was the struggle for freedom and independence. After a 'war of independence' and a protracted correspondence between de Valera and Lloyd George, it was finally agreed at the end of September 1921 that talks should take place in October, 'with a view to ascertaining how the asociation of Ireland with the community of nations known as the British Empire may best be reconciled with Irish national aspirations'.[32]

In analysing the Irish proposals and the negotiations, it is important to bear in mind that there are distinctions between aspirations and policy, and that negotiation involves not only compromise but also an element of asking for more than one expects. This is all the more significant if one remembers that it was neither defence nor neutrality that caused problems in either London or Dublin, but rather the vexed questions of Oath and Empire, and—certainly during the negotiations, if not the subsequent Dáil debates—Partition. Fanning, Murphy, and particularly Longford (amongst others) are all agreed that defence and neutrality were 'not central to the treaty split and to the tragic events leading to civil war'.[33] As Longford puts it, in 'their hearts the Irish had always recognized that Defence touched Ireland's honour least and British security in British eyes most'.[34] None the less, significant weight was attached to neutrality at the beginning of the negotiations. This is evidenced both by the draft Irish proposals with which the Irish left Dublin—Draft Treaty A[35]—and by discussions at the second plenary session on the first afternoon (11 October 1921) of the Conference.[36]

Draft Treaty A consisted of 'Outlines for *ideas* and *principles* only.

[30] De Valera, 11 Apr. 1919, reproduced in *Speeches and Statements*, 26–8.

[31] e.g. in attitudes to the North Atlantic Treaty in 1949: see below, ch. 6.

[32] Much of the correspondence, and Lloyd George's letter of 29 Sept. 1921 using this phrase, is reproduced in Macardle, 431–79, esp. 478–9.

[33] Fanning, 'Neutrality', 29. See also John A. Murphy, *Ireland in the Twentieth Century* (Dublin, 1975), 33, and Lord Longford, *Peace by Ordeal* (London, 1972), 90–1, 145.

[34] Longford, 148.

[35] 'Draft Treaty A' is reproduced in Macardle, 863–5 (app. 16).

[36] See Longford, 124, and Thomas Jones, *Whitehall Diary*, ii: *Ireland 1918–1925*, ed. Keith Middlemas (OUP, 1971), 121–2.

Wording tentative and rough', since the wording would be refined once agreement upon principles was reached. In terms of neutrality, most attention is usually focused, correctly, upon Article V:

Ireland accepts and the British Commonwealth guarantees the perpetual neutrality of Ireland and the integrity and inviolability of Irish territory; and both in its own interest and in friendly regard to the strategic interests of the British Commonwealth binds itself to enter into no compact, and to take no action, nor permit any action to be taken, inconsistent with the obligation of preserving its own neutrality and inviolability and to repel with force any attempt to violate its territory or to use its territorial waters for warlike purposes.

Article XI also made reference to neutrality in that the British were to seek recognition of Ireland's neutrality by others. Fully one-third of the draft dealt with these issues.

While proponents of Irish 'traditional neutrality' naturally focus upon these articles, less attention is usually paid to Article II, which, it might be argued, compromises that neutrality in that Ireland would agree 'to become an external associate of the states of the British Commonwealth. As an associate Ireland's status shall be that of equality with the sovereign partner states of the Commonwealth'.

This is particularly significant because of British views on the rights of Commonwealth states.[37] It is also noteworthy that the first Irish proposals submitted to the British on 24 October were significantly different from the original Draft Treaty A, which was never presented. The memorandum of 24 October proposed, in a critical section, that 'Ireland shall be recognised as a *free* State, that the British Commonwealth shall guarantee Ireland's *freedom* and integrity'.[38] Longford suggests that it was Collins who 'had the word "neutral" altered to "free" ', and (says Longford) this was 'without apparently much change in the meaning'. Longford supports this view by arguing that 'freedom' would make 'clear once and for all that England had no right of occupation in time of war', while 'some scope would apparently be left Ireland to join in a war; she would not therefore, from a military point of view, be completely sterilised as she would be under neutrality'.[39] Clearly the change of wording is significant: it emphasizes the importance of the perception

---

[37] See below, pp. 90–1 and 94–5 and n. 51.
[38] Jones, 141, wrongly refers to this as 'Draft Treaty A'. For the memo see Macardle, 866–8 (emphasis added).
[39] Longford, 144.

that the 'Irish struggle has always been for freedom—freedom from English occupation, from English domination—not for freedom with any particular label attached to it'.[40]

Even so, there were a number of verbal exchanges on the issues of defence and neutrality, even on the first afternoon of negotiations, when Griffith raised the question of permanent Irish neutrality guaranteed by England. However, it is clear that the general tenor of the verbal exchanges was rather different from that of the various Irish memorandums. Moreover, the British were adamant that neutrality meant secession, and as such, and for other reasons, was not acceptable.

Indeed, the question was complicated by the discussions over the form of relationship between Ireland, Britain, and the Commonwealth. For example, at one stage in these discussions, Griffith advised Lloyd George that, in association with the Crown, Britain, and the Dominions, the Irish would be 'Something more than allies—not temporary but permanent allies', and that Ireland understood matters of 'common concern' to mean 'war and peace, trade, all the large issues. It is a matter of drafting.' Indeed, Griffith said 'I would regard defence of our country and your country' as a matter of 'common concern'. Griffith also informed Lloyd George, after having been told that no country would recognize Irish neutrality if Britain had the harbours, that in principle the Irish had 'no objection to taking those safeguards which are necessary to your security', although 'working out of details might be very difficult'.[41] As Longford comments, 'Not much more was likely to be heard of the Irish claims to neutrality; Britain had won on Defence.'[42]

In the final agreement,[43] the relevant clauses on defence and facilities are contained in Articles 6–8 and in the Annex, while Articles 1–3 attempted to define the position of Ireland, its Commonwealth responsibilities, and its relationship to the Imperial Parliament. On these questions Ireland was to be similar to Canada, Australia, New Zealand, and South Africa, except that *vis-à-vis* the Imperial Parliament the Canadian model was largely to apply. Article 6 gave Britain predominant responsibility for 'the defence by sea of Great Britain and Ireland', until the Irish Free State 'undertakes her own coastal defence', by agreement with Britain. These arrangements were to be reviewed after five years, 'with a

---

[40] M. Collins, 32.

[41] For details of these exchanges see Jones, 142–4, and Longford, 146–8.

[42] Longford, 148; but for further exchanges see ibid., 90–1, 213–17; Macardle, 519, 530–1, 578–9; and Jones, 142 ff.

[43] For the Treaty see Macardle, app. 21, pp. 880–5.

view to the undertaking by Ireland of a share in her own coastal defence'. However, there was no guarantee that Britain would accept alternative arrangements after five years or agree to an Irish contribution. Article 7 was in clear contradiction with any Irish aspiration to neutrality, since in peacetime Britain was to be given certain port facilities, while 'In time of war or of strained relations with a Foreign Power' the Irish accepted that the British should have 'such harbour and other facilities' as they 'may require for the purposes of such defence as aforesaid'. In Article 8, if the Irish established a military force it would 'not exceed in size such proportion of the military establishments maintained in Great Britain as that which the population of Ireland bears to the population of Great Britain'.

These provisions ruled out Irish abstention from a British war, impartiality, and the ability to fulfil neutral rights and duties. In addition, not only would Ireland lack the right to be neutral, it would also lack the power to be so, because of Article 8 (and the lack of its own navy). Any notion of 'defence against help' was now a bitter irony. The British might forgo an active Irish contribution to their war effort in terms of men etc., but remained throughout emphatic that membership in the Empire involved automatic Irish involvement in British conflicts. No Dominion could be neutral; for Ireland, especially, there could be no neutrality.[44]

The treaty split the Irish cabinet and parliament but it was accepted by a majority. Much of this debate and controversy avoided defence and neutrality altogether, which is perhaps another sign of its relative importance. Only Childers dwelt upon these issues, relating them to the question of independence. He argued that Ireland would not be like Canada, given the cession of the ports and British defence of Irish coasts. Indeed, what was the 'use of talking of responsibility for making treaties and alliances with foreign nations which may involve a country in war', when Ireland remained 'under British authority and under the British Crown'? Ireland, it appeared to Childers, would almost inevitably be pulled into British wars though legal obligations and military ties.[45]

Although de Valera complained that the Treaty as signed differed

[44] Longford still held this view nearly twenty years after the Treaty and after much constitutional evolution within both Ireland and Commonwealth: see Longford, 302–3. It is interesting that what came to be the 'Simonstown solution' in South Africa was not considered: see Nicholas Mansergh, *Survey of British Commonwealth Affairs: Problems of External Policy 1931–1939* (OUP, 1952), 257.

[45] Dáil Éireann, Official Report, *Debate on the Treaty between Great Britain and Ireland signed in London on 6 December 1921* (Dublin, 1922), 37–8, *passim*.

from the draft treaty which the delegates took with them, it is clear that his own 'Document No. 2' in December 1921 was also significantly different, in that it omitted the very specific reference to neutrality.[46] Incidentally, it is interesting that this was at least the second occasion during the crucial six months of negotiations and debate on which there was a private proposal (which was not taken up) to include the word 'neutrality' in the formal documents. It was not the only objective, and it could be bartered against other objectives.

Even de Valera's own idea, which came to be known as 'external association', was problematic for neutrality. This was so because it was intertwined with defence (war and treaties being matters of 'common concern'), because the Irish had guaranteed not to allow themselves to be used in ways inimical to British security, and because the association seemed of an amorphous nature, at a time when Commonwealth involvement was understood to imply commitments to Britain. It should be noted that these problems arose irrespective of the ports or other issues.

Before independence in 1922, Irish attitudes to neutrality and defence were clearly complex, and there was no one consistent tradition.

EVOLVING POLICY: THE POLITICAL DIMENSION

For the first ten years of the new state's life, policy-making was in the hands of supporters of and sympathizers with the Treaty. A consequence of exclusion from power was that de Valera's party, Fianna Fáil, on coming into government in 1932, initially had other, more pressing preoccupations than foreign policy, with the crucial exception of the bilateral relations with Britain. Indeed, Fanning argues, 'neutrality [was not] high on the agenda of de Valera's First Fianna Fáil government when it came to power in 1932. Articles 6 and 7 of the Treaty . . . escaped unscathed in the early thirties when de Valera was busily engaged in rewriting much of the rest of the Treaty as he thought it should have been written in the first place.'[47] The overriding initial preoccupations were freedom and independence, to give concrete expression to Michael Collins's famous aphorism that the Treaty gave 'not the

---

[46] Much controversy surrounds this document. The Treaty was 'Document No. 1'. For details of the document and de Valera's expositions upon it see Macardle, app. 22, pp. 886–91, and de Valera, *Speeches and Statements*, 80–7.

[47] Fanning, 'Neutrality', 29.

ultimate freedom that all nations aspire and develop to, but the freedom to achieve it'.[48]

The initial constraints on the new Irish regime in the 1920s were both internal and external. On the one hand there was an attempt to placate anti-Treaty elements, but on the other the British had also to be placated. This latter was important because the constitution of the new Ireland had to be acceptable to the British, and indeed was eventually embodied in British law.[49] The Constitution of the Irish Free State (Saorstát Éireann), as finally approved, certainly constrained the Irish, since the accompanying Constituent Act made it clear that if any article or amendment, as law made thereunder, 'is in any respect repugnant to any of the provisions of the Scheduled Treaty [i.e. Articles of Agreement for a Treaty between Great Britain and Ireland], it shall, to the extent only of such repugnancy, be absolutely void and inoperative. . . .' At first sight Article 49, 'Save in the case of actual invasion, the Irish Free State (Saorstát Éireann) shall not be committed to active participation in any war without the assent of the Oireachtas', would appear to allow for neutrality. However, this must be read in conjunction with the Constitutent Act. Moreover, it is interesting that the Constitution, as adopted, specifies 'active participation'. The use of the adjective is presumably deliberate, which presumably implies that passive participation does not require such consent. Moreover, the British Lord Chancellor was keen to reassure Britain about Article 49, and clearly stated that there was 'no question here of neutrality: it may be said that, by their giving facilities, neutrality goes'.[50]

None the less, no final settlement had been attained, and those who had supported the Treaty were therefore committed to stretching its terms as far as possible in order to expand the scope of Irish freedom and independence. In this the Irish benefited not only from their own efforts (e.g. in registering the Treaty of 1921 with the League of Nations in 1924 over British objections) but also from the aspirations, drive, and actions of the older Dominions. The following years saw a successive widening of Dominion freedom and power.[51]

---

[48] Dáil Éireann, *Debate on the Treaty*, 29–35.

[49] See for the relevant documentation and the Constitution: Irish Free State (Agreement) Act 1922 (31 Mar. 1922); An Act to Provide for the Constitution of the Irish Free State (5 Dec. 1922); An Act to Make Such Provisions as are Consequential on or incidental to the Establishment of the Irish Free State (5 Dec. 1922).

[50] Quoted in Macardle, 747.

[51] For an impressive literature on Anglo-Irish and Commonwealth relations and on the role of

It was perhaps the Statute of Westminster which put the stamp on the developments of the preceding years—the Imperial Conferences of 1926 and 1930, the Irish acceptance of invitations to conferences and signing of treaties on their own initiative (1928-9), and the Report on the Operation of Dominion Legislation in 1929, amongst other things. The Statute of Westminster defined the Commonwealth as a 'free association' of members, implying that a state could leave. Furthermore, in future no British laws were to extend to the Dominions, unless the Dominion consented.[52] In effect, Ireland was now only to be bound by moral obligations and the normal conventions relating to international treaties.[53]

The unilateral steps of de Valera were more dramatic than the painstaking diplomacy in Commonwealth meetings, but they did not significantly alter the degree of independence in foreign policy. Indeed, somewhat paradoxically, the clarity of that independence in external eyes was kept rather clouded by the terms of the Executive Authority (External Relations) Act of 1936, whereby the King was to continue to have a strictly formal role in diplomatic accreditation and the signing of international treaties, albeit 'as and when advised' by the Irish Executive Council.[54]

The 1937 Constitution affirmed Irish independence, and contained marked differences from the 1922 Constitution. For example, Article 28.3.1 stated that 'War shall not be declared and the State shall not participate in any war save with the assent of Dáil Éireann.'[55] In the changed environment no subtle distinction between active and passive participation was necessary, but further ambiguity remained after 1937 with respect to the position of Ireland in the Commonwealth. The Irish regarded themselves as outside it and only externally associated with it, while Britain and the Dominions decided only after much

the Irish in the evolution of the Commonwealth, and for differing views on these questions, see: W. K. Hancock, *Survey of British Commonwealth Affairs: Problems of Nationality 1918-1936* (OUP, 1937); N. Mansergh, *Survey, 1931-9*; id., *Survey of British Commonwealth Affairs: Problems of Wartime Co-operation and Post-war Change, 1930-52* (1958); D. W. Harkness, *The Restless Dominion: The Irish Free State and the British Commonwealth of Nations, 1921-31* (London, 1969); Deirdre McMahon, *Republicans and Imperialists: Anglo-Irish Relations in the 1930s* (New Haven, Conn., 1984); and Paul Canning, *British Policy Towards Ireland 1921-1941* (OUP, 1985).

[52] For the Statute of Westminster, see Nicholas Mansergh (ed.), *Documents and Speeches on British Commonwealth Affairs 1931-1952* (OUP, 1953), 1-4.

[53] This was confirmed by *Moore v. Attorney-General for the Irish Free State* (1935); see Mansergh, *Survey 1931-9*, 28, 292-3.

[54] Executive Authority (External Relations) Act 1936.

[55] 'Bunreacht na hÉireann', 29 Dec. 1937; see also Article 29 on 'International Relations'.

agonizing that they were 'prepared to treat the new Constitution as not affecting a fundamental alteration in the position of the Irish Free State'.[56] This issue was of more than semantic or symbolic importance, since arguments were still occurring within the Commonwealth as to whether the Dominions had the right to decide the issue of peace or war themselves, notwithstanding the evolution of doctrine culminating in the Statute of Westminster.

This dispute continued despite the fact that the 1937 Imperial Conference had 'recognized that it is the sole responsibility of the several Parliaments of the British Commonwealth to decide the nature and scope of their own defence policy',[57] and that, as Mansergh has argued, in the 'supreme issue of war and peace the Commonwealth had henceforward to rely not, as in 1914, upon a unity constitutionally imposed from above, but upon a unity of wills'.[58] For Ireland the question was particularly difficult because of geographical proximity to Britain, and because, as Lyons puts it,

neutrality, after all, was not just the instinctive reaction of a small power to keep clear of the quarrels of big powers, it was the outward and visible sign of absolute sovereignty. To be free to choose between peace and war was the mark of independence, to be free to choose between peace and a *British* war demonstrated to all the world just how complete that independence really was.[59]

This was very important to an Ireland so close to Britain, with internal and external confusion over its precise constitutional position and degree of freedom, and to an Ireland which, in 1939, had diplomatic relations with only nine states,[60] its letters of accreditation still being signed by the King. But most of all it was important to an Ireland which had divided over the treaty, over whether it gave the 'freedom to achieve freedom', and over the Oath and Empire, and which wished to assert the sovereignty and independence proclaimed in the 1937 Constitution.

The problem for the Irish was that a 'politically independent Irish state . . . posed a strategic problem for successive British governments,

---

[56] Statement published in *The Times*, 30 Dec. 1937, and reproduced in Mansergh, *Survey 1931-9*, 305-6. De Valera did not protest, but disagreed, continuing to regard Ireland as externally associated.

[57] *Summary of Proceedings: Imperial Conference 1937* (Cmd. 5482; London, 1937), §§ IX and X, reproduced in Mansergh, *Documents and Speeches*, 163-9.

[58] Mansergh, *Survey 1931-9*, 87.

[59] Lyons, 554 (emphasis in original).

[60] Britain, United States of America, Holy See, France, Germany, Belgium, Spain, Italy and Canada—in order of date of establishment.

concerned to protect their Atlantic flank',[61] despite de Valera's oft-repeated pledge that 'our territory will never be permitted to be used as a base for attack upon Britain'.[62] This pledge was not a commitment to partcipate in a British war, nor was it a commitment to alliance. In one sense it was fully compatible with an aspiration to neutrality, since the central Irish concern was simply with defending its independence and sovereignty (and potential neutrality), although this had the by-product of offering additional security to Britain.[63] However, a potential belligerent could construe this guarantee differently, since in that same speech of April 1938, de Valera commented that 'an independent Ireland would have interests, very many interests, in common with Great Britain. In providing for our defence of our own interests, we would also of necessity be providing to a certain extent for British defence of British interests.'[64]

Over a decade earlier the government of William Cosgrave had considered those common interests, examining the possibility of 'some foreign Power' using 'our geographical position either as a base for an offensive against Great Britain or against sea-borne traffic between ports in Saorstát Éireann and other countries' (the only contingencies specifically referred to). The document which the Cabinet considered argued that the central precept of Irish defence policy must be that the army be 'so organised, trained and equipped as to render it capable, should the necessity arise, of full and complete co-ordination with the forces of the British Government in the defence of Saorstát territory whether against actual hostilities or against violation of neutrality on the part of a common enemy'.[65] This oblique reference to neutrality clearly illustrates a desire to keep that option open, but the tenor of the document as a whole places greater emphasis upon 'full and complete co-ordination' with British forces. In a Dáil debate in February 1927 Desmond FitzGerald, apparently following the 1925 document, had declared that 'We need not blink the fact that it is quite possible, in the event of a general attack on these islands—it is perfectly obvious—our army must co-operate with the British Army.' When asked whether Ireland could

[61] Keatinge, Formulation, 5.

[62] Parliamentary Debates: Dáil Éireann: Official Report (hereafter Dáil Debates) 56 (1935), cols. 2086–116. See the Feb. 1920 'interview', in de Valera, Speeches and Statements, 32–4; 'Document No. 2', in Macardle, 886–91; and Dáil Debates 71 (1938), 32–48.

[63] De Valera, Dáil Debates, 71 (1938), 34–6.

[64] Ibid. 37.

[65] The Cabinet met on 13 Nov. 1925: a schedule entitled 'Defence Policy' is attached to Cabinet minutes 2/225.

be neutral if the United Kingdom alone were attacked, or whether it would be 'bound up in' an attack by conceiving of itself 'as part of the defence forces of the British islands', FitzGerald did not reply directly, simply stating that he had been speaking of a general attack, and that in any case it would be for the Dáil to decide.[66] It is interesting that, while not always explicit, the expectation that British and Irish forces would co-operate was to some extent enduring.

The possibility of a formal defence arrangement or alliance was certainly not as remote as might be suggested by the Irish obsession with neutrality (if such it was). Indeed, in May 1935, in a rather enigmatic phrase, de Valera himself had said 'We can make trade treaties . . . I can even conceive conditions in which we could make defence treaties.'[67] Of course, one problem which permeates this whole issue is the difficulty of evaluating such rhetorical statements: were they reflections of a genuine policy position or merely trial balloons for potential negotiations, and what was the envisaged content of any such agreement? These questions are particularly pertinent in the context of discussions in 1938 to end the Anglo-Irish 'economic war' and to arrange for a settlement on the issue of the ports. It is the conventional wisdom that by 1938 de Valera was committed to neutrality as the appropriate policy for Ireland in any forthcoming war, and sought the return of the ports to make such a policy viable (or at least more viable). Indeed, in later years de Valera himself regarded the return of the ports as 'his greatest political achievement . . . because of its importance in the context of neutrality'.[68] On the other hand, in January 1938 de Valera 'indicated that he would then be willing to conclude a naval agreement to Britain's satisfaction' if Britain would settle the Partition issue;[69] and in February 1938 he acknowledged that if Partition were later settled satisfactorily ' "he would be able to go a long way" ' towards the defence agreement then being contemplated'. Indeed, at the same meeting, he told the British that some in Ireland 'would urge that "defence should be made a lever" in order to bring effective pressure on Britain over Partition'.[70] It may be that de Valera was at least persuaded of tactical advantages in such a ploy,

---

[66] *Dáil Debates*, 18 (1927), 399.

[67] *Dáil Debates*, 56 (1935), 2116.

[68] John Bowman, *De Valera and the Ulster Question 1917–1973* (OUP, 1982), 181.

[69] T. Ryle Dwyer, *Irish Neutrality and the USA 1939–47* (Dublin, 1977), 11–12, although no precise evidence is cited. Cf. Longford and O'Neill, 313–14; Bowman, 175; and de Valera, *Speeches and Statements*, 358–62.

[70] Bowman, 174.

since it was 'at this same time . . . that the policy of neutrality began to be linked with the question of partition'.[71]

Malcolm MacDonald, who became Dominions Secretary in 1935 (and was also influential in Anglo-Irish relations during the Second World War believed that for 'de Valera, Irish control of the ports was not only a symbol of independence but an *establishment* of independence'.[72] Neutrality was an objective at the talks, but the achievement of sovereignty was a higher priority. There was, it should be noted, no guarantee of co-operation, even if Partition were ended. Nor was there an unconditional assertion of neutrality in the negotiations of 1938.

In the negotiations in 1936–8 de Valera clearly envisaged (according to Fisk) some defence relationship, if only the 'possibility of making a request for British defence experts, a common defence plan and interchangeable equipment "because our forces would co-operate together" '. There was even talk of the construction of a factory for munitions in the Free State. But de Valera said that the Irish people were 'nervous of being dragged into some Imperialist war' which Britain might wage.[73] It was the Irish who formally proposed discussion 'in regard to economic and other measures to be adopted in time of war'.[74] No such deal was struck, largely because de Valera was able to get the ports and the ending of the tariff war without one, while there was no movement on Partition. None the less, talk of a defence arrangement was not abandoned until a late stage in the 1938 negotiations, and at one point a draft agreement on defence was placed before delegates.[75]

When de Valera spoke in the Dáil introducing the motion in favour of the return of the ports and an end to the Anglo-Irish economic war, he made no specific mention of neutrality. Rather, on 27 April 1938 he emphasized independence and sovereignty. He also sought to make the point that

we have got these defences unconditionally . . . There has been no bargain . . . there is no secret understanding. But there is a belief, I am certain . . . that it is far better for Britain, far more advantageous for Britain, to have a free

---

[71] Conor Cruise O'Brien, 'Ireland in International Affairs', in Owen Dudley Edwards (ed.), *Conor Cruise O'Brien Introduces Ireland* (London, 1969), 120.

[72] Interview with Fisk, 18 Apr. 1978: see Robert Fisk, *In Time of War: Ireland, Ulster and the Price of Neutrality 1939–1945* (London, 1983), 34 (emphasis in original).

[73] Ibid. 32, citing P R O C A B 24/271, MacDonald to Cabinet, 12 Oct. 1937.

[74] Ibid. 34, citing S P O C A B 1/8, Cabinet minutes, 23 Nov. 1937, and the Irish Cabinet's attitude.

[75] Ibid. 34–5.

Ireland by its side than an Ireland that would be unfriendly because of liberties which Britain denied.[76]

Perhaps the omission of a reference to neutrality was a gesture towards British sensibilities until after the British had ratified the agreement, since after that de Valera was more direct in his references to the issue. None the less, in an important speech of 13 July 1938 to the Dáil,[77] although he was explicit in the 'desire not to get into a war if [the Irish] can keep out of it', de Valera's actual assertion of neutrality as an objective was highly equivocal:

Assuming other things were equal, *if* there were any chance of our neutrality in general being *possible*, we would *probably* say that we want to remain neutral. I *do not know* that you can follow that up by saying in any war but, in general, our desire would be for neutrality *as far as possible*.

This is a remarkable section of a speech normally considered to be a statement of neutrality.

De Valera asserted 'we have no commitments, we can keep out of war, we can be neutral if we want . . . There are no advance commitments on us to take any side.' But he went on to consider the situation 'in which our rights, or liberties, or interests generally were being attacked by some State other than Britain'. In response, de Valera was convinced that Britain would have to act to help Ireland in Britain's own interest 'because of her geographic position'. Britain would act 'not in our interests . . . [but for] immediate selfish interest'. As a result, Ireland 'may be able to . . . count on assistance'.

Now here is the rub: de Valera asked 'Would we want such assistance?' He doubted whether Ireland could, unaided, effectively resist 'a frontal and straightforward attack from any foreign State'. Given, therefore, that it would be in Britain's interest to help and that Ireland would require such help, 'commonsense dictates that we should try to provide in advance so that that assistance would be of the greatest possible benefit to us'. This being so, consultation with Britain might be 'necessary and advisable . . .'.

While de Valera had played hard to get earlier in the year, by the summer of 1938 it was clearly the Irish who were placing the emphasis upon some arrangement, be it tacit or formal. In August 1938 Dulanty, the Irish High Commissioner to Britain, asked 'if he could attend the

---

[76] *Dáil Debates*, 71 (1938), 32–48. Chamberlain seemed to concur in the House of Commons on 5 May 1938, although Churchill did not: see *Commons Debates*, 335 (1938), 1072–8, 1094–1105.

[77] *Dáil Debates*, 72 (1938), 696–703 (emphasis added).

meetings of the Cabinet's Committee for Imperial Defence',[78] and in September he began to attend 'the daily briefings for the High Commissioners given by Malcolm MacDonald in the Dominions Office'.[79] That same summer, the Irish also requested copies of the British Government's War Book measures.[80] This activity by officials would be exceedingly curious without the sanction of de Valera, given that he was not only Taoiseach at the time, but also Minister for External Affairs. De Valera himself met with the British Minister for Co-ordination of Defence, Sir Thomas Inskip, on 8 September 1938, and made it clear he was anxious to attain 'help in deciding what were the matters that needed attention and on the type of defences required'.[81]

Despite hesitations, two senior Irish army officers were sent to London in October for secret talks. Again the primary objective was information, for example on how the ports might best be defended. Apparently the British felt that these discussions were 'very satisfactory'.[82]

Even so, there were to be no more such military talks in the pre-war period, although the Irish did suggest that the British recommend a French officer who could become the principal military adviser to the Irish army. As explained to the British, 'political expediency made the appointment of a British officer impossible' and therefore the Irish wanted 'the next best thing in securing a high military officer of our ally. The appointment of such an officer would be a clear indication to Germany and the world that Eire was on the side of the Western democracies.'[83]

Despite these talks and exchanges, de Valera was making it clear that Partition remained the problem, that in 'the event of war the attitude of Ireland would be very different if partition still existed from what it would be were Ireland one, and many of the steps which he would like to take in the event of our being at war would be impossible for him so long as partition lasted'.[84] In the talks that took place in the late 1930s it is evident that the Irish position was not unambiguously one of neutrality. The 'traditional neutral' image is therefore open to question. This is true

[78] Deirdre McMahon, 'Ireland, the Dominions and the Munich Crisis', *Irish Studies in International Affairs*, 1/1 (1979), 35.   [79] Ibid. 30.

[80] Ibid. 35.

[81] Ibid., and see Fisk, 59–61. For the general relationship in the 1930s see McMahon, *Republicans, passim*.

[82] See McMahon, 'Ireland', 35, and Fisk, 61–2. The Irish Deputy Prime Minister (An Tánaiste), Sean T. O'Kelly, was one of those with doubts.

[83] Fisk, 68. The British felt unable to agree.

[84] Ibid. 63 ff., for this and what de Valera told Chamberlain in the spring of 1939.

also if one examines the attitude of the Irish to the League of Nations, and collective security and neutrality in that context, especially given the Irish commitment to collective security.

The Irish saw League membership as an assertion of statehood and independence, and sought to make this manifest by their activities at the League, e.g. by the insistence in 1924 on registering the 1921 Treaty. A sign that independence was regarded as the key was the affirmation by Kevin O'Higgins, as early as 1923, that despite support for the League participation in any war, including a League war, would require the Dáil's consent under the new Constitution.[85] However, unlike Switzerland, Ireland never appears to have sought or attained a neutrality reservation, although the Swiss had established the precedent in 1920.[86] Up until 1935–6 the Irish were committed to the League and, moreover, knew full well the nature of the commitments and obligations involved. This route to security took precedence over the aspiration to neutrality, which only re-emerged significantly in 1935–6.

De Valera had demonstrated his commitment when he addressed the League Assembly as Acting President in September 1932 and spoke of the need to 'show unmistakably that the Covenant of the League is a solemn pact, the obligations of which no State, great or small, will find it possible to ignore'.[87] In fact de Valera laid great stress upon upholding the Covenant and upon united collective action.

Three years later, de Valera was arguing that the

theory of the absolute sovereignty of States, interpreted to mean that a State is above all law, must be abandoned . . . peace and order [are] impossible . . . if States may hold that self-interest is for them the supreme law, and that they are subject to no other control . . . The rule of unanimity for decision and legislation must go . . . There must . . . be some tribunal by which the law shall be interpreted and applied, and, finally, there must be some means by which its judgments can be enforced against a State.

It must be acknowledged that de Valera described this as 'the ideal' and

---

[85] *Dáil Debates*, 5 (1923), 423. For most of the period the League did not generate much Irish interest: see Keatinge, *A Place*, 152–7, and Stephen Barcroft, 'The International Civil Servant: The League of Nations Career of Sean Lester 1929–1947' (Trinity College, Dublin, Ph.D. thesis, 1972). See also id., 'Irish Foreign Policy at the League of Nations 1929–1936', *Irish Studies in International Affairs*, 1/1 (1979).

[86] See Nils Ørvik, *The Decline of Neutrality*, 2nd edn. (London, 1971), 122, and Peter Lyon, *Neutralism* (Leicester, 1963), 152.

[87] 'Address opening the 13th League Assembly', 26 Sept. 1932, reproduced in *Peace and War: Speeches by Mr De Valera on International Affairs (1932–1938)* (Dublin, 1944), 11. For the whole speech see pp. 5–14.

conceded that the League was 'very far from coming up to the ideal'.
None the less, this speech hardly epitomizes a recalcitrant member. In
closing, de Valera spoke of the need to maintain the League, and to do
that 'we must live up to its obligations'.[88]

Four days later de Valera emphasized that the Irish by their 'own
choice and without compulsion . . . entered into the obligations of the
Covenant. We shall fulfil these obligations in the letter and in the spirit.
We have given our word and we shall keep it.'[89] Ireland was ready to pay
the price for peace. As a submission to the Irish Cabinet in September
1935 makes clear, while aware that military action under the Covenant
was unlikely to occur, de Valera did acknowledge that 'it would be
contrary to the spirit of the Covenant for the member concerned to
refuse to take part . . . [in] collective military action to be taken by the
League'.[90] Indeed, de Valera's biographers even suggest that 'Had
World War II come from a joint decision of the League of Nations his
attitude would, no doubt, have been modified.'[91]

This attitude prevailed until the League failed to apply the military
sanctions he had supported earlier. In September 1935 de Valera was
emphatic that the Abyssinian crisis meant that the 'final test of the
League . . . has come'.[92] As a result of the test, Irish attitudes changed,
and henceforth there was a search for alternative means of safeguarding
security. Indeed, in a debate on the Estimate for External Affairs in June
1936, de Valera went so far as to ask the Chair 'if it would be appropriate
at this stage to discuss the question as to whether or not we should
withdraw from the League'.[93]

After 1935 de Valera spoke of 'bitter humiliation' regarding the
League, and began to make it clear that there could no longer be 'an
obligation to go to war to maintain the principles of the League'.
Ireland, along with other small states, could only resolve 'not to become
the tools of any great Power', and they should all 'resist with whatever
strength they may possess every attempt to force them into a war against

---

[88] 'The League and Peace: Broadcast to the United States', 12 Sept. 1935, ibid. 39–43.

[89] 'The Abyssinian Crisis' (speech to the League Assembly), 16 Sept. 1935, ibid. 44–8. On
4 Oct. de Valera reiterated that on coming into office Fianna Fáil could have renounced the
obligations, but they decided otherwise: 'Abyssinian War: Broadcast from Radio Éireann', ibid.
49–53.

[90] 24 Sept. 1935, Cabinet File S8083 (State Paper Office of Ireland).

[91] Longford and O'Neill, 347. See also O'Brien, 'International Affairs', 115, and cf. Keatinge,
A Place, 156.

[92] To League Assembly, 16 Sept. 1935, in de Valera, *Peace and War*, 45.

[93] *Dáil Debates*, 62 (1936), 2650 ff.

their will'.[94] This was not equivalent to saying that the Irish would necessarily avoid involvement, if it was by their own decision.

After 1935 the Irish attitude to security clearly changed, and only now, after four years and after de Valera had been 'busily engaged in rewriting much of the rest of the Treaty', was attention turned to the ports issue.[95] Only then did it come to be argued that British occupation of the ports provided others with a reason to ignore Irish neutrality, that it was not Irish will that 'would be effective in keeping a position of neutrality but the will of other people',[96] and that Ireland 'could be treated as an automatic belligerent'.[97] Only now did the cry 'We want to be neutral'[98] become clearer, although even then there was the complication of the relationship and the negotiations with Britain in the period between 1936 and 1939.

A further complication is that, while the Irish had made great strides in the politico-legal area, there still remained the problems of economic sovereignty and military self-sufficiency.

SELF-SUFFICIENCY: THE ECONOMIC DIMENSION

Whatever the interpretation of 'Sinn Féin', it is usually asociated with the concept of 'self-reliance',[99] and this attitude remained a Fianna Fáil ideal, namely 'an Ireland self-contained and self-supporting economically'.[100] De Valera's biographers have argued that his views on this matter were related to his view that Ireland should be neutral, that his 'economic policy was calculated to make that possible. It was part of a pattern of self-sufficiency.'[101] However, the problem is that there was a real difference between rhetoric and actual policy, and that even in rhetoric the stress upon self-sufficiency was almost always linked to the aspiration to economic and political independence, as seen in the Fianna Fáil pledge 'not merely to try to secure independence politically in this

---

[94] 'Withdrawal of Sanctions', 2 July 1936, in de Valera, *Peace and War*, 54–9.

[95] Fanning, 'Neutrality', 29.

[96] De Valera, in *Dáil Debates*, 67 (1937), 721.

[97] Longford, 303.

[98] De Valera, in *Dáil Debates*, 62 (1936), 2650 ff. For 1932–8 see Paul Francis O'Malley, 'The Origins of Irish Neutrality in World War II 1932–1938' (University of Boston, Ph.D. thesis, 1980).

[99] Lyons, 256; Longford and O'Neill, 90.

[100] As it was put in de Valera's motion to the Sinn Féin *Ard-Fhéis*, 10 Mar. 1926. It is at this meeting that de Valera resigned as President of Sinn Féin: de Valera, *Speeches and Statements*, 127–8.

[101] Longford and O'Neill, 267.

country, but to try and secure its economic independence also'.[102] That was the real rationale of self-sufficiency, and other rationales were not persistently advanced and so remained peripheral.

By any measure the degree of economic dependence upon the United Kingdom was severe, as was the degree of general Irish dependence on trade with others. This is illustrated by Tables 4.1 and 4.2. Although

Table 4.1. Irish Imports and Exports from and to Great Britain and Northern Ireland 1924–1939 (%)

Year	Imports	Exports/Re-exports
1924	81.1	98.1
1925	81.1	97.2
1926	75.6	96.7
1927	77.4	95.8
1928	77.9	96.2
1929	78.1	92.3
1930	80.1	91.4
1931	80.8	96.3
1932	76.6	96.2
1933	69.9	93.9
1934	66.7	93.3
1935	72.4	91.7
1936	51.9	91.5
1937	48.7	90.8
1938	50.5	92.6
1939	55.7	93.6

Sources: Ireland: Statistical Abstract, 1931, table 82, p. 63; 1935, table 97, p. 75; 1938, table 98, p. 87; 1945, table 93, p. 100.

the import pattern does reveal a significant decline over the years in reliance upon British goods (down from 81.1% in 1924 to 50.5% in 1938, the last full year before the war), there is only a marginal decline with regard to exports (98.1% in 1924 to 92.6% in 1938). The earlier figure of 98.1% reveals in effect total dependence for export markets on Britain, while even by 1938 the level remains high enough to constitute virtual dependence. While Table 4.2, with its declining percentages, appears more reassuring, it is as well to recall Hancock's com-

[102] De Valera speech to Fianna Fáil *Ard-Fhéis*, 8 Nov. 1932, in *Speeches and Statements*, 223–9, esp. 227 (from which I take the quotation in the text).

ment concerning the 1932–8 dispute: 'Great Britain and the Irish Free State deliberately inflicted economic damage upon each other. That damage, undoubtedly, was not light. Yet it had not been able to do more than scratch the grapplings binding the two economies together.'[103]

Table 4.2. Ireland: Foreign Trade Dependence 1926–1938

Year	Merchandise exp.[a]	Merchandise imp.[a]	Exp. of goods & services[a]	Imp. of goods & services[a]
1926	26.8	39.8	n.a.	n.a.
1929	29.3	38.0	n.a.	n.a.
1931	24.7	34.4	38.7	37.7
1938	15.1	25.8	27.4	26.2

[a] As % of GNP at current factor cost.

Sources: T. K. Whitaker, 'Monetary Integration: Reflections on Irish Experience', *Quarterly Bulletin* (Central Bank of Ireland; Winter 1973), 69. He cites Kieran A. Kennedy, *Productivity and Industrial Growth: The Irish Experience* (OUP, 1971) as his source.

De Valera clearly saw the dangers inherent in such dependency, and at both the beginning and the end of the economic war sought to argue that Britain was using its economic predominance for political purposes. To illustrate the Irish concern about being squeezed by Britain, de Valera used the analogy of a wall, arguing that 'a good way would be to approach it as if this country were surrounded by a wall . . . what I mean is how we could maintain our population if by any chance we were cut off . . . we have the food that is necessary here . . . '[104]

It must be acknowledged that the Anglo-Irish dispute illustrates that the high degree of economic dependence of Ireland upon the United Kingdom did not lead to political servility on the part of the Irish towards the United Kingdom. The Irish were aided in their counter-dependency strategy by the constraints exercised upon the

---

[103] W. K. Hancock, 367–8; and note T. K. Whitaker's observation that in the 1930s foreign trade was reduced both absolutely and as a percentage of GNP: 'Monetary Integration: Reflections on Irish Experience', *Quarterly Bulletin* (Central Bank of Ireland) (Winter 1973), 68.

[104] De Valera, in *Dáil Debates*, 25 (1928), 474 ff. See also his speeches to Fianna Fáil Ard-Fhéis, 8 Nov. 1933, in *Speeches and Statements*, 245–58, esp. 248; and to the Dáil, *Dáil Debates*, 41 (Apr. 1932), 906–19.

United Kingdom by other factors, while the generally interdependent nature of the relationship also imposed costs upon the United Kingdom if any significant rupture occurred.[105]

According to Longford and O'Neill, Irish neutrality in the Second World War 'would scarcely have been possible if it had not been for the extent to which self-sufficiency had been achieved',[106] and they claim that the policy of 'self-sufficiency . . . was to be a crucial factor in the years of World War II'.[107] But less partial authorities are rather more equivocal in their judgment, while even de Valera was less sanguine than Longford and O'Neill. In direct reference to these questions in 1941 de Valera was anxious to emphasize the progress that had been made in the 1930s, but he acknowledged that

the war came and found us still far from our goal of self-sufficiency. We were still importing considerable quantities of wheat, fertilisers and many such fundamental raw materials as pig-iron, steel, timber, paper, vegetable oils, as well as coal and liquid fuels for our factories, for our field tractors and for transport. Tea has come to be regarded almost as the national beverage, and it all reaches us, of course, from abroad . . . [108]

While progress was made in the pre-war period towards self-sufficiency, it was not spectacular[109] and significant gaps remained. An internal memorandum of 16 April 1939 acknowledged Ireland's lack of self-sufficiency, and continued dependence upon Britain. Virtually all Irish foreign investment was in British securities, and while the proportion of imports received from Britain had declined, many of the remaining imports from Britain were of 'essential supplies . . . which we cannot provide ourselves'. As the report noted, the country depended 'entirely on other countries for the shipping space necessary to carry our entire imports of wheat, maize, petroleum, timber, and any other "bulk" cargoes from abroad'. Clearly, 'if war should break out we are very largely at the mercy of other countries, and particularly of the

---

[105] On 'counterdependence' see Marshall R. Singer, *Weak States in a World of Powers: The Dynamics of International Relationships* (New York, 1972), 42–3; and on interdependence generally, Robert O. Keohane and Joseph S. Nye, *Power and Interdependence: World Politics in Transition* (Boston, 1977), 8–11, *passim*.   [106] Longford and O'Neill, 331.

[107] Ibid. 334; see also their p. 349.

[108] De Valera, radio broadcast to United States, St Patrick's Day 1941, in *Speeches and Statements*, 453.

[109] T. K. Whitaker, 'From Protection to Free Trade: The Irish Experience', *Administration*, 21/4 (Winter 1973), 412. More generally see Raymond James Raymond, 'The Economics of Neutrality: The United States, Great Britain and Ireland's War Economy: 1937–1945', 2 vols. (University of Kansas, Ph.D. thesis, 1980).

United Kingdom, in respect of our external trade, and . . . the economic activities of this country could in such circumstances be completely paralysed'. This document also reveals the exact percentages of Irish raw materials provided by the UK: 100 per cent of coal, 94 of iron piping, 84 of pig-iron, 78 of aluminium, 74 of copper plates and sheets, and 51 of cattle feed-stuffs.[110] No wonder that in February 1939 de Valera had to express his fear to the Dáil that it was 'possible that, despite any declarations on our part of our desire to keep out of these conflicts, if we desired and tried to carry on the trade which is essential to our economic life here, we would be regarded as a combatant, and our neutrality would not be respected'.[111]

Moreover, although some 'effort had been made to set up a proper Irish merchant marine before the war', it had been thwarted.[112] Not surprisingly Keatinge is somewhat sardonic in his comment on 'the lack of a viable national shipping line—for a supposedly self-sufficient state mostly surrounded by sea!'.[113] Similarly thwarted were continuing efforts in the 1930s to provide an independent source of petrol supply, until, ironically, 'with war imminent, the oil refinery project had to be shelved . . .'.[114] This also may indicate that few really saw the link between self-sufficiency and the potential position of Ireland in a war, even if the connection does occasionally appear in rhetoric.

According to Farrell, the 'administrative process of preparing the Irish economy for war conditions began in 1938', although apparently the Irish 'administrative machine had begun making preparations to organise for a major international emergency since the mid-thirties'.[115] A review of the principal Irish industries took place and sought to encourage them 'to prepare for an emergency'. Not unnaturally the main emphasis was on securing and building up supplies. The response was generally positive but somewhat mixed, since, for example, 'the oil distributors . . . did little to develop extra reserves'.[116] In 1939 the 'case for a major reorganisation of governmental functions and priorities became more urgent. It was also increasingly evident . . . that it was time to regularise arrangements for securing supplies; informal

---

[110] SPO S11394, Dept. of Industry and Commerce, 18 Apr. 1939, memo to Taoiseach and ministers. [111] De Valera, in *Dáil Debates*, 74 (1939), 719.

[112] Joseph T. Carroll, *Ireland in the War Years 1939–1945* (Newton Abbot, 1975), 89.

[113] Keatinge, *A Place*, 137.

[114] Brian Farrell, *Sean Lemass* (Dublin, 1983), 49–50. This was ironic, since, as Carroll notes (p. 90), because of the proposed oil refinery 'Ireland had probably the most modern oil-tanker fleet in the world when war broke out', but they were transferred to the British register!

[115] Farrell, 47, 51; he does not explain or elaborate upon the discrepancy. [116] Ibid. 51.

assurances by British civil servants should be replaced by "an agreement between the two governments".' None the less, it appears that de Valera was slow to move, since 'it was only with the actual outbreak of war that [he] bowed to the inevitable, regrouped his cabinet and created a new Department of Supplies', with Lemass as its Minister.[117]

Despite the clear aspirations expressed between 1927 and 1932 (and both before and after this period), the actual record of achievement was mixed.

SELF-SUFFICIENCY: THE DEFENCE DIMENSION

Contrary to the argument of Fisk that an 'authentic policy of neutrality' merely involves a 'desire to maintain the country's commercial life', to 'safeguard its political integrity', while 'taking only minimum defence precautions', genuine neutrality (as has been demonstrated earlier) demands much more.[118] A concern to defend diligently a neutral state's rights, for example, is an integral requirement of a policy 'for neutrality' and ought, therefore, to have been a significant factor in the defence policy of Ireland. In abstract terms, Irish leaders appear to have recognized these needs. In March 1939, for example, Frank Aiken said that Ireland could not have neutrality merely by wishing for it; that there was 'no use in trying to substitute a wishbone for a backbone'.[119]

Perhaps one of the most surprising things concerning Irish defence is that while much attention has been paid to the island as single entity, very little, if any, attention has apparently been paid to the island *qua* island. This is especially significant for an island deficient in resources, lacking self-sufficiency, and dependent upon foreign trade. Particularly revealing concerning Irish attitudes to the sea is the reported statement of the Irish representative 'at the Naval Conference of 1936, that the Irish Free State had no concern with the treaty as she possessed no navy and had no intention of possessing one'.[120] Of course, the Irish were initially constrained by the 1921 Treaty, but no serious effort was made to develop a navy, even in the period from 1935 to 1939 when she was legally free to do so, nor did the Irish pursue this matter with the British

[117] Farrell, 53. Farrell quotes from a document prepared by John Leydon in the files of the Dept. of Industry and Commerce.

[118] Fisk, 84, and see above, ch. 2.

[119] *Dáil Debates*, 74 (1939), 2318. Aiken was Minister of Defence (1932–9), Minister for Co-ordination of Defensive Measures (1939–45), Minister of Finance (1945–8), and Minister of External Affairs (1951–4, 1957–69).

[120] Cited in W. K. Hancock, 289 n. 2.

in the way that a range of other issues was pursued. It appears that the main reason for this persistent Irish attitude was a belief that they were defended already by the British navy.[121]

Secondly, there was hesitation because of the degree of expenditure involved. An awareness of financial constraints was made apparent in the related matter of the ports. Speaking in the debate on the 1938 agreement and the return of the ports, William Cosgrave, the President of the Executive Council between 1922 and 1932, sought to argue that his government 'could have taken over these ports six or seven years ago'. However, he explained that he 'hesitated to do it. For what reason? At that time the cost would have involved the people of this country in an expenditure of between £350,000 and £500,000.'[122] Depending upon which year is used, this would have been equivalent to between 17.8 and 28.4 per cent of Irish defence expenditure at the time.[123] Even the de Valera government was not to prove enthusiastic about such defence expenditure: de Valera told MacDonald that while he and 'strong nationalists' would be glad to gain control of the ports, 'he feared such a proposal would not be accepted if the Irish had to pay maintenance costs'![124]

More generally in the 1930s old arguments were revived concerning the most appropriate basis of Irish defence. In brief the argument revolved around whether it was more sensible to rely upon naval and air defences, or, as Fianna Fáil proposed, land forces. Fine Gael argued that while it was true that Ireland had one land frontier across which it could be attacked, there was also the possibility of attack by air and/or sea. Therefore, 'the defence of the country had to be oriented towards having a strong navy and air force capable of preventing an invasion from sea, or at least capable of causing heavy losses, with an adequate air support'.[125]

Initially, at least, the Fianna Fáil government was committed primarily to land forces, although as the 1930s came to an end there was some effort to improve the air force, or Air Corps. None the less, it remained small. Even by 1939 Ireland had 'very little air cover'.[126] According to Fisk, 'by the autumn of 1939, the Irish Air Corps

---

[121] A belief confirmed for some by the subsequent war experience. See O'Higgins, in *Dáil Debates*, 105 (1947), 52.

[122] Cosgrave, ibid. 71(1938), 49–50.

[123] See H. M. Shehab, 'Irish Defence Policy 1922–1950' (Trinity College, Dublin, M.Litt. thesis, 1975), 297, for Irish defence expenditure in 1927/8 and 1928/9.

[124] 4 Oct. 1937, conversation with MacDonald: see Fisk, 32.

[125] Dr Thomas O'Higgins, in *Dáil Debates*, 50 (1934), 1140.

[126] Lt.-Col. P. D. Kavanagh (ed.), *The Irish Army Handbook 1973* (Dublin, 1973) 12.

comprised four Gloster Gladiators, fifteen Miles Magisters, three Walrus amphibious aircraft, six Lysanders and an assortment of Vickers Vespas, Avro 636s, de Havilland Dragons and Avro Ansons. Only the Gladiators could be regarded as fighter aircraft of any consequence.'[127] Although over the same period the number of Flying Officers also increased, doubling from seventeen in 1936 to thirty-four in 1939,[128] Ireland remained exceedingly vulnerable. This vulnerability provided an important incentive for non-involvement in war, particularly since some of the Irish were alive to the horrendous prospect of massive aerial bombardment of their 'mega-cephalic capital city, with all the consequences that that entails',[129] although it was only in July 1939 that air-raid precautions for householders were considered by the Cabinet.[130]

This lack of defence pertained not only to the air: 'Ireland's territorial waters were virtually undefended' also.[131] Even after the return of the ports there were only two vessels, which were 'operated by the Department of Agriculture on fishery protection duties'.[132] It appears that de Valera may have been more interested in measures such as coast-watching and a coastal patrol service than in a genuine navy, but even these activities came under pressure from the Department of Finance. While there had been some plans for a new coastal patrol service, by February 1939 the Department of the Taoiseach was suggesting that its proposed size could be halved.[133] Ireland was clearly not in a position in 1939 to exercise, by any reasonable interpretation, 'due diligence' in the protection and maintenance of neutral rights, nor indeed was it capable of adequately fulfilling neutral duties.[134] It was relying upon the sufferance and forbearance of others.

In fact, Irish defence policy in the 1930s rested upon deterrence through making the cost of occupation too high, rather than through denial or retaliation against the aggressor's homeland. Clearly the memories of the War of Independence (1919–21) and before, when the British found the resistance of the people, flying columns, and guerrillas to difficult to overcome at reasonable cost, were in the minds of Fianna Fáil leaders. In 1934 Fianna Fáil, thinking along these lines, established

[127] Fisk, 66, citing a letter from the Dept. of Defence, Dublin, 4 Apr. 1979.

[128] *Ireland: Statistical Abstract*, 1939 (Dublin, 1939), table 176a, p. 149.

[129] Col. J. J. O'Connell had warned of this danger in 'The Vulnerability of Ireland in War', *Studies* (Mar. 1938): see Fisk, 136.   [130] Fisk, 138–9.

[131] Capt. J. Sheehan, *Defence Forces Handbook* (Dublin, n.d.), 63.

[132] Kavanagh, *Handbook 1973*, 48. See also Francis E. McMurtrie (ed.), *Jane's Fighting Ships 1939* (London, 1939), 115.   [133] Fisk, 85.

[134] See 'Overseas Reactions to the Crisis, III: Ireland', in *Round Table*, 29/113 (Dec. 1938), 35–6.

a new 'Volunteer Force', which greatly increased the number of part-time reserves.[135]

The army which Fianna Fáil inherited was certainly small, numbering only 5,793 in 1932 and 5,763 in 1934,[136] and Aiken proposed to effect an increase by the establishment of the Volunteer force, which could be grafted on. Such a force had a reasonable basis if the objective was not so much to stop the invader at the sea-shore but either to deter or to eject by making invasion too costly. Aiken hoped that 'such a type of organization is sufficient to make even strong neighbours respect a country, and we hope to make ours respected'.[137] By 1935 Ireland had a 'Reserve' of 6,483 men and 11,531 in the new Volunteers, although by March 1939 these figures had drifted down to 5,100 and 9,952 respectively, which compared to 7,263 'Regulars'.[138] 'At the outbreak of the Second World War on 2 September 1939 the composition of the Defence Forces was as follows: regulars—630 officers, 1,412 NCOs, and 5,452 privates; the A and B reservists—194 officers, 544 NCOs, and 4,328 privates; Volunteers—327 officers, 557 NCOs, and 6,429 privates.[139] This adds up to 19,873 for all ranks.

Could Ireland reasonably hope to be able to ensure that no portion of its territory could be occupied and used as a base by third parties? The answer was surely no, given the limited nature of Irish defence capabilities—no navy, a small air force, and a total of less than 20,000 in the armed forces.

A further issue was Ireland's financial commitment to defence. Table 4.3 illustrates Irish expenditure on defence between 1922/3 and 1939/40.[140] After the civil war there was clearly a progressive decline for several years. Even when this was arrested, the increases were only marginal until 1939/40. The statistical evidence is hardly consistent with the June 1936 commitment to undertake all necessary expense or indeed to mobilize the 'full strength of this nation'.[141]

Indeed, after the agreement about the ports in April 1938 and the failure to come to a defence agreement with Britain, 'there is evidence

---

[135] Sheehan, 8–11.

[136] *Ireland: Statistical Abstract*, 1935 (Dublin, 1935), table 169, p. 125.

[137] Aiken, *Dáil Debates*, 50 (1934), 1130–5 for his arguments on introducing the new force. For a brief account of the force see Sheehan, 8–10.

[138] *Ireland: Statistical Abstract*, 1935, p. 125; and 1939, table 176, p. 149.

[139] Kavanagh, *Handbook 1973*, 12.

[140] These figures differ marginally from Shehab, 297, app. II, which is based on *Published Estimates for Public Services* (Dublin, 1922–51).

[141] De Valera, in *Dáil Debates*, 62 (1936), 2654–60 (quotation from col. 2659); 71 (1938), 32–48.

Table 4.3.   Irish Defence Expenditure 1922/3–1939/40

Year	Expenditure (£m.)[a]	% of govt. expenditure[b]
1922/3	7.502	27.8
1923/4	10.581	29.9
1924/5	2.994	12.2
1925/6	2.596	11.1
1926/7	2.352	9.8
1927/8	2.018	9.1
1928/9	1.737	8.1
1929/30	1.334	6.3
1930/1	1.133	5.5
1931/2	1.161	5.4
1932/3	1.179	4.9
1933/4	1.209	4.6
1934/5	1.324	5.0
1935/6	1.352	5.2
1936/7	1.376	5.2
1937/8	1.469	5.3
1938/9	1.766	6.2
1939/40	2.973	10.1

[a] According to the Tables, these figures are actual amounts issued in each year.

[b] Or, at any rate, of Total Supply Services.

Sources: Ireland: Statistical Abstract, 1931, table 155, pp. 128–31; 1935, table 173, pp. 130–3; 1937, table 179, pp. 134–7; 1945, table 171, pp. 180–3.

that de Valera . . . was ready to pare down even the limited defence scheme which he, Aiken and other ministers had prepared in case of war'.[142] A number of plans made in 1938 suffered reductions over the winter of 1938–9—arms for rifle battalions, the proposed coastal patrol service, the arming of the new field brigades, and the number of Swedish armoured cars to be purchased.[143]

None the less, in the spring of 1939 the government did announce plans to improve the defence situation, largely by allocating £5.5m. for expenditure on the acquisition of capital equipment and stores. This planned expenditure included £1m. on aircraft, and a further £1m. on anti-aircraft guns and ammunition. It also involved plans for aerodromes,

[142] Fisk, 84–5.
[143] See S P O S10868A Dept. of Finance and S P O S10823 Dept. of Taoiseach.

a munitions factory, and increase in army size, and the new coastal patrol service and mine-sweeping.[144] However, the problem was that since Europe stood on the brink of war, it was virtually impossible for Ireland to acquire the proposed equipment and stores.[145] According to the figures on *actual* defence expenditure, by 1939–40 defence expenditure was only up £1.5m. from 1937–38.[146]

Despite the talk of self-sufficiency, the Irish were not in a position to arm or supply themselves with home-produced equipment. When war broke out, Ireland had no source of war supplies within its shores,[147] even though Desmond FitzGerald, the Minister of Defence, had argued in 1931 that 'no country which lacks any part of the raw materials necessary for the manufacture of warlike stores is capable of being free'.[148] Between 1931 and 1939 little or nothing was done to remedy the situation.

Some in the Fine Gael opposition, acknowledging this dependence, particularly upon Britain, appeared to opt for Commonwealth solidarity, arguing that Ireland would be virtually powerless unless she had 'a guarantee of assistance from Great Britain', and they asked about the possibility of a unified Anglo-Irish command to meet an attack and the possibility of a new arrangement with the British regarding the defence of the ports.[149] Thus, by the late 1930s the Fine Gael opposition was still sceptical about Ireland's ability to go it alone, with Dr O'Higgins saying that while prepared to try neutrality, he 'was never a firm believer in the feasibility or benefits of neutrality'.[150]

The dilemma between the demands of neutrality and geographical situation remained acute for the Fianna Fáil government, as it had for its predecessors. As we have already seen, on 13 July 1938 de Valera made an important speech to the Dáil on the problems of Irish neutrality,[151] much of which echoed the FitzGerald speech of 1927. De Valera wondered, 'Would Britain just stand aside and allow us to be attacked by an outside State?' The answer was clearly in the negative, especially if an

[144] 'Ireland's Vital Problems', *Round Table*, 29/115 (June 1939), 586.
[145] See Dr T. O'Higgins, *Dáil Debates*, 74 (1939), 182 ff.
[146] See Shehab, 297; and above, table 4.3.
[147] See G. A. Hayes-McCoy, 'Irish Defence Policy 1938–51', in K. B. Nowlan and T. Desmond Williams, *Ireland in the War Years and After 1939–51* (Dublin, 1969), 40.
[148] *Dáil Debates*, 37 (1931), 1126.
[149] James Dillon, ibid. 62 (1936), 2673, although later events showed that he was atypical. See also General Mulcahy, ibid. 74 (1939), 2688–95.
[150] Ibid. 77 (1939), 463; 77 (1939), 1197.
[151] Ibid. 72 (1938), 696 ff. for subsequent quotations.

enemy 'was likely to get possession of our territory from which they would be in a position to menace British interests or rights'. In such a case, 'there is no doubt that Britain would have an interest and an immediate interest because of her geographic position', a factor reinforced by the 'certain association' existing between the two countries, although that was secondary. Crucially, Britain would act 'not in our interest . . . [but] for some immediate selfish interest'. Therefore, if attacked, 'it is not unreasonable that we should—if we wanted it, count on assistance'. De Valera then turned to the question of whether Ireland would ask. This depended 'on the circumstances . . . whether we thought it advisable to act alone or not. If we considered that we had an advantage in acting alone we would act alone in all probability.' But, in an admission of dependency and lack of military self-sufficiency, de Valera argued that Irish defence planning should be based on the proposition 'not alone, but with assistance'; and he acknowledged that 'if we had a great Continental power attacking us we would recognize that we would need such assistance, because of ourselves we probably would not be able, in fact I think it is almost certain, to meet a frontal and straightforward attack from any foreign State', although Ireland would resist. As a consequence of such thoughts, de Valera felt it acceptable to talk with the British to discover 'their plans in such a case' and to 'prepare our plans accordingly'. Before concluding he said that a strong Britain was a shelter for Ireland, and that as a consequence Ireland had 'an interest in seeing that sheltering position was maintained'. Clearly 'a direct attack upon Great Britain, even though it was not a direct attack upon us, but which might remove from us the shelter or protection that we had up to then, would be a matter of serious importance to our people'.

No wonder some argued that

'the real defences of Ireland were not those which might be put up by her people—the defences, that is, on which the government declared itself to rely—but rather the British navy, and the fact that Ireland is geographically remote from central Europe. It would be quite wrong . . . to minimize the effect which another people's battleships and aeroplanes and the all-important matter of distance had on the situation'.[152]

The Irish relied upon a protective umbrella supplied by the British.

152 Hayes-McCoy, 39; and see also 'Mr De Valera's Victory', Round Table, 28/112 (1937–8), 751.

'THE EXPECTATIONS OF OTHERS' OR THE 'RECOGNITION OF IRISH NEUTRALITY'

In July 1938 de Valera had clearly acknowledged how important it was that others should recognize, tolerate, and accept the neutrality of a country if its position were to be viable and sustainable. He was aware that herein 'lay the trouble'.[153] In the 1930s the Irish assessment of their own future prospects was vexed. One problem was that they themselves were not sure if they could sustain neutrality, partly for economic reasons but also for political reasons. For example, John Dulanty, the Irish High Commissioner in London, told Sir Thomas Inskip, the Secretary of State for the Dominions, that he thought that 'in a week Eire would come in on [the British] side as a result of attacks on shipping'.[154] Crucial was their dependency upon Britain. However, if the Irish were not confident, then how could other states be confident that the Irish would be either desirous or capable of upholding strict neutrality? Before 1938 this problem was clearly aggravated by the ports issue. But even after the return of the ports, some clearly felt there must be a catch.[155]

To some extent the factors that caused the Irish to doubt the position were also uppermost in British minds; Inskip, for one, did not think that Irish neutrality could survive, given that Ireland was dependent upon trade, especially agricultural trade, with Britain.[156] At the very least there would be attacks on lines of communication and Anglo-Irish transport.

Complicating the issue was the question of Irish membership of the Commonwealth. While Mansergh has convincingly argued that by 1939 the Dominions were free to make their own decisions regarding peace and war,[157] to some extent the changes had been so recent that the states themselves apparently did not yet appreciate this situation. The problems are well illustrated by a memorandum written by Anthony Eden, the British Dominion Secretary, shortly after the outbreak of war. Britain did not want to recognize Ireland as neutral while it regarded her as a Commonwealth member, but equally did not wish to assert that Ireland was no longer such a member.[158] Given these ambiguities and

---

[153] De Valera, *Dáil Debates*, 72 (1938), 696 ff.   [154] Carroll, 12.

[155] De Valera went to great lengths to emphasize that there were no secret understandings or conditions: *Dáil Debates* 71 (1938), 32–48. Why he was concerned is explained in Fisk, 62.

[156] P R O F O 800/30, Inskip to de Valera, 8 Sept. 1938.

[157] Mansergh, *Survey 1931–9*, 87.

[158] P R O C A B 66/1 W P (39) 34, Eden memo, 16 Sept. 1939. See also P R O F O 800/300, for the paper by Malkin, the Foreign Office Legal Adviser, which supported Irish rights in this regard, and P R O F O 800/310 for Churchill's riposte. For further argument see P R O F O 800/310, *passim*, P R O C A B 65/1, and P R O C A B 67/2.

perplexities, the question of the 'expectations of others' was hardly clear-cut.[159] This was even more so in view of the vexed problem of the ports: not only the Irish wondered if it were too good to be true that these should have been returned without any concessions to Britain. Thus while Longford and O'Neill are emphatic that 'No hint was ever dropped by de Valera to encourage the idea that Ireland would participate in the war', they are prepared to admit that Chamberlain may perhaps have misunderstood de Valera.[160]

If the British attitude to Irish neutrality on the eve of war lacked a certain clarity, the case is somewhat more straightforward regarding the Germans. On 26 August the civil service head of the Irish Department of External Affairs, Walshe, met the German Minister in Eire, Dr Hempel, for lunch and made it clear that 'Ireland would remain neutral except in the case of a definite attack, for example dropping bombs on Irish towns.'[161] Walshe expressed concern about trade with Britain, especially given its 'vital importance to Ireland for obtaining supplies of essential consumer goods', and asked that, if Ireland were involved indirectly because of 'German acts of war against Britain . . . any suffering incurred should be kept to a minimum'.

The German expectations regarding Ireland were made quite clear in the reply that Hempel received from Ribbentrop.[162] Ribbentrop explicitly asked Hempel to see de Valera and make a specific statement, in which the Germans asserted they were

determined to refrain from any hostile action against Irish territory and to respect her integrity, provided that Ireland, for her part, maintains unimpeachable neutrality towards us in any conflict. Only if this condition should no longer obtain as a result of a decision of the Irish Government themselves, or by pressure exerted on Ireland from other quarters, should we be compelled as a matter of course, as far as Ireland was concerned too, to safeguard our interests in the sphere of warfare in such a way as the situation then arising might demand of us . . . [Germany was] of course, aware of the difficulties involved in the geographical position of Ireland.

[159] One further problem was the complex issue of British, Irish, and Commonwealth citizens and subjects: see Nicholas Mansergh, 'Ireland: The Republic outside the Commonwealth', *International Affairs*, 28/3 (July 1952).

[160] Longford and O'Neill, 343; but see also p. 353, and Maffey report (PRO CAB 66/2) of 21 Oct. 1939, when Maffey implied that Britain had certain expectations.

[161] *Documents on German Foreign Policy 1918–1945*, ser. D (1937–1945) (hereafter *DGFP*), vii: *The Last Days of Peace August 9 – September 3, 1939* (London, 1956), doc. 303, 'The Minister in Eire to the Foreign Minister', p. 311.

[162] Ibid., doc. 428, 'The Foreign Minister to the Legation in Eire' (29 Aug. 1939), pp. 422–3.

Naturally, this statement was highly conditional. Moreover, the Germans were seeking 'unimpeachable neutrality', which it might reasonably be argued meant something specific to the Germans, since elsewhere German theorists had developed the concept of 'integral neutrality', that is, that neutrality of the state was insufficient of itself and had to be complemented by neutrality of the people.[163]

Hempel duly delivered the statement in a meeting with de Valera on 31 August 1939.[164] De Valera repeated his statement of 16 February to the Dáil that Ireland wished to remain neutral.[165] It is interesting that de Valera made something of the phrase 'unimpeachable neutrality', apparently fearing that 'translated as "non-objectionable" ' it might easily give Germany 'cause for objections'. According to Hempel, de Valera then

said that in spite of the Irish Government's sincere desire to observe neutrality equally towards both belligerents, Ireland's dependence on Britain for trade vital to Ireland on the one hand, and on the other the possibility of intervention by Britain if the independence of Ireland involved an immediate danger for Great Britain, rendered it inevitable for the Irish Government to show *a certain consideration for Britain.*

De Valera then warned Hempel of dangers regarding violation of Irish territorial waters or exploitation of radical nationalist sentiment. A further warning, incompatible with neutrality, was given regarding 'any hostile action against the population on the other side of the Northern Ireland frontier who wanted to return to the Irish State'. It is extremely difficult to see how this could be reconciled with a neutral stance since it implied that the Irish might react to an attack upon territory which the Germans might legitimately regard as British.

Hempel was clearly impressed, in the sense that his 'general impression was one of a sincere effort to keep Ireland out of the conflict', although he also perceived great fear. Before the meeting closed de Valera proposed identical and simultaneous announcements that there were 'friendly German–Irish relations' and that the Germans 'had promised respect for Irish neutrality'.[166] The Germans were prepared to

---

163 Joechim Joesten, 'Phases in Swedish Neutrality', *Foreign Affairs*, 23/2 (Jan. 1945), 327–8.

164 *DGFP* vii, doc. 484, 'The Minister in Eire to the Foreign Ministry' (31 Aug. 1939), pp. 471–2. The paragraph is based on this report (emphasis added).

165 Hempel had reported this in 'A143 of February 23, 1939' to Berlin but the report is not published in *DGFP* vii, although referred to in a footnote (see p. 471 n. 3).

166 See references in last note.

accept this, as long as it was clear that, after their 'promise is referred to, the words "conditional on a corresponding attitude by Ireland" must be added'.[167] They were therefore prepared to accept the Irish position regarding neutrality, but their reiterated insistence upon the conditional nature of their recognition of Irish neutrality leaves the impression that they did not really expect it to survive.

THE IRISH AND NEUTRALITY: ATTITUDES AND POLICY BEFORE 3 SEPTEMBER 1939

It is of major significance that, contrary to the cited literature and much Irish opinion, there is a clear distinction to be drawn between the Irish position(s), albeit variously expressed and not always consistent, and the requirements both of the classical theory of neutrality, as understood by international law and convention, and of what subsequently came to be understood as the principal and necessary components of a policy 'for neutrality'.

The object was simply to stay out of the war, not necessarily following an impartial policy, or a policy conditional upon insistence on and respect for neutral rights and duties, or a policy limited by well-known rules and obligations. Rather, it was a policy based upon bending with the wind through discrimination and compromise. Ireland wished to avoid involvement at almost any cost and by all means. All of this was starkly revealed when de Valera spoke to the Dáil in the first weeks of the war, when he said

Our attitude we hope to keep not by adherence to some theoretical, abstract idea of neutrality or anything like that, but by addressing ourselves to the practical question that we do not want to get involved in this war, and we merely want to keep our people safe from such consequences as we would be involved in by being in the war.[168]

This is non-belligerency, not neutrality, and in this Ireland was behaving like the other small European states, including Sweden. These states pursued 'one single object'—to stay out of the war to come, not conditionally, by insistence on rights and duties, but almost at any cost

---

[167] *DGFP* vii, doc. 527, 'The State Secretary to the Legation in Eire' (1 Sept. 1939), p. 504. See also ibid., doc. 499, 'The Minister in Eire to the Foreign Ministry' (1 Sept. 1939), p. 482.

[168] *Dáil Debates*, 77 (1939), 592. See also ibid. 72 (1938), 696, and Carroll, 12, who quotes from de Valera's broadcast on the outbreak of war: 'the aim of our policy . . . to keep our people out of a war'.

and by all means.[169] The lone exception was Switzerland, which deliberately sought to assert its previously clearly defined status.[170]

The notion of 'a traditional policy of the Irish state since independence' must be questioned. At best the evidence for it is equivocal, and at worst, it is equally possible to posit an alternative tradition, quite apart from the question of non-belligerency. It can reasonably be argued that those with government responsibility in Ireland have always taken a more pragmatic view, and that such pragmatism had even been displayed by de Valera.[171] Finally, of course, there was the clear admission by de Valera to Hempel of the discriminatory and partial nature of Irish policy in the forthcoming war. As Kevin O'Higgins had put it on 17 February 1927, neutrality might be 'a consummation devoutly to be wished for, but . . . we are unable to alter the geographical relations between this State and Great Britain and we are unable to alter the strategical aspects of the matter . . .'[172]

---

[169] Ørvik, *Decline of Neutrality*, 189–90.

[170] Ibid. 188.

[171] Even Longford and O'Neill, 348, describe his speech to the Dáil on 2 Sept. 1939 as 'a pragmatic approach based on Ireland's interests and on the circumstances of Irish public opinion'.

[172] O'Higgins, *Dáil Debates*, 18 (Feb. 1927), 656; but he repeated the point several times (654–8).

5

'Unneutral Neutral Eire' or Non-Belligerent Ireland?

APART from Smyllie, whose phrase provides part of this chapter's title,[1] chronological accounts of Irish policy and the policy of others towards Ireland between September 1939 and May 1945 have taken as axiomatic that Ireland was 'One of the Neutrals'.[2] However, it is possible to challenge this consensus if one moves from the simply chronological to a more analytical perspective. One then sees the value of Smyllie's assertion that 'Eire was nonbelligerent . . . but she was never neutral in the generally accepted sense of the term'.[3]

An almost infinite list of factors influencing the Irish position can be drawn up. The principal influences have been evident in much of the foregoing, including the desire of a newly independent state to assert its sovereignty; Partition; lack of defence; hostility to participation in British wars; and a general disposition to fear the lack of influence of small states and the general immorality of Great Powers. This historical background was of vital importance, as were the associated internal dynamics of the Irish situation.

After all, the IRA had engaged in a bombing campaign in the United Kingdom in January 1939, and at least 'one faction in Fianna Fáil approved of the hallowed republican maxim that "England's difficulty was Ireland's opportunity." Its first wartime *Ard Fhéis* [annual conference or meeting] heard delegates advocate the use of force against Northern Ireland.'[4] On the other hand, de Valera had to contend with

---

[1] R. M. Smyllie, 'Unneutral Neutral Eire', *Foreign Affairs*, 24/2 (Jan. 1946).

[2] e.g. Lord Longford and T. P. O'Neill, *Eamon de Valera* (London, 1970), 347–68. An exception is Smyllie; other chronological accounts include Robert Fisk, *In Time of War: Ireland, Ulster and the Price of Neutrality 1939–45* (London, 1983); T. Ryle Dwyer, *Irish Neutrality and the USA 1939–47* (Dublin, 1977); Joseph T. Carroll, *Ireland in the War Years 1939–1945* (Newton Abbot, 1975); John Bowman, *De Valera and the Ulster Question 1917–1973* (OUP, 1982); Bernard Share, *The Emergency: Neutral Ireland 1939–1945* (Dublin, 1978); Nicholas Mansergh, *Survey of British Commonwealth Affairs: Problems of Wartime Co-operation and Post-war Change 1930–1952* (OUP, 1958); V. P. Hogan, 'The Neutrality of Ireland in World War II', (University of Notre Dame, thesis, 1953); Kevin B. Nowlan and T. Desmond Williams (eds.), *Ireland in the War Years and After 1939–1951* (Dublin, 1969); and Constance Howard, 'Eire', in A. J. Toynbee and V. M. Toynbee (eds.), *Survey of International Affairs 1939–46: The War and the Neutrals* (OUP, 1956).

[3] Smyllie, 324.

[4] Bowman, 208.

many others whose sympathies were clearly pro-Commonwealth and for involvement.[5] In view of this divide and the recent civil war, internal unity was a factor not to be underestimated, and there was widespread acceptance that neutrality was the course of action most likely to unite the people of Eire.

It can be argued that such was the support for the proposed course that 'there was no discussion in the Dáil of the issues involved, or of the factors which should determine Irish policy'.[6] Even after the United States' entry into the war de Valera still felt that 'Our circumstances of history . . . [and] partition . . . made any other policy impracticable. Any other policy would have divided our people, and for a divided people to fling itself into this war would be to commit suicide.'[7] However, unanimity was only achieved by a stress upon the difference between Irish sympathies and interests.[8]

The historical background and the internal dimension were also crucial because of the significance of symbols in Irish political history and life. Arguably, the divide over the Treaty and the Civil War had been about the symbols of 'Republic' and 'Oath'. Concepts and symbols in Ireland were always liable to have a particular interpretation and significance attached to them. Even towards the end of the war the British Representative, Maffey, would complain that de Valera was concerned with 'the symbols of neutrality and independence. It was obvious that he attached immense importance to this symbolic factor.'[9] Yet it is also clear that the commitment to independence was more than merely 'symbolic'.

The outbreak of the Second World War was to prove the acid test[10] of many of the questions facing Ireland about its position and was, in fact, to resolve many of the ambiguities, although in some cases only with hindsight. It must be remembered that, as of September 1939, 'Irish neutrality . . . was by no means clearly established—in the sense, for example, that Swiss neutrality was universally recognized',[11] and, as noted earlier, many internal and external observers doubted whether it

---

[5] Most notably James Dillon TD, but there were others. Dillon was Deputy Leader of Fine Gael.

[6] Nicholas Mansergh, *Survey of British Commonwealth Affairs: Problems of External Policy 1931-1939* (OUP, 1952), 403.

[7] Speech in Cork on 14 Dec. 1941, in de Valera, *Ireland's Stand: Being a Selection of the Speeches of Éamon de Valera during the War (1939-1945)*, 2nd edn. (Dublin, 1946), 56-7.

[8] De Valera, *Dáil Debates*, 77 (1939), 1-8.

[9] PRO FO 371 42679, Maffey memo, 22 Feb. 1944.

[10] John A. Murphy, *Ireland in the Twentieth Century* (Dublin, 1975), 101.

[11] T. Desmond Williams, 'Ireland in the War,' in Nowlan and Williams, 15.

could or would ever be implemented. Moreover, neutrality was not enshrined in the new 1937 Constitution or in the amendment to the Constitution rushed through on the outbreak of war, although occasionally in the literature there are loose references to 'legislation affirming Ireland's neutrality for the duration of the conflict'.[12] The First Amendment to the Constitution Bill sought to clarify the original phrase 'in time of war' (Article 28.3.3.), to make it clear that this included situations 'when there is taking place an armed conflict in which the State is not a participant but in respect of which each of the Houses of the Oireachtas shall have resolved that, arising out of such armed conflict, a national emergency exists affecting the vital interests of the State'.[13]

De Valera himself in introducing the amendment spoke of it as 'indirectly' indicating the policy of the government, that is, 'to keep this country, if at all possible, out of' war.[14] However, as either the original or the revised version stands, there is no necessary implication of neutrality, and the word is not used. Its inclusion would certainly have strengthened the Irish position, and its omission tends to lend support to the view that neutrality was a means rather than an end. Clearly, far from putting itself in a position where it could not choose to go to war, Ireland had in effect closed no doors and no options. It could be neutral, non-belligerent, or belligerent within the terms of the framework of the decisions of the summer of 1939.

To distinguish between rhetoric and policy, orthodoxy and reality, the period of the Second World War will now be examined in the light of the first set of variables proposed at the end of Chapter 3, namely the rights and duties of neutrality; the recognition of Ireland's status by belligerents and others; the disavowal of external help; and the freedom of decision and action.

RIGHTS AND DUTIES

As neutrality evolved, rights, duties, and—crucially—impartiality were emphasized. In Ireland there was some grasp of these matters. Aiken, for example, although referring to the 'old Hague Convention', clearly

---

[12] Murphy, *Ireland in the Twentieth Century*, 100. See also Williams, 'Ireland in the War', in Nowlan and Williams, 15.

[13] 'Bunreacht na hÉireann', Article 28.3.3. The 1937 Constitution allowed amendment before June 1941 without a referendum.

[14] *Dáil Debates*, 77 (1939), 1–8.

grasped the need to avoid breaching 'the impartial conduct which neutrality imposes'.[15] De Valera also saw the need 'to avoid giving to any of the belligerents any cause, any proper cause, of complaint'.[16]

The Irish were aware that a simple declaration of neutrality was not enough, that it was necessary to make clear a determination 'to stand by their own rights, conscious of the fact that they did not wish to injure anybody, or throw their weight, from the belligerent point of view, on the one side or the other'.[17] They also knew that, with regard to neutrality, 'you have to defend it and uphold it. The upholding of neutrality, if you are sincere about it, means that you will have to fight for your life against one side or the other—whichever attacks you.'[18]

An initial manifestation of the Irish approach was an *aide-mémoire* handed to the British on 12 September 1939 on the subject of neutrality.[19] The memorandum made explicit reference to the Hague Convention of 1907 on the rights of neutral powers, announced in formal terms prohibitions against vessels of war and submarines of the belligerents in Irish waters, and forbade the use of Irish airspace to their military aircraft. It applied equally to all of the belligerent powers, and was based upon international law. Indeed, Eden had to advise the British Cabinet that 'it would hardly be possible to offer any serious criticism of the proposals set out in the memorandum',[20] although Maffey, the British Representative in Dublin, made clear to de Valera that 'this rigid *aide-mémoire*, dotting the "i's" and crossing the "t's" in the way of stringent rules affecting British ships and aircraft had been read with profound feelings of disappointment'.[21]

The problem was that the formal position was undermined simultaneously by the Irish themselves in both words and actions. Ireland would and did 'show a certain consideration for Britain'.[22] While Hempel may have felt at the beginning of October 1939 that there had been 'careful, consistent adherence to' the declaration of Irish neutrality,[23] the strict

[15] In his memo to colleagues, 'Neutrality, Censorship and Democracy', 23 Jan. 1940: SPO S11586A.

[16] *Dáil Debates*, 77 (1939), 1–8 (quotation from col. 4).

[17] Ibid. 5.

[18] *Dáil Debates*, 91 (1943), 2124.

[19] PRO CAB 66/1, app. I, 12 Sept. 1939. At British request it was not published for over a year.

[20] PRO CAB 66/1, Eden memo, 16 Sept. 1939.

[21] PRO CAB 66/1, app. II, Maffey, 14 Sept. 1939.

[22] *DGFP* vii (1956), doc. 484, 'The Minister in Eire to the Foreign Ministry' (31 Aug. 1939), pp. 471–2.

[23] *DGFP* viii (1954), doc. 216, 'The Minister in Eire to the Foreign Ministry' (8 Oct. 1939), p. 241.

letter of neutrality law—and certainly its spirit—was already being eroded by the Irish. Already a British plane which came down at Skerry had been allowed to depart 'without interference', while a British plane at Ventry Bay had managed—or been allowed—to get away.[24]

While some may regard Irish behaviour as scrupulous with regard to the 'forms of neutrality',[25] there is a much greater consensus that Irish behaviour was friendly or benevolent. De Valera himself stated that while 'we proclaimed our neutrality . . . it has all the time been a friendly neutrality',[26] and immediately after the entry of America into the war, in a famous speech in Cork on 14 December 1941, while emphasizing the reasons for Irish neutrality and that the 'policy of the State remains unchanged', he did continue: 'We can only be a friendly neutral.'[27] Again, subsequent to the American Note in 1944, de Valera complained that the American government did not seem to realize 'the uniformly friendly character of Irish neutrality in relation to the United States and of the measures which had been taken by the Irish Government, within the limits of their power, to safeguard American interests', although he did make the point in conclusion that the Irish government 'must, in all circumstances, protect the neutrality of the Irish State'.[28] Only Smyllie appears to raise the question of whether such expressions and behaviour were consistent with neutrality.[29]

Despite these statements and Irish behaviour, de Valera sought to emphasize to Hempel 'Eire's continued adherence to strict neutrality' and that this was being 'so far' respected by the English. He made clear that Ireland would fight against either England or Germany if they invaded and, in an effort to appear impartial, assured Hempel that 'Except for the minimum of loose connection with the British Empire provided for constitutionally, which was exclusively intended to facilitate the future return of Northern Ireland to the Irish State, and except for the strong economic dependence of Ireland on England, Ireland stands in exactly the same position toward [Germany] as toward England.'[30] In fact, the Irish were not impartial. The Germans were

[24] P R O C A B 66/1, app. II, Maffey, 14 Sept. 1939.

[25] See Murphy, *Ireland in the Twentieth Century*, 101; Carroll, 171; F. S. L. Lyons, *Ireland Since the Famine* (London, 1973), 557; G. A. Hayes-McCoy, 'Irish Defence Policy 1938–51', in Nowlan and Williams, 49.

[26] *Dáil Debates*, 83 (1941), 971–2.

[27] De Valera, *Ireland's Stand*, 56.

[28] Ibid. 105–9; his reply was handed to the State Department on 7 Mar. 1944.

[29] See Smyllie, *passim*.

[30] *DGFP* ix (1956), doc. 310, 'The Minister in Eire to the Foreign Ministry' (23 May 1940), pp. 422–4.

prepared to accept this, because what they regarded as Ireland's 'understanding neutral attitude' was to their advantage.[31]

With respect to the foregoing, it could be argued that 'sympathy was one thing and positive action was another',[32] but in fact the Irish expressions of sympathy were not confined to words but reflected the way in which Ireland was actually partial given its geographical and economic position. Moreover, words and actions cannot be completely divorced, since words can create expectations or suspicions on the part of others. Indeed, in a memorandum to colleagues in January 1940 Aiken had argued that partiality in propaganda could 'be regarded as an act of war'. A belligerent might 'regard it as a departure from the impartial conduct which neutrality imposes'.[33] This was Aiken's justification for tough domestic censorship. It is interesting that, according to Hempel, 'Germany's view was that taking sides was not permissible in neutral countries and that they should remain silent . . . And it was not in accordance with strict neutrality that Mr de Valera should have protested' about the invasion of Holland and Belgium.[34]

Before turning to specific instances of Irish overt action and behaviour, one must consider two factors which offer some support for the 'neutral' argument. Firstly, Ireland did abstain from belligerency during the Second World War, although like many other non-belligerents it suffered the occasional damage of war.[35] Secondly, the Irish consistently resisted threats and blandishments to involve them as belligerents. It might then be argued that the Irish retained a sufficient degree of independence, sovereignty, and freedom of decision and action to enable it to say 'no'. However, this can be exaggerated, since Irish non-belligerency was only really possible because of 'strategic factors outside the Irish government's control . . . Ireland was never of critical strategic value to any of the belligerents.'[36] As de Valera himself was to admit in 1946, outside circumstances and personalities were decisive; indeed, Irish neutrality 'depended ultimately upon the will of, perhaps, two men'.[37]

The real pressure came from the Allies, initially over the question of

[31] Ibid. doc. 506, 'The Minister in Eire to the Foreign Ministry' (21 June 1940), pp. 637–40; Carroll, 37.

[32] Mansergh, Survey 1931–9, 405.

[33] SPO S11586A, 23 Jan. 1940.

[34] See Hempel's recollections published in the Sunday Press for 22 Dec. 1963, cited in Fisk, 149.

[35] In the summer of 1940 three girls were killed when German bombs fell on a Wexford creamery; in Jan. 1941 German bombs fell near Drogheda, in Dublin, and in counties Wexford, Carlow, Wicklow, and Kildare. Further bombs fell on Dublin in May 1941.

[36] Patrick Keatinge, A Place Among the Nations: Issues of Irish Foreign Policy (Dublin, 1978), 89.

[37] Dáil Debates, 102 (1946), 1463–78 (quotation from p. 1465).

the access to the ports and then over the American Note affair in spring 1944, when the Allies called for Axis representatives to be removed and complained about espionage.[38] The blandishments were usually in the form of some arrangement for a united Ireland. One particular example was the British plan of 26 June 1940.[39] However, the Irish would not accept these offers, because, as de Valera put it in a letter to Chamberlain, the 'plan would commit us definitely to an immediate abandonment of our neutrality. On the other hand, it gives no guarantee that in the end we would have a united Ireland.'[40]

Churchill raised the ports issue publicly in the autumn of 1940, referring to the inability to 'use the south and west coasts of Ireland to refuel' as 'a most heavy and grievous burden', made worse by the irony that it made more difficult the protection of the 'trade by which Ireland as well as Great Britain lives'.[41] Although not in itself a direct or immediate threat, it troubled the Irish, coming as it did after private pressure. Therefore, de Valera responded by emphasizing that there could 'be no question of the handing over of these ports as long as this State remains neutral. There can be no question of leasing these ports. They are ours. They are within our sovereignty.'[42]

On certain major issues touching upon the core of sovereignty, the Irish dug in their heels. On issues not so central to sovereignty, they were prepared to act and behave in 'unneutral' ways or as a 'non-belligerent' rather than as a neutral. If abstention is to be understood as offering no partial assistance to either belligerent, the Irish did not conform to this criterion, since their sympathies did spill over into partial acts.

It may be argued that the charge of partiality is mitigated by German acquiescence, and by the fact that, despite favours for Britain, the British were denied the ports—making the Irish attitude balanced overall. But this would be to ignore the fact that the Germans were watchful against blatant partiality and that, in some other cases, they were clearly not always aware or fully aware of the partiality. Moreover, partiality to one

---

[38] See de Valera, *Ireland's Stand*, 103–9, for the original American Note of 21 Feb. 1944 and de Valera's reply of 7 Mar. 1944.

[39] PRO CAB 66/9 WP (40) 233, annex I, 'Proposals taken by MacDonald to Dublin', 26 June 1940; annex II, MacDonald's report to Cabinet of meeting of 27 June 1940; and annex III, 'Text of communication handed to Mr. de Valera', 29 June 1940.

[40] PRO CAB 66/9 WP (40) 251, de Valera to Chamberlain, 4 July 1940. See also Bowman, 218–39, 252, and *passim*.

[41] Churchill, in *Common's Debates*, 356 (1940), col. 1243.

[42] De Valera, *Dáil Debates*, 81 (1940), 582–6.

side or the other is not simply to be added up and judged acceptable if the score comes out evenly at the bottom. There can be little doubt that the Irish engaged in unneutral acts and in partial behaviour.

In his meeting on 20 September 1939 with Maffey, de Valera's attitude exhibited a clear but subtle distinction between form and substance.[43] He agreed that the Irish coast-watching service would wireless *en clair* information on the presence and location of German U-boats. Superficially this was in conformity with impartiality, since any belligerent could theoretically receive and act upon the information; but given the geography of the war and Ireland's location it was exceedingly partial in substance. Indeed, within a short time Hempel was advising that 'Submarines should avoid Irish territorial waters.'[44] Later a similar arrangement was apparently made about movements of German aircraft, although in this case at 'British request the radio messages were made in code'.[45] This would appear to breach both the form and substance of neutrality.

Something similar occurred with regard to censorship, although this time operating in favour of Germany. While not even factual and documented accounts of German atrocities were allowed to be published, there was no similar restriction with regard to the enduring problem of Partition, partly because it was regarded as unconnected with the war and an internal issue.[46] As one of the constant victims of the censorship wrote after the war, 'In theory the censorship was entirely neutral; in practice it worked almost exclusively against the Allies.'[47]

Given the inadequate nature and level of their defences, the Irish were unable effectively to prohibit violations of their airspace and territorial waters, despite the contents of the 1939 *aide-mémoire*. The Irish record was not totally consistent throughout the war, as on occasions British aircraft were fired upon by Irish anti-aircraft gunners, while the more general pattern was that, rather than being defended, Irish airspace was quite accessible, there being at least, 160 recognized violations.[48]

Initially, British aircrews who crashed in the twenty-six counties were interned and then released. Subsequently, British and American crews were returned to Northern Ireland without being interned. The

[43] PRO DO 35/1107, Maffey, 20 Sept. 1939.

[44] *DGFP* viii, doc. 216, 'The Minister in Eire to the Foreign Ministry' (8 Oct. 1939), pp. 241-2.

[45] Carroll, 21.

[46] Fisk, 146-7.

[47] Smyllie, 322. Smylie was editor of the *Irish Times* during the war.

[48] See Fisk, 152; Carroll, 121-2; and PRO CAB 66/2, Maffey to Eden, 26 Oct. 1939.

Irish distinguished 'operational' from 'training' flights, and the Americans were always regarded as being on the latter, despite the frequency of their infringements of Irish airspace. The Irish distinction between types of flight was partial,[49] and no Germans were released for the duration. In addition to these cases, de Valera allowed RAF flying-boats a corridor beside Lough Erne to fly over Irish territory.

The Irish also had difficulties with their territorial waters, despite the injunction in the 1939 *aide-mémoire* that no 'vessels of war, whether surface or submarine craft' should enter Irish territorial waters, unless in distress,[50] and the publication in September 1940 of prohibitions upon belligerent ships in Irish waters.[51] De Valera agreed that British warships should be allowed to pursue and attack hostile submarines infringing Irish territorial waters and neutrality, 'whatever the regulations may be'.[52] Certainly, the British did take the precaution of covertly patrolling the Irish coast at times. It is also clear that German U-boats operated close to Irish shores on occasion.

In some other areas the Irish were more scrupulous, most notoriously when on 2 May 1945 de Valera and Walshe called upon Hempel to express condolence at the death of Hitler.[53] The Irish also ultimately rejected a trade agreement with Britain in the summer and autumn of 1940, despite the fact that the talks had opened on the initiative of the Irish at the end of April. The reason for the breakdown was that the Irish felt that the proposed terms on offer were incompatible with their neutrality.[54] A trade agreement *per se* need not have violated neutrality, in view of the traditional Anglo-Irish relationship, but the Irish were concerned at the British request for transshipment and storage rights, while even more significantly Churchill became British Prime Minister and the Germans advanced to the Channel ports. Pragmatism clearly played a role.

Shipping was something of a sore point for the Irish. At the beginning of the war the Irish had voluntarily transferred to Britain seven modern oil-tankers and subsequently had agreed, in order to avoid competition and at Britain's request, to charter ships through the British

[49] Longford and O'Neill, 401, note the repeated protests of Hempel over this, and say that he presented a formal note of protest on 27 July 1943.

[50] PRO CAB 66/1, Dulanty, 12 Sept. 1939.

[51] SPO S12026A, Emergency Powers (51) Order, Sept. 1940.

[52] Quotation in text from Longford and O'Neill, 354; cf. Fisk, 150; Carroll, 21—although it is not clear whether this agreement was tacit or explicit.

[53] For de Valera's reasoning see Longford and O'Neill, 411–12.

[54] Carroll, 83–4; Brian Farrell, *Sean Lemass* (Dublin, 1983), 60.

Ministry of Shipping's Charter Office. Although the real hardships came after 1940, the Irish already felt that they were receiving something of a raw deal. Even more problematic was the point that for some time Irish ships, and neutral ships engaged in Irish trade, took part in British convoys. Furthermore, the Irish do not always appear to have been vigorous in protesting about their shipping losses; at least, this was a stated reason at the end of 1943 for the American rejection of an Irish request for 'permission to purchase another ship as a replacement for the two ships chartered in 1941, which had been lost while carrying wheat to Ireland'.[55] On the other hand, clearly there were cases when the Irish government did protest.

The complexities in the Irish position are further seen in the issue of co-operation with the Allies over intelligence.[56] While there is some conflict of evidence, it does appear that close contact was maintained, with senior Irish officials meeting their British and American counterparts. Information from captured German agents was also handed over. Dwyer has even claimed that Walshe 'offered to allow the United States to station agents in Ireland'.[57] In spite of the lack of hard facts, there was certainly co-operation, and thus partiality.

A similar *de facto* partiality was evident in the contribution allowed by the Irish to the British war-effort in terms of manpower for the British armed forces and industrial and agricultural production. As Smyllie put it,

Mr de Valera easily might have followed the example of other neutral countries by passing a Foreign Enlistment Act, making it an offense, punishable by loss of all civil rights, to join the fighting services of any of the belligerent Powers. He did nothing of the kind. All through the war, Irishmen were completely free to join the British Forces; and . . . they did so in comparatively large numbers . . . [58]

It is impossible to be precise about the numbers involved, but the consensus appears to be that around 40,000 people from the twenty-six counties served in the British forces. Some 10 per cent of these volunteers

---

[55] Dwyer, *Neutrality*, 178.
[56] See e.g. Nigel West, *MI5 British Security Service Operations 1909-1945* (London, 1981), 309, 316, and id., *MI6 British Secret Intelligence Service Operations 1909-1945* (London, 1983), 206, 228-9. See also Williams, 'Ireland', in Nowlan and Williams, 21; Carroll, 35, 41-4, 157; and Longford and O'Neill, 398, 405.
[57] Dwyer, 148, 198.
[58] Smyllie, 320. For a discussion of the various estimates see Fisk, 451-2; Murphy, *Ireland in the Twentieth Century*, 103; Carroll, 109; and Mansergh, *Survey 1930-52*, 164.

deserted the Irish Army to join the British Army, taking with them their training.[59] Mansergh suggests that 'If their enlistment did not infringe the letter of Irish neutrality, it materially strengthened the forces at the disposal of the British Commonwealth.'[60] In fact, it did infringe neutrality by its partiality.

A related question was the contribution by Irish manpower to British production. Again, estimates vary, but it was probably of the order of 150,000–180,000.[61] Originally the Irish government did nothing to stop the traffic, even if they did not officially encourage it. Although certain advertisements were prohibited from Irish newspapers, the government ordered 'that the British Ministry of Labour's *National Clearing House Gazette* should be displayed at employment exchanges throughout Ireland'.[62] As the war progressed certain restrictions were placed on emigration, although not for reasons of neutrality but rather because of concerns about the state of the domestic economy.[63] Although a distinction might be drawn between State and citizens, the degree of complicity of the Irish state in this material assistance cannot be ignored. This partiality far outweighs the impartiality represented by banning collections for Spitfires.

Northern Ireland provided other sensitive and difficult issues for the Irish, given Article Two of their Constitution and de Valera's public claim in May 1941 that the 'Six Counties are a part of Ireland . . . Their inhabitants are Irishmen, and no Act of Parliament can alter this fact.'[64] Article Three of the Constitution, limiting Dublin's jurisdiction to the twenty-six counties 'Pending the re-integration of the national territory',[65] might have provided a basis for ignoring belligerent actions in the six counties, but such action was not ignored. Dublin complained about the possibility of conscription being introduced and about the American presence. This latter led David Gray, the American representative in Dublin, to ask why de Valera 'protested American troops coming as friends for the protection of Ireland, and did not protest German bombers coming to Belfast and killing Irish nationals'.[66] De

---

[59] See Smyllie, 321 and Carroll, 118.
[60] Mansergh, *Survey 1930–52*, 164.
[61] Smyllie, 321; Carroll, 109; Dwyer, *Neutrality*, 147.
[62] Dwyer, *Neutrality*, 19.
[63] See James F. Meehan, 'The Irish Economy during the War', in Nowlan and Williams, 32, and Carroll, 109.
[64] *Dáil Debates*, 83 (1941), 971–2.
[65] 'Bunreacht na hÉireann', Article 3.
[66] Quoted by Dwyer, *Neutrality*, 152; and see also ibid. 143.

Valera saw the presence of American troops in terms of Irish sovereignty,[67] but the problem was made worse by the fear that his protests could have stirred up trouble for the GIs from the nationalist minority in Ulster, which would have been difficult to reconcile with either abstention or impartiality.

A complication was the thought that occurred to Irish and other minds, of what to do if the Germans should invade Northern Ireland and proclaim themselves liberators. De Valera told Gray that if this happened, 'what I could do I do not know'. The Irish Labour Party would not countenance aiding the British in such a situation, while Fine Gael would have. Fianna Fáil had no ready answer.[68] The issue is of interest since one factor in neutrality is the expectation of belligerents as to what a neutral might do in certain situations; this situation did not arise only because the Allies were strong enough to prevent it.

Most of the 'active' measures undertaken by Ireland were actually negative: they refused to yield to pressure. While these refusals were frequent, the Irish position was somewhat undermined by the fact that de Valera himself realized that 'We are a small nation, we are quite aware that in modern wars the equipment and armaments required are *far beyond* the possibilities of a small nation',[69] although again it was made clear that '*Any* attempt to bring pressure to bear on us by any side . . . could only lead to bloodshed', since Ireland would defend its rights 'in regard to these ports against whoever shall attack them, as we shall defend our rights in regard to every other part of our territory', and 'if we have to die for it, we shall be dying in that cause'.[70] Indeed, in a private interview with the Canadian High Commissioner, de Valera emphasized that the Irish would resist the Allied threat to 'the *sovereignty* of Eire'. If that sovereignty were interfered with, 'the army and the country would fight, and were even now preparing for eventualities. He intended to summon the Dáil and receive their endorsement of this renewal of the old struggle, this time against England, against America, against anybody . . .'[71] On occasion the words were matched by action; thus the army was put on alert on the night of the American Note.

When they were speaking publicly to the nature of Irish preparations, it was natural that politcians usually put some emphasis upon Irish strength. Thus, in November 1940 de Valera was keen to make clear that

---

67 See press statement, 27 Jan. 1942, reproduced in de Valera's *Speeches and Statements by Éamon De Valera 1917-73*, ed. Maurice Moynihan (Dublin, 1980), 465.   68 Bowman, 211-12.
69 *Dáil Debates*, 91 (1943), 2124 (emphasis added).
70 Ibid. 81 (1940), 586 (emphasis added).
71 See P R O F O 371 42679, Maffey, 22 Feb. 1944 (emphasis added).

Ireland had 'at present in men and material a stronger defensive force than ever existed in this island before, and we are constantly strengthening it'. However, in the same passage de Valera had also had to admit that Irish equipment was not complete, although he argued that this was 'not our fault'.[72]

Clearly, the Irish defence effort was substantially increased over the period from 1938/9 to 1945/6. The increase is marked both in amount and as a proportion of 'Total Supply Services', as Table 5.1 indicates. The figures show sharp increases between 1939/40 and 1941/2, after which expenditure levelled off, although it peaked in gross terms in 1942/3. However, the effect is somewhat modified by the substantial rise in the cost of living over the period.[73] The figures tend to support the argument that it was only with the overthrow of France that 'for the first time, de Valera and the Opposition parties set about attempting to introduce some kind of effective defence force',[74] that the 'emergency became a reality'.[75] It was only in May 1940 that certain infantry battalions were placed on a war footing, as were an anti-aircraft brigade and two companies of engineers.[76] It was during this period that de Valera sought American help, established the inter-party Defence Conference,

Table 5.1. Irish Defence Expenditure 1938/9–1945/6

Year	Expenditure (£m.)[a]	% of govt. expenditure[b]
1938/9	1.766	6.2
1939/40	2.973	10.1
1940/1	6.682	20.35
1941/2	8.155	22.9
1942/3	8.394	22.0
1943/4	8.189	20.5
1944/5	8.147	18.7
1945/6	8.768	18.4

  [a] Actual amounts issued in each year.
  [b] Or, at least, percentage of 'Total Supply Services'.

Source: Ireland: Statistical Abstract, 1946, table 174, pp. 152–5.

[72] 19 Nov. 1940, United Press interview, in de Valera, *Ireland's Stand*, 31–2.

[73] Using 1914 = 100 as base, the cost of living index in May of each year 1939–45 was as follows: 1939–172; 1940–204; 1941–220; 1942–240; 1943–275; 1944–292; 1945–292. See *Ireland: Statistical Abstract* 1946 (P. 7745; Dublin, 1947), table 238, p. 195.

[74] Williams, 'Ireland', in Nowlan and Williams, 17.   [75] Hayes-McCoy, ibid. 47.

[76] SPO CAB 2/3, Cabinet minutes, 17 May 1940. It was only in July 1940 that it was agreed to manufacture mines for Irish ports: SPO S12014A, Cabinet minutes, 2 July 1940.

intensified action against the IRA, and suggested Anglo-Irish military talks. It was on 28 May that a new security force was created—the Local Security Force (LSF)—and between 31 May, when recruiting for LSF began, and 16 June 1940 44,870 men were enrolled. It was only in June that general recruiting began in earnest. At the beginning of June, the Defence Forces (Temporary Provisions) (No. 2) Bill passed through all its stages in two days. It provided for enlistment for the duration of the emergency, billeting, the placing of troops on active service, and certain other contingencies.[77] Yet, despite the activities of 2 September 1939, it was only on 7 June 1940 that the Irish government declared that a state of emergency existed, and it was not until November that a supplementary army estimate for £3m. was adopted.

Until the crisis in 1940, numbers in the army were comparatively small. In September 1939 the Reserve had been called out on permanent service, as were the Volunteers. The Reserves nominally comprised 5,066 officers and men, the Volunteers 7,223, and in addition to these there were 7,494 Regulars.[78] However, of the Reserves and Volunteers, 2,053 exemptions were granted by Christmas 1939, and by the end of 1939 the Cabinet was committed for financial reasons to reduce the numbers permanently on service to 'the smallest number of troops necessary to garrison fixed positions'—and that meant below 15,350.[79] By April 1940 'one way and another, there were 1,256 officers and 15,900 other ranks on permanent service', a total of 17,156, although apparently even then 'the authorities began to wonder, in the slang of the time, *if their journey was really necessary*'.[80] In a revealing comment the editor of the *Defence Forces Handbook*, Capt. J. Sheehan, states that by the 'end of 1940 the army had more or less completed its expansion to a war-time footing'.[81] The end of 1940 seems rather late to be ready for war, especially given the excitements of the summer, the fear of invasion, and the vexed issue of the ports.

The LSF trained regularly and by 1942 had 98,429 men, 103,530 by 1943, and 96,152 by 1944, with the estimate that these strengths were 90 per cent effective.[82] While these figures appear impressive, it remains

[77] *Dáil Debates*, 80 (1940), 1522 ff., for the debate. Carroll argues that the call-up 'found the army seriously unprepared', with e.g. not enough blankets (p. 32).

[78] Lt. Col. P. D. Kavanagh (ed.), *The Irish Army Handbook 1973* (Dublin, 1973), 12–13.

[79] SPO CAB 2/3, Cabinet minutes, 11 Dec. 1939.

[80] Kavanagh, *Handbook 1973*, 13 (emphasis in original).

[81] Capt. J. Sheehan, *Defence Forces Handbook* (Dublin, n.d.), 11.

[82] Ibid. 11–12. For the Cabinet's views on the role of the LSF see SPO CAB 2/3, Cabinet minutes, 28 May 1940.

true that in 1942 the number of Irishmen on permanent service was 38,787 (all ranks), and in the summer of 1944 36,211 (all ranks).[83] In other words, the effective Irish figure was about half of the quarter of a million men that de Valera had hoped for. One possibly significant factor, as Gray reported being told by de Valera himself, was that de Valera dared not arm the Volunteer force, because of fears about IRA infiltration.[84]

Even if given the benefit of the doubt, the effective size of the Irish defence forces remained small, a problem compounded by the fact that although the 'recruits . . . were forthcoming . . . the arms were not'.[85] In 1940 de Valera was very conscious of Ireland's 'nakedness of defence', and felt that in such circumstances the government 'could not have it on their consciences' that they had taken Ireland to war.[86] A somewhat jaundiced opposition member of the Defence Conference, Dr T. O'Higgins, had observed privately in March 1941 that 'We have 100,000 LSF men with empty hands—as helpless as any civilians', while 20,000 of the LSF had 'rifles of a bore that limits the supply of ammunition to less than 100 rounds or about a couple of hours service'. Ireland had 'no aerial fighters worth mentioning and no anti-aircraft ground defences'.[87]

Irish weakness was most dramatic with respect to the navy or the Marine Defence Service. At the outbreak of war neither existed. *Fort Rannoch* and *Muirchú*, the fishery protection vessels, became Public Armed Vessels in January 1940, and the first Motor Torpedo Boat (MTB) arrived a week earlier. This and subsequent MTBs were built by Thorneycrofts in Britain. Within two years the number of MTBs had increased to six, but they were very small and were unsuited to rough seas.[88] There was also the schooner *Issault*, which was purchased as a training ship, and the barge SS *Shark*, which was designated as a 'mine

---

[83] Sheehan, 11.

[84] Quoted in Bowman, 225. Hempel also saw the IRA as a factor in this: *DGFP* doc. 310, 'The Minister in Eire to the Foreign Ministry' (23 May 1940), pp. 422–4. For de Valera's aspiration for a force of a quarter of a million men see United Press interview, 19 Nov. 1940, in *Ireland's Stand*, 31–2.

[85] Fisk, 137.

[86] In conversation with MacDonald: PRO PREM 3/131/1, MacDonald memo, 21–2 June 1940.

[87] Quoted in Fisk 211, from UCD Archives, Mulcahy papers P7/C/114, O'Higgins, 3 Mar. 1941.

[88] For details see Francis E. McMurtrie (ed.), *Jane's Fighting Ships 1944–45* (London, 1944), 128a, and Capt. T. McKenna, 'Thank God We're Surrounded by Water', *An Cosantóir* (Apr. 1973).

planter'.[89] With respect to the sea 'active' measures from Ireland were lacking.

With respect to the skies Ireland did a little better but still fell short of sufficiently vigorous 'active' measures. Ireland did have a number of planes of various types by the autumn of 1939, but most were of little or no use in the war of 1939–45 because of the technological developments that had taken place, and perhaps only the Gloucester Gladiators were of practical significance.[90] During the war itself no significant fighter aircraft were acquired—only six Hawker Hinds in 1940 and a further ten Hawker trainers in the summer of 1941. Again the British were the suppliers. The only other acquisitions were those repaired and pressed into service by the Air Corps from the 163 belligerent aircraft which crashed in Eire. This produced a Fairey Battle and a Lockheed Hudson, as well as a couple of Hurricanes.[91] Of course, aerial defence also involved anti-aircraft guns, but the Irish remained short of them, although in November 1941 the British let Ireland have twelve 3.7-inch anti-aircraft guns. None the less, they were too few and failed to stop the high level of incursions or indeed the bombing of Eire.

As for the Irish Army, it was 'Lightly armed, with very little aircover and no armour, [and] was not a formidable force'.[92] Once the war was under-way, supplies became a critical problem. The Americans tended to argue that they only had enough for their own rearmament and for those fighting aggression,[93] the British that no arms could be given unless they were 'assured that it was Southern Ireland's intention to enter the war'.[94] The Germans were also a possible source, but in that case there were both substantial problems of transport and fears about British sensitivities and reactions.[95] It seemed that everyone was only willing to give arms in return for some measure which violated Irish neutrality. Despite the occasional bile in British and American responses, Britain was Ireland's chief source of supply, and later on the Americans supplied rifles. But Ireland still only had a couple of tanks, less than thirty armoured cars, and in addition some armoured vehicles adapted by the

[89] Sheehan, 63.

[90] See above, p. 110.

[91] See Carroll, 119–20; Sheehan, 60–1; and Lt.-Col. M. Cassidy, 'A Short History of the Air Corps', *An Cosantoir* (May 1980).

[92] Kavanagh, *Handbook 1973*, 12.

[93] Cordell Hull, *The Memoirs of Cordell Hull*, ii (London, 1948), 1353–4.

[94] PRO PREM 3/131/3, Churchill to Cranborne, 31 Jan. 1941.

[95] *DGFP* xi (1961), doc. 523, 'The Minister in Ireland to the Foreign Ministry' (17 Dec. 1940), pp. 882–3.

Irish from Ford and Dodge chassis. Its armour was inadequate—and it was deficient in tanks, anti-tank guns, anti-aircraft guns, machine-guns, rifles, and ammunition, and was further handicapped by the antiquity of some of the equipment.[96]

It is difficult to say categorically what constitutes sufficient resources, but at sea and in the air the Irish clearly did not have 'enough', since they were incapable of preventing invasions into territorial waters and airspace, or violations of their neutrality. Their relative defencelessness meant that on occasion they did bend. On land the situation was somewhat different, since throughout the duration the land area of the twenty-six counties remained inviolate. There was perhaps an element of deterrence, but the crucial factors appear to have been the geo-political ones.[97] Certainly, the Irish could have made wholesale occupation unprofitable, and even partial occupation of e.g. the ports would have been relatively expensive in men, time, and resources—a factor the British chiefs of staff had taken into account in 1936.[98]

Ireland's active measures were not wholeheartedly or vigorously pursued. With respect to 'due diligence' the Irish clearly defaulted, particularly in the air and at sea. The Irish objective was simply to avoid participation in the war. That is not neutrality.

RECOGNITION OF NEUTRAL STATUS

In his speech to the specially convened Dáil on 2 September 1939, de Valera attempted to make clear that Ireland would seek to pursue a policy of neutrality.[99] On the other hand many internal and external observers doubted whether such an Irish policy could ever be implemented: there was no such tradition; Ireland appeared to be in an ambiguous juridical position; and there were questions concerning the political, military, and economic viability of such a policy.

For the most part the Germans accepted Irish neutrality, although there were some violations. Irish rights were breached by U-boats, by occasional bombing, and by such practices as aerial reconnaissance,

[96] For details of what the Irish received and what they possessed see PRO CAB 66/27, Chiefs of Staff to War Cabinet, annex I, 6 Aug. 1942; Hayes-McCoy, in Nowlan and Williams, 48; Carroll, 81; and Denis J. McCarthy, 'Armour in the War Years,' *An Cosantoir* (Mar. 1975).

[97] In Dec. 1940 the German Naval Staff, on 'The Question of Supporting Ireland Against Britain', had argued e.g. against an invasion of Ireland while Britain remained supreme at sea. See Mansergh, *Survey 1930–52*, 70–2.

[98] PRO CAB 53/6, Committee on Imperial Defence, 6 July 1936.

[99] *Dáil Debates*, 77 (1939), 1–8; and see also ibid., 74 (1939), 707–23.

which, incidentally, led the Irish to fire on German planes.[100] The Germans also found it difficult to abjure some involvement with the more militant of Irish republicans and there was also some espionage activity.[101] In 1940 and 1941 there was some discussion and planning of an attack upon Eire, but this was largely envisaged as 'diversionary' and of a lower priority than the main target of Operation Sealion, Britain.[102]

On 17 June 1940 Hempel was asked by Walshe 'to declare that we would not make a landing in Ireland'. Hempel said that such a request 'could only meet with a negative reaction on my part and I added that such a declaration was impossible in the present military situation'.[103] However, within a month the Germans were more reassuring, saying that 'As long as Ireland conducts herself in a neutral fashion it can be counted on with absolute certainty that Germany will respect her neutrality unconditionally.'[104] In 1941 Hitler himself apparently argued that 'Eire's neutrality must be respected. A neutral Irish Free State is of greater value to us than a hostile Ireland', although he recognized that certain marginal encroachments could not be avoided.[105] It was fortunate for the Irish that, although Hempel was aware that 'Irish neutrality was weighted on the Allied side . . . he did not believe such breaches of impartiality warranted German retaliation',[106] and that geography and the Allied forces remained strong enough to prevent the Germans from interfering.

The initial British discomfiture was clearly revealed in the Eden memorandum of 16 September 1939 on the legal and constitutional position.[107] The British never simply accepted the 1939 Irish aide-mémoire and throughout the war refused to recognize the Irish

---

[100] *DGFP* vii, doc. 428, 'The Foreign Minister to the Legation in Eire' (29 Aug. 1939), pp. 422–3; doc. 527, 'The State Secretary to the Legation in Eire' (1 Sept. 1939), p. 504; Fisk, 199–200.

[101] See Enno Stephan, *Spies in Ireland* (London, 1965), and Carolle J. Carter, *The Shamrock and the Swastika: German Espionage in Ireland in World War II* (Palo Alto, Calif., 1977).

[102] See John W. Blake, *Northern Ireland in the Second World War* (Belfast, 1956), 154–5; Dwyer, *Neutrality*, 75; and Fisk, 189–200, 226–7.

[103] *DGFP* ix, doc. 473, 'The Minister in Eire to the Foreign Ministry' (17 June 1940), pp. 601–3.

[104] *DGFP* x, (1957), doc. 149, 'The Foreign Minister to the Legation in Eire' (11 July 1940), pp. 184–5.

[105] General Kurt Student, 'Airfields around Belfast as Paratroop Objectives', in the *Irish Independent* for 26 Apr. 1949, quoted by Fisk, 226–7. Student had published 'A German Airborne Attack on the North' the previous day. An order of 1 Jan. 1942 told the navy to observe Irish neutrality, although the order was occasionally deliberately flouted: fisk 277, citing supp. 3 to German Standing War Orders 104 and 105.

[106] Murphy, *Ireland in the Twentieth Century*, 102.

[107] P R O C A B 66/1 W P (39) 34, Eden memo, 16 Sept. 1939.

position formally. Moreover, there was lacking not only a guarantee of respect for Irish neutrality but also a guarantee not to invade Irish territory: this latter omission was quite deliberate. Early in 1941 the Irish were told that the question was 'academic' but, none the less, 'in a war like this it is impossible to foresee what might develop. A situation of life and death might arise in which it might be essential, in our view, to the survival of the liberties of Britain and Southern Ireland too that we should have the use of the ports.'[108]

On occasion there was a certain apparent *de facto* recognition of the Irish position and a certain ambiguity of language—for example, when on 17 June 1940 MacDonald spoke to de Valera of Ireland's 'immediate abandonment of neutrality' in return for co-operation in advance against a possible German invasion.[109] Moreover, one of the British proposals put forward by MacDonald during negotiations contained the idea that 'Eire [was] to *remain neutral*, at any rate for the time being'.[110] More indicative of British attitudes was the continuing belief that it might be possible to do a deal over unity, the ports, or the supply of equipment. While this deal was rebuffed, it is of significance that it was at least subject to negotiation, thus giving some sustenance to British hopes.

The Americans also refused to guarantee the Irish position, and even before entry into the war were not sympathetic to it. As a later formulation puts it, the American government 'did not question the determination or the right of the Irish people to maintain their neutrality, but between a policy of this character and one which potentially at least gave real encouragement to Germany there was a clear distinction'.[111] The United States remained antipathetic and returned to charges concerning the nature of Irish neutrality, although Roosevelt in February 1942 did send reassurances to de Valera there was not, and 'is not now, the slightest thought or intention of invading Irish territory or threatening Irish security'.[112] This was repeated in the wake of Irish fears over the American Note in 1944.[113] The Note specifically charged 'that

---

[108] PRO PREM 3/131/3,Cranborne to Churchill, 30 Jan. 1941; and for other examples of British views on this see PRO CAB 66/10, Caldecote to Cabinet, 20 July 1940; PRO PREM 3/131/5, report of Duff Cooper speech of 7 May 1941; PRO PREM 3/131/7, Maffey memo, 14 Mar. 1941; and Winston Churchill, *The Second World War*, iii. *The Grand Alliance* (London, 1950), 641.

[109] PRO PREM 3/131/1, MacDonald memo, 17 June 1940.

[110] Ibid., MacDonald memo, 21–2 June 1940 (emphasis added).

[111] Hull, 1353–4, for US attitudes; cf. Dwyer, *Neutrality*, 100.

[112] Carroll, 117.

[113] Longford and O'Neill, 406. For accounts of 'The Note Affair' see Longford and O'Neill, 403–8; Carroll, 139–59; and Dwyer, 179–200.

despite the declared desire of the Irish Government that its neutrality should not operate in favour of either of the belligerents, it has in fact operated and continues to operate in favour of the Axis Powers and against the United Nations on whom [Irish] security and the maintenance of [the Irish] national economy depend'.[114] The British concurred with the Americans.

In 1940 Hempel was confident that 'the Army, together with the nationalist population, would be prepared to carry on strong resistance in the form of guerrilla warfare against an English attack',[115] although in November 1939 he had explicitly warned that, if the British took action against the harbours, the Irish government *'might put up armed resistance or it might not, in view of the small size of the armed forces'*.[116] Ribbentrop was annoyed at an Irish rejection of German arms, and believed that this implied that Irish resistance to a British attack was hardly likely to be all it was made out to be.[117]

Hempel was aware that the position of the United States was crucial; he warned in October 1939 that 'a possible abandoning of American neutrality would constitute a threat to Irish neutrality',[118] and a month later commented that, while American entry into the war was 'not expected for the time being', such 'a step would exert a decisive influence on the situation here'.[119] The American representative in Dublin, David Gray, initially felt the same, since de Valera had told him that American entry into the war 'would alter our situation over-night'.[120]

The Allies also occasionally had hopes with respect to Irish opinion, possible internal divisions within the Fianna Fáil government, the possibilities of an alternative, more congenial, government, and the cultivation of Mr James Dillon TD. While some of these thoughts were chimerical, there was also some foundation for certain hopes along these lines. In October 1939 Maffey and Hempel both agreed that neutrality

---

114 The Note and de Valera's reply are reproduced in de Valera, *Ireland's Stand*, 103–9.

115 *DGFP* ix, doc. 310, 'The Minister in Eire to the Foreign Ministry' (23 May 1940), pp. 422–4.

116 *DGFP* viii, doc. 401, 'The Minister in Eire to the Foreign Ministry' (30 Nov. 1939), pp. 466–7 (emphasis added).

117 Carroll, 75; and see *DGFP* xi, doc. 523, 'The Minister in Ireland to the Foreign Ministry' (17 Dec. 1940), pp. 882–3; ibid. xii, *DGFP* xii (1962), doc. 79, 'The Foreign Minister to the Legation in Ireland' (24 Feb. 1941), pp. 152–3; and ibid., doc. 150, 'The Minister in Ireland to the Foreign Ministry' (11 Mar. 1941), pp. 270–1.

118 *DGFP* viii, doc. 216, 'The Minister in Eire to the Foreign Ministry' (8 Oct. 1939), pp. 241–2.

119 Ibid., doc. 401, 'The Minister in Eire to the Foreign Ministry' (30 Nov. 1939), pp. 466–7.

120 Gray to Roosevelt, 19 June 1940, quoted in Bowman, 234.

enjoyed public support, but the degree of Irish unanimity can be exaggerated.[121] For example, although a senior Fine Gael politician claimed in 1940 that entry into the war would be opposed by 'perhaps more than half of' Fianna Fáil, 'one third of Fine Gael and perhaps the whole of Labour', this does suggest that the abandonment of neutrality did have some support.[122] This came about despite the fact that neutrality was fortified by censorship.

For some, private doubts revolved around the moral issue of abstention from a war against Nazism; for others, the doubts involved the practical grounds of viability and expediency of the policy. There was no organized group of 'doubters' and those holding such views did not always do so consistently or with the same strength. For example, doubts concerning viability and expediency rose significantly with the fall of France. The most consistent opponent of the government's policy was James Dillon TD, deputy Leader of Fine Gael until he was forced to resign on the issue in February 1942, when he suggested that 'Whatever the sacrifice, whatever America may want from us to protect her from her enemies, she will get for the asking.'[123]

While the shadow cabinet refused to support Dillon's motion in March 1941 to seek a declaration of war, it was interested in a bargain over Northern Ireland. The great constraint was the perception of public opinion. In fact there was more concern over neutrality among the shadow cabinet than its public utterances suggested.[124] Cosgrave had repudiated Dillon in public but in private was somewhat more flexible. After all, he had written to de Valera in July 1940 (for the first time in eighteen years), pointing out that 'If the Government in changing circumstances feel it necessary to depart from the policy of neutrality in which they have had our support up to the present, my colleagues and I would be prepared to give them our fullest support in such a change of policy.' De Valera did not act upon this hint, and Cosgrave's reply emphasized that his original 'letter had been written, not to suggest a change of policy but to indicate what would be his party's view if the Government felt obliged to abandon neutrality'.[125]

---

[121] PRO CAB 66/2, Maffey to Eden, 23 Oct. 1939, and DGFP viii, doc. 216, 'The Minister in Eire to the Foreign Ministry' (8 Oct. 1939), pp. 241-2.

[122] UCD Archives, Mulcahy papers, P7 a/210 memo, 4 and 5 July 1940, quoted by Bowman, 237.

[123] PRO PREM 3/131/7, extract of a Dillon speech, attached to Maffey letter, 10 Mar. 1941; cf. Carroll, 116.

[124] See Dwyer, Neutrality, 131; Fisk, 260, 383; and Bowman, 242-3.

[125] See Longford and O'Neill, 370-1, for Cosgrave's letter to de Valera on 9 July 1940 and a paraphrase of de Valera's reply of 16 July 1940.

In private with Maffey in October 1942, Cosgrave observed that no Irish government could abandon neutrality, because support for the policy was increasing rather than diminishing. Maffey had to report that 'the conversation revealed the present firm and unyielding adherence of all parties to the policy of neutrality', although it is interesting that, in repudiating Dillon, Cosgrave used the expression 'at the moment', and Maffey reported 'the present' adherence.[126] Even in Fianna Fáil some, Lemass perhaps included, were ready at least to discuss some of the British offers.[127]

During the 1943 election campaign Fine Gael was nevertheless careful to insist that it supported neutrality, although there were hints of the need for closer co-operation with Britain after the war. Fianna Fáil sought to use neutrality for their own purposes, suggesting that 'If you vote Fianna Fáil, the bombs won't fall' and that neutrality would be endangered if they were not returned. De Valera told audiences: 'Remember that this nation is being watched, and if you turn down the Government, foreign people will represent it as a turning down of the policies for which the Government has generally stood.'[128] Despite this, the Fianna Fáil vote fell significantly in 1943 compared to 1938.[129] Although this primarily reflected domestic factors, it was hardly a ringing endorsement of de Valera.

As for the 1944 election, the *Round Table* correspondent reported in July that the 'campaign was remarkable . . . for the discreet silence which was observed on topics which to an outsider might well have seemed all-important for the future of Eire . . . Neutrality was not an issue.'[130] Little was said about the future, although in the spring of 1944 General Mulcahy had argued that Eire should become a full member of the Commonwealth again when the war was over—a departure from his party's policy. In 1944 Mulcahy also advocated an Anglo-Irish military alliance as a future plank in the party's platform.[131] In 1944 Fianna Fáil recovered support, although not back to the 1938 level. Most of the votes appear to have come from Labour,[132] and as such were not

---

126 According to Dwyer, *Neutrality*, 161.

127 See e.g. PRO PREM 3/131/1, MacDonald memo of meeting with de Valera, Aiken, and Lemass of 27 June 1940.

128 See 'Ireland', in *Round Table* 33/131 (July 1943), 373–6, esp. p. 374 (from which I take the quotation in the text); Murphy, *Ireland in the Twentieth Century*, 109–10; Murphy, 'The Irish Party System', in Nowlan and Williams, 151–7; and Carroll, 122 and 129.

129 Basil Chubb, *The Government and Politics of Ireland* (OUP, 1974), table B.5, p. 334.

130 'Ireland', *Round Table*, 34/135 (July 1944), 363–5.

131 Murphy, 'The Irish Party System', 153.

132 Chubb, 334.

necessarily related to neutrality, although the crisis concerning the Note does appear to have enhanced de Valera's position. However, with regard to attitudes to neutrality, it must be remembered that thousands of Irishmen voted with their feet by going to Britain.

DISAVOWAL OF EXTERNAL HELP

For the Irish there was uncertainty as to who the enemy might be. Indeed, this uncertainty 'contributed to a rather schizophrenic feeling in the army with the men in the 1st Division in the south mentally anticipating a German landing, and those in the 2nd Division in the northern part of the country facing towards the border with the possibility of having to oppose a British invasion'.[133] If there was uncertainty about the source of possible invasion, what was the attitude to receiving and accepting help from others?

At the height of the German successes in 1940, de Valera asked to see Hempel and warned him that fears about German intentions concerning Ireland had increased, but that Ireland stood by its pledge not to become a base against Britain. He then went on: 'If it came to an invasion then Ireland would inevitably become a battlefield for the belligerents. *In an English invasion we would fight with Irishmen against the English, in a German invasion the English would fight along with the Irish.*'[134] Indeed, whenever this subject came up the Irish catechismal response was to focus, as de Valera did in his talk with Hempel, upon 'invasion'. There was to be no physical presence by German or British armies until the other side had invaded.

The Germans periodically enquired whether the Irish would welcome help either to forestall or in response to a British invasion, with the assurance that the 'Reich Government would be in a position to give Ireland vigorous support and would be inclined to do so'.[135] On 3 December 1940 Hitler himself decided that Hempel should find out 'whether de Valera desires support', and this was coupled with the offer of the British arms left in France.[136] In response to such offers the Irish

---

[133] This is a succinct summation of a complex and varying situation: Carroll, 119. De Valera had tried to make clear that 'If attacked, we are at war with whoever attacks us': United Press interview, 19 Nov. 1940, in *Ireland's Stand*, 32.

[134] *DGFP* ix, doc. 506, 'The Minister in Eire to the Foreign Ministry' (21 June 1940), pp. 637–40 (emphasis added).

[135] *DGFP* xi, doc. 407, 'The Foreign Minister to the Legation in Ireland' (26 Nov. 1940), pp. 718–19.

[136] Fisk, 193.

were very circumspect, at least at an official level, fearing British discovery and response. For those reasons they declined, 'until a British attack, which was unlikely for the time being, had become a fact'.[137] De Valera felt that 'I don't think we have to make provision now. Should it really happen, I think Germany is so efficient that they could find ways and means.'[138] However, Hempel occasionally worried that even in the event of a British attack de Valera might not call upon the Germans.[139] One senior Irish army officer, Major-General Hugo McNeill, the General Officer Commanding the 2nd Division (the troops on the Northern border), met with the German Counsellor in Dublin to solicit German arms and assistance, but again this appears to have been in the event of a British invasion.[140]

With regard to the British, the Irish shied away from formal arrangements, partly because de Valera felt that any arrangement, 'no matter how independent it left both parties, would inevitably be interpreted by outsiders as making them allies'.[141] Indeed, in 1940 de Valera refused an invitation to go to London, for much the same reason.[142] None the less, German success aroused Irish fears, and talks about defence co-operation did take place. On 23 May 1940 the Irish suggested that 'immediate secret contacts should be established between the Irish military authorities and the service chiefs in [Britain] with a view to concerting the military action which would be taken when the occasion arises'.[143] It was Walshe and Col. Archer who attended the meeting that day in London with the Permanent Under-Secretary of the Dominions Office (Machtig) and British navy, army, and air force officers to explore possible avenues of German attack;[144] and they showed the British Lt.-Col. Dudley Clarke around Dublin. Incidentally, Clarke subsequently reported on the satisfactory nature of the arrangements for co-ordination, and said that his visit had been encouraging. It was also agreed that the British should appoint a military attaché to their

[137] DGFP xi, doc. 523, 'The Minister to the Foreign Ministry' (17 Dec. 1940), pp. 882–3.

[138] Dr E. Hempel (as told to John Murdoch), 'Ireland on the Brink', in the Sunday Press, 17 Nov. 1963, quoted in Fisk, 218.

[139] DGFP ix, doc. 310, 'The Minister in Eire to the Foreign Ministry' (23 May 1940), pp. 422–4.

[140] Carter, Shamrock, 162–6, 173; Stephan, 208–9.

[141] Longford and O'Neill, 316.

[142] Ibid. 365.

[143] See British Chiefs of Staff, Committee on Eire, memo of 30 May 1940: PRO CAB 66/8, Chiefs of Staff minutes.

[144] PRO PREM 3/130, Minutes of Machtig–Walshe meetings, 23 and 24 May 1940. Each side conferred with their government between meetings.

Dublin mission, albeit in a civilian guise.[145] The British chiefs of staff told their own Cabinet at the end of the month that the Irish had been told that 'they may expect to receive direct support as far as land forces are concerned from [the] General Officer Commanding [the] Northern Ireland district. Staff officers from headquarters, Northern Ireland, have attended the conversations in Dublin and detailed planning is now proceeding. There have also been talks on how the RAF can help from United Kingdom bases.' The British Cabinet sanctioned the action of the chiefs of staff on 1 June 1940.[146] After this excitement the impetus was lost.[147]

Throughout this period the Irish repeatedly qualified their willingness to accept British help. The original Irish suggestion of 23 May made clear that the political situation in Eire was such that there was no question of inviting in British troops before fighting between Ireland and Germany had actually begun. On 17 June 1940 MacDonald referred to the Irish reservation, making it clear that this might mean help arriving too late, and proposing an immediate pre-invasion invitation.[148] The Irish were unyielding, and, according to Bowman,

there were strong arguments against acceptance. Any abandonment of neutrality in advance of a German invasion, would create a rift in the Fianna Fáil party and cabinet . . . it seemed likely to the cabinet that some British troops would be attacked by republican extremists; in the event of a German invasion, a government which had invited prior British aid, would be open to the charge that it was the British presence which had precipitated the attack; further, there was a suspicion in de Valera's mind, at least, that if the British ever returned to the Treaty ports—even by invitation—they might never leave; moreover, Germany, at this hour in the war, seemed invincible; and, lastly, there was Ulster . . . Was de Valera not being cast in the role of Redmond?[149]

The real question is whether the Irish reservation was sufficient to save their policy of neutrality. Preparations for and expectations of help

---

[145] Details of Clarke's trip are in Carroll, 43–4. Carroll had access to the uncensored manuscript of Clarke's memoirs, *Seven Assignments* (London, 1948).

[146] PRO CAB66/8, Chiefs of Staff minutes, 30 May 1940. For a wider discussion see Fisk, 203–10, 213, 217, 228, 234, and Blake, 156–7.

[147] Partly because co-operation became embroiled in the exchanges over unity, neutrality, and defence between MacDonald and de Valera in June 1940.

[148] For these negotiations see PRO PREM3/130, Minutes of Machtig–Walshe meeting, 24 May 1940; PRO PREM3/131/1, MacDonald memo 17 June 1940; ibid., MacDonald memo, 21–2 June 1940.

[149] Bowman, 235.

certainly ran counter to the principles underpinning a policy 'for neutrality', as followed by Austria, Sweden, and Switzerland, and, although lacking a formal treaty, it might be regarded as nearer to the Finnish position after the 1948 treaty with the Soviet Union. A further problem for the Irish was the asymmetrical nature of their preparations and expectations, since the number of talks with the British showed a clear partiality. In October 1940 discussions began again, while in March 1941 plans for combined resistance were revitalized.[150] In addition, some specialist Irish personnel were sent for training in Britain, while the British sent experts to Ireland to give advice.[151]

This period of liaison continued until the threat of the German invasion was deemed to have passed, and bitterness entered Anglo-American relations with Ireland in the winter of 1943–4. However, between March 1941 and that time the 'improved liaison between the army staffs north and south eventually eased the Irish army's shortage of modern equipment and there were frequent secret rendezvous on the border when Irish army lorries which had gone north with hams, eggs and butter returned south with badly needed military supplies'.[152]

Thus, during the war there was no consistent Irish disavowal of external help, particularly in relation to the question of preparing for, and expecting, assistance from others in the event of an attack. There still remained a belief in the 'protective umbrella'.

FREEDOM OF DECISION AND ACTION

Much of the foregoing has dealt with the constraints upon Irish policy-makers because of their economic and military dependency upon others. Crucially, the 'availability of supplies of anything depended on many matters which were outside the control of "the Irish". They depended increasingly, as the war wore on, on the degree of cordiality between Ireland and the major allies.'[153] The dependency resulted from the simple fact that, as de Valera told the nation in January 1941, 'Ours is an island country. Everything which we use and do not produce ourselves comes to us in ships across the seas. We have few ships of our own and little

---

[150] Carroll, 96. Carroll is adamant that de Valera was always told about the meetings and had a report afterwards on them.

[151] See e.g. SPO CAB 2/4, Cabinet minutes, 8 Oct. 1941, and Fisk, 235.

[152] Carroll, 312.

[153] Meehan, in Nowlan and Williams, 31. For a fuller account of the economic dimension see Raymond James Raymond, 'The Economics of Neutrality: The United States, Great Britain and Ireland's War Economy 1937–1945', 2 vols. (University of Kansas, Ph.D. thesis, 1980).

hope of purchasing any.' De Valera went on: 'we must *now* create for ourselves a war economy capable of withstanding the economic stresses that we shall henceforth feel acutely'.[154] Perceptive listeners might have wondered at the lapse of time since September 1939—or even before that, when war seemed likely. Indeed, de Valera had not even taken action on a memorandum drawn up by his own department in 1935 which noted that in a war any significant interruption of supplies 'of petrol and other fuels and lubricating oils would practically bring road transport in this country to a standstill in a short time'. All supplies of raw materials would be 'critical'.[155] There was also a warning from the Department of Industry and Commerce in April 1939 concerning Irish dependence on other countries' shipping for imports of 'wheat, maize, petroleum . . . and any other "bulk" cargoes from abroad'. It had concluded that 'if war should break out we are very largely at the mercy of other countries, and particularly of the United Kingdom, in respect of our external trade, and that the economic activities of this country could in such circumstances be completely paralysed'.[156] Despite all the rhetoric about self-sufficiency, Ireland had no 'strategic reserve'. Consequently, third parties saw room for influence and manoeuvre, and doubted not only the credibility of Irish neutrality but also the real extent of the Irish freedom of action and decision.

However, the formal position on key issues was clear. Ireland was not constrained or obligated by any military alliance or commitment, any formal agreement about the ports, or any formal treaty in the political area, although in some minds questions did remain about the nature of the relationship with the Commonwealth.[157] The Irish retained that essential ingredient of political sovereignty, namely the right and ability to say yes or no.[158]

Although there are well-known pitfalls in a legalistic approach to sovereignty, it remains true that after the constitutional upheavals of the 1930s the Irish themselves were in no doubt about their sovereign right to declare war. The 1937 Constitution stated: 'War shall not be declared

---

[154] De Valera, radio broadcast to the nation, 29 Jan. 1941, in *Ireland's Stand*, 40–5. See also Frank Forde, *The Long Watch: The History of the Irish Mercantile Marine in World War Two* (Dublin, 1981).

[155] SPO S28208, Dept. of the President, memo 'War: Essential Materials', 4 Dec. 1935. The nomenclature 'President' refers to the situation before the 1937 Constitution.

[156] SPO S11394, Dept. of Industry and Commerce, 18 Apr. 1939.

[157] e.g. Mulcahy and Dillon.

[158] Cf. James, 'Ground Rule', 12: 'Sovereign states are those territorially-based entities which are independent in terms of their constitutional arrangements.'

and the State shall not participate in any war save with the assent of Dáil Éireann' (28.3.1°). The provisions of Article 28 are crucial, for they meant that Irish participation could not be delivered solely by the government or even by the head of government, except in case of actual invasion. This was of critical importance with respect both to credibility and to the perceived freedom of action and decision. Equally importantly, the Constitution also stated clearly that 'Every international agreement to which the State becomes a party shall be laid before Dáil Éireann' (29.5.1°), which made any agreement on the ports more difficult.[159]

The Irish clearly faced a number of difficulties. In addition to those discussed, de Valera recognized in his broadcast of 29 January 1941 that 'another danger . . . presented itself . . . the economic one'. He went on to make his famous comment that the 'belligerents in blockading each other are blockading us'. What worried him at that time was that suffering might compel the nation to give way to pressure. He felt that it need not, but only if the people made 'whatever adjustments in our economic life the new situation may demand'.[160] It was because of this vulnerability and indeed dependence that Gray thought that Irish neutrality was ridiculous.[161] De Valera himself recognized the problem of getting supplies and of meeting the high cost of them, urging his people 'to try to get our own home substitutes for the things we imported'.[162] He also explicitly recognized that the British controlled shipping space, which they could 'deny to us if they choose leaving us in a dependent position'.[163]

It might well be argued that too much is made of Irish dependency, since neither it nor their lack of resources and supplies, reached such a level as to force them 'to give way to pressure'. However, this would be to ignore the further question of whether it was Irish action and resources that were decisive, or whether the Irish were able to resist pressure merely because it never became too great. For example, at the height of their success in June 1940 the Germans were cautious about blockading Ireland, partly because they believed 'she can subsist in a pinch'.[164] This clearly suggests that Irish resources, especially food, would be such that a blockade would not lead to a change in Irish

159 See 'Bunreacht na hÉireann', Articles 28 and 29, and also Articles 1, 5, and 15.

160 De Valera, radio broadcast to the nation, 29 Jan. 1941, in *Ireland's Stand*, 40–5.

161 Dwyer, *Neutrality*, 133.

162 De Valera, speech at Galway, 12 May 1940, in *Ireland's Stand*, 19.

163 De Valera, Christmas Day broadcast to the US, 1940, ibid. 37.

164 See *DGFP* ix, doc. 367, memo by Ambassador Ritter (1 June 1940), pp. 500–1, and doc. 396, 'The High Command of the Navy to the Foreign Ministry' (6 June 1940), pp. 524–5. This latter document also contains Hitler's views on the subject.

political policy. If the Germans were somewhat constrained, so too were the British; yet they did embark upon a policy of deliberate sanctions early in 1941.[165] Further measures were taken later in the war, e.g. on petroleum in 1943 and on a range of commodities before the launching of the second front in 1944. But the British War Cabinet's Committee on Economic Policy towards Eire, formed in 1942, apparently had as its general policy 'keeping Eire's economy going on a minimum basis'.[166] Carroll rightly concludes that it was 'never, therefore, starvation but a question of constantly reminding the Irish that they owed their survival to Britain but had refused to pull their weight and so must expect to pay some price in personal comfort'.[167]

The potential power of Britain was daunting. In July 1940 the Irish Interdepartmental Committee on Emergency Measures worried that more than a quarter of a million Irish people could be made idle if the country was cut off for a significant period,[168] while a year later Gray was writing to Roosevelt that 'If Britain completely shuts off coal and gasoline this place would be a disorganised and howling wilderness in three months.'[169] The pattern of Irish trade was one problem. During the period 1939–45 the figures for Irish trade with Britain (as illustrated in Table 5.2) show a crippling dependence, particularly on the export side. But even on the import side, the impact of the war was dramatic (as is demonstrated in Table 5.3). While in some sectors (e.g. sugar), the impact of trade dislocation was mitigated by increased domestic production, this was not possible in all areas (e.g. tea, coal, iron and steel, oils, fertilizers, and seed). Indeed, 'by 1943 the community had 25 per cent of its nominal requirements of tea, 20 per cent of its requirements of petrol, less than 15 per cent of its paraffin, 16 per cent of its gas coal, no domestic coal whatever and 22 per cent of its textiles'.[170] Elements of the normal staple diet—bread, butter, and tea—became scarce and expensive, while what was available, namely meat, was also expensive. Despite this, the worst never quite came to the worst, and 'apart from tea and white bread the Irish were better fed than the British with meat, bacon, butter and eggs . . . for those who could afford them'.[171]

It was Irish good fortune to live, as de Valera put it, on a 'fertile

---

[165] For their origin and rationale see PRO CAB66/14, Wood memo, 6 Dec. 1940.

[166] See Carroll, 78–94, on these measures and British policy.

[167] Ibid. 92. For Irish reactions see PRO CAB72/25, Dulanty to Attlee, 23 Feb. 1943.

[168] SPO S11980, Report of the Interdepartmental Committee on Emergency Measures, 4 July 1940.

[169] Letter of 11 Aug. 1941, quoted by Dwyer, *Neutrality*, 133.

[170] Meehan, in Nowlan and Williams, 36.   [171] Carroll, 92.

Table 5.2. Irish Imports and Exports from and to Great Britain and Northern Ireland and its Allies 1939–1945 (%)

	1939	1940	1941	1942	1943	1944	1945
Imports							
British	55.7	53.1	71.5	57.3	50.6	47.0	47.5
British allies[a]	15.3	20.2	15.5	25.3	25.9	30.8	25.9
TOTAL	71.0	73.3	87.0	82.6	76.5	77.8	73.4
Exports							
Britain	93.6	96.0	97.1	98.8	98.8	98.8	97.9
British allies[a]	1.4	2.0	2.6	1.1	1.0	1.0	1.0
TOTAL	95.0	98.0	99.7	99.9	99.8	99.8	98.9

[a] Including for this purpose the United States, even before 1942.

Source: Ireland: Statistical Abstract, 1946, table 94, p. 84.

island'. As a result he felt 'no one should starve. We can have abundance of the best food if we set out now to produce it ourselves.' He also explicitly told farmers that 'every extra acre they grow' was 'giving the nation added strength to pursue unwaveringly its own policy, and to resist pressure, should pressure be attempted by any side'.[172] Compulsory tillage was introduced, and 'crop and turf' output rose by over 30 per cent during the war.[173]

Meehan judged that 'the economy just managed to keep going; and above all, the policy of neutrality was not prejudiced by economic weakness',[174] a judgement shared by Longford and O'Neill.[175] On the other hand, Carroll believes that early in 1941 de Valera made 'a definite pro-British shift in policy', the British economic campaign having brought home 'the country's dependence on British goodwill for essential supplies', and he cites the renewed interest in military co-operation as evidence.[176] While there is supporting evidence for Carroll's view,[177] the Irish did not yield on their fundamental line of policy. Yet Allied forbearance meant that the Irish were never put to the full test, and de Valera had subsequently to admit that Irish neutrality hung upon the 'slender thread' of the goodwill of Roosevelt and Churchill.[178]

[172] De Valera, radio broadcast to the nation, 29 Jan. 1941, in *Ireland's Stand*, 41–2.
[173] *Ireland: Statistical Abstract*, 1946, table 50, p. 59.
[174] Meehan, in Nowlan and Williams, 38.
[175] Longford and O'Neill, 378.   [176] Carroll, 95–6.
[177] The supply position led to de Valera considering going to London for trade talks in Mar. 1940: SPO S118846A.
[178] *Dáil Debates*, 102 (1946), 1465. De Valera did not name the two until Dillon intervened.

Table 5.3. Quantity of Imports in Key Economic Sectors 1939–1945

Article	1939	1940	1941	1942	1943	1944	1945
Cereals/feeding-stuffs (cwt)							
Wheat	7,257,581	6,637,177	1,000,014	3,897,906	1,942,202	4,462,682	4,567,718
Barley	338,713	275,277	—	19,684	4,552	736,970	764,190
Oats	285	121,269	110	—	95,621	2	355,677
Maize	8,160,980	5,782,519	789,004	—	—	—	n.a.[a]
Wheaten flour	96,322	79,611	30,769	10,353	577	668	n.a.[a]
Other food (lb)							
Sugar	899,553	1,803,144	5	25,062	351,091	18	8,818
Tea	21,858,693	23,605,229	11,203,771	11,610,025	6,144,209	6,216,032	7,824,137
Non-metalliferous mine products (ton)							
Coal	2,875,773	2,757,318	1,487,920	1,048,636	1,015,371	734,654	920,573
Iron/steel (ton)							
Pig-iron	7,566	4,012	939	2,994	2,749	2,301	1,597
Steel bar-rods	13,609	10,904	2,161	1,130	1,045	1,527	8,692
Non-ferrous metals (cwt)							
Aluminium	6,025	6,340	450	53	59	52	5,977
Lead	63,053	30,766	7,173	3,634	5,064	6,699	11,500

Machinery/vehicles (no.)							
Agric. machinery	8,984	8,744	1,637	1,470	441	1,317	4,661
Tractors	572	769	31	65	138	387	1,066
Ships/boats and parts	—	—	—	—	—	—	—
Aeroplanes	—	—	—	—	—	—	—
Oils (gall.)							
Gas/fuel-oil	11,623,035	11,473,077	8,652,951	6,132,927	6,103,093	6,470,282	6,284,045
Oils/motor-spirit	39,021,517	32,343,909	17,814,232	14,090,493	10,831,209	12,916,818	14,925,890
Fertilizer (ton)							
Rock-phosphate	88,986	73,624	6,776	—	18,370	27,525	18,240
Seeds for sowing (cwt)							
Wheat	614,973	205,172	176,509	44,252	250	—	n.a.[a]

[a] Data not available or not available in comparable form.

Sources: Ireland: Statistical Abstract, 1945, table 97, pp. 104–19; 1946, table 98, pp. 88–95.

CONCLUSION

Ireland did not fulfil all the criteria 'of' or 'for' neutrality, even during the war, despite Keatinge's claim that this period saw 'the most clear-cut manifestation of neutrality in Irish history'.[179] More important than neutrality *per se* was the imperative of proving to the world and itself its independence. Even in 1944, when Ireland could have joined the Allies with little risk to itself, de Valera felt that 'Irish independence of action had to be preserved'.[180] On 7 February 1939 in a crucial speech to the Irish Senate on Irish unity, de Valera had stressed the need for independence of action and the importance of Article One of the Constitution, with its basis affirmation of sovereignty. He 'would not sacrifice that right, because without that right you have not freedom at all'.[181]

There was also an abhorrence of war and of participation in British wars, reflecting a 'dumb but powerful urge among the people for peace at any price', an urge which provided much of the strength of neutrality.[182] While thousands felt differently and contributed to the British war-effort, this popular sentiment influenced de Valera heavily. In May 1940, for example, he commented that having been scourged by whips, the Irish wanted 'no scourging with scorpions instead'. In view of this, he had the 'desire and intention to save our people from the horrors of this war'.[183] Some time later he reaffirmed that it was his 'duty to Ireland to try to keep out of this war'.[184] Conscious of the effects of bombing, he noted that London for all its defences was suffering, and wondered 'what would happen to Dublin, Cork and other Irish cities relatively unprotected'. No country should court such dangers, so that while the Irish would be mindful of the international situation, 'Our principal purpose now must be to save our own people.'[185]

Neutrality was merely a vehicle to satisfy these fundamental urges, although they were actually met by non-belligerency. The period 1939–45 saw highly pragmatic policy-making. Despite this, the Irish experience in these years generated a powerful myth of Irish neutrality.

179 Patrick Keatinge, *A Singular Stance: Irish Neutrality in the 1980s* (Dublin, 1984), 17.

180 Longford and O'Neill, 405. De Valera had told the Dáil in Nov. 1943 that 'There is no question . . . of trying to get up on the band-wagon': *Dáil Debates*, 91 (1943), 2130.

181 De Valera, in *Parliamentary Debates: Seanad Éireann: Official Report* (hereafter, *Seanad Debates*), 22 (1939), 1510–35.

182 Carroll, 178; see also Conor Cruise O'Brien, 'Ireland in International Affairs', in Owen Dudley Edwards (ed.), *Conor Cruise O'Brien Introduces Ireland* (London, 1969), 122.

183 De Valera, speech at Galway, 12 May 1940, in *Ireland's Stand*, 21.

184 De Valera, radio broadcast to US, Christmas Day 1941, in *Speeches and Statements*, 463–4.

185 De Valera, United Press interview, 19 Nov 1940, reproduced in *Ireland's Stand*, 29.

Important in this regard was the actual success in keeping Ireland out of the war, which had been achieved under the label of neutrality. While Irish policy had been *ad hoc* and pragmatic, de Valera had 'carried it through so successfully and brilliantly that for many people, including his political opponents, neutrality became a veritable creed'.[186] For most Irishmen it was perceived as a specifically Irish success, the crowning glory of independence, and the confirmation of distinctiveness from Britain. Consequently, neutrality was elevated beyond the realms of normal political debate and acquired an almost hallowed status, despite its absence from the Constitution.

Influential in this process was the Irish world-view, distorted as a result of isolation and censorship. The end of the war saw anti-American protests in Dublin (which possibly had some relevance for the decision on the Atlantic Pact four years later), and the Irish 'were less informed than almost any other people' in Western Europe.[187] There is general consensus that this ignorance had deleterious effects which are perhaps captured most graphically by F.S.L. Lyons's observation that it was 'as if an entire people had been condemned to live in Plato's cave, with their backs to the fire of life and deriving their only knowledge of what went on outside from the flickering shadows thrown on the wall. . . . When . . . they emerged, dazzled, from the cave into the light of day, it was to a new and vastly different world.'[188] As Constance Howard observed, 'the dream had become more real than the hard facts',[189] and as a consequence, according to Dr O'Higgins, the Irish brought up 'a generation blissfully unconscious of facts . . . We have magnified our immunity from war and our neutral position into a major . . . achievement.'[190]

These factors were reinforced by the linking of neutrality with partition, which emerged most clearly in de Valera's famous reply to Churchill on 16 May 1945, when de Valera asked whether a partitioned England would have fought on behalf of the partitioner. To many, this speech was de Valera's finest hour, and it was 'the final, crucial episode in . . . [the] transformation of Irish perceptions of neutrality'.[191]

[186] Carroll, 178. See also Mansergh's comment that what 'had begun as a policy had ended by becoming a symbol', *Survey 1930–52*, 163, and O'Brien, 'International Affairs', 123.

[187] Douglas Gageby, 'The Media', in J. J. Lee (ed.), *Ireland 1945–70* (Dublin, 1979), 125.

[188] Lyons, 557–8.

[189] Howard, in Toynbee and Toynbee, 256. A prominent future Fine Gael politician, Alexis FitzGerald, was to describe neutrality as a 'narcotic': quoted in Bowman, 255.

[190] Dr T. F. O'Higgins, *Dáil Debates*, 94 (1944), 1448.

[191] Ronan Fanning, 'Irish Neutrality: An Historical Review', *Irish Studies in International Affairs*, 1/3 (1982), 32. For de Valera's speech see *Speeches and Statements*, 470–7.

The myth, then, became an established part of Irish political culture, despite its flawed basis. The actual position of Ireland was *sui generis,* and even Keatinge accepts that 'the use of the term neutrality is best qualified in the Irish context',[192] requiring to be seen 'in its specifically Irish context'.[193] Geographical proximity, resource deficiencies, and consequent dependence upon Britain meant 'a certain consideration' for Britain, and non-belligerency rather than neutrality.

[192] Keatinge, *Singular Stance,* 56.
[193] Ibid. 7.

6

'Erstwhile Isolationist'?
1945–1955

MOST of the causes and rationales behind Irish policy did not disappear with the ending of the Second World War. Rather, the foundations of what Lyon describes as an 'erstwhile isolationist's approach',[1] came to be exacerbated by the fact that in Ireland the psychological effect of the war was 'eventually to prove far more significant'[2] than the material effects, and by developments in the immediate post-war period. Some of these developments were within and some beyond Irish control. They served further to entrench the myth of a tradition of Irish neutrality, contributing to 'the process whereby neutrality acquired the sanctity of a dogma that was not merely uncontested but uncontestable. Perhaps "mystery of faith" would be more appropriate than "dogma" since it had still failed to acquire ideological foundations.'[3] This process was aided by Ireland's limited international role, circumscribed because of its exclusion from the embryonic United Nations, although the extent of Irish abstention from international affairs in the post-war decade can be exaggerated. None the less, there was a degree of insularity, and reality failed to penetrate the psyche of either Irish politicians or the Irish public. The legacy of the war, and its apparent confirmation in the period from 1945 to 1955, has been a crucial factor in Irish policy ever since.

The termination of hostilities in 1945 removed a necessary condition of neutrality as classically understood, although 'the emergency' in Ireland continued for another generation. Moreover, the legacy of the wartime years was so potent that the term 'neutrality' continued to have a pervasive influence in Ireland as a description of Irish policy in the years of peace after 1945. Irish policy in that period will, therefore, now be analysed using the criteria already applied to the war years in a modified form to appraise it as a policy 'for' rather than 'of' neutrality. In this period also, although it would be proleptic to analyse Irish policy in

---

[1] Peter Lyon, *Neutralism* (Leicester, 1963), 103.

[2] F. S. L. Lyons, *Ireland Since the Famine*, 2nd edn. (London, 1974), 557.

[3] Ronan Fanning, 'Irish Neutrality: An Historical Review', *Irish Studies in International Affairs*, 1/3 (1982), 35.

terms of non-alignment, two new variables derived from the 'political' pillar of non-alignment will be applied, especially since they reflect the fact that non-alignment is best seen as an attitude of mind or identity rather than as a particular policy.

DUE DILIGENCE

The conclusion of the war did nothing to resolve what for many Irishmen was the fundamental problem regarding the inviolability or otherwise of Irish territory and sovereignty, namely the British presence in Northern Ireland. Indeed, the war years had exacerbated the problem. Partition remained for de Valera and others 'the burning question' that would 'dominate every political issue' in the country, whether 'in times of crisis or in times of no crisis'.[4]

While this issue was to have a dramatic impact upon Irish security policy, the initial concerns in 1944–5 were with the defence of the twenty-six counties, and with planning for both demobilization and the future shape, size and role of the Irish defence forces. It was in fact an Irish General Staff submission to government in August 1944[5] which examined these issues and which, together with the decisions taken on it, 'formed the basis for . . . post-war reorganisation and the size and shape of the army for more than a decade'.[6] The General Staff made a number of assumptions about the basis of future defence policy, which de Valera subsequently told them could be 'taken as substantially representing the Government's defence policy', although modifications might prove 'necessary at a later stage'.[7] There were essentially four major assumptions:

(a) That the State will endeavour to remain neutral in future wars.

(b) That the defence forces will be organised, trained, equipped and maintained on the basis of operating on and in defence of our own territory.

(c) That in the event of Great Britain being involved in another major war, our defence forces would be sufficiently strong to enable the Government to assume complete responsibility for defence of this country so that Great Britain and her allies could not justify a claim that it was necessary to occupy our

    [4] De Valera, Dáil Debates, 122 (1950), 1540–1.
    [5] SPO S13620, memo on the defence forces, submitted by Lt.-Gen. D. MacCionnaith, 23 Aug. 1944.
    [6] Lt.-Col. P. D. Kavanagh (ed.), The Irish Army Handbook 1973 (Dublin, 1973), 15.
    [7] SPO S13620 B, notes of meeting held in the Taoiseach's room, Government Buildings, 2 Jan. 1946, p. 1.

territory or part thereof to protect both this country and Great Britain from invasion by another Great Power.

(d) That the defence forces to be raised, equipped and maintained should be sufficiently strong to ensure that on the one hand Great Britain's enemies would be deterred from attempting to invade this country for the purpose of defeating Great Britain, and on the other, that Great Britain and her allies would be deterred from attempting to invade this country for the purpose of securing bases from which to attack their opponents.

The memorandum then went on 'to consider the most practicable method of implementing' the foregoing.[8]

The General Staff clearly appreciated both the need to have such strength that a belligerent in another war (such as Britain) would not perceive any need to act against Ireland, and the responsibility of a neutral to take active measures to meet the requirements of neutrality. The political debate over the next decade revolved around the extent to which this recognition of principles was to be translated into policy and capability.

Not all members of Dáil Éireann accepted as axiomatic that the Irish State needed an army in the traditional sense. For example, Mr Coogan thought that the army should be organized on a gendarmerie basis, as simply 'a reserve for the civil authority'.[9] Dr O'Higgins, Fine Gael's spokesman on defence and later a Minister of Defence, was himself sceptical of the need for a large army, although he wished the resources to be allocated to air and naval protection instead.[10] In addition, when in opposition he occasionally gave the impression that he saw the main purpose of the army as preserving internal peace, although he acknowledged a ceremonial function and saw advantages in having 'a small nucleus which would be capable of expansion in times of greater emergency'.[11]

For Fianna Fáil this orientation was anathema, since it meant 'your defence will then have to be provided for outside'. Moreover, garrisoning by foreign troops would be necessary 'at the very commencement of . . . operations and any chance you have of maintaining neutrality goes'.[12] Fine Gael disputed this, believing that Britain would never invade and that, therefore, the only danger to Ireland was from an

[8] Ibid. 3.
[9] Coogan, in Dáil Debates, 105 (1947), 68–71.
[10] O'Higgins, ibid. 97 (1945), 1449–51.
[11] O'Higgins, ibid. 105 (1947), 50–1, 62; also ibid. 104 (1947), 447 ff.
[12] Major V. de Valera (Éamon's son), ibid. 105 (1947), 106.

enemy powerful enough to defeat Britain.[13] In that eventuality they felt that there was little that Ireland could do. This line of reasoning was of dubious historical validity and was itself hardly compatible with neutrality. When in opposition Fianna Fáil claimed that the Inter-Party governments (1948–51 and 1954–7) had allowed doubts to arise as to whether Ireland was capable of protecting itself, and as to its neutrality, *inter alia*.[14] As their spokesman put it in June 1955,

If we are really serious about preserving the neutrality of this State, then we ought at least provide the means by which we can protect that neutrality. No nation will take our statements that we are a neutral nation seriously if we do not ourselves make an effort . . . by keeping the Army at the highest possible strength . . . [15]

Fianna Fáil also claimed that wartime neutrality was respected 'mainly by reason of . . . the forces which were there'.[16]

In government all parties paid lip-service to possessing 'a defence force capable of operating in defence of the national territory', with sufficient strength, training, and equipment to allow the Irish government 'to assume complete responsibility for the defence of the country'.[17] However, they also had to contend with the recognition that 'for a country such as this', the objective of 'providing a Defence Force to resist and repel any aggressor' was beyond them. Despite this, Major de Valera, Fianna Fáil's most articulate spokesman on defence, was adamant that the alternative was not to do nothing, since defence was one of the privileges of independence. While absolute defence might be out of the question, 'a more modest view of the problem' was reasonable, involving the objective of minimizing the danger of interference.[18] None the less, in actual policy and provision ambivalence persisted. When asked in 1951 whether Ireland could protect its neutrality, the Inter-Party Minister for Defence, General MacEoin, replied 'I think so', and said that the country would put up 'a very decent show', holding out longer than an opponent might expect:[19] this was not a very positive statement.

---

13 O'Higgins, ibid. 50–1.
14 Traynor, ibid. 125 (1951), 1754.
15 Traynor, ibid. 151 (1955), 1663.
16 Traynor, ibid. 110 (1948), 728.
17 Traynor, ibid. 104 (1947), 434. See also O'Higgins, ibid. 120 (1950), 591, and Traynor, ibid. 100 (1946), 583.
18 Major V. de Valera, ibid. 132 (1952), 674.
19 General MacEoin, ibid. 124 (1951), 1948.

The Irish did recognize that in the new international environment Ireland occupied a pivotal position, lying as it did 'right across the communications of the North Atlantic', so that it 'could not ignore the storm breaking'.[20] Consequently, Oscar Traynor, Fianna Fáil's shadow spokesman on defence in 1951 and subsequently minister, argued that if Ireland left a vacuum and failed to ensure that its territory could not be used by others, 'then it is almost certain that we would find this State of ours in the hands of one or other of the belligerents',[21] not through malevolence on their part, but rather because there would be 'no other military way out' for them, 'as a protection for themselves', in the words of Major de Valera.[22]

The official answer to these problems was deterrence, since Ireland could not necessarily stop an invader, but could, arguably, 'have such a force as would compel any belligerent . . . to deploy relatively large forces . . . [making] the cost both in men and materials relatively high for them'. If Ireland could have sufficient forces to pose problems for a putative belligerent, it could deter him.[23] Some deputies even quoted with approbation the Swedish example.[24] In the Irish case, the hope was to deter partly by making it clear that the costs of continued occupation would be high. Moreover, the Irish explicitly took comfort in the scenario of marginal attack, denying that the full weight of an aggressor was likely to fall upon Ireland,[25] since any attack would be incidental to another operation.[26]

The problem of deciding what constituted 'sufficient' defence forces was further complicated by a division of opinion over the likelihood of war and over where the threat to Ireland came from. On coming into office in 1948 the Inter-Party government established a Cabinet committee to examine the possibility of war,[27] and this concluded that Ireland was 'facing a period of peace and not a period of war'.[28] This influenced

---

[20] Major V. de Valera, ibid. 120 (1950), 629.

[21] Traynor, ibid. 125 (1951), 1754–5.

[22] Major V. de Valera, ibid. 100 (1946), 639. See also Colley, ibid. 110 (1948), 753, 119 (1950), 814.

[23] Major V. de Valera, ibid. 114 (1949), 2015–16. See his contributions also ibid. 120 (1950), 631, 132 (1952), 673 ff.

[24] e.g. Colley, ibid. 110 (1948), 753–4.

[25] É. de Valera, ibid. 122 (1950), 1831 ff.

[26] Major V. de Valera, ibid. 132 (1952), 824.

[27] It comprised An Tánáiste and the Ministers of Finance, Defence, External Affairs, Agriculture, and Industry and Commerce. It attempted to consolidate the experience of 1939–45 and to draft legislative bills in the event of another war: see the reports, ibid. 122 (1950), 1851, 122 (1950), 2022.

[28] O'Higgins, ibid. 114 (1949), 2037; and see also ibid. 114 (1949), 712–16.

policy towards army strength, resources, and roles. Fianna Fáil were less sanguine, fearing especially that there would not again be the 'favourable accident' of 1939–40, which allowed for a build-up of forces, and that the world situation was inherently dangerous.[29] Fianna Fáil were also less sanguine about the likelihood of Britain and/or America not invading, in view of their refusal during the Second World War to give guarantees to respect Irish neutrality.[30] The Inter-Party government was more relaxed about the situation, believing it to be 'beyond question' that Britain would 'never . . . lay a finger on this country'.[31]

In view of this background of rhetoric, it is revealing to examine what actually happened with respect to defence expenditure, equipment procurement, and defence-force strength. Table 6.1 provides evidence of the financial effort: allowing for 1946 and 1947 as periods of adjustment, on average between 1948 and 1955 defence accounted for 6.19% of government expenditure, with some tendency to increase slightly under Fianna Fáil and decrease under Inter-Party governments. By comparison, according to figures given in the Dáil in 1949 and 1950, the Swedes were spending 19–25%, the Swiss 25–30%, the Spanish 30–40%, the Belgians 11%, and the Dutch 22% of total government expenditure on defence.[32] The Irish figure was clearly distinctly smaller than that of both fellow 'neutrals' and small alliance members.

The Irish situation was made worse by the problem of 'warlike stores'. While money was allocated for this purpose—in the period 1946–50, between £397,545 and £117,888 annually,—in the 1947/8 budgetary year only £4,000 was actually spent, and in the following year only £73,000, since the equipment could not be obtained.[33] To some extent the picture changed towards the end of the period, with £4.5m. being spent between March 1952 and June 1955,[34] but over the ten-year period the amount was pitifully small, especially since it was admitted in

[29] É. de Valera, ibid. 119 (1950), 815–16. Major V. de Valera, felt the same: ibid. 114 (1949), 2017 ff.; 112 (1948), 978.

[30] See Traynor, ibid. 110 (1948), 727, 132 (1952), 982–4 and É. de Valera, ibid. 119 (1950), 818.

[31] O'Higgins, ibid. 105 (1947), 49–50.

[32] See Aiken, ibid. 114 (1949), 1969–70, and Major de Valera, ibid. 120 (1950), 693–4.

[33] See O'Higgins, ibid. 114 (1949), 1954–5. See also ibid. 100 (1946), 586; 105 (1947), 42; 120 (1950), 598; 126 (1951), 1178 ff.; 132 (1952), 331 ff.; 136 (1953), 2060; 138 (1953), 1310; 151 (1955), 1589. In 1949 Major de Valera claimed (ibid. 114 (1949), 2025 ff.) that, in the fifteen years before the Second World War, the average shortfall between money allocated and money spent on defence equipment was 11%, so the post-war phenomenon was not new, only more marked.

[34] General MacEoin, ibid. 151 (1955), 1589.

Table 6.1.   Amounts Issued in Each Year for Defence 1946–1955

Period	Year	Government	£	%[a]
To 18.2.48	1946	Fianna Fáil	8,768,712	18.46
	1947	,, ,,	4,983,022	9.43
To 14.6.51	1948	Inter-Party	3,671,891	6.27
	1949	,, ,,	3,674,322	5.68
	1950	,, ,,	3,679,172	5.02
	1951	,, ,,	4,204,303	5.56
To 2.6.54	1952	Fianna Fáil	5,116,519	5.66
	1953	,, ,,	7,037,767	7.54
	1954	,, ,,	7,864,730	7.50
From 2.6.54	1955	Inter-Party	6,667,966	6.32

Note: There may be variations each year in terms of which services came under the Defence heading but these are minor.

[a] % of amounts issued from the Exchequer for Supply Services.

Sources: *Ireland: Statistical Abstract*, 1950, table 182, pp. 144–7; 1955, table 226, pp. 234–7.

1946 that Ireland lacked sufficient armoured vehicles, guns and carriages, parts for rifles and machine guns, and other items.[35]

The size of the Permanent Defence Force (PDF) hardly gives a better impression, as is shown in the following list:[36]

Date	Numbers
1.4.46	13,040
1.3.47	8,750
30.4.48	8,511
1.3.49	8,006
31.3.50	8,113
31.3.51	7,880
31.5.52	10,004
31.3.53	10,562
31.3.54	10,412
31.3.55	9,692

[35] Traynor, ibid. 99 (1946), 2127.
[36] The figures are from *Ireland: Statistical Abstract*, 1955 (Pr. 3018: Dublin, 1956), table 211, p. 220; *Dáil Debates*, 104 (1947), 1732; 111 (1948), 1360; 114 (1949), 2225; and 120 (1950), 522. For 1946, 1947, and 1948 there were additionally 1,286, 1,188, and 86 members respectively of the 'Construction Corps', but these were not regarded as soldiers *per se*.

This hardly suggests a strong force, particularly if one considers the number of men actually capable of being put in the field. On the other hand, official policy made much of the large number of men already trained (as a result of the war) in reserve, who could be quickly called up.[37] However, this was a diminishing asset, so that by 1955 there were only 4,406 in the First Line Reserve and 19,980 in the Second Line Reserve.[38] Moreover, after 1946 the peacetime establishment was officially fixed at 12,860 officers and men in the PDF, with some subsequent minor modifications, but there was continually a shortfall of at least about 20 per cent in the actual numbers in service.[39] Altogether PDF and Reserves were well short of the figures contained in the General Staff plans of 1944, which envisaged total forces of between 60,000 and 120,000.[40] In addition, there was sometimes large-scale absenteeism from training among the reserve forces, especially the Second Line Reserve.[41]

There was thus a failure to fulfil self-assigned objectives, a problem compounded by the General Staff's unease about relying upon a voluntary system of recruitment. In 1944–5 the General Staff had warned the government of the difficulties of rapidly expanding a small cadre.[42] In fact, compulsory military training was more seriously considered than public statements imply,[43] but it was rejected, and although the problems of the size of the army and of the reserves were often debated, little of substance was achieved.[44]

The situation was even worse with regard to Irish air and naval services, despite the fact that the country was an island. Traynor and others knew that if they were 'serious in regard to the policy of neutrality . . . the least that would be expected from a nation with a coastline such as we possess would be that we should be capable of patrolling that

[37] O'Higgins, ibid. 113 (1948), 1460.

[38] *Ireland: Statistical Abstract, 1955* (Pr. 3018; Dublin, 1956), table 211, p. 220.

[39] Traynor, *Dáil Debates*, 104 (1947), 429. The figure was reduced to 12,500 within a couple of years only to be increased to 12,743 by Fianna Fáil in 1951: ibid. 126 (1951), 1178.

[40] SPO S13620 memo, on the defence forces, 5–6, and app. 1.

[41] O'Higgins, in *Dáil Debates*, 119 (1950), 885–7.

[42] SPO S13620, memo on the defence forces, 7–8, 12–17.

[43] See e.g. SPO S13620B, notes of meeting held in the Taoiseach's room, 2 Jan. 1946; SPO S13620, addendum 1; and *Dáil Debates*, 110 (1948), 882 ff., 919; 114 (1949), 2025, 2040; 119 (1950), 884; 120 (1950), 593 ff., 719; 126 (1951), 1199; 132 (1952), 537; 138 (1953), 2379; 139 (1953), 348.

[44] For the flavour of the debate see *Dáil Debates* 99 (1946), 2130, 2142, 2163, 2173; 104 (1947), 429, 707–9; 110 (1948), 722, 822, 910; 114 (1949), 2017 ff.; 120 (1950), 593 and 605; 132 (1952), 685; 138 (1953), 2416; 151 (1955), 1587, 1659, 1667.

coastline and ensuring that it would not in any way be used to the detriment of other countries'.[45] But little was actually done.

In October 1945 the General Staff had recommended the immediate 'purchase of two corvettes, to be followed by the annual purchase of one corvette until six have been acquired', and detailed the tasks that the new naval service should perform.[46] In discussions on the submission, ministers appear to have been concerned about whether the service 'would give value for the money expended on it', and only three corvettes were agreed to, with doubts as to whether the Cabinet would agree to more.[47] Three corvettes were purchased from Britain late in 1946, and by the early fifties they comprised the Irish Naval Service, remaining 'the mainstay of the service right up to the nineteen seventies'.[48] It was impossible for such a navy to fulfil the tasks originally assigned by both General Staff and successive governments.

In 1944 the General Staff had also planned for a 'small air force'[49] of perhaps '10 fighter squadrons', with a first step being an actual purchase of five.[50] In discussions on the plan de Valera made clear that 'ordinarily this country would not possess sufficient aircraft for war purposes'.[51] In the following years purchases were made of Spitfires, Seafires, Ansons, and reconditioned Magisters, and by the summer of 1953 it was announced that all aircraft in use by the Air Corps had been purchased since 1946 and all had been new when purchased.[52] However, the force was now dated and in addition it was decided only in 1953 to provide concrete runways at Baldonnel.[53] In the summer of 1955 plans were put into operation to purchase three jet trainers and four piston-engined trainer aircraft.[54] In the early fifties the Air Corps had between twenty and thirty-two aircraft.

The Irish clearly failed to meet the requirements of 'due diligence': indeed, in conversations with the American Secretary of State and the President in March 1951, the Inter-Party Minister for External Affairs,

[45] Traynor, ibid. 151 (1955), 1597; and see O'Higgins, ibid. 100 (1946), 607; 105 (1947), 50. At other times both were Minister for Defence.

[46] SPO S13620, memo on the defence forces; addendum 2, 8, passim.

[47] SPO S13620 B, notes of meeting held in the Taoiseach's room, 2 Jan. 1946, pp. 5–7.

[48] Capt. J. Sheehan (ed.), Defence Forces Handbook (Dublin, n.d.), 63.

[49] SPO S1362, memo on the defence forces, 5.

[50] Ibid., app. 1, 34–6.

[51] SPO S13620 B, notes of meeting held in the Taoiseach's room, 2 Jan. 1946, p. 2, SPO S13620.

[52] See Traynor, in Dáil Debates, 100 (1946), 587; 105 (1947), 45, and 139 (1953), 673, and General MacEoin, ibid. 151 (1955), 1590. See also Sheehan, 61.

[53] Dáil Debates, 141 (1953), 178.

[54] General MacEoin, ibid. 151 (1955), 1590.

Sean MacBride, admitted that 'Ireland was unable to defend itself', and was 'quite defenceless'.[55]

RECOGNITION OF NEUTRAL STATUS

In spite of everything, Ireland was not isolated from the world. By 1952–3 it was making payments to thirty-three international organizations[56] and had some form of diplomatic representation in eighteen states, although some of their representatives were accredited to more than one state.[57] However, a striking feature of Ireland's diplomatic profile was the lack of representation in the Soviet Union and Eastern Europe, a factor which did affect Soviet perceptions of the Irish.[58] The perceptions of others may also have been influenced by the fact that, with the ending of the war, the practice resumed of using the King's signature on letters of credence, a practice which lasted until the Republic of Ireland Act came into operation on Easter Day 1949.[59]

An early test of the Irish position after the war and of others' perceptions of it, came with the question of membership of the United Nations. On a number of occasions in the summer of 1946 de Valera specifically invoked the 'attitude taken by the other neutral States' as a model for Ireland, initially when he advocated a lack of urgency in making an application,[60] but a month later when he urged the need for decision.[61] While the Swiss position was described as unique, de Valera also told the Dáil that 'Sweden is in a practically analogous position to ours . . . Her parliament has agreed in principle [to apply for membership]'.[62]

De Valera told the Dáil that the Potsdam Agreement suggested that Ireland would be accepted,[63] but his own department, the Depart-

---

55 Memo of conversation: call of Minister for External Affairs, Sean MacBride, 13 Mar. 1951, Box 66, Acheson Papers, Truman Library (T L); and Memo of conversation, 23 Mar. 1951, ibid. Some Dáil Deputies felt the same: Dáil Debates, 139 (1953), 437.

56 Dáil Debates, 143 (1953), 2426.   57 Ibid. 143 (1953), 1738; 179 (1959), 64.

58 See below, p. 165.

59 See Nicholas Mansergh, Survey of British Commonwealth Affairs: Problems of Wartime Co-operation and Post-war Change 1930–1952 (O U P, 1958), 268 ff., and Dillon in Dáil Debates, 101 (1946), 2181–2, 106 (1947), 2326.

60 É. de Valera, Dáil Debates, 101 (1946), 2452. For a discussion of Irish entry see Norman MacQueen, 'Ireland's Entry to the United Nations 1946–1956', in Tom Gallagher and James O'Connell, Contemporary Irish Studies (Manchester, 1983).

61 É. de Valera, Dáil Debates, 102 (1946), 1469–70. On the change see Irish Times, 22 July 1946, in S P O S13750 A.   62 É. de Valera, Dáil Debates, 102 (1946), 1325.

63 É. de Valera, ibid. 102 (1946), 1311; he referred specifically to the Potsdam Agreement.

ment of External Affairs, had already told the government that, despite Potsdam, 'candidatures are apt to be regarded not so much on their merits as from the point of view of their probable effect on the distribution of political forces and voting power within the organization'.[64] This assessment proved correct, and the Soviets vetoed the Irish application. It is interesting that, by way of contrast, the Swedish application proved acceptable.[65] The Irish were vetoed four times by the Soviets. The Soviet arguments were the absence of conventional bilateral relations,[66] Irish failure to aid the laying of the foundations of the organization, and Irish 'open sympathy with the Axis and with Franco Spain'. Therefore, the Irish lacked 'the qualities which are required by the Charter'.[67] In 1955 Ireland was finally admitted as a result of a 'package deal', a deal which was 'So intricate . . . that Ireland's membership was in doubt up to the last moment', with the Soviets nearly vetoing again 'all the Western nominees'.[68] The Irish were clearly perceived by the Soviets as part of the hostile camp.

The leader of the other camp, the United States, was influenced in its attitudes to Ireland by the experiences of 1941–5 and also by its perception that it was itself now in another 'real war'.[69] Despite the experiences during World War II, the United States had as its avowed objective, 'to ensure the collaboration of Ireland as an ally with the Western Powers in any future conflict'.[70] The US Legation in Dublin did not believe this to be unachievable, if 'properly presented and the moment well chosen', since important elements of Irish opinion were 'not disposed to support a policy of neutrality in terms of present day threats to peace'. The Irish would not accept the humiliation of capitulation to British terms, but 'something could perhaps be achieved' by an American or Canadian approach.[71] Indeed, even when it became clear

64 SPO S13750, Dept. of External Affairs, memo for the Govt., 11 July 1946.

65 On the general background see MacQueen, 68–9, and Inis L. Claude, *Swords into Plowshares: The Problems and Progress of International Organisations*, 3rd edn. (London, 1965), 81–3. Claude suggests that the Soviets vetoed what they regarded as 'potential adherents to the Western grouping'.   66 MacQueen, 'Ireland's Entry', 68, citing UN doc. S/PV 57, 29 Aug. 1946.

67 *Irish Press*, 31 July 1947, reporting on the UN membership committee meeting at Lake Success on 30 July 1947.   68 MacQueen, 'Ireland's Entry', 71; Claude, 85.

69 For an elaboration of this view see NSC 68/2, 'Report by the National Security Council on United States Objectives and Programs for National Security', 30 Sept. 1950, President's Secretary's Files, Box 209, Truman Papers, TL.

70 State Dept. Policy Statement on Ireland 1948, RG84, Box 702, Washington National Records Center (WNRC).

71 State Dept. Policy Statement on Ireland: memo from the Dublin Legation, 7 Dec. 1948, RG84, Box 702, WNRC.

that the government would not sign the North Atlantic Treaty, George Garrett, the head of the US Legation, was still sure that if he had been 'permitted to go to higher places . . . I could have cracked the situation and avoided the impasse as it has now materialized'.[72] He also reported that MacBride had told him that he was committed to accepting the Atlantic Pact provisions 'if [the] Partition issue [was] removed . . . there was no question whatsoever about this'.[73]

As of 1 April 1949 the CIA believed that Ireland was 'already ideologically aligned with the West . . . strongly Catholic and anti-Communist, and, in spite of military weakness and the Partition issue, would probably not remain neutral in an East–West war'. It did acknowledge that the Irish attitude might not change in 'anything short of war', and that Irish participation might provoke 'civil disorder'. None the less, it argued that even de Valera was not likely to insist upon neutrality in a 'Holy War', while MacBride did not believe that 'Ireland would remain neutral in the event of war'.[74]

The Irish rejection of the North Atlantic Treaty changed the American perception, as is shown by a National Security Council (NSC) Staff Study in October 1950. Considering whether the United States should offer inducements to Ireland to join NATO or some bilateral arrangement, the NSC decided against. This was partly so as not to encourage others to seek bilateral arrangements rather than NATO membership, but also because, while Irish neutrality 'undoubtedly would be more benevolent' than in 1939–45, there were 'no indications that the Irish would abandon neutrality even if by so doing a strong contribution to the anti-communist forces would be made'. In any case, the 'denial of Ireland to enemy forces is already encompassed in existing NATO commitments'.[75] This 1950 decision was still considered valid in November 1960.[76]

While such assessments were being made, the possibility of a deal of arms for a bilateral agreement was discussed, apparently on the initiative of Garrett. It was proposed that the British offer technical assistance and

[72] Garrett to Hickerson, Director, Office of European Affairs, State Dept., 8 Apr. 1949, RG84, Box 703, WNRC.

[73] Garrett to Secretary of State, 18 Mar. 1949, RG84, Box 703, WNRC.

[74] CIA: Ireland SR-48, President's Secretary's Files, Intelligence File, Truman Papers, TL.

[75] NSC Staff Study, 'The Position of the United States Regarding Irish Membership in the NATO and Military Assistance to Ireland Under a Bilateral Arrangement', 17 Oct. 1950, NSC 83/1, President's Secretary's Files, Truman Papers, TL. See also NSC 83, which is attached to it. This view was adopted by the NSC.

[76] Memo., James S. Lay, jun., Executive Secretary, NSC, to the NSC, 10 Nov. 1960: attached to copy of NSC 83/1, ibid.

military aid. Most interestingly, Garrett wrote to President Truman that in 'the event this proposal was approved, MacBride . . . volunteered to make an all-out effort to secure bipartisan support for a bilateral treaty of defence'. Garrett felt that this 'would . . . bring Ireland into the defence picture' against the communists.[77] Subsequently, in 1951, in meetings with the American Secretary of State and the President, MacBride raised 'the subject of the desirability of some military assistance being provided for Ireland', and advised the Americans on how best to carry on the struggle against communism. He repeated that, but for the political difficulties caused by Partition, Ireland would join NATO.[78]

Any American doubts about Ireland were removed when the Fianna Fáil government rejected the amendment to the Economic Co-operation Act of 1948 which came about with the Mutual Security Act passed by Congress in 1951. The 1951 Act made future American assistance conditional upon the recipient's willingness to contribute to the 'defensive strength of the free world'.[79] Ireland told the Americans that it could not accept this condition, 'altering its established foreign policy . . . by . . . undertaking to render military assistance to other nations'.[80] Ireland was now putting a price on its principles, albeit that the price was small, since the bulk of assistance had already been received.[81]

A factor in other states' perception of Ireland was Irish Catholicism. For example, this appears to have encouraged Spanish officials to see Ireland as a possible member of 'a neutral bloc' for the 'defence of the Catholic religion and resistance to Communism', since 'Ireland was an essentially Catholic' country.[82] The Irish did not wish to become involved with Spain, Portugal, and the Argentine, but the perception of

---

[77] Garrett to Truman, 10 July 1950, Official File 218, Truman Papers, TL.

[78] Memo of conversation between MacBride and Acheson 13 Mar. 1951; and Acheson: memo of conversation of 23 Mar. 1951, Box 66, Acheson Papers, TL.

[79] Mutual Security Act 1951.

[80] Aide-mémoire of Matthews (Head of Dublin Legation): Aiken, conversation of 7 Jan. 1951, in SPO S15231 A. This file contains other relevant material on this issue: e.g. Aiken, in letters, told the Americans that 'Partition . . . dominates . . . [the Irish] approach to all questions of external policy.'

[81] Even with the suspension of aid, it was expected that Ireland would receive 'the benefit of the entire authorized commodity program', some $146.2m., although $900,000 of technical assistance was to be lost, in addition to some currency complications. See memo from Theodore Tannenwald, jun., Office of the Director for Mutual Security, to Charles Murphy, White House, 25 Feb. 1952, Official File 218, Truman Papers, TL.

[82] John A. Belton, Irish Legation in Madrid, reporting conversation with Director of the Foreign Political Section of the Spanish Foreign Office: Senor Erice said it was a 'purely personal' idea (Belton to The Secretary, Dept. of External Affairs, 8 Apr. 1948, S14291 A/1).

Ireland as Catholic was strong.[83] It was also valid, since in 1946 94.3 per cent of the population were Roman Catholic, a figure which did not significantly alter for a generation, while there was also a practising rate of over 80 per cent.[84] Irish Catholics were strongly concerned about the persecution of the Church in Eastern Europe and in Far Eastern countries where Irish missionaries were active. The influence of the Vatican and Pius XII was strong. This affected others' perceptions all the more, in view of the activities of 'professional Catholics', who were always ready to raise the spectre of atheistic Communism; such Catholicism was 'anti-Soviet in a sense in which it was not anti-Nazi'.[85]

On the other hand, despite occasional hiccups, there was a strong identity of values with the United States, and MacBride even claimed that Ireland supported the 'cardinal principles' of American policy,[86] although the CIA regarded Aiken as 'extremely anti-British and anti-American'.[87] Most of the Irish political élite agreed with MacBride that Irish 'sympathies . . . lie clearly with the nations of Western Europe',[88] and that Ireland was 'an essentially democratic and freedom-loving country . . . anxious to play her full part in protecting and preserving Christian civilization, and the democratic way of life', albeit thwarted by Partition.[89] Ireland agreed 'with the general aim of the . . . Atlantic Pact',[90] and in 1955 Liam Cosgrave, Minister for External Affairs, reiterated Irish commitment to 'a policy of co-operation with peoples who, like ourselves, have a Christian and democratic way of life'.[91] His Taoiseach, John A. Costello, had affirmed that Ireland was not ethically neutral but had a duty to help the West,

[83] e.g. American officials asked the Vatican if it would give 'indirect advice' to Ireland on the Atlantic Pact. The Vatican did make known its views to the Irish. See correspondence between Gowen and Ranney, Ranney and Garrett, Ranney to Gowen, and Gowen to Ranney in RG84, Box 703, W N R C. Ranney was in the State Dept. Division of British Commonwealth Affairs and Gowen was one of Truman's representatives to the Vatican.

[84] See Basil Chubb, *The Government and Politics of Ireland* (O U P, 1974), table A.10, p. 328, and J. H. Whyte, *Church and State in Modern Ireland 1923–1979*, 2nd edn. (Dublin, 1980), 5–6, 382.

[85] Nicholas Mansergh, 'Ireland: The Republic Outside the Commonwealth', *International Affairs*, 28/3 (July 1952), 288. See also Michael O'Corcora and Ronald J. Hill, 'The Soviet Union in Irish Foreign Policy', *International Affairs*, 58/2 (Spring 1982); Marcus Wheeler, 'Soviet Interest in Ireland', *Survey*, 21/3 (1975); Michael MacGreil, *Prejudice and Tolerance in Ireland* (Dublin, 1977); and CIA SR-48. See *Dáil Debates*, 103 (1946), 1322–402, for a debate on the imprisonment of Archbishop Stepinac in Yugoslavia.

[86] MacBride to U S National Press Club, in *Eire-Ireland* (Bulletin of the Dept. of External Affairs), 78 (2 Apr. 1951).   [87] CIA SR-48.

[88] MacBride, *Dáil Debates*, 112 (1948), 903.

[89] MacBride, ibid. 114 (1949), 323–6.

[90] MacBride, ibid.

[91] Cosgrave, ibid. 152 (1955), 540.

and that its influence would 'always be directed against the threat of Communism'.[92]

However, while Ireland was hostile to some countries and supportive of others, there were limits to how far the Irish would go to offer support against the threat of Communism.

DISAVOWAL OF EXTERNAL HELP

To some extent treatment of this variable has been implicit in the foregoing discussion, particularly with regard to the clear evidence of Irish sympathies and the lack of 'due diligence'. It could be argued that this latter was based upon implicit assumptions, particularly in Fine Gael, about British attitudes and behaviour and the degree to which Ireland had been and was protected by 'the second mightiest navy in the world . . . That is our naval defence'.[93]

Certainly, there was no explicit disavowal of this 'protective umbrella', and it can be argued that the Irish did not rule out the acceptance of help. While the question of attitudes to alliances will be dealt with in the following section, it is relevant to note in the current context that in opposition two sometime Ministers for Defence, General MacEoin and Oscar Traynor, acknowledged that Ireland would need and accept help if attacked: Traynor, of Fianna Fáil, while arguing that Ireland must have a strong army and a deterrent capability, acknowledged that 'it would be a question, as it was in the past, of retaining our territory for the longest possible time until such time as we could receive help from one of the other interested parties in a world strife'.[94] Furthermore, Major de Valera repeatedly attempted to show that 'whether . . . neutral . . . or whether you envisage co-operation with the Western Powers',[95] the desiderata of Irish policy and 'the general plan for its implementation can and should be so framed as to fit either situation'.[96]

Dr O'Higgins (another sometime Minister for Defence) occasionally seemed willing to go further,[97] while General Mulcahy, the Fine Gael

---

[92] Costello, speech to Fine Gael Ard Fhéis 1951, reported in Eire-Ireland, 72 (13 Feb. 1951). See also a Costello speech in the Dáil: Dáil Debates, 152 (1955), 566 ff.

[93] O'Higgins, Dáil Debates, 105 (1947), 52.

[94] Traynor, ibid. 151 (1955), 1665; and cf. MacEoin, ibid. 132 (1952), 504 ff.

[95] Major V. de Valera, ibid. 114 (1949), 2015.

[96] Major V. de Valera, ibid. 120 (1950), 627.

[97] See O'Higgins, ibid. 72 (1938), 773; 105 (1947), 52, and 104 (1947), 407. In 1938 he had said that if 'we are going to stand alone, and absolutely alone, the most reasonable defence policy for us is absolute disarmament . . .' (loc. cit.).

leader in 1947, argued that Ireland was 'unique in the world' if it thought it could defend itself with its own resources. Lack of consultation with friends meant that money spent on defence was being wasted. For Mulcahy, 'if we do not realise the lines on which they are thinking we are simply going to act irresponsibly'.[98] Others complained of a lack 'even of a gentleman's agreement',[99] or proposed co-operation with the British and American navies,[100] or suggested a defence arrangement with Britain and common defence of the British Isles.[101]

Fianna Fáil complained that Fine Gael appeared to be flirting with such ideas, and asked 'Is there any alliance?'[102] In April 1950, as Minister for Defence, O'Higgins poured scorn on such suggestions, denying 'Emphatically' and 'categorically' that such arrangements had been made and reminding the House that any arrangement would in any case require Dáil approval.[103] However, he limited his reply to formal arrangements and it is interesting that in December 1948 the US Legation in Dublin was noting the '[not] infrequent visits made to the Irish Chief of Staff by the GOC Belfast and vice versa'.[104] None the less, the Taoiseach was adamant that no Irish representative 'either directly or indirectly, by implication or otherwise, entered into any commitment on defence matters with any other country'.[105] Despite this, it is clear that contact between the military of both states occurred, and the links were reinforced by numbers of Irish officers being sent on courses in both Britain and the United States.[106]

In fact, the Irish were acting in a highly pragmatic way, since there was no question of a principled foreclosure of assistance. While formal plans do not appear to have been laid, the Irish were clearly keeping the door open and trying to maintain their freedom of decision and action. Unfortunately, such a policy faced a number of constraints.

---

[98] General Mulcahy, ibid. 105 (1947), 97–104 (the quotation is from 104); cf. ibid. 104 (1947), 729.   [99] Coogan, ibid. 105 (1947), 65.

[100] Coogan, ibid. 104 (1947), 561.

[101] Capt. Giles, ibid. 105 (1947), 84.

[102] Traynor, ibid. 119 (1950), 804; Moran, ibid. 104 (1947) 720.

[103] O'Higgins, ibid. 120 (1950), 587–8.

[104] American Legation memo by Chapin, 7 Dec. 1948, RG84, Box 702, WNRC.

[105] Costello, Dáil Debates, 113 (1948), 1123. In 1946 Traynor similarly denied any arrangements or steps relating Irish defence to that of others with an interest in the Atlantic: ibid. 103 (1946), 1101.

[106] The Irish government were anxious for their officers to receive training abroad. The problem of language meant that it was overwhelmingly to Britain and the US that officers went, and a degree of familiarity was probably established. See Traynor, ibid. 100 (1946), 657; 103 (1946), 1101 ff.; Dillon, ibid. 99 (1946), 2180; and O'Higgins, ibid. 132 (1952), 558 ff.

FREEDOM OF DECISION AND ACTION

One problem for Ireland was that while its 'legal status' was 'that of a neutral . . . laws have never been able to contravene economic forces', and that the Americans, for example, regarded Britain and Ireland as economic 'Siamese twins',[107] or, in CIA terms, Ireland as an 'economic satellite' of Britain.[108] This was the situation, despite all the previous talk of self-sufficiency—indeed, this term disappeared from the Irish political lexicon.

The main problem was the financial and economic dependence upon Britain, as is demonstrated in Table 6.2. Over the period 1946–55, on average 51.5 per cent of Irish imports were from Britain and 88 per cent of exports to Britain. The dependence upon Britain was exacerbated by financial ties, so that when Britain devalued in 1949 so too did Ireland. A further complication was Ireland's 'meager endowment of natural resources' and the consequent need to import all their petrol and 75 per cent of their coal, to take two examples. A saving grace, as in the war years, was that there was over 90 per cent self-sufficiency in food, although even in this sector 'wheat for flour, animal feed-stuffs, and fertilizers' needed to be imported.[109] While food caused no apprehensions, there was concern at the lack of an economic base in other areas.[110] For example, Aiken noted that if Ireland lacked a properly equipped army, 'if we have not got a reasonable amount of the essentials of life within our shores . . . the decision will be made by somebody else and we will be kicked around'. It was, therefore, necessary to organize not only 'national military defences but our economic defences' so as to be capable of making 'our own decision' and having a reasonable chance of sticking to it 'during the war, in spite of what anybody else may say'.[111]

In fact, post-war planning appears to have taken little cognizance of economic defence,[112] and this is shown most clearly by the attitude to

---

[107] State Dept. Policy Statement on Ireland, 1948: records of the US Legation at Dublin, Irish Delegation memo, 7 Dec. 1948, RG84, Box 702, WNRC.

[108] CIA SR-48, p. 108; and see Patrick Keatinge, *A Place Among the Nations: Issues of Irish Foreign Policy* (Dublin, 1978), p. 139, and Donald Harman Akenson, *The United States and Ireland* (Cambridge, Mass., 1973), 111–12.   [109] CIA SR-48, p. 20.

[110] Costello, *Dáil Debates*, 122 (1950), 2006–7; cf. MacBride, in the *Irish Independent*, 9 Apr. 1949; Major V. de Valera, in *Dáil Debates*, 132 (1952), 817 ff.; 120 (1950), 670, and Capt. Giles, ibid. 132 (1952), 371.

[111] Aiken, ibid. 119 (1950), 827.

[112] Although Major V. de Valera spoke on the topic regularly: ibid. 119 (1950), 827–8; 120 (1950), 668–70.

Table 6.2. Irish Exports and Imports from and to Great Britain and
Northern Ireland 1946-1955 (%)

Year	Imports	Exports
1946	52.2	92.3
1947	41.5	88.6
1948	53.9	87.3
1949	57.3	89.9
1950	52.9	86.7
1951	46.8	84.0
1952	50.9	86.1
1953	50.7	90.5
1954	55.7	88.6
1955	52.7	87.2

Sources: Ireland: Statistical Abstract, 1950, table 100, p. 82; 1956, table 112, p. 130.

arms production. The General Staff in 1944 had mentioned the need for a munitions factory,[113] but the Fianna Fáil government decided to defer the issue,[114] despite the fact that Ireland was 'not able to produce a .22 bullet or even a shot-gun cartridge', and that all equipment and ammunition 'came from across the water'.[115] Even by 1950 all bullets and rifles came from 'outside the shores' of Ireland.[116] The Fianna Fáil government reopened the issue of a munitions factory in 1951, but nothing came of it,[117] essentially because of the lack of raw materials and the conclusion that three days' working would meet the army's annual requirements.[118] Even de Valera, on a visit to America in 1948, had to admit that as a small nation, Ireland was 'unable to provide its own means of defence', and could only obtain supplies if this suited the purposes of the Great Powers.[119] The problem for Ireland was that for most of the period it did not so suit their purposes; in view of their own preoccupations they did not wish to meet Irish requirements, so that only 'driblets' of supplies were received.[120]

113 SPO S13620, memo on the defence forces, 27-8.

114 SPO S13620 B, notes of meeting held in the Taoiseach's room, 2 Jan. 1946.

115 Capt. Giles, in *Dáil Debates*, 99 (1946), 2195.

116 O'Higgins, ibid. 119 (1950), 888.

117 Traynor, ibid. 127 (1951), 278.   118 O'Higgins, ibid. 132 (1952), 357.

119 É. de Valera, speech on 3 Apr. 1948, New York, in his *Speeches and Statements by Éamon de Valera 1917-73* ed. Maurice Moynihan (Dublin, 1980), 502.

120 O'Higgins, *Dáil Debates*, 120 (1950), 589; and see O'Higgins, ibid. 114 (1949), 2034; 132 (1952), 350-1; 139 (1953), 431; and General Mulcahy, ibid. 99 (1946), 2158.

As the Korean situation eased, so too did the Irish problem: a Supplementary Estimate was introduced in March 1953 for weapon procurement,[121] and it was confessed in that summer that a 'heavy leeway' had to be made up.[122] However, there were contrary fears of obsolescence and worries about the rising cost of equipment,[123] so that within two years the new Inter-Party government was suggesting 'a cautious attitude towards the purchase of conventional weapons of the heavier and less mobile types', and in 1954 both Fianna Fáil and Inter-Party governments cut back equipment-purchase estimates.[124] Moreover, shipping continued to be a problem.[125] All in all, it is difficult to see how the Irish could have performed their avowed policy of relying on their 'own strength to hold this island against anybody'.[126]

Economic autarky received further blows from the change in Europe away from protectionism towards liberalization, and the impetus to international economic co-operation provided by the Marshall Plan announcement of June 1947.[127] Initially the Irish had doubts about these developments, and Sean Lemass attacked the fallacious notion that economies are complementary rather than competitive.[128] Moreover, de Valera was wary of surrendering any independence, arguing that it would be 'most unwise for our people to enter into a political federation which would mean that you had a European Parliament deciding the economic circumstances, for example, of our life here'. Ireland 'did not strive to get out of that domination of our affairs by outside force or we did not get out of that position to get into a worse one', although Ireland would co-operate to the extent commensurate 'with our liberty to look after the fundamental things'.[129]

In fact, participation in the European Recovery Programme and the OEEC were judged to be acceptable, but perhaps more important was the realization that Ireland could not raise her living standards unless she looked beyond the confined home market. Albeit hesitantly and while trying to maintain protectionist tariffs, she signed a 'host of binational economic agreements' with European states.[130]

[121] Traynor, ibid. 136 (1953), 2061.   [122] Traynor, ibid. 138 (1953), 1309 ff.

[123] O'Higgins, ibid. 113 (1948), 1459–60.

[124] General MacEoin, ibid. 151 (1955), 1589.

[125] É. de Valera, ibid. 122 (1950), 1831–40; 119 (1950), 815.

[126] O'Higgins, ibid. 119 (1950), 884.

[127] Akenson, 109.

[128] For the debate on the Convention of European Economic Co-operation and the contributions by Lemass and MacBride see *Dáil Debates*, 111 (1948), 1979–2077.

[129] É. de Valera, ibid. 152 (1955), 548–9.

[130] Akenson, 109–10; but Lyons, p. 625, argues that Ireland did not abandon protectionism.

Interestingly, Partition was not allowed to obtrude into these economic developments.

However, the aspiration to independence remained powerful. As de Valera put it in July 1950, 'What could be regarded as of greater value than the maintenance and integrity of this State . . . of our independence . . . our way of life . . .?'[131] In fact, some were already beginning to answer by pointing to economic prosperity,[132] and it can be argued that the difficulties encountered in the economic realm only served to provide an added edge to the desire to assert unequivocally sovereignty in the political sphere. This preoccupation was not the preserve of one party, and it was also inextricably intertwined with 'the first object' of the domestic and foreign policies of Fianna Fáil and Inter-Party governments, the ending of Partition.[133]

This period, then, saw a marked concentration upon and agitation regarding Partition, epitomized by de Valera's anti-Partition campaign after leaving office in 1948.[134] This agitation fundamentally shaped the political environment within which other questions were debated and decided. The period 1946–55 saw a reinforcement of the symbiosis between this issue and the avowed aspiration 'to keep out of any entanglements . . . any wars . . .'. [135] However, this relationship was influenced by a changing external environment, where European inter-dependence was growing. Moreover, the Irish had a number of other objectives, such as a concern with the maintenance of international peace and security, prosperity, and global order and justice.[136] They thus found themselves having to reconcile a number of objectives rather than paying exclusive attention to one or two. The question of Irish attitudes to membership of the United Nations was an early manifestation of some of the difficulties which these concerns produced.

In July 1946, for example, de Valera presented the issue of UN membership as essentially involving one question: was membership the course 'most likely to preserve the independence of this country?' Yet, in the next paragraph, the key question appeared to be: 'are we more

See also Patrick Lynch, 'The Irish Economy since the War, 1946–51', in Kevin B. Nowlan and T. Desmond Williams (eds.), *Ireland in the War Years and After* (Dublin, 1969), 190.

131 É. de Valera, *Dáil Debates*, 122 (1950), 1831–40 (quotation in text from col. 1833).

132 Akenson, 107–29.

133 Nicholas Mansergh, 'Irish Foreign Policy 1945–51', in Nowlan and Williams, 136.

134 Keatinge, *A Place*, 112–13; id., *The Formulation of Irish Foreign Policy* (Dublin, 1973), 285.

135 O'Higgins, *Dáil Debates*, 105 (1947), 49–50.

136 See Keatinge, *A Place, passim.*

likely to keep out of war by joining an organisation of this sort' or by remaining outside?[137] De Valera appeared to equate the two questions, but there is no necessary equation, and the objectives could have proved contradictory.

A full study of the obligations of membership was undertaken, and these were made clear to both government and Dáil. The discussion was based on a rather literal reading of the Charter, which tended to emphasize the obligations, since no one was sure how the United Nations might evolve, especially with respect to Article 43 and the negotiation of military agreements between the Security Council and member states. According to the Department of External Affairs, it was clear that 'once the Security Council has decided that enforcement measures should be taken, the members are obliged to carry out the . . . decision'. Incidentally, the possible existence of the Military Staff Committee was one of a number of matters which were not regarded as giving rise 'to any major question of principle'.[138] The Attorney-General believed that Ireland was obliged to negotiate a military agreement, and was, moreover, concerned that the Charter involved members agreeing, 'inter alia, to engage in war on the call of the Security Council', a situation which clashed with the Dáil's constitutional rights in that regard.[139] Despite such briefings, the Fianna Fáil Cabinet favoured membership.[140]

De Valera specifically brought to the attention of the Dáil Articles 25, 33–7, and 43–5, making clear the perceived obligation to make a military agreement, and stating that 'If the Security Council decides that action should be taken against a particular State, and that action leads to war, we must participate in that action and enter the war.' There was no question of accepting 'the advantages of collective security and of avoiding obligations'. As to the constitutional issue, the Dáil would have to deal with that when it arose, bearing in mind that international undertakings should be honoured.[141] If anything, de Valera drew a 'worst-case scenario' and the Dáil still agreed to membership.

137 É. de Valera, Dáil Debates, 102 (1946), 1465. The previous day he argued that membership would neither help nor hinder unity: ibid. 1324.

138 SPO S13750, memo for the Govt., Dept. of External Affairs, 'Membership of the United Nations Organisation', 11 July 1946.

139 SPO S13750, 'Membership of United Nations', Ard-Aighne [Attorney-General], 18 July 1946.

140 The Cabinet decided to apply on 30 July 1946, SPO S13750.

141 É. de Valera, Dáil Debates, 102 (1946), 1315 ff.

The Dáil appreciated that membership 'may undoubtedly involve us in war in certain contingencies' but was generally supportive.[142] Despite concern as to whether the calls upon Ireland would be
disproportionate to its resources,[143] there was a general willingness to
accord collective security a higher priority than neutrality. It was
recognized that collective security demanded that Ireland be 'really loyal
members', committed to taking 'collective action with other people'
and ready to engage, if necessary, in 'a war of enforcement'. The Irish
accepted that they might have 'to face the waging of war in order to
prevent war'[144] and that traditional sovereignty was 'not consistent with
the idea of collective security', since in a system of collective security you
surrendered 'the right to do at any time just as you please', being
'prepared to accept some deciding authority other than your own
will'.[145]

Not all Dáil members supported membership. Those against were
concerned that the Irish had 'sold our right to declare our position as
one of neutrality',[146] that Ireland would be involved in war,[147] and
that, unlike in 1939–45, the ports and airfields would be used by a
belligerent.[148] However, opponents lost the argument, essentially because of a pervasive belief that the United Nations and collective security
afforded a better prospect of peace than did neutrality.

The initial failure to achieve entry led to the accrual of doubts about
the organization itself, as did the first decade of its operations.[149] De
Valera, MacBride, and Costello all considered the possibility of with-
drawing the Irish application, and the actual entry aroused little enthusiasm.[150] Costello announced entry on 15 December 1955, noting that,
since the 1946 debates, the Korean War had made clear that Article 43,
with its requirement to make available armed forces, was not mandatory.[151] It should be noted that Irish disenchantment with the United
Nations stemmed from concern at its weakness, not its strength.

[142] Coogan, ibid., 102 (1946), 1381.

[143] See e.g. O'Higgins, ibid., 102 (1946), 1401–3; but General Mulcahy was more sanguine,
ibid. 1330.   [144] É. de Valera, ibid. 1466–7; and see also ibid. 101 (1946), 2450–1.

[145] É. de Valera, ibid. 102 (1946), 1312–13.

[146] Maguire, ibid. 1414.   [147] Cafferky, ibid. 1368–9.

[148] Oliver J. Flanagan, ibid. 1395–8. He was against it for other reasons also.

[149] There was distaste for the notion of a 'deal' to achieve entry, and anger at the insult to
national dignity: Cogan ibid., 104 (1947), 4, and 117 (1949), 999.

[150] See É. de Valera, ibid. 886, and the speech of 3 Apr. 1948 in New York, in his
Speeches and Statements, 504; MacBride, Dáil Debates, 112 (1948), 903–4: Costello, in Eire-
Ireland, 77 (19 Mar. 1951); and Finan, Dáil Debates, 138 (1953), 734, for a backbench view.

[151] For the announcement and exchanges between Costello and de Valera on whether a debate
was necessary see Dáil Debates, 153 (1955), 1601–8.

The Irish were also confronted with conflicting pressures and the need to decide policy with respect to their attitude to help, as already discussed, and to bilateral and regional security arrangements. Some in Ireland appreciated the significance of their geographical proximity to Britain and their key position in the Atlantic.[152] Many accepted that Irish security 'would be bound up with Britain's security',[153] and Cogan noted that even if one had a 'very deep quarrel' with neighbours, if a fire broke out, all would co-operate to extinguish it.[154] Moreover, some backbenchers drew attention to the fact that Ireland was a thirty-two-county nation,[155] that defence would be stronger if the whole nation made common cause against communism, and that co-operative schemes on drainage and railways already existed.[156] Some in the North clearly felt the same and in January 1949 the Northern Ireland Premier proposed talks on a joint defence arrangement on the basis of the constitutional status quo.[157] Over two years earlier, in July 1946, there were brief Anglo-Irish exchanges on the 'old question' of a deal involving defence and unity, but they petered out, as had previous exchanges.[158] The British were fearful that 'any suggestion that we are prepared to give the matter consideration, is . . . certain to lead to serious trouble'.[159] For his part de Valera retained his scepticism about the British ability to deliver,[160] and warned the Dáil more generally about the dangers of 'entering into arrangements which involve military alliances', since Irish 'history is there with a warning finger to us as to what is likely to happen if we do it'.[161] Moreover, independence was regarded as a right to be acquired, not bargained over.[162]

A further bilateral possibility was an arrangement 'with the most powerful of all the nations that stand for the protection of freedom', especially in view of the historical Irish–American ties.[163] If the United

[152] e.g. Major V. de Valera, ibid. 114 (1949), 2011–12.

[153] MacBride interview to United Press, 12 Feb. 1949, S P O S14291 A/1.

[154] Cogan, in *Dáil Debates*, 120 (1950), 700 ff.; but Mr Hickey interjected 'Surely you are helping John Bull when you do that?'

[155] MacCarthy, ibid. 152 (1955), 118.

[156] See e.g. Capt. Giles, although he acknowledged some difficulties, ibid. 132 (1952), 368–71, and 139 (1953), 387.   [157] *Irish Times*, 19 Feb. 1949.

[158] Norman Archer, an official at the Dublin British embassy, reported on this conversation. For fuller details see John Bowman, *De Valera and the Ulster Question 1917–1973* (O U P, 1982), 262–4, citing P R O D O 35/1228/W. X.101/154.

[159] Bowman, 264, citing Addison, Cabinet memo, 'Eire and Northern Ireland', 18 Oct. 1946, P R O C A B 129/13, C P (46) 391.

[160] É. de Valera, *Dáil Debates*, 152 (1955), 550–2.

[161] É. de Valera, ibid. 550–2.

[162] É. de Valera, *Irish Times*, 17 Mar. 1951. De Valera said that there could be no 'bargaining of that sort'.   [163] Cogan, *Dáil Debates*, 120 (1950), 700.

States called for talks, should not the Irish at least enter into discussions to see what was involved and what the United States might offer in return?[164] As already noted, in private MacBride did seek to explore certain possibilities, but just as the British were wary of trouble in such arrangements, so too the Americans feared that any such bilateral deal with the Irish would undermine American pressure for 'collective defence' and might deter others from joining the new North Atlantic Treaty, as well as creating 'friction and resentment' with NAT signatories.[165] While the Inter-Party government might have favoured some arrangement, principally perhaps to secure equipment,[166] Fianna Fáil tended to feel that if the West felt threatened it should support Ireland, even without a formal treaty.[167] In addition, in 1953 de Valera claimed that a majority would be against a bilateral treaty with the Americans, especially if it involved American bases in Ireland.[168]

Many in Ireland felt it impossible to 'consider entering into any . . . military commitment . . . for joint defence so long as she is denied . . . national unity and freedom'.[169] Ireland could not 'possibly ally itself with an army that occupies portion of its territory'.[170] Partition was 'the keystone' in the 'arch of foreign policy' thrown across 'the chasm that separated a small neutral from . . . belligerent powers'.[171] This feeling was especially pertinent because of de Valera's anti-Partition campaign and the atmosphere created by the Republic of Ireland Act and the British riposte, the Ireland Act, which confirmed the status quo regarding Partition.[172] This atmosphere influenced a makeshift coalition, lacking in confidence,[173] which occupied government between 1948 and 1951, and was composed of an ideologically diffuse grouping, even including the strongly republican Clann na Poblachta.

The factors militating against Irish support for bilateral arrangements

---

[164] Cogan, ibid. 177 (1949), 998–9.

[165] NSC 83/1, NSC Staff Study on 'The Position of the United States Regarding Irish Membership in NATO and Military Assistance to Ireland Under a Bilateral Arrangement', 17 Oct. 1950.

[166] See Dillon, Dáil Debates, 99 (1946), 2179, although he was in oppossition at the time.

[167] É. de Valera, ibid. 120 (1950), 723–6.

[168] É. de Valera, in an interview with United Press International: see Eire-Ireland, 208 (9 Nov. 1953).

[169] Aiken, in letter to Francis P. Matthews, US Legation in Dublin, 24 Dec. 1951, SPO S15231 A.

[170] O'Higgins, Dáil Debates, 119 (1950), 884.

[171] Lyons, 590.

[172] For an excellent account of this episode see Mansergh, Survey 1930–52, 262–304.

[173] The American Legation certainly were struck by this particular point: see Chapin to Acheson, 4 Mar. 1949, RG84, Box 703, WNRC. See also Lyons, 590.

also operated with respect to multilateral regional arrangements. Again, because of the division of the world into two opposing camps, several leading Irish figures called for some Irish relationship with the Western-minded States. Mulcahy, for example, talked of the need for regional conceptions of defence policy,[174] while Dillon wanted Irish involvement in a United States–Commonwealth arrangement, which might be open to certain European states. Such an arrangement would 'build a citadel for independence . . . and above all [allow] . . . the undying freedom of Bishops to discharge the duties of their pastoral office'.[175] Mulcahy, Dillon, and O'Higgins, whose sympathy was strongly with the British, were all in the Inter-Party government.[176]

Fianna Fáil opposed such ideas for the reasons already advanced regarding bilateral arrangements, and because of a general antipathy towards alliances: alliances involved recompensing partners as well as receiving help,[177] and one's partners would remain primarily interested in themselves.[178] Particularly important was the view that small nations should be cautious when entering alliances because such entry could bring them 'willy-nilly, into . . . wars'. Ireland 'would not be consulted in how a war would be started . . . when it was ended . . . [or] the terms on which it should end'.[179] Moreover, defeat for a small nation meant that it would be 'utterly destroyed—effaced from the earth'.[180]

In the planning for the Atlantic Pact in 1948, Ireland was usually mentioned in the lists of those to be invited to participate, albeit possibly as 'limited members, with 'graded membership'.[181] Ireland was also considered for full membership, and on 14 April the Canadian Under-Secretary of State asked the Irish High Commissioner in Ottawa how

---

[174] General Mulcahy, *Dáil Debates*, 104 (1947), 441–4.

[175] Dillon, ibid. 101 (1946), 2190–1. See also ibid. 104 (1947), 471, and 106 (1947), 2388. Coogan occasionally spoke in a similar vein: ibid. 102 (1946), 1341, 1388–9; 104 (1947), 557–9. See also 'Ireland and the Atlantic Pact', *Round Table*, 39/155 (June 1949).

[176] So too was Patrick McGilligan as Minister for Finance. On 1 Nov. 1948 he circulated privately to Fine Gael colleagues in Cabinet a memo in which he recommended joining the Brussels treaty and entering negotiations with the Commonwealth on mutual defence: Patrick McGilligan Papers, University College Dublin Archives, P35/c/185. I am grateful to Professor Raymond Raymond for bringing this to my attention.

[177] É. de Valera, *Dáil Debates*, 110 (1948), 911–12.

[178] É. de Valera, ibid. 122 (1950), 1831–40.

[179] É. de Valera, ibid. 152 (1955), 548.

[180] É. de Valera, speech on 3 Apr. 1948, New York, in his *Speeches and Statements*, 502 and cf. *Dáil Debates*, 120 (1950), 712.

[181] See Sir Nicholas Henderson, *The Birth of NATO* (Boulder, Colo., 1983), 17, 48–50, 55, 61–2, 77–8. Graded members would be able to remain neutral until their partners determined that their belligerency would be more helpful.

the Irish would respond 'to a proposal on the lines . . . of the basic commitment in the Rio Pact' for the 'Atlantic Nations'.[182] The report of the conversation was circulated to all Cabinet members and what ensued forced the Irish, instead of simply talking about their attitude, to make a decision concerning regional security arrangements. While there is a dearth of information about the Cabinet's discussions,[183] it is extremely revealing that at no stage did any Irish official statement simply declare membership in the proposed Atlantic Pact to be unacceptable because of Irish neutrality. Indeed, other reasons were advanced and neutrality *per se* appears to have played little part in the decision.

Discussion of the issue did not occur at a propitious moment, because of the furore over Partition in 1948–9, although several members of the coalition government were sympathetic in principle to some kind of regional security arrangement, and it has been claimed that 'a Fine Gael government, *with a safe majority of its own* . . . would eventually have committed itself to NATO'.[184] Certainly the American Legation in Dublin felt that Costello might be sympathetic[185] and it also reported on the privately expressed 'dissatisfaction over the course of events' by ministers,[186] and the 'disillusionment' of many Fine Gael supporters.[187] However, the decision was by no means straightforward, since other elements in the coalition, especially the Clann na Poblachta, had fought the 1948 election primarily on the issues of the establishment of an Irish republic, and an end to Partition, as well as on social radicalism.[188] Moreover, the Irish Labour Party had a traditional attachment to neutrality.[189] Thus, while the American Legation felt that it could have

---

[182] Report of meeting between J. J. Hearne, Irish High Commissioner, and Pearson, Canadian Under-Secretary, on 14 Apr. 1948: SPO S14291 A/1.

[183] The relevant State Paper Office files (SPO S14291, S14291 A/1, and S14291 A/2) contain, apart from speeches and press cuttings, only the Hearne report of the Pearson warning.

[184] Conor Cruise O'Brien, 'Ireland in International Affairs', in Owen Dudley Edwards (ed.), *Conor Cruise O'Brien Introduces Ireland* (London, 1969), 124–5 (emphasis in original). Lyons, 592, suggests that they 'might' have.

[185] Garrett, reporting to Hickerson at the State Dept. said that Archbishop MacQuaid thought it worth approaching Costello, 11 Feb. 1949: Decimal File of the Dept. of State 840.20/2-1149, National Archives Building, Washington, DC (NAB).

[186] Garrett to Acheson, 12 Apr. 1949, RG84, Box 703, WNRC. He also reported that not all of Fianna Fáil 'was' happy with the Irish position.

[187] Chapin to Acheson, 4 Mar. 1949, RG84, Box 703, WNRC.

[188] The two Clann na Poblachta ministers were MacBride (whom Akenson, p. 122, has described as 'an Anglophobe', and Lyons, p. 560, as one of the 'die-hard republicans') and Dr Noel Browne, who in later years vehemently opposed Irish entry to the European Community because it was, amongst other things, a threat to neutrality.

[189] See the contribution by Johnson, the Labour Leader, in *Dáil Debates*, 18 (1927), 625–40.

mobilized support for some arrangement, there were difficulties, especially given the political attitude to Partition. In addition, after sixteen years in opposition coalition members appear to have put a premium on keeping de Valera out, especially since for some of them he was a greater enemy than either Britain or Russia.[190] Furthermore, de Valera's anti-Partition campaign posed the danger that the coalition would be out-flanked on the national question, a risk which they sought to avoid. While it would be mistaken to argue that de Valera had such prescience that he would actually have engaged on such a campaign 'to forestall attempts to involve Ireland in future military alliances', his emphasis made any movement towards such involvement far more difficult and had the effect of contributing to Irish abstention.[191]

In this environment it was not clear what the Irish response to any invitation to adhere to the Atlantic Pact would be. Ultimately they declined, but the key question is whether this was because of expediency or principle, and—if the latter—did the principle concern Partition or neutrality?

On 7 January 1949 the Americans handed MacBride an *aide-mémoire* on the proposed Pact, which invited Ireland to help draft the treaty and to be one of the 'original signatories'. The *aide-mémoire* spelt out the proposed obligations, specifically that 'all parties would take such action as might be necessary to restore and assure the security of the area' by a 'definite obligation' to contribute to collective defence both before and after any attack, although such a contribution would be commensurate with the 'resources and geographic location' of the state. Crucially, it was suggested that the obligations 'would not necessarily involve in every case declaration of war in the event of armed attack', since in democracies it was usually a 'parliamentary prerogative' to declare war, and there might be advantages to the alliance if not all members were involved in a war.[192]

On 8 February 1949 the Irish replied by reaffirming Irish commitment to democracy, freedom, and Christianity, but also arguing that a corollary was concern for human rights and national self-determination. The Irish wished to play their 'full part' in protecting such values and were in agreement 'with the general aim of the proposed Treaty'.

---

190 'Ireland and the Atlantic Pact', *Round Table*, 216.

191 O'Brien, 'International Affairs', 125; and cf. also Keatinge, *A Place*, 92.

192 For this *aide-mémoire*, and the further *aide-mémoire* of 8 Feb., 25 May, and 3 June 1949, and a verbal reply to the Irish Minister in Washington on 31 Mar. 1949, see *Texts Concerning Ireland's Position in Relation to the North Atlantic Treaty* (P. 9934; Dublin, 1950) (hereafter *Texts re NAT*). The US *aide-mémoire* is at pp. 3–4.

However, Partition involved a denial of Irish territorial integrity, and the 'elementary democratic right of national self-determination', as well as allowing 'undemocratic practices' in Northern Ireland. British occupation of six of Ireland's 'north-eastern counties' against the will of the Irish people meant that

> any military alliance with, or commitment involving military action jointly with, the State that is responsible for the unnatural division of Ireland, which occupies a portion of our country with its armed forces, and which supports undemocratic institutions in the north-eastern corner of Ireland, would be entirely repugnant and unacceptable to the Irish people. No Irish Government, whatever its political views, could participate with Britain in a military alliance while this situation continues, without running counter to the national sentiment of the Irish people. If it did, it would run the risk of having to face, in the event of a crisis, the likelihood of civil conflict within its own jurisdiction.

It was argued that on a small island only an integrated defence under a single authority with popular support had a chance of success, and that Partition denied to the Dublin government the productive capacity of 'the industrial area of the country', thus weakening its capacity. Alliance with the occupying power would lack 'the necessary sympathy and support' of the people. Nevertheless, there was no hostility to Britain, and it was 'inconceivable . . . [that] Ireland should ever be a source of danger . . . to Britain in time of war'. On the contrary, a united Ireland would be in the interests of Britain and the other participating states. Given this, the Irish sought American help to resolve Partition.[193] In sum, Partition was the central objection, partly because of its undemocratic aspects and partly because of its economic, political, and military consequences. With some variation, these arguments were repeated over the following months and years.

The allies' reply was simply that the Pact was 'not a suitable framework' in which to resolve bilateral Anglo-Irish difficulties and that Partition was 'not considered . . . [to be] connected in any way with membership' in the Pact.[194] MacBride took umbrage at this and tried for over two years to persuade the United States to intervene and take up the Irish case.[195] He failed.

---

[193] All quotations are from the Irish *aide-mémoire* of 8 Feb. 1949, ibid. 4–7.

[194] Verbal reply to Irish Minister in Washington, Nunan, on 31 Mar. 1949, ibid. 7.

[195] See e.g. Garrett to Acheson, 24 May 1949, RG84, Box 703, W N R C; Acheson, memo of conversation with MacBride, 11 Apr. 1949, ibid., and memo of conversations of 13 Mar. 1951, MacBride and Acheson, and 23 Mar. 1951, MacBride, Acheson, and Truman, in Acheson Papers, Box 66, T L. For some of the background see Garrett to Acheson, 2 Feb. 1949, RG84, Box 702; Chapin to Acheson, 4 Mar. 1949; Garrett to Acheson, 18 Mar. 1949; Garrett to Acheson, 21 Mar.

On 4 April 1949, in the presence of the Irish Minister in Washington, the North Atlantic Treaty was signed.[196] Nearly two months later the Irish government made a full and considered reply to the American position. Before reiterating the previous arguments, it argued that the British 'Ireland Bill' appeared, amongst other things, to be 'specifically designed to bring the six north-eastern counties of Ireland within the scope of the mutual undertakings' regarding territorial integrity in the North Atlantic Treaty, and thereby attempted to accord Partition 'a new measure of international guarantee and recognition'. The Irish thereby rejected the alleged lack of connection between adherence and Partition, and insisted that Partition was 'the sole obstacle to Ireland's participation in the Atlantic Pact'.[197] Again there was no reference to neutrality and again Washington refused to rise to the bait regarding Partition.[198] It is interesting that the Irish sought agreement to make these exchanges public, thus making it a matter of international knowledge that they had only one objection to participation in the Atlantic Pact.[199]

Partition was undoubtedly the key factor, although Raymond has tried to establish that it was used 'as a reason . . . merely in legitimation of a policy dictated by political expediency', as a 'useful smokescreen' against the failure of the coalition's domestic programme.[200] Clearly a number of factors were relevant, but the role of Partition ought not to be underestimated, in view of the political environment of 1948-9 and MacBride's background of involvement with the IRA. Moreover, even when discussions were first broached with the High Commissioner in Ottawa, Partition had been indirectly alluded to as a problem.[201] Before and after the question became public, ministers told the Dáil 'time and again', according to O'Higgins, that successive

---

1949; Hickerson to Garrett, 14 Apr. 1949; Garrett to Acheson, 8 Apr. 1949, all in RG84, Box 703, WNRC; and Garrett to Hickerson, 11 Feb. 1949, Decimal File of the Dept. of State 840.20/2-449, NAB.

[196] The Irish presence was noted by the Irish press: see Garrett to Acheson, 5 Apr. 1949, RG84, Box 703, WNRC.

[197] Irish aide-mémoire, 25 May 1949, Texts re NAT, 8-10 (emphasis added).

[198] US aide-mémoire, 3 June 1949, ibid. 10-11.

[199] The French were initially opposed, the Belgians reluctant, and the US 'neutral' about agreeing: see Ranney-Wapler, Counselor, French Embassy, memo of conversation, 13 Sept. 1949, RG84, Box 703, WNRC.

[200] Raymond James Raymond, 'Irish Neutrality: Ideology or Pragmatism?', International Affairs, 60/1 (Winter 1983-4), 36-9.

[201] J. J. Hearne, Irish High Commissioner, in response to Pearson, 14 Apr. 1948, SPO S14291 A/1.

governments had argued that 'alliance is unthinkable and impossible for a divided partitioned country'.[202] In July 1948 MacBride had said that Partition prevented Ireland from taking its rightful place in a number of developments,[203] a view with which de Valera concurred, since it was 'ridiculous that we should be asked to join in' to create a large bloc, 'whilst Ireland was deliberately kept cut in two'.[204] The American Legation also privately reported that 'the government . . . [was] opposed to signing while the question of partition remained unresolved',[205] and the CIA reported that feeling over Partition was 'genuine, not artificial; constant, not occasional. If political parties keep the issue before the people, it is because they cannot do otherwise and continue to exist.'[206]

MacBride told the Americans privately that if Partition were ended 'there was no rpt. no question whatsoever' but that Ireland would accept the Pact's provisions,[207] and in April 1949 he was reported in the *Irish Press* as saying that Ireland 'would join the Atlantic Pact as a full charter member immediately after British forces were withdrawn from the Six Counties', since it would then be maintaining its own 'territorial integrity and political independence'.[208] Moreover, he thought that in such a situation the Irish people would be united behind the treaty.[209] O'Higgins described membership as 'the natural thing' if circumstances were different.[210] De Valera suggested that a proper basis of Anglo-Irish relations would lead to 'the normal reaction here' concerning the Pact,[211] and that, given independence and unity, Ireland would 'probably have the same inducements to join as other nations',[212] and that in such circumstances 'he would advocate entrance into the Pact'.[213] These utterances suggest a belief in Dublin in the possibility of a deal involving unity and participation, and also significantly lack any reference to neutrality as a reason for abstention.

With respect to a deal, the Irish politician simply failed 'to appreciate

202 O'Higgins, in *Dáil Debates*, 113 (1948), 1341.
203 MacBride, ibid. 112 (1948), 903 ff.
204 É. de Valera, ibid. 931.
205 Garrett to Acheson, 2 Feb. 1949, RG84, Box 702, WNRC.
206 CIA SR-48, p. 15.
207 Garrett to Acheson, 18 Mar. 1949, RG84, Box 703, WNRC.
208 *Irish Press*, 23 Apr. 1949.
209 *Irish Independent*, 9 Apr. 1949.
210 O'Higgins, *Dáil Debates*, 120 (1950), 590–1.
211 É. de Valera, press conference, 18 June 1951, SPO S14291 A/2.
212 É. de Valera, statement, 16 Mar. 1951, ibid.
213 Both *Irish Times* and *Irish Independent* on 22 Mar. 1949 carried this report.

or evaluate with proper emphasis the interest that is taken abroad in matters affecting Ireland'—a particular failing, the Americans believed, of MacBride[214]—although, in addition, the wartime pressure led the Irish to exaggerate the Allies' need of them. In reality, an NSC study in October 1950 concluded that, while Ireland was 'Strategically located' and afforded 'valuable sites' for air and naval operations, those sites were 'not considered essential at this time', certainly not so essential as to jeopardize the principle of collective defence. Irish participation would be welcome if 'unqualified'.[215] Few in Ireland appreciated this basic assessment.[216] If some were ready to bargain, only a few insisted that neutrality was a principle not to be bargained away. Despite the almost incidental role of neutrality in the debate, the shibboleth of 'no NATO' subsequently became closely identified with neutrality.

Even those who, like Raymond, attack the conventional wisdom regarding the role of Partition do not seek instead to suggest that there was a principled adhesion to neutrality. Rather, Raymond cites the fear of a 'loss of independence in foreign policy'.[217] It is possible to support this argument by reference to the attitude of An Tánaiste, William Norton, who wished Ireland 'to detach' itself 'from the groups and the blocs of power',[218] and de Valera himself, who claimed that Ireland gained respect in the 1930s because it was 'taking an independent attitude'.[219]

On the other hand, there is little evidence in the period 1945–55 of any consistent attempt to evolve a distinctive Irish position. Although MacBride made clear his view that 'Europe cannot continue for ever to live as an armed camp' and needed 'an ideal round which [Europeans] can rally' as an alternative to communism, he was unable to give the Americans any concrete suggestions when asked to elaborate.[220] Moreover, he acknowledged that alliance was 'wholly right' in certain circumstances.[221] In addition, perhaps to compensate for non-participation in the Atlantic alliance, MacBride went out of his way to

214 Chapin to Acheson, on 4 and 21 Mar. 1949; Garrett to Acheson, on 18 and 21 Mar. 1949, RG84, Box 703, WNRC.

215 NSC Staff Study, NSC 83/1, 17 Oct. 1950.

216 See e.g. Brigadier O. Gowan, addressing the Literary and Philosophical Society, University College, Cork, reported in the *Irish Times*, 19 Feb. 1951, SPO S14291; and *Round Table*, 'Ireland and the Atlantic Pact'.

217 Raymond, 'Irish Neutrality', 39–40.

218 Norton, *Dáil Debates*, 102 (1946), 1350.

219 É. de Valera, ibid. 101 (1946), 2448.

220 MacBride to Garrett, 19 Mar. 1949, RG84, Box 703, WNRC.

221 Acheson, memo of conversation with MacBride, 11 Apr. 1949, RG84, Box 703, WNRC.

decry anti-Americanism,[222] and to support American foreign policy in general: he expressed regret, for example, that American efforts in Korea should be misinterpreted as military aggression.[223] None the less, for Irishmen who formed the political élite of 1945–51, independence was the main preoccupation.

Raymond also draws attention to other issues, such as economic fears and worries over the possibility of foreign bases on Irish soil. He suggests that it was believed that 'additional military expenditure of the order of IR £14–20 million' would be required after membership, at a time of constraint upon defence spending.[224] If this was a factor, it is surprising that there is no evidence of the Irish seeking financial aid from the Americans to ameliorate it. Similarly, another argument that the installation of bases would increase the prospect of Ireland becoming a target takes no account of the fact that an aggressor would first need to overcome British air defence. Perhaps more significant was a calculation that Ireland could 'secure all the advantages of being within the ambit of the Pact without any of the disadvantages of subscribing to its terms'.[225] Equally important is that Irish participation was never considered vital enough to generate sufficient allied pressure upon them. Being 'une île derrière une île', had certain advantages.

None of the above arguments points to principled neutrality *per se*. For all those who mentioned it, an equal number complained that Eire was fiddling 'not only while Rome but all Christianity trembled on the brink of a Red inferno'.[226] What really mattered was Partition and independence, partly because many of the Irish political élite actually cared about it and partly because after years in the political wilderness the Coalition parties did not wish to be outflanked on the national question by de Valera, but wished rather to deprive the opposition of issues.[227] The principle of Partition was reinforced by expediency, but neutrality hardly came into play.

Parallel with these debates were the many developments and initiatives concerning European integration. While Ireland abstained from the Brussels Treaty of 1948[228] and from the ECSC, it was a founder member of the OEEC and the Council of Europe, and unofficial Irish representatives were present at the Congress of Europe at The Hague in

---

[222] MacBride, *Dáil Debates*, 136 (1953), 1170.   [223] MacBride, ibid., 122 (1950), 1603–4.
[224] Raymond, 'Irish Neutrality', 39–40.
[225] *Round Table*, 'Ireland and the Atlantic Pact'.
[226] Cogan, *Dáil Debates*, 117 (1949), 999.
[227] This view was put very strongly by Chapin to Acheson, 4 Mar. 1949, RG84, Box 703, WNRC.   [228] Despite Patrick McGilligan's memo of 1 Nov. 1948: see above, n. 176.

May 1948.[229] The Irish attitude appeared to revolve around a distinction between high and low politics, with abstention not only from defence organizations but also from those which touched on the integrity of the State and the sensitive issue of sovereignty. The Council of Europe and OEEC were acceptable, since they imposed 'no obligations which are inconsistent with our national rights', while, as has been seen, it was felt that NATO did, because of the possible danger to 'territorial integrity'.[230] The Irish also favoured the OEEC and Council of Europe because of their basis of unanimity.[231] While MacBride appeared to support European integration in principle, he was also a nationalist, so that, although he accepted that few could object to surrendering 'a part of their national sovereignty', if by so doing 'they could avoid utter destruction' and war, he could also see that sovereignty was 'a matter for consideration' and that the rights of small nations needed to be safeguarded.[232]

De Valera was anxious to distinguish military from non-military co-operation, although he was somewhat wary even of the latter, believing that Ireland 'would not be wise . . . in entering into a full-blooded political federation'. None the less, he recognized that Ireland had 'interests . . . in common with other countries', and should therefore co-operate so long as it was 'consistent with our own reasonable well-being' and Ireland was not precluded from building up its own economy.[233] Partly for this reason, the Irish tended to follow the British minimalist and *ad hoc* approach, steering clear of any transfer of sovereignty and lacking the continental sense of need and urgency regarding European unity.[234] In addition, of course, 'neither coal nor steel played any major role in the Irish economy (other than imports)', so that Ireland was not an obvious candidate for the ECSC.[235]

---

[229] Senators Douglas and Butler, and Professor Tierney.

[230] É. de Valera, in an Associated Press interview, 2 Apr. 1952, in response to a specific question as to why Ireland could participate in some but not other organizations: SPO S14291 A/2.

[231] For MacBride's contributions and the debate generally on these issues see *Dáil Debates*, 111 (1948), 1979-2077; 117 (1949), 694-716, 741-8.

[232] MacBride in the Seanad debate on The Hague Congress, *Seanad Debates*, 35 (1948), 809 ff. See also *Dáil Debates*, 111 (1948), 1989, 2067; 117 (1949), 694; 122 (1950), 1590-607.

[233] É. de Valera, in *Dáil Debates*, 152 (1955), 548-50; see also ibid. 120 (1950), 1608; 117 (1949), 707-11.

[234] See e.g. Gerald Boland in *Assembly Debates*, 6th Ordinary Session (3rd part), 33rd sitting, 6 (1954), 933.

[235] Miriam Hederman, *The Road to Europe: Irish Attitudes 1948-61* (Dublin, 1983), 36 and passim; and Denis Maher, *The Tortuous Path: The Course of Ireland's Entry into the EEC 1948-73*

Partition was felt to be important, and it became routine to raise it as a grievance in the Consultative Assembly of the Council of Europe[236]—so routine, in fact, that it dominated Irish contributions to the debate on a European army in August 1950, with severe denunciations of a European 'freedom army'[237] while Ireland was still 'not free'. Even before Churchill was able to put his motion de Valera joined with Norton in a tirade, and all four Irish members voted against Churchill's motion.[238] On the other hand, the Irish do not appear to have complained too much when the change in rules allowed the Consultative Assembly to discuss certain 'political problems connected with the security of Europe', and they did not vote against the motion.[239]

Next to nothing was said concerning the 'European army' or the EDC within Ireland itself,[240] although Miriam Hederman suggests that the latter 'was regarded with some favour in Irish circles which followed the debate "on the mainland" ', since 'the new idea of a genuinely multi-national defence had no particular prejudices to overcome'. But fundamentally it was regarded as suitable for others, not Ireland, in view of the Irish position and the unacceptability of 'the concept of Irish soldiers serving with, under and over British soldiers', albeit that they would be only part of a collective force.[241] In fact, the EDC was never an issue.

In December 1954 the Consultative Assembly discussed the Paris Agreements leading to the WEU. The Irish members generally supported it, although Boland said that he intervened diffidently, given Irish inability to take part in the movement for European defence. None the less, he had a 'personal interest' in the question, 'realising that a strong Western Europe is the best guarantee for the preservation of peace'. He also described himself as 'feeling that on this subject I was more an

---

(Dublin, 1986), for a general review of Irish attitudes to Europe. Aiken, incidentally, welcomed the Schuman initiative, although he did not believe in the 'sector appproach', *Assembly Debates*, 2nd session, 19th sitting (1950), 1030-2.

[236] It became known as the 'sore thumb' policy: see Lyons, 591.

[237] Norton, *Keesing's Contemporary Archives*, viii (1950-2), 11085.

[238] É. de Valera, ibid. 11086. Hederman, 37, argues that MacBride would have voted differently, but offers no evidence.

[239] Although Oliver J. Flanagan spoke against the idea in the Dáil, arguing for neutrality: *Dáil Debates*, 138 (1953), 813–17. See also A. H. Robertson, *The Council of Europe*, 2nd edn. (London, 1961), 46–7; and report of the Committee of Ministers, 1951, in *Documents of the Consultative Assembly 1951* (Strasburg 1951), doc. 5; and *Documents of the Consultative Assembly 1950*, (Strasburg 1950), pt. ii, doc. 4, and pt. iii, doc. 8.

[240] For an example of a rare mention see *Dáil Debates* 128 (1951), 549.

[241] Hederman, 38 and 47.

observer than a Representative'.[242] Another Irish member implied that he objected to the stretching of 'the Statute . . . by bringing in the question of defence', and referred to defence as 'the cancer in the heart of the Council of Europe' and a diversion from its 'primary aims' of rebuilding ravaged Europe in the economic, cultural, social, and ultimately political fields. None the less, he still expressed support for 'an integrated European defence system under a specialized authority'.[243]

Fundamentally, however, these proposals generated none of the excitement of the 1948–50 debates about the Atlantic Pact; indeed, those debates appear to have prevented a genuine debate about the European dimension, a situation which lasted for over a decade.

LACK OF ISOLATIONISM

Despite the foregoing focus upon the Irish position, Ireland was not at the centre of events in the post-war decade. Indeed, by 1948 Ireland was 'almost wholly isolated from the mainstream of world events and without the means to influence them': the exclusion from the United Nations, coming so soon after Ireland's wartime abstention, had 'led to considerable diplomatic isolation'.[244] The Irish were involved in Europe, but their pursuit of the 'sore thumb' strategy of raising Partition at every opportunity gave the impression that they were introspective and somewhat detached. They appeared 'content to let the world go by, heeding it only when necessity forced . . . [them] to do so', and their outlook was 'essentially isolationist'.[245] The preoccupation with domestic issues, Partition, and Anglo-Irish questions led to 'little positive thinking' about foreign policy,[246] a situation further exacerbated by resource constraints, geography and the ideological divide in the world.

On the other hand, the Irish, aware of the millions of Irish living abroad—'the missionaries . . . the Wild Geese, the diaspora'[247]—felt that they had an influence 'far in excess of . . . mere physical size and the smallness of . . . population', because of their 'spiritual dominion'.[248]

242 Boland, *Assembly Debates*, 6th Ordinary Session, 3, 33rd sitting, 6 (Dec. 1954), 932.
243 Crosbie, ibid. 958–9.
244 Keatinge, *Formulation*, 29.
245 Michael Macdonagh, 'Ireland's Attitude to External Affairs', *Studies*, 48 (1959), 78.
246 Ibid.
247 Douglas Gageby, 'The Media', in J. J. Lee, *Ireland 1945–70* (Dublin, 1979), 129.
248 Costello, in his Montreal speech, 1 Sept. 1948, in his *Ireland in International Affairs* (Dublin, 1948), 28–9.

De Valera himself thought that Irish 'spiritual' resources allowed a materially small Ireland to 'play a very important part in international affairs'.[249] In addition, there was a feeling that the Irish freedom struggle was a model for others, especially since Ireland lacked 'any imperialistic ambitions'[250] or involvement in 'power politics'.[251] There was also an awareness that 'even if it were desired to maintain a policy of complete isolation, this . . . [was] no longer possible' in the shrinking post-war world.[252]

Yet, if the Irish had perceptions of influence, the lack of constructive thinking meant that there was little distinctive and positive Irish contribution to the world. Instead, it was a case of what the Irish were against, with only faint glimmerings of an aspiration not to be as identified with one camp in the cold war struggle as the overwhelming welter of their statements suggested. There was an even fainter glimmering of an aspiration to be part of a third force, with backbenchers occasionally floating the suggestion of Irish participation in a 'barrier . . . to prevent . . . America and Russia . . . from involving the world in war', although the proposed composition of this barrier varied widely.[253] Some hoped that the British Commonwealth might organize a third force of neutral nations,[254] while other suggestions involved a league of small nations[255] or of small specifically European countries,[256] or even a league of the disarming.[257]

During this period the Irish made no significant efforts at mediation. The MacBride version of mediation saw Ireland as a link between Western Europe and the United States,[258] while with respect to the Korean War, de Valera argued that 'we cannot stop the conflict' but only try to 'survive as a nation through it'.[259] More generally, the Irish had 'little sympathy for the neutralist attitudes . . . being advocated, principally by India' at that time.[260] Most, like MacBride, preferred to think of Ireland, the United States, and Western Europe as 'we'.[261] For many in

[249] É. de Valera, *Dáil Debates*, 152 (1955), 547.
[250] MacBride, ibid. 152 (1955), 557.
[251] O'Higgins, ibid. 102 (1946), 1405.
[252] MacBride, ibid. 152 (1955), 555.
[253] Capt. Cowan, ibid. 136 (1953), 2070; 139 (1953), 370 ff.
[254] Capt. Cowan, ibid.
[255] Blowick, ibid. 138 (1953), 749.
[256] Desmond, ibid. 152 (1955), 563.
[257] Kyne, ibid. 139 (1953), 437.
[258] MacBride, *Seanad Debates*, 35 (1948), 804, *Dáil Debates*, 136 (1953), 1170.
[259] É. de Valera, *Dáil Debates*, 122 (1950), 1833.
[260] Patrick Keatinge, *A Singular Stance: Irish Neutrality in the 1980s* (Dublin, 1984), 22.
[261] MacBride to Garrett, 19 Mar. 1949, RG84, Box 703, WNRC.

Ireland the cold war had the characteristics of a holy war, a struggle between the Cross and the anti-Christ.[262] While a few felt that Ireland 'should keep . . . [its] nose out of the business of other nations',[263] in such a situation most Irishmen were neither indifferent nor impartial.

A glimmering of an aspiration for a distinctive Irish position and contribution can be seen in MacBride's search for an 'ideal which had stronger influence and attraction than Communistic ideology', but he was unable to put substance into the ideal, except to lament increasing materialism and the armed division of Europe.[264] Despite the breast-beating, the Irish contribution to the solution of the world's problems was negligible, and by 1951 there was 'very little evidence' that the Irish government cared.[265] Ireland was no innovator or mould-breaker. It was no incipient leader of a third force. While somewhat detached, it belonged to the 'old world', not the non-aligned world.

Moreover, the Irish were not impartial in the great rivalry between East and West. Their sympathies were clearly very much with the West, although, like the Austrians, Swiss, and Swedes, they were unwilling to contribute materially to the Western cause or to the preservation of the values which that cause espoused. In many respects Irish quiescence was somewhat akin to the behaviour of the passive Swiss and the preoccupied Austrians; the Swedes took more active precautions.

ATTITUDE TO NATIONAL IDENTITY

It is noteworthy that the debate 'about identity, legitimacy, symbolism, [and] status' not only 'underlay all Ireland's early efforts in the international field', as O'Brien suggests, but stretched into the post-war period as the pervasive basis of Irish policy.[266] In 1945, for example, Dillon and de Valera were still involved in heated exchanges over the 'dictionary Republic' and Ireland's status in the Commonwealth.[267] Moreover, the goal of Sinn Féin of a free, independent, and united republic had still not been achieved, and neither had self-sufficiency and

262 Capt. Giles, *Dáil Debates*, 110 (1948), 855; 125 (1951), 1811-12. See also O'Higgins, ibid. 110 (1948), 719; Collins, ibid. 120 (1950), 617; Dillon, ibid. 138 (1953), 817.

263 McQuillan, ibid. 152 (1955), 575.

264 Garrett to Acheson, reporting conversation with MacBride on 18 Mar. 1949, RG84, Box 703, WNRC; Acheson, memo of conversation with MacBride, 11 Apr. 1949, ibid. See also MacBride in the Dáil, *Dáil Debates*, 152 (1955), 557; and Costello, in his speech in Montreal, Ireland in International Affairs, 28-9.

265 T. Desmond Williams, 'Conclusion', in Nowlan and Williams, 204.

266 O'Brien, 'International Affairs', 104.

267 See *Dáil Debates*, 97 (1946), 2568-75.

economic independence. Even in 1972 an Irish foreign minister still saw the basic issues of policy as 'the assertion of . . . identity' and 'the recognition of that identity by others',[268] and in the post-war period as a whole the Irish worried about 'Ireland's right to pursue her own foreign policy' and establish 'her full sovereignty'.[269] While these concerns permeated the whole period and were interwoven with a range of other issues, they were particularly important in 1949, when the Ireland Act produced 'the ultimate paroxysms of anti-partitionist fervour'.[270]

CONCLUSION

In the period from 1945 to 1955 there was a striking lack of assertions that the fundamental Irish policy was one 'for neutrality'. Rather, leaders such as de Valera and MacBride argued that Irish policy was thus only 'so long as' Partition existed.[271] Irrespective of party, no government was willing to provide the wherewithal 'for neutrality'. There was no single aspiration in the direction of such a policy, since some were ready to countenance some form of agreement with others concerning security. Just as non-participation in war is not equivalent to neutrality, neither is non-participation in alliances a sufficient condition for it. It is rather the case that the post-war decade saw the foundation of a position which was *sui generis*.

---

[268] Hillery, ibid. 260 (1972), 384 ff.

[269] Williams, 'Conclusion', in Nowlan and Williams, 204.

[270] Keatinge, *A Place*, 113.

[271] É. de Valera used this expression in a press conference, 18 June 1951, in SPO S14291 A/2; MacBride, in an important Dáil speech, used the phrase 'as long as': *Dáil Debates*, 114 (1949), 324.

7

'Bloody Mavericks' or Partners?
1956–1972

AFTER a decade of relative isolation, the Irish were forced to decide whether they would be 'bloody mavericks'[1] or rather partners with other Western states. The quiescence of Irish policy in the mid-fifties was disturbed by Irish entry into the United Nations in December 1955 and the need to work out 'nothing less than the basic principle on which . . . policy towards the outside world is to be based'.[2] Within a few years this task was made yet more difficult by the need to take a stand on the possible nature of a relationship with the European Economic Community and on the obligations which might follow any such relationship. In addition, the embryonic concept of non-alignment was attractive to some Irish minds,[3] and, combined with the legacy of neutrality, needed to be taken into account. Consequently, the period 1956–72 saw a renewal of debate and of the need for decision regarding the foundations of Irish policy. Further questioning arose with the eruption of the troubles in Northern Ireland in 1968–9.

DUE DILIGENCE

In the spring of 1964 the General Staff's post-war plan was described as 'archaic', since in 'no year since that plan was formulated have we had or were we ever in reach of having the number of men envisaged'.[4] Throughout the period the overall shortfall between number of men in the PDF and the peacetime establishment of 12,915 averaged 33 per cent, with an average of 13 per cent for officers and 37 per cent for other ranks[5] (the detailed figures for each year are shown in Table 7.1). By their own criterion, then, the Irish failed to provide enough men. While

---

[1] Conor Cruise O'Brien, *To Katanga and Back* (London, 1965), 36.

[2] Liam Cosgrave, Minister for External Affairs, *Dáil Debates*, 159 (1956), 138.

[3] The Belgrade conference took place in the same year as the decision to apply to the EEC.

[4] McQuillan, *Dáil Debates*, 208 (1964), 674; 214 (1965), 1409 ff.; Cosgrave, ibid. 244 (1970), 1699.

[5] Gen. MacEoin, Minister for Defence, ibid. 156 (1956), 268 ff.; Boland, Minister for Defence, ibid. 166 (1958), 865; 181 (1960), 781; Bartley, Minister for Defence, ibid. 195 (1965), 1086.

ministers bemoaned the shortfall,[6] it was to some extent a matter of policy, since the general opinion was that defence was only 'one of many State services' and that 'if more is given to one, the others must do with less—unless, of course, extra revenue can be procured'.[7] By 1971 every 1,000 men cost £1m. per annum,[8] and certainly the Irish felt that 'small countries such as ours are forced by circumstances to do with the military forces they can maintain'.[9]

Table 7.1.   Number of Officers and Men in the Permanent Defence Force 1956–1972

Year	Numbers	Shortfall from 12,915 (%)
1956	8,735	32.4
1957	8,846	31.5
1958	8,130	37.0
1959	9,188	28.8
1960	8,965	30.6
1961	8,868	31.3
1962	8,451	34.6
1963	8,449	34.6
1964	8,221	36.3
1965	8,199	36.5
1966	8,159	36.8
1967	8,331	35.5
1968	8,312	35.6
1969	8,232	36.3
1970	8,574	33.6
1971	8,663	32.9
1972	9,932	23.1

Sources: *Ireland: Statistical Abstract*, 1958, table 222, p. 230; 1962, table 247, p. 259; 1967, table 234, p. 266; 1970–71, table 227, p. 275; 1974 and 1975, table 220, p. 235.

The smallness of the PDF created a number of problems, since there were hardly enough men to cope with everyday tasks, especially given occa-

---

[6] See Hilliard, Minister for Defence, ibid. 222 (1966), 941.
[7] Cronin, Minister for Defence, ibid. 257 (1971), 2155 ff.; and see also Peter Jay, 'Public Expenditure and Administration', *Political Quarterly*, 41 (June 1970), 196.
[8] Cronin, *Dáil Debates*, 251 (1971), 681.
[9] Hilliard, ibid. 222 (1966), 941.

sional periods of internment duty and border patrols.[10] Moreover, the number of men actually available for patrols at certain times was only a part of the overall total.[11] The numbers in Ireland were further depleted by contributions to UN peace-keeping operations, despite doubts as to whether the dwindling army could meet such commitments.[12] For certain periods between 1960 and 1965 the figures for personnel abroad and personnel in Ireland were as shown in Table 7.2. While the percentage might seem small, the more significant figure is the number left in Ireland, which was generally lower than the (insufficient) strength of the period 1945–55; and of those left in Ireland a number similar to those abroad were preparing to go abroad. In 1964 Tully asked whether the army left in the country was 'in [a] position to carry out duties for which [it was] intended or are we slowly proving that . . . we do not need an Army?'[13] The official reply was that UN service provided valuable experience for an army which had not seen action for over a generation.[14] In all some 3,934 Irishmen served in ONUC and somewhat more in UNFICYP.[15]

The First Line Reserve numbered only between 5,128 in 1957 and 1,333 in 1972, while the Second Line Reserve numbered between a high of 21,033 in 1960 and a low of 17,623 in 1972.[16] Of the latter Reserve, only half trained regularly,[17] so for most of the period the Irish had some 20,000–22,000 reasonably effective and trained troops. This was well below their own planning assumptions. One consequence of the small size of the Irish defence forces was that, with 'the troubles' in Northern

[10] See Boland, ibid. 161 (1957), 870 ff. In 1958 Boland, as Minister for Defence, asserted that 7,500 was the minimum viable size of PDF: ibid. 166 (1958), 865 ff. In 1962 another Defence Minister, Bartley, suggested that a non-commissioned strength of 8,000 was desirable: ibid. 195 (1962), 1086 ff.

[11] Owing to administration and routine back-up duties.

[12] Traynor, ibid. 156 (1956), 273 ff.; Bartley, Minister for Defence, ibid. 208 (1964), 588 ff.

[13] Tully, ibid. 208 (1964), 1112; cf. 214 (1965), 1296.

[14] Boland, Minister for Defence, ibid. 187 (1961), 1187 ff.

[15] 15 Irish soldiers died in peace-keeping action between 1960 and 1972, and a further 20 were killed while overseas with peace-keeping forces. See Capt. J. Sheehan (ed.), The Defence Forces Handbook (Dublin, n.d.), 81–2, and Dáil Debates, 200 (1963), 985; 234 (1968), 1423.

[16] Figures for each year can be found in: Ireland: Statistical Abstract, 1958 (Pr. 4564; Dublin, 1958), table 222, p. 230; ibid., 1962 (Pr. 6571; Dublin, 1962), table 247, p. 259; ibid., 1967 (Pr. 9587; Dublin, 1967), table 234, p. 266; ibid., 1970–71 (Pr. 1974; Dublin, 1974), table 227, p. 275; ibid., 1974 and 1975 (Pr. 6072; Dublin, 1977), table 220, p. 235.

[17] 1966 Hilliard admitted that only about 10,000 out of 18,000 went for training: Dáil Debates, 222 (1966), 941.

Table 7.2.   Numbers Serving with United Nations 1960–1965

Date	Commitment	Irish involved	% of PDF	No. in Ireland
Aug. 1960– Jan. 1961	ONUC[a]	1,395	15.56	7,570
May 1961	ONUC	988	11.14	7,880
Dec. 1961– May 1962	ONUC	715	8.06	8,153
May–Nov. 1962	ONUC	723	8.55	7,728
Nov. 1962– Apr. 1963	ONUC	826	9.77	7,625
Aug.–Oct. 1964	UNFICYP[b]	1,005	12.22	7,216
Apr.–July 1965	UNFICYP	1,044	12.73	7,155

[a] Opération des Nations Unies au Congo.
[b] United Nations Force in Cyprus.

Sources: Capt. J. Sheehan, *Defence Forces Handbook* (Dublin n.d.), app. B, 79–80; and sources for Table 7.1 above.

Ireland, elements of the First and Second Line Reserve had to be called up for guard duty.[18]

Part of the explanation for the scale of the Irish defence effort was a general sense of inadequacy. Replying to criticisms of cutbacks during the 1956 Defence Vote for 1956–7, the Minister, General MacEoin, argued that 'to defend this small island would require nearly as much if not more defensive equipment than Britain requires to defend itself.'[19] In view of this attitude and the constant emphasis upon living 'within our means',[20] it is not surprising that little was done. The general pattern of expenditure in the period 1956–72 was one of declining resources (in real terms) being allocated to defence, and of even less of government spending going to defence than had been the case in the period 1948–55: this is shown in Table 7.3. This level of effort did attract internal criticism. While official policy emphasized that Irish policy continued to be based on deterrence—that the more force an aggressor had to use or contemplate using, the 'more likely we will retain our neutrality',[21] that the 'hostilities that might affect us would be only part of a much larger

---

[18] See Tully, ibid. 244 (1970), 1690 ff., and Gibbons, Minister for Defence, 244 (1970), 2093 ff.   [19] Gen. MacEoin, Minister for Defence, ibid. 156 (1956), 378.
[20] Gen. MacEoin, ibid.; Cosgrave, ibid. 222 (1966), 882.
[21] Boland, Minister for Defence, ibid. 164 (1957), 1470; cf. Cronin, Minister for Defence, 257 (1971), 2155 ff.

scheme', and that Ireland 'can still even be neutral', since there was no reason why a great power should 'suddenly single out this island for annihilation'[22]—senior backbenchers and future Ministers for Defence argued that there was no real defence,[23] and that to 'talk about our having any defence at all is a joke. We have a small Army which probably is adequate to quell a civil commotion . . . That is all we have.'[24] In the mid-sixties some felt that there was little need for a traditional army, and wanted the PDF to become a 'sort of auxiliary to the Garda',[25] or called for the amalgamation of the Justice and Defence Departments.[26] Although this was a minority view, it reflected widespread doubts about the strength and role of the PDF.

Table 7.3.   Irish Defence Expenditure 1956-1972

Year	Defence exp. (£m.)	% Supply services	% GNP
1956	6.494	6.1	1.16
1957	6.355	5.8	1.10
1958	6.094	5.5	1.01
1959	6.090	5.4	0.96
1960	6.591	5.7	0.98
1961	7.108	5.6	0.98
1962	7.459	5.2	0.96
1963	8.235	5.2	0.98
1964	8.505	4.9	0.90
1965	11.396	5.5	1.12
1966	11.910	5.2	1.11
1967	10.418	4.2	0.97
1968	11.184	4.0	0.84
1969	12.212	3.7	0.82
1970	14.184	3.7	0.85
1971	18.681	4.1	0.98
1972	19.165	3.9	0.84

Sources: Ireland: Statistical Abstract, 1958, table 239, p. 245; 1962, table 251, p. 266; table 263, p. 274; 1967, table 238, p. 273; table 250, pp. 280–1; 1970–71, table 231, p. 281; table 243, pp. 288–9; 1974 and 1975, table 224, p. 241; table 236, p. 252.

[22] Major de Valera, ibid. 156 (1956), 305–12.
[23] Oliver J. Flanagan, ibid. 175 (1959), 70 ff.
[24] Donegan, ibid. 247 (1970), 1733.
[25] Sherwin, ibid. 208 (1964), 637 ff.
[26] P. O'Donnell, ibid. 227 (1967), 588. See also Sherwin's observation that the Swiss had 'no standing army but only a part-time army', ibid. 201 (1963), 670 ff.

It was generally accepted that 'there must be an army';[27] and according to official policy, its size and role was 'not calculated' upon the premiss of 'participating in world war', but rather upon merely '[defending] our territory against occupation as far as that is possible'. In 1957 four roles were identified for the PDF, namely to maintain internal security; if possible, to prevent occupation by others; to warn of attacks; and, if possible, to assist in civil defence. The preservation and maintenance of neutrality *per se* was not a specific role, although it was argued that the ability to perform the other roles would help with this.[28] For most of the period the stress was upon the PDF as the 'protector of sovereignty and independence',[29] and of 'territorial integrity'.[30] These responsibilities were not to be left to others.[31] Subsequently other roles were added, such as contributing to UN peace-keeping and fishery protection.[32] Although the emphasis changed somewhat, it did not result in higher priority being given to the requirements of neutrality but rather to those of internal security, so that by 1972 it was argued that 'the primary role of the Army is the defence of the State against external aggression and helping the Civil Power'.[33] A difficulty for the Irish was that, although they recognized that it 'would be unreasonable to expect the Great Powers to allow a military vacuum to develop here',[34] this recognition was not translated into operational policy and resources.

Financial constraints, for example, were reflected in the problem of equipment, where it was repeatedly stressed that Irish efforts had to be 'within our resources'.[35] One argument was that in the nuclear age Ireland could not compete, since its equipment was as obsolete 'as the bow and arrow',[36] and another was the cost of updating that equipment. Irish shortcomings with equipment were revealed during UN service in the Congo, when Irish forces were able to compare their equipment

27 Corish, ibid. 201 (1963), 635.

28 Boland, Minister for Defence, ibid. 164 (1957), 1470 ff.

29 Gen. MacEoin, Minister for Defence, ibid. 156 (1956), 375.

30 Boland, Minister for Defence, ibid. 188 (1961), 152.

31 Major de Valera, ibid. 156 (1956), 305–12; Boland, Minister for Defence, ibid. 188 (1961), 151–2.

32 See FitzGerald, ibid. 245 (1970), 867 ff.; Hilliard, Minister for Defence, ibid. 234 (1968), 1474 ff.

33 Cronin, Minister for Defence, ibid. 258 (1972), 703 ff.; see also ibid. 245 (1970), 710; 257 (1971), 2155 ff.

34 Boland, Minister for Defence, ibid. 188 (1961), 151–2.

35 Bartley, Minister for Defence, ibid. 195 (1962), 1289; MacEoin, Minister for Defence, 156 (1956), 378–9.

36 Coogan, ibid. 156 (1956), 346; cf. Sherwin and Booth, ibid. 194 (1962), 526; 166 (1958), 908.

with others.[37] This led to the purchase of small arms and FN sub-machine-guns.[38] But problems persisted, with the lack of modern equipment for training the reserves[39] and the lack of suitable transport and communication systems for the PDF.[40] In 1970 the newest truck in the Curragh military base was fifteen years old,[41] and many of the other vehicles were thin-skinned. The 'troubles' in Northern Ireland led to Supplementary Estimates for additional equipment and transport. In 1971 it was £1.7m. (namely 10 per cent of the original Estimate),[42] and in 1972 £1.985m. (an additional $11\frac{1}{2}$ per cent).[43] This was hardly sufficient to offset the extra costs of inflation.[44]

These general problems had a specific impact upon the Air Corps and the Naval Service. The Air Corps was unable to stop incursions into Irish airspace: most notably, in 1971 it failed to do anything when an RAF Canberra flew in Irish airspace for an hour, approaching within twenty miles of Dublin and flying over crucial lines of communication around Mount Oriel.[45] Such was the Air Corps's condition that Mark Clinton asked in that same year whether it was to remain in existence, although he felt it should.[46] It allegedly had four roles—military duties, Aer Lingus training, aerial surveys for Ordnance Survey, and responsibility for helicopters[47]—but was too ill-equipped for any substantial role, and there was little which its forty-eight pilots could do to protect Ireland.[48]

Similarly, there was little which the Naval Service could do with its three corvettes. In 1957 the Minister had to admit that, although the defence plan provided for seaward defence, the Naval Service was not

[37] Sherwin, ibid. 195 (1962), 1146.

[38] Bartley, Minister for Defence, ibid. 194 (1962), 521, 536 ff. According to Davern, ibid. 245 (1970), 831, it was only experience in the Congo that made the Dept. of Defence realize that the .303 rifle was twenty years out of date.

[39] Davern, ibid. 258 (1972), 658 ff.

[40] Part of a general indictment: Cooney, ibid. 251 (1971), 230–1: Dr Byrne, ibid. 257 (1971), 2225 ff.

[41] Clinton, ibid. 257 (1971), 2168 ff.

[42] Cronin, Minister for Defence, ibid. 258 (1972), 703 ff.; and see Clinton, ibid. 257 (1971), 2167 ff.

[43] Cronin, ibid. 259 (1972), 2069 ff.

[44] A point made by Dr Byrne, ibid. 257 (1971), 2225 ff.

[45] Ibid. For details of Air Corps see ibid. 156 (1956), 316 ff., 344; 161 (1957), 870–80; 164 (1957), 1457 ff.; 166 (1958), 902 ff.; 181 (1960), 781; 187 (1961), 1216 ff; 192 (1961), 504; 203 (1963), 687; 231 (1967), 1336; 243 (1969), 1185; 257 (1971), 2155, 2225 ff.; 260 (1972), 317, 2191; Lt-Col. P. D. Kavanagh, *The Irish Army Handbook 1973* (Dublin, 1973), 47–8; Sheehan, 61.

[46] Clinton, *Dáil Debates*, 257 (1971), 2181.

[47] Bartley, Minister for Defence, ibid. 201 (1963), 616; 188 (1961), 153.

[48] As of Dec. 1969, Gibbons, Minister for Defence, ibid. 243 (1969), 1185.

geared for that role and was merely protecting Irish fisheries.[49] Despite this, the three corvettes remained *the* Naval Service until 1968-71, when they were withdrawn from service.[50] They could not perform their official tasks (anti-submarine patrols, minesweeping, seaward defence of the ports, control of maritime activities within Irish territorial waters, fishery protection, and the protection of ships);[51] nor could they fulfil what was officially the main reason for their existence, namely that if Ireland 'had not a Naval Service some other country would claim to be protecting our waters', and thereby influence the traffic to Irish ports.[52] The corvettes were increasingly ageing, slow, and unreliable.[53] Their retention was in marked contrast to the view of Traynor in 1956, that if Ireland wished to demonstrate its sincerity about neutrality it should purchase a new vessel every year for ten years.[54] The problem was that by 1965-8 it was estimated that the cost would be between £1m. and 1.4m. for each vessel, so that ten would have cost more than one year's total budget for defence.[55]

At one stage in 1969, owing to a combination of the condition of vessels and inadequate numbers of personnel, not one Naval Service vessel was capable of being put to sea, and the Irish had to rely upon an unarmed fishery-research vessel.[56] This situation was repeated in the spring of 1970.[57] Little wonder that a Minister for Defence, a few years earlier, had to admit that he was not satisfied that the Naval Service would be of any real use in an emergency.[58] In 1971 three coastal minesweepers built in the mid-fifties were purchased from Britain,[59] and

---

[49] Boland, Minister for Defence, ibid. 161 (1957), 870; 166 (1958), 961; 188 (1961), 152; see also Dr Byrne, ibid. 245 (1970), 815 ff.; Tully, ibid. 195 (1962), 1131-42; Esmonde, ibid. 245 (1970), 855 ff.; Hilliard, Minister for Defence, ibid. 234 (1968), 1476 ff.

[50] Sheehan, 63.

[51] Bartley, Minister for Defence, *Dáil Debates*, 214 (1965), 1595-6; Boland, Minister for Defence, ibid. 166 (1958), 961; Esmonde, ibid. 175 (1959), 21.

[52] Kavanagh, ibid. 258 (1972), 682.

[53] For description of vessels and complaints see ibid. 192 (1961), 1187; 196 (1962), 959; 201 (1963), 719, 828; 207 (1964), 325; 208 (1964), 642; 212 (1964), 469; 214 (1965), 1271; 217 (1965), 708, 1283, 1840, 1914, 1922, 1930; 234 (1968), 1423; 236 (1968), 2362.

[54] Traynor, ibid. 156 (1956), 278.

[55] Hilliard, Minister for Defence, ibid. 234 (1968), 1477; Bartley, Minister for Defence, ibid. 214 (1965), 1583 ff.

[56] Gibbons, Minister for Defence, ibid. 243 (1969), 1187, 1944.

[57] Gibbons, ibid. 244 (1970), 2033.

[58] Hilliard, Minister for Defence, ibid. 227 (1967), 1403. By 1969 no other European naval service was still using Flower-class corvettes: Gibbons, Minister for Defence, ibid. 242 (1969), 1537-9.

[59] Gibbons, ibid. 249 (1970), 875. These ships had been held in reserve by the British for some years and required attention to a number of defects.

in May 1972 the Naval Service took delivery of a purpose-built fishery-protection vessel, the *Deirdre*.[60] Subsequently further efforts were made, but generally between 1956 and 1972 the Naval Service was a 'joke'.[61]

In this period the Irish again failed to meet either their own criteria of adequate defence or the requirements of 'due diligence'. Moreover, at the time of crisis in Northern Ireland in 1969–70 the PDF was unprepared. For example, in the two years ending 31 March 1972 there were eighty-eight known border-incursions by the British Army,[62] and by February 1972 twenty-seven confirmed overflights.[63] Although the government protested, little positive action was taken, despite a recognition that some incursions were deliberate.[64] In addition, in the winter of 1970–1 the British boarded a number of Irish vessels in Carlingford Lough, looking for arms. While some TDs called for 'defensive measures to protect Irish vessels', and the deployment of Irish naval vessels to the area,[65] a government minister dismissed such ideas as empty gestures.[66] In an Adjournment Debate, Richie Ryan argued that Irish vessels were 'entitled to the full protection of the military forces' of the State, and called 'if necessary' for 'armed forces aboard Irish vessels', ready to arrest and intern 'troops who forcibly [entered] Irish vessels or Irish soil'.[67] The government preferred the 'velvet glove approach' and did not use the recently acquired British minesweepers for action.[68] There was a clear failure to uphold the sovereignty and integrity of the State, and more generally, as will be discussed in a later section, a clear inability to intervene militarily in the North.

RECOGNITION OF NEUTRAL STATUS

Apart from the establishment of a UN mission in January 1956, entry into the United Nations did not produce any expansion of Irish

[60] Cronin, Minister for Defence, ibid. 256 (1971), 1310; Gibbons, ibid. 242 (1969), 491; Sheehan, 63–4.

[61] Booth, *Dáil Debates*, 214 (1965), 1353; Dowling, ibid. 227 (1967), 1359. For a history of Naval Service see *An Cosantoir* (Apr. 1973), which was given over to the Naval Service. It is worth noting that in 1964 Irish territorial waters were expanded to 15,136 m.²: *Dáil Debates*, 213 (1964), 921.

[62] Lenihan, Minister for Transport and Power, for Minister for Foreign Affairs, *Dáil Debates*, 260 (1972), 1793.

[63] Lenihan, ibid. 258 (1972), 1202–3.

[64] Lynch, Taoiseach, ibid. 256 (1971), 283; cf. ibid. 251 (1971), 1487.

[65] Ryan, ibid. 252 (1971), 1769 ff.

[66] Lenihan, standing in for Hillery, ibid. 252 (1971), 2059.

[67] Ryan, ibid. 2112 ff.

[68] Lenihan, standing in for Hillery, ibid. 2118 ff.

diplomatic representation. Subsequent modest expansion appears to have been predominantly influenced by trade considerations.[69] In the mid-sixties the pattern of Irish representation was challenged, particularly by the Irish Labour Party, which drew attention to the vacuum regarding Eastern Europe.[70] Trade seems to have influenced them, although the official position was that the volume of trade did not warrant the cost of formal diplomatic representation.[71] Some in Fine Gael not only derided the trade argument, but also argued that the Soviets represented the antithesis of everything which the Irish believed in, so that the Irish should not 'suckle the Russian bear'.[72] Labour representatives did introduce the question: 'How can we suggest that we are neutral? What is the meaning of neutrality if we have no diplomatic relations with the damned on the other side?',[73] but when the situation did change, with diplomatic relations established in 1973, it appears to have been more to do with Irish entry into the European Community, and with trade, than with considerations of neutrality.

As for the Soviets, in 1959 they accused the Irish of not being independent agents, but of acting as tools and agents of another country.[74] The following year they opposed the candidacy of F. H. Boland for the Presidency of the General Assembly: their candidate was from Poland, and 'the West's was from Ireland'.[75] Later it appears that the Soviets did not send the Irish a Note indicating that they regarded membership of the European Community as incompatible with neutrality, although Finland, Austria, Sweden, and Switzerland did receive such Notes.[76]

During this period the Irish did not participate in either the first non-aligned summit at Belgrade or subsequent non-aligned meetings. In June 1961 the Dáil was twice told that no invitation to Belgrade had been received, but it is unclear whether President Sukarno of Indo-

---

[69] For details of expansion see ibid. 179 (1959), 64; 232 (1968), 862–4; and for Irish policy on recognition and representation, 222 (1966), 1; 194 (1962), 1442. See also Patrick Keatinge, *A Place Among the Nations: Issues of Irish Foreign Policy* (Dublin, 1978), app. 2, pp. 270–1.

[70] O'Leary, *Dáil Debates*, 226 (1967), 886.

[71] Aiken, ibid. 232 (1968), 1717.

[72] Ryan, ibid. 260 (1972), 406 ff.; Coogan, ibid. 504.

[73] O'Leary, ibid. 480.

[74] For Aiken's replies see *Ireland at the United Nations 1959: Speeches by Mr Frank Aiken* (Dublin [1960]) (other volumes referred to as *Ireland/UN* with year), speech delivered to General Assembly, 20 Oct. 1959, pp. 36–7, and speech to General Committee, 9 Oct. 1959, pp. 29–35.

[75] Strobe Talbott (ed.), *Khrushchev Remembers: The Last Testament* (London, 1974), 470. O'Brien, *Katanga*, 46, refers to Boland as 'the successful Western-sponsored candidate' in an 'Eastern European year'.

[76] This speculation is raised by Adam Roberts, 'Can Neutrality Be Defended?', in Bill McSweeney (ed.), *Ireland and the Threat of Nuclear War* (Dublin, 1985), 25.

nesia had made informal soundings on a visit to Dublin earlier in the year.[77] The lack of any Irish participation or invitation reveals how the Irish position was perceived elsewhere. In the following year, moreover, the Irish supported the United States during the Cuban missile crisis, and did not participate in meetings of what were referred to as forty-five 'unaligned' and 'Afro-Asian states'.[78] Many in Ireland were suspicious of the non-aligned movement, seeing behind it Communist sympathizers.[79]

Evidence of a more positive perception of the Irish position is provided by the invitations to contribute to the peace-keeping forces established by the United Nations, which suggest a view of Ireland as having 'no ties, commitments or obligations to any other nation or group of nations'—as neutral and therefore acceptable.[80] Certainly Irish politicians perceived it in this light.[81] Similarly, Conor Cruise O'Brien has postulated that Dag Hammarskjöld chose him to be the Representative of the United Nations in Katanga because the choice narrowed 'to a European neutral'.[82] Some in Ireland saw similar perceptions behind Boland's election to the General Assembly Presidency in 1960 and Ireland's election to the Security Council in 1962.[83]

In fact, the claims associated with acceptability for peace-keeping are highly tendentious. MacQueen has argued that Ireland only superficially met the criteria regarding so-called 'middle powers', and that the 'middle power' argument is itself based on a misinterpretation, since at crucial junctures the United Nations itself 'was not politically neutral between East and West'.[84] Moreover, an examination of major participants in UN peace-keeping and observer missions up to 1970 reveals that out of 12 operations, the most frequent contributors were as follows: Sweden—10; Canada—9; Denmark—8; Ireland and Norway—7 each;

---

77 See *Dáil Debates*, 190 (1961), 5, 1097 and 209 (1964), 868.

78 Costello, ibid. 197 (1962), 409.

79 Costello, ibid. 191 (1961), 551 ff.

80 McQuillan, ibid, 208 (1964), 1103 ff.; Cosgrave, 194 (1962), 1355 ff. See also Brian Farrell, *Sean Lemass* (Dublin, 1983), 118.

81 Corish, *Dáil Debates*, 208 (1964), 1075 ff.; Lemass, Taoiseach, 183 (1960), 1875 ff.

82 O'Brien, *Katanga*, 52–3.

83 Cf. Andrew Boyd, *Fifteen Men on a Powder Keg* (London, 1971), 108–12.

84 Norman MacQueen, 'Irish Neutrality: The United Nations and the Peace-keeping Experience 1945–1969' (New University of Ulster, D.Phil. thesis, 1981), 223–4 (see also pp. 207–17); Larry L. Fabian, *Soldiers without Enemies: Preparing the United Nations for Peace-keeping* (Washington, DC, 1971), 88, *passim*; J. van Doorn and J. H. Mans, 'United Nations Forces: On Legitimacy and Effectiveness of International Military Operations', in J. van Doorn (ed.), *Armed Forces and Society* (The Hague, 1968), 353, *passim*.

and India, Italy, Netherlands, and New Zealand—6 each. Six of the nine were alliance members. Out of the total list of participants, only Yugoslavia 'could be said to be identifiably non-Western', while nearly all NATO members, but no Warsaw Pact states, took part.[85] MacQueen concludes that, contrary to Irish conventional wisdom, peace-keeping was 'a Western conception', viewed, moreover, with suspicion by the communists.[86] Peace-keeping participation was not equivalent to an international acceptance of independent position, but only a few in Ireland recognized this.

Only a minority, for example, recognized that participation in the Opération des Nations Unies au Congo could involve a sacrifice of Ireland's alleged non-committed standing, since it might be regarded as supporting colonialism.[87] It is interesting that MacQueen observes that the Congo experience demonstrated 'the fundamental differences in perspective and interests between the Afro-Asian small powers and those of Western Europe'.[88]

Perceptions of Ireland may also have been influenced by various changes in Irish behaviour and by pronouncements at the United Nations itself. O'Brien argues, for example, that while Ireland was initially regarded by the United States as 'Absolutely safe on straight East–West issues',[89] a change occurred in 1957 when Aiken became Minister, firstly with his statement on disengagement in Europe, and secondly (and more importantly) in the Irish vote to allow a discussion of the question of Chinese representation.[90] This latter, according to O'Brien, was regarded as a reliable indicator of votes on a range of issues,[91] and led to an American perception of Ireland as one of 'the bloody mavericks'.[92] O'Brien argues that this only lasted four years, since in 1961 the Irish voted for a different American formula, so that observers could subsequently predict that Ireland 'would now be aligned with . . . the United States. In this expectation these observers were not disappointed.'[93] There is some other evidence (discussed in a later

[85] MacQueen, 'Neutrality', 215; cf. Fabian, 226.
[86] MacQueen, 'Neutrality', 217–18.
[87] Browne, Dáil Debates, 186 (1961), 853 ff.
[88] MacQueen, 'Neutrality', 336.
[89] O'Brien, describing part of a 'Manipulator's Manual', in his Katanga, 29–30.
[90] Ibid. 30 and id., Ireland, the United Nations and Southern Africa, public lecture, 20 July 1967; Dublin, 1967), 3.
[91] O'Brien, Ireland, the United Nations and Southern Africa, 3.
[92] O'Brien Katanga, 36.
[93] O'Brien, Ireland, the United Nations and Southern Africa, 5; cf. MacQueen, 'Neutrality', 156.

section) that the Irish position, or at least alignment, did change about this time.

Those who tried to discern the true nature of the Irish position had the additional problem that there were divergent publicly expressed Irish views. For example, early in 1960 the Taoiseach, Sean Lemass, drew important distinctions between the Afro-Asians who refused to take a position on East–West issues and stressed anti-colonialism, and the ' "independent" countries such as Sweden and Ireland', who wished to judge according to the criteria of the Charter.[94] However, in October of the same year Aiken, as Minister for External Affairs, spoke to the General Assembly of the role which 'we smaller . . . independent . . . uncommitted countries, call us what you will . . . We, the recently emerged' could play.[95] A year later Aiken denied using the word 'uncommitted', and claimed that he had stressed that Ireland was 'independent'.[96] This ambiguity of view was present in the Irish UN delegation itself, so that although 'all important matters' were decided by the chairman of the delegation, there were variations in the Irish position according to committee, issue, and representation.[97]

Added to the problems was the manner in which the Irish distanced themselves from the Afro-Asians on certain aspects of the colonial, South African, and Rhodesian questions. While the Irish knew 'what imperialism is and what resistance to it involves'[98] from their own history, and although the principle of self-determination 'ought to be the great master principle by which this Assembly should be guided',[99] they believed in gradualism and preparation for self-government,[100] so that peoples should not 'immediately and without preparation of any kind' be 'thrown on their own resources', since this might lead to 'tyranny and exploitation'.[101]

There was a disparagement of the Afro-Asians 'proposing unrealistic resolutions'.[102] Remembering the problems which the League of

---

[94] Lemass, address to Cambridge University Liberal Club, 31 Jan. 1960: text in *Eire-Ireland*, (Bulletin of the Dept. of External Affairs), 468 (1 Feb. 1960). Ten years later, Lemass still felt that the distinction was valid: see his 'Small States in International Organisations', in A. Schou and A. O. Brundtland (eds.), *Small States in International Relations* (Uppsala, 1971), 117.

[95] Speech by Aiken to General Assembly, 6 Oct. 1960, in *Ireland/UN 1960*, 11–12.

[96] Aiken, *Dáil Debates*, 191 (1961), 672–9.

[97] O'Brien, *Katanga*, 37–40, 46–7.

[98] Speech by Aiken to General Assembly, 6 Oct. 1960, in *Ireland/UN 1960*, 13.

[99] Statement by Aiken to General Assembly, 20 Sept. 1957, in *Ireland/UN 1957*, 24.

[100] MacQueen, 'Neutrality', 119–20.

[101] Aiken, *Dáil Debates*, 171 (1958), 1266.

[102] Keatinge, *A Place*, 175.

Nations had over Italy, the Irish also had doubts as to the efficacy of sanctions. Although they complied with the mandatory sanctions against Rhodesia and prohibited sales of arms to South Africa, this was not done with any confidence.[103] Fundamentally, the Irish would have preferred 'separate [votes] on the contentious issues', and when this was rejected they failed to support a number of resolutions.[104]

Difficulties in others' perceptions of the Irish were exacerbated by the 1961 decision to apply for membership of the EEC, particularly since on this issue 'Ireland definitely parted company with the European neutrals.'[105] This was clearly recognized in Europe. In February 1963 the EEC Commission referred to 'the three neutral countries' as Austria, Sweden, and Switzerland, and dealt with Ireland in another context,[106] while in 1962–3 the Consultative Assembly of the Council of Europe, in examining the problem of the relationship between neutrals and the Community, made no mention of Ireland in its committee analyses and reports. Ireland was not cited as an example of a neutral which had been able to reconcile neutrality and membership.[107] In fact, few European politicians argued this.[108] One exception was Maurice Schumann, the French Foreign Minister, who argued that it was 'wrong to say that joining the Community involved a change in Ireland's neutral policy', on the grounds that the Community was purely economic.[109] More generally, there was hostility to neutral membership, since it implied dilution of the political objectives of the Community.

The distinction between Ireland and 'the three neutral countries' was perceived by some in Ireland, who concluded that Irish 'so-called neu-

---

[103] See *Dáil Debates*, 188 (1961), 175; 191 (1961), 479; 196 (1962), 1459; 197 (1962), 1463; 203 (1963), 981; 211 (1964), 20; 214 (1965), 754; 226 (1967), 972; 232 (1968), 1768; 241 (1969), 2278.

[104] Aiken, ibid. 203 (1963), 982. More generally see Peter Willetts, *The Nonaligned Movement: The Origins of a Third World Alliance* (London, 1978), *passim*.

[105] Hanspeter Neuhold, 'Permanent Neutrality in Contemporary International Relations: A Comparative Perspective', *Irish Studies in International Affairs* 1/3 (1982), 14.

[106] EEC Commission, *Report to the European Parliament on the State of Negotiations with the United Kingdom* (Brussels, 26 Feb. 1963), 97.

[107] See e.g. 'Report on the General Policy of the Council of Europe', (rapporteur: Mr Maurice Macmillan), with 1962 Struye Report; and 'Report on the General Policy of the Council of Europe' (rapporteur: Mr Pflimlin), with 1963 Struye Report.

[108] See 1962 Struye Report, 21–6; Miriam Camps, *Britain and the European Community 1955–1963* (OUP, 1965), 422, 498; Spaak in *Assembly Debates*, 15th Ordinary Session (1st part), 1 (1963), Sittings 1–8, pp. 33–6; Tully, *Dáil Debates*, 230 (1967), 1097; Lynch, ibid. 196 (1962), 3435; Browne, ibid. 255 (1971), 2121, 2465.

[109] Quoted in *Irish Independent*, 21 Oct. 1971; by Hillery, *Dáil Debates*, 259 (1972) 2445. For others see Ryan, ibid. 257 (1971), 1286 ff.

trality is a joke and a joke in poor taste'.[110] There were queries as to why the Irish government was not co-ordinating its approach with that of Austria, Sweden, and Switzerland, to 'ensure that in common Ireland may ensure her neutrality in future'.[111] The answer was that it was not deemed useful to co-ordinate policy with non-applicants,[112] and, moreover, that Ireland had 'no traditional policy of neutrality . . . like countries such as Sweden, Switzerland and Austria, who have declared themselves to have permanent policies of neutrality'. Rather, in the Irish case, it was for the Dáil to decide 'in the light of the circumstances prevailing' at the time.[113]

DISAVOWAL OF EXTERNAL HELP

The Irish position and debate on this subject remained little changed from that of the previous period. Other arguments arose in connection with the nature of Ireland's relationship to the European Community, and will be dealt with in the following section, which discusses freedom of decision and action.[114] Mostly they concerned the extent to which Ireland would have to help others, not the converse situation.

However, one thing which did emerge with respect to 'disavowal of help', was an explicit admission by the Taoiseach, Sean Lemass, in 1962 that it would be highly undesirable to give the impression that the Irish regarded NATO membership as discreditable, since 'the existence of NATO is necessary for the preservation of peace and for the defence of the countries of Western Europe, *including this country*. Although we are not members of NATO, we are in full agreement with its aims.'[115] In 1969 Richard Burke berated those who found it convenient to be derogatory about NATO, since the Irish at times 'were very glad of its umbrella of protection'.[116] Some backbenchers continued to assume, in view of the lack of Irish 'due diligence', that the Irish system must be based upon co-operation with both Britain and America in the event of an attack.[117] It was argued the Irish would be unwise to cut themselves

---

[110] O'Leary, *Dáil Debates*, 226 (1967), 883.
[111] Ibid. 235 (1968), 1215.
[112] Ibid.
[113] Lynch, Taoiseach, ibid. 241 (1969), 632. He had earlier acknowledged that 'our neutrality is not of the same nature as theirs': ibid. 157.
[114] See the following section on Freedom of Decision and Action.
[115] Lemass, Taoiseach, ibid. 193 (1962), 4 ff. (emphasis added).
[116] Richard Burke, future Cabinet and Commission member, ibid, 241 (1969), 1972 ff.
[117] McQuillan, ibid. 188 (1961), 108 ff.

off completely from co-operative planning, since if hostilities commenced Ireland would undoubtedly be part of the general scheme of the defence of Western Europe.[118] Official policy was to disavow such reasoning, and during this period there was no apparent question of an alliance or defence arrangement, nor of any deals on the basis of neutrality in exchange for unity.[119]

One specific question arising was that of foreign military bases.[120] The government claimed that these were not being considered: in particular, in 1962 it strongly denied a rumour that it was considering a proposal to allow American bases in Ireland in exchange for the freedom of Northern Ireland.[121] What did occur was the landing of a significant number of foreign military aircraft at Shannon: between 1 January and 20 July 1967 there were 167 such landings, with aircraft from the United States, Canada, France, West Germany, Belgium, Israel, Iran, and Saudi Arabia.[122] Although this is not definitive evidence, it does suggest an informal Irish orientation.

In general, however, the Irish remained opposed to foreign military bases, whether on Irish soil or situated on the territory of other nations. Frank Aiken spoke out repeatedly on this issue at the United Nations, for example, in his disengagement proposal of 1957,[123] and in his so-called 'areas of law' proposals.[124] He was particularly critical of the Cubans in 1962, arguing that instead of introducing new foreign bases into the area they should have followed the Irish example of allowing 'under no circumstances . . . [their] country to be used as a base for attack against [a] neighbour'.[125]

FREEDOM OF DECISION AND ACTION

Despite many years of official policy and rhetoric, Ireland had not attained economic self-sufficiency. It remained a very open economy,

---

[118] Russell, ibid. 187 (1961), 1246–51. See also William FitzGerald, *Irish Unification and NATO* (Dublin, 1982), 41, 49, 64, *passim*.

[119] However, Irish personnel continued to attend courses abroad, predominantly in Britain and the United States.   [120] Browne, ibid. 247 (1970), 1715; Tully, ibid. 248 (1970), 68.

[121] Lemass, Taoiseach, ibid. 195 (1962), 1 ff. Bases had a symbolic importance, owing to the issue of the ports: Tully, ibid. 248 (1970), 68 ff.

[122] This is the only period for which figures are available. It includes the period of the Six Day War between Israel and its neighbours. Cf. Hilliard, Minister for Defence, ibid. 230 (1967), 429.

[123] Aiken, speech to General Assembly, 10 Sept. 1957, *Ireland/UN 1957*, 8–10.

[124] Aiken, speech to General Assembly, 14 Aug. 1958, in *Ireland/UN 1958*, 7–9, 14; speech, 20 Sept. 1957, in *Ireland/UN 1957*, 15; speech to First Committee, 28 Oct. 1960, in *Ireland/UN 1960*, 32.

[125] Aiken, speech to Security Council, 24 Oct. 1962, in *Ireland/UN 1962*, 23–30.

still 'extremely dependent on foreign trade',[126] and this dependency increased in the period 1956–72, as is shown in Table 7.4. Such dependence had a decisive effect upon Ireland's economic choices,[127] and the situation was exacerbated by the continuing 'monetary union in the form of a fixed link between the Irish pound and sterling', so that the Irish again devalued at the same time and by the same amount as the British.[128] Although the significance to Ireland of trade with the United Kingdom declined somewhat between 1956 and 1972, it remained extraordinarily high, as can be seen in Table 7.5.

The dependence upon one state is the critical distinction between the Irish pattern of trade and that of 'the three neutral countries'.[129] At key moments of decision the Irish were importing about two-thirds of their requirements from Britain and the Six, and exporting over three-quarters of their exports to those same countries. Once Britain decided to apply for EEC membership, the Irish faced the daunting prospect of being at a competitive disadvantage because of customs tariffs in large key markets, with little possibility of finding an alternative market.[130]

Table 7.4. Ireland: Foreign Trade Dependence 1955–1972

Year	Merchandise[a]		Goods/Services[a]	
	Exp.	Imp.	Exp.	Imp.
1955	22.8	42.7	37.2	44.5
1960	25.9	38.4	39.8	39.9
1965	27.2	43.7	39.7	45.0
1970	32.4	47.0[b]	46.2	50.7[b]
1972	33.8	44.1	44.0	46.9

[a] As % of GNP at current factor cost.
[b] Distorted by exceptional imports of aircraft.

Source: T. K. Whitaker, 'Monetary Integration: Reflections on Irish Experience', *Quarterly Bulletin* (Central Bank of Ireland; Winter 1973), p. 69.

[126] T. K. Whitaker, 'Monetary Integration: Reflections on Irish Experience', *Quarterly Bulletin* (Central Bank of Ireland; Winter 1973), 68–9; and see also Dermot McAleese, 'The Foreign Sector', in Norman J. Gibson and John E. Spence (eds.), *Economic Activity in Ireland: A Study of Two Open Economies* (Dublin, 1976).
[127] McAleese, 'Foreign Sector', 116.
[128] Whitaker, 'Integration', 68.
[129] See above, Table 3.1.
[130] Not all accepted the lack of alternatives. See e.g. app. A, in Raymond Crotty, *Ireland and the Common Market: An Economic Analysis of the Effects of Membership* (Dublin, 1971), 43–53.

Table 7.5. Trade by Areas in Selected Years

	1956[a]	1961[b]	1967[c]	1969[d]	1972[e]
Imports % from:					
Great Britain/Northern Ireland	57.8	50.8	50.2	52.6	51.0
Rest of EFTA[a]	n.a.[f]	3.2	3.8	5.8	6.7
EEC members[a]	11.0	13.5	14.6	15.6	17.5
Dollar Countries	10.9	10.2	10.8	10.8	9.1
Eastern Europe	< 1	1.0	1.5	1.0	1.0
Exports % to:					
Great Britain/Northern Ireland	76.2	74.3	72.1	65.4	60.8
Rest of EFTA[a]	n.a.[f]	1.0	1.1	1.7	2.4
EEC members[a]	9.0	6.3	8.5	11.1	16.8
Dollar Countries	3.5	9.1	10.8	12.5	12.0
Eastern Europe	< 1	< 1	< 1	< 1	< 1

[a] The figures are for trade with the eventual member states of EFTA and EEC.

[b] First application to EEC.

[c] Second application to EEC.

[d] Revitalized application to EEC.

[e] Last year before entry to EEC.

[f] Figures not available in Statistical Abstract.

Sources: Ireland: Statistical Abstract, 1958, tables 114 and 115, p. 135, table 121, p. 139; 1962, tables 131 and 132, p. 155, table 138, p. 159; 1969, tables 123 and 124, p. 149, table 130, p. 153; 1970–71, tables 118 and 119, p. 151, table 125, p. 155; and 1972–73, tables 114 and 115, p. 154, table 121, p. 161.

Equally significant—and again a key feature distinguishing Ireland from 'the three neutral countries'—was the size of the agricultural sector. In 1961, 1967, 1969, and 1972, agricultural, forestry, and fishing produce accounted for 51.8, 53, 46.5 and 41.8 per cent respectively of Irish Domestic Exports,[131] while the agricultural figures for 1969 of Austria, Sweden, and Switzerland were 4.1, 2.4 and 2.9 per cent respectively of total exports.[132] Agriculture, including additionally processed

---

[131] *Ireland Statistical Abstract*, 1962, table 137, p. 153; ibid., 1969 (Prl. 1101), table 129, p. 153; ibid., 1970–71, table 124, p. 155; ibid., 1974 and 1975, table 119, p. 151.

[132] According to Senator O'Higgins, *Seanad Debates*, 72 (1972), 800.

products, approached 75 per cent of the Irish export trade, and nearly all of it was exported to Britain.[133] In 1969 Garret FitzGerald commented that such dependence upon another state was a 'serious undermining of the true independence of a country like ours . . . we are not independent economically'.[134] Lemass also felt that 'the historic task' of their generation was to secure economic independence,[135] and that a failure to do so 'would set the political gains to nought'.[136]

The extent of the influence of dependence upon Britain was further seen in the government White Paper of 30 June 1961 on the 'European Economic Community'. A major factor in determining Irish policy was the proportion of external trade with Britain, and any Irish–EEC relationship would have to take that into account. Irish national interest might be best served by joining if the United Kingdom was a member, but 'would not be served by joining . . . if the United Kingdom remained outside'. Ireland had to 'avoid any action which might adversely effect . . . the special trading relations' with Britain. Ireland might seek membership or association, but a decision could only be made when it was clear if Britain was joining and on what conditions.[137]

Lemass told the Dáil that if Britain applied, 'we also will apply, while at the same time informing them of our difficulty in accepting, in the present stage of our development, the full obligations of membership'.[138] If Ireland's trading partners joined 'together in an economic union, we cannot be outside it', since there would be 'no economic future for this country if we were to be cut off . . . [from] all our European markets' by a uniform tariff applying to Irish exports. It was not a 'choice of joining . . . or leaving things as they are', since the status quo was disappearing.[139] Generally, the Dáil accepted that there was little or no alternative to membership, with Browne arguing that the Dáil no longer had real freedom of decision, being merely a puppet.[140] Others also complained that, although allegedly a sovereign state, they had no real choice, and had less control over their destiny than

---

[133] *Economic Development* (Pr. 4803; Dublin, 1958), 15.

[134] FitzGerald, in *Dáil Debates*, 241 (1969), 1998 ff.; and see McAleese, 'Foreign Sector', 146.

[135] Lemass, in *Dáil Debates*, 175 (1959), 938.

[136] T. K. Whitaker, 'From Protection to Free Trade: The Irish Experience', *Administration*, 21/4 (Winter 1973), 421.

[137] *European Economic Community* (Pr. 6106; Dublin, 1961), 7–8.

[138] Lemass, *Dáil Debates*, 191 (1961), 205 ff. Corish described it as 'Hobson's choice', ibid. 232.

[139] Lemass, ibid. 266.

[140] Browne, ibid. 292.

they had in 1922.[141] Ireland was dependent 'on the decisions taken in Britain and elsewhere over which . . . [it had] no control'.[142]

That lack of control was further emphasized by de Gaulle's veto of British entry in 1963, when Lemass had to admit that the Irish position was dependent upon how relations between Britain, the Community, and others evolved.[143] Again, the Irish could not determine their position 'until the position concerning the British application, and Britain's future commercial policy' were known.[144] It is not surprising that in 1967 Lemass announced that 'our own application for membership should follow closely on that of Britain'.[145] The primacy of economic considerations is further shown by the key role at this time of the departments of Finance, and Industry and Commerce, rather than that of External Affairs.[146]

The Irish did 'continue to plan and prepare . . . [for] entry'.[147] They continued with the change of direction in economic policy initiated in 1955–6.[148] A reassessment of Irish economic progress culminated in the historic White Paper on 'Economic Development' in 1958, which acknowledged that previous policies 'have not resulted in a viable economy', and that a 'sense of anxiety is, indeed, justified'. In view of this and developments in Europe, the government concluded that 'sooner or later, protection will have to go and the challenge of free trade be accepted. There is really no other choice for a country working to keep pace materially with the rest of Europe.'[149]

Despite the problems with the EEC, therefore, there could be no turning back for the Irish, especially since the Six began tariff-reductions in January 1959 and the British pursued the idea of a free-trade industrial area in Europe, culminating in the foundation of EFTA in 1960. The Irish sought informal and partial interim agreements with the EEC and

---

141 McQuillan, ibid. 641 ff.

142 Costello, ibid. 199 (1963), 974 ff. This was especially important since, as Foreign Minister, Hillery referred to the EEC decision as possibly the most significant decision of a generation, perhaps even since 1922; ibid. 260 (1972), 293.

143 Lemass, ibid. 199 (1963), 617 ff.

144 Ibid. 932.

145 Ibid. 228 (1967), 550, 790; see also Cosgrave, ibid. 799 ff.

146 See Brigid Burns and Trevor C. Salmon, 'Policy-Making Coordination in Ireland on European Community Issues', *Journal of Common Market Studies*, 15/4 (June 1977), 277–8; and Patrick Keatinge, *The Formulation of Irish Foreign Policy* (Dublin, 1973), 129–31.

147 Lemass, *Dáil Debates*, 199 (1963), 617 ff.

148 On 11 Oct. 1955 Lemass made an important speech to Comh-Chomhairle Átha Cliath in Clery's Ballroom: see Farrell, 92–3; Whitaker, 'Protection', 415–16.

149 *Economic Development*, 2.

EFTA, but they were unsuccessful, and were thus excluded from EFTA. This followed the British insistence that EFTA be for developed economies only (the Irish having explained their weaknesses and inability fully to participate in a free-trade area during the negotiations led by Maudling, the British minister, under the auspices of the OEEC), and that agriculture be excluded. Consequently, Lemass took the view that 'participation in EFTA cannot be expected to offer substantial advantages to us'. The Irish would have no additional rights in the British market, and the exclusion of agriculture outweighed any putative advantage of free trade with the other members.[150]

Instead, in 1965 the Irish accepted the Anglo-Irish Free Trade Area Agreement. This was generally in Britain's favour, reflecting the asymmetrical bargaining-positions of the two sides.[151] It was partly the need to change that situation, where Britain could act as 'referee and umpire', which made the Community attractive, since, if both were members, they both would be 'subject to the European institutions' and Ireland would be safer than in 'the big jungle of the world'.[152] However, the Irish still felt constrained, confronted with the fact that 'in the world today there is no such thing as a really independent nation',[153] and that reduced dependence upon Britain was simply 'at the cost of increasing their dependence on the markets of Western Europe and the United States'.[154] This was shown by the pattern of investment in Ireland after the replacement of the Control of Manufacturers Act by the Industrial Development (Encouragement of External Investment) Act. Investment from the United States and West Germany amounted to 46 per cent and Britain accounted for 29 per cent of total foreign investment. There was now an acceptance of foreign penetration of the Irish economy;[155] incidentally, this raised the question of whether Irish subsidiaries of multinational firms would have to comply with NATO restrictions on trade in 'strategic goods' with Eastern Europe.[156]

The Irish could see little alternative to the EEC, but they initially

[150] For Ireland and EFTA see Garret FitzGerald, in *Seanad Debates*, 61 (1966), 1833 ff.; Lemass, *Dáil Debates*, 189 (1961), 295 ff.; and Farrell, 110. See also Miriam Hederman, *The Road to Europe: Irish Attitudes 1948–61* (Dublin, 1983), *passim*.

[151] See Garret FitzGerald, in a speech of May 1971, 'Ireland and the EEC', in *Ireland, Britain and Europe* (London, 1971), 30–1.

[152] Senator Dooge, *Seanad Debates*, 69 (1971), 1347.

[153] FitzGerald, *Dáil Debates*, 241 (1969), 2148 ff.

[154] McAleese, 'Foreign Sector', 146.

[155] See Keatinge, *A Place*, 140–2.

[156] This possibility is raised by Michael O'Corcora and Ronald J. Hill, 'The Soviet Union in Irish Foreign Policy', *International Affairs*, 58/2 (Spring 1982), 268–9.

failed to gain entry, for reasons not directly concerning them (although there were doubts about their preparedness).[157] In the 1961 White Paper both association and membership were considered as possibilities.[158] To some extent the matter was again beyond Irish control, in view of the Community ambivalence regarding association, but the Irish themselves also quickly decided that only membership would give them 'a voice in the formulation of policies and ensure access on a footing of equality', as well as allowing 'possible recourse to sources of assistance'.[159] Crucially, participation in the Common Agricultural Policy offered assured and remunerative markets for Irish agricultural produce. On the other hand, it was recognized that membership 'on the basis only of full obligations . . . would create a critical situation'.[160]

However, no substantive decisions were required, until there were further changes in circumstances, again taking place beyond Irish control. The Hague summit of December 1969 led for the first time to substantive negotiations concerning an Irish application. That Ireland continued to be dependent upon Britain was evident in the White Paper of January 1972, *The Accession of Ireland to the European Communities*. If Britain joined and Ireland remained aloof, 'the results for industry would be very serious, to say the least and, for agriculture, disastrous'. It was not a realistic alternative, bearing in mind the limitations imposed by 'the key position of agriculture' and 'the critical dependence on external trade'. An examination of a range of alternatives concluded that these involved 'such major disadvantages as to cause serious damage to our economic growth, to employment and to our standard of living'.[161] Irish choice was therefore constrained, as Aiken had admitted earlier, by forces 'operating in Europe . . . which are beyond our sole control, beyond direction by our single will'.[162] It was against this background that the debate about the implications of membership of the Community took place.

Another feature of that background was that speculation regarding what might happen if Ireland joined involved 'an hypothesis about an

---

[157] For a review of the response of the Six, the initial Irish memorandum and a critique of the Irish govt.'s approach, see Garret FitzGerald, in *Seanad Debates*, 61 (1966), 1833 ff. For general background see Hederman, *passim*, and Trevor C. Salmon, 'Ireland', in Carol and Kenneth Twitchett, *Building Europe: Britain's Partners in the EEC* (London, 1981), *passim*.

[158] *European Economic Community*, 7–8.

[159] Ibid. 34–5.

[160] Lemass, *Dáil Debates*, 191 (1961), 274.

[161] *The Accession of Ireland to the European Communities* (Prl. 2064; Dublin, 1972), 61–8.

[162] Aiken, *Dáil Debates*, 191 (1961), 664.

hypothesis'.[163] As a consequence of this, and of a changing external environment, the Irish attitude over the years 1961–72 encompassed several changes of emphasis, depending upon their perception of what was required of them at certain times. When it was expedient to stress commitment to the European cause, including defence, this was done; but at other times such commitment became conditional and was expressed mutedly. Questions associated with defence were somewhat 'peripheral' to the main debate,[164] although between 1961 and 1972 about a hundred parliamentary questions, in addition to points in debate, adjournment debates, and motions, were asked in the Dáil about NATO membership, the defence commitment which Community membership might involve, and a number of related issues, such as attitudes to the WEU.

On the one hand, it became clear that there was no enthusiasm for joining any existing system of alliance. For example, in 1961 the Dáil was assured that 'Irrespective of Partition' there were reasons for abstaining from NATO.[165] Particularly significant, apart from the freedom from having to clear in advance every word or action with other states, was the ability 'to make suggestions . . . that a member of a bloc could not make',[166] so as to contribute to reducing tensions by, for example, nuclear non-proliferation proposals and contributions to UN peace-keeping.[167] Rather than help alliances destroy each other, the Irish should 'try to win the peace'.[168] On the other hand, within days of such statements the Irish applied to join what some regarded as 'one of the most powerful groups and blocs' in the world, namely the European Community.[169] The government denied that the Community was a bloc (and even queried whether this was a correct description of the United States),[170] arguing that there was 'no commitment to belong to any bloc or to take part in any conflict involved in negotiating membership of the Community'.[171] Ireland was still 'neutral as between blocs . . . neutral in conflict', and no incompatibility existed between that and

---

[163] Gibbons, Minister for Defence, ibid. 245 (1970), 901.
[164] Keatinge, A Place, 95. For a review of the issues see Hederman, passim, and Salmon, 'Ireland', in C. and K. Twitchett, passim.
[165] Aiken, Dáil Debates, 189 (1961), 461.
[166] Ibid. 194 (1962), 1418; 191 (1961), 672 ff.
[167] Ibid. 189 (1961), 461.
[168] Ibid. 230 (1967), 890.
[169] Costello, ibid. 194 (1962), 1326.
[170] Aiken, ibid. 194 (1962), 1420.
[171] Hillery, ibid. 255 (1971), 2122.

Community membership, or between that and the commitment to 'take part in the defence of Europe just as now we defend our own territory', since it involved 'absolutely no question at this time of participating on one side or another in a bloc or taking part in any conflict'.[172]

Yet tensions did emerge between what many saw as Ireland's traditional position and the apparent obligations of Community membership. These tensions were exacerbated initially by a number of statements by the Taoiseach, Sean Lemass. In accordance with his conviction of the primary importance of Irish economic interests, he attempted to weaken the idea that neutrality was indispensable, announcing, for example, that 'there is no neutrality and we are not neutral'.[173] If help from Ireland was crucial to a Western victory, 'could we in the last resort refuse it . . .?', especially since everybody knew Ireland was on the democratic side.[174] Ireland could help NATO even if not a member,[175] and by 1962 Lemass was arguing that it was 'not in the national interest to represent [Article 4 of North Atlantic Treaty] as implying an undertaking to preserve [the] Partition situation', because there were similar phrases in the UN Charter and League Covenant (although he still felt that the arguments of the 1950 White Paper were relevant).[176] NATO membership was not discreditable: indeed, NATO helped defend Ireland.[177] Although no Cabinet committee looked at NATO membership at that time,[178] Lemass did arrange for the Minister for Lands, Michael Moran, to air the issue.[179] Moran noted that all current EEC members were also members of NATO, and that they had come together, at least partly, because of common policies on foreign and defence issues. Lemass, he said, had made it clear that there was no policy laid down with respect to neutrality between Communism and freedom, and that neutrality in that 'context is not a policy to which we would ever wish to appear committed'.[180] Lemass himself

---

[172] Hillery, ibid. 2122.

[173] *Irish Times*, 20 Aug. 1960.

[174] Lemass, address to the Solicitors' Apprentices Debating Society, on the motion 'The morality of neutrality', in *Eire-Ireland*, 506 (5 Dec. 1960).

[175] Id., interview with the *Scotsman*, repr. in *Eire-Ireland*, 516 (20 Feb. 1961).

[176] Id., *Dáil Debates*, 193 (1962), 4 ff., 1321–4. In the latter, Lemass admitted that he had only recently read the North Atlantic Treaty, although McQuillan (pp. 1315 ff.) quoted a statement by Lemass, reported by the *Irish Press*, 26 Sept. 1953, citing territorial integrity as a reason for not joining NATO.

[177] Lemass, ibid. 4 ff.

[178] Bartley, Minister for Defence, ibid. 194 (1962), 989.

[179] Farrell, 106.

[180] Lemass's version of the speech is in *Dáil Debates*, 193 (1962), 4 ff.; Moran's ibid. 966.

emphasized that Ireland recognized 'that a military commitment will be an inevitable consequence of our joining the Common Market and ultimately we would be *prepared to yield even the technical label of neutrality.* We are prepared to go into this integrated Europe without any reservation as to how far this will take us in the field of foreign policy and defence.'[181] Neutrality was no longer an aspiration or a fundamental principle.

In the autumn of 1962 Lemass made clear to the Dáil the willingness to co-operate 'without qualification' in achieving the wider objectives of the Community,[182] having said this to the EEC Council of Ministers in January 1962. Ireland, he declared, accepted the general aims of NATO, the ideal of European unity, and 'the conceptions embodied in the Treaty of Rome and the Bonn Declaration . . . of the duties, obligations and responsibilities which European unity would impose'.[183] In subscribing to the Bonn Declaration, Lemass accepted that 'only a united Europe, allied to the United States of America and to other free peoples, is in a position to face the dangers that menace the existence of Europe and of the whole free world'. This also involved accepting the need to create conditions allowing for a 'common policy' with the aim of political union and strengthening the Atlantic Alliance.[184]

The Irish application was made without any reservation regarding the supranational implications of membership,[185] or request for any discussion of possible provisos for neutrality. In the summer of 1969 the government was again emphatic that it had 'no reservations whatever about our application . . . We know there are political and economic obligations and that whenever the defence of Europe arises we will play our part.'[186] Did 'no reservations' mean literally that? Lemass, on occasion, also tried to argue that the Irish motives for their application were 'primarily political'—especially the desire to play a role in building

---

181 As cited in the Dáil by Browne, ibid. 199 (1963), 1149 and FitzGerald, ibid. 327 (1981), 1423 (emphasis added).

182 Lemass, ibid. 197 (1962), 15.

183 Statement by Lemass to Council of Ministers, Brussels, 18 Jan. 1962, reproduced in *European Economic Community: Developments Subsequent to White Paper of 30 June 1961* (Pr. 6613; Dublin, 1962), 63–4.

184 Lemass read the Bonn Declaration in full to the Dáil and reiterated the government's acceptance of it: *Dáil Debates*, 193 (1982), 15–18.

185 Lemass, ibid. 220 (1966), 1613.

186 Hillery, ibid. 241 (1969), 884; and see Browne, ibid. 199 (1963), 1149 ff.

Europe—and that this involved accepting the wide scope of the provisions of the Treaty of Rome.[187]

This approach may have been a corrective to an initial Irish memorandum submitted on 4 July 1961, which had raised doubts about Irish political commitment and ability to cope with full membership. Although another memorandum was substituted for it,[188] Lemass may have used hyperbole to advance the Irish cause. None the less, as a matter of public and international record, Ireland accepted the letter and spirit both of the Community treaties and of the Bonn Declaration. It might be argued that NATO was completely irrelevant to its EEC application,[189] and that no one had requested Irish membership,[190] but the tenor of Irish statements suggests that, for Lemass, the economic arguments were so strong that he was prepared to yield neutrality.

Unfortunately, it was uncertain whether the treaties and Community membership involved a defence commitment. If the Irish joined, 'Would we have to take part in a war?'[191] The official reply was that the treaties contained no military provisions,[192] had no requirement to join alliances,[193] and said nothing about neutrality.[194] Obligations contrary to neutrality were not 'mentioned directly or indirectly' by the EEC.[195] No military or defence commitments were 'involved in Ireland's acceptance of these Treaties'.[196] The Irish argued that any attempt to impose non-economic matters would be *ultra vires*, and that any defence treaty would require Irish consent—indeed, a referendum—if it involved raising an army or decisions about going to war.[197] Any Irish response on these matters would be voluntary. It was also asserted that the Treaty of Accession contained no recognition or guarantee of territorial boundaries.[198]

---

[187] Lemass, ibid. 197 (1962), 19; he was being specifically questioned on this.

[188] See FitzGerald, *Seanad Debates*, 61 (1966), 1833 ff.

[189] Lemass, *Dáil Debates*, 193 (1962), 4 ff.

[190] Lemass, ibid. 197 (1962), 15; and see ibid. 195 (1962), 457; 197 (1962), 14; 259 (1972), 2444 ff.

[191] Blowick, ibid. 191 (1961), 2619.

[192] Lemass, ibid. 195 (1962), 890.

[193] Lynch, Taoiseach, ibid. 227 (1967), 4; Lemass, ibid. 192 (1961), 140.

[194] Hillery, ibid. 249 (1970), 263.

[195] Ibid. In the summer of 1961 it had been acknowledged that some EFTA members felt 'unable to subscribe to the Rome Treaty because of its possible political implications', but although this was a factor to be considered, it was stressed again that the treaty said nothing directly about defence: Lemass, ibid. 189 (1961), 958.

[196] *The Accession of Ireland to the European Communities*, 57.

[197] Ibid., and cf. Lemass, *Dáil Debates*, 193 (1962), 1483, and debate on Third Amendment to the Constitution Bill, ibid. 258 (1972), 393 ff.

[198] Lynch, Taoiseach, ibid. 260 (1972), 1248.

This legalistic approach can be challenged on both specific and general grounds, as indeed it was by Austria, Sweden, and Switzerland. Moreover, a recent study has concluded that 'there was no formal exclusion of defence from the Community agenda in the Treaty of Rome', and that the Community 'could expand into defence without actually violating the Treaty of Rome if its members so chose', especially given Article 235, which allowed the Community, under certain circumstances, to move into new areas.[199] Such moves would require Irish consent but it is not clear that they would be *ultra vires* or require a referendum. In addition, many feared that Ireland would be unable to choose freely, since membership would be like 'jumping on to a moving escalator from which one will never be allowed to get off . . . In ten years' time we shall be so totally economically committed to the infrastructure of the EEC and our trade will be so firmly based . . . that if . . . a decision is taken of a political or military kind', Ireland would in reality have lost the option of refusal.[200] Economic association was bound to lead to some form of political and military involvement, and legalistic safeguards would be no genuine safeguard.

This was why Labour rejected the Fine Gael amendment to the Third Amendment of the Constitution Bill (1971). The original bill provided for Irish membership of the Communities and, as originally drafted, said that no provision of the Constitution could invalidate 'laws enacted, acts done or measures adopted by the State *consequent on* membership of the Communities'. The amendment substituted 'necessitated by the obligations of' for 'consequent on' and was successfully and specifically introduced to preserve a narrow interpretation of the treaties and to ensure that any defence treaty arising out of Community membership would have to be put to the people. Labour continued to argue that the *de facto* position would outweigh the *de jure* one.[201]

Within Ireland scant attention was paid to the specific articles which worried the three neutral countries, although attention was focused upon the Preamble and likely political and defence obligations. While it remained unclear what those obligations would be, many realized that 'it would be less than frank if we imagined that defence was not at the

[199] Trevor Taylor, *European Defence Co-operation* (Chatham House Papers 24; London, 1984), 17–18; and *EEC Treaty*, Articles 224–6, 235.

[200] Thornley, *Dáil Debates*, 258 (1972), 449.

[201] For the debate see ibid. 257 (1971), 1095–142, 1286–555, 1720–32, 258 (1972), 393–484, 519–621 (emphasis added). It is worth noting that in 1962 the Dáil had been told there would be no referendum on any change in Ireland's militarily neutral position, since Ireland was a parliamentary democracy: Lemass, ibid. 193 (1962), 19.

forefront of the thinking behind the drafting of the Rome Treaty',[202] and therefore that as dutiful members the Irish had to shoulder 'our share of responsibility for securing its well-being'. Those 'participating in the new Europe . . . must be prepared to assist, if necessary, in its defence', although as a member Ireland would have a voice in shaping those developments.[203]

Successive government declarations did not help to clarify this issue: they emphasized the legal position when referring to neutrality, but Irish moral and political obligations when referring to Community commitment. A distinction was also drawn between current and future commitments, and between the Community and an alliance. No little ambiguity existed on these questions, but underneath the statements lay a public recognition and acceptance that at some time in the future, and conditional upon certain developments, Ireland would join in the defence of the Community. The problem arose from a reluctance to accept the corollary, namely that such a position involved the abandonment of neutrality. Instead, Taoiseach Lynch tried to argue that he did 'not think . . . the word "neutrality" is relevant' in the context of Community membership, since neutrality 'would not be relevant in the context of our being attacked by anybody: we would defend ourselves'. In an admitted departure from previous policy, it was accepted that Ireland would 'be interested in the defence of the territories embraced by the communities. There is no question of neutrality there.'[204] Ireland told its prospective partners that it would be prepared to assist in Community defence, 'if this became necessary, at any time'.[205]

Lynch also emphasized the conditional nature of Irish neutrality, that it was not traditional like the three neutral countries and that the Irish were free to 'make up our minds as to our neutrality in certain circumstances'. Lynch believed that, in a 'war between atheistic communism . . . and the way of life we know', neither Dáil nor people would 'permit us to be neutral'.[206] Scorn was now poured on the way in which *ad hoc* wartime neutrality had become 'inculcated in some people', as 'an

---

[202] Cosgrave, ibid. 228 (1967), 801; Cosgrave was leader of the opposition and in 1973 became Taoiseach.

[203] Cosgrave, ibid. 247 (1970), 1668; 199 (1963), 1188 ff.

[204] Lynch, ibid. 241 (1969), 1157.

[205] Although 'at any time' was specified to mean a particular future period when the Community had developed and there was a common defence force: Hillery, Minister for Foreign Affairs, ibid. 246 (1970), 1373. He also acknowledged that this was a departure from previous policy.

[206] Lynch, ibid. 241 (1969), 631 ff.

idea that . . . was a policy for all time in all circumstances';[207] it was an 'accident', introduced for 'reasons . . . which are not relevant today'; it was a 'practical expedient'.[208] Past decisions would not 'in any way impede . . . Parliament from taking a decision that would make us non-neutral in other circumstances', specifically as EEC obligations developed.[209] Ireland had 'never adopted a permanent policy of neutrality in a doctrinaire or ideological sense'.[210] Although Hillery on one occasion spoke of neutrality as 'Traditional since the last war', this was part of a rebuttal of the wider traditional argument,[211] and more generally, it came to be argued that Ireland had 'never been neutral' since 1945, because of its role 'in international organisations and making decisions and taking our own independent line'.[212] Entry into the UN was 'not the action of a country with a tradition of neutrality',[213] since Ireland was 'now on the side of all peace-loving countries'.[214]

In view of such developments, it was highly tendentious to argue that they had 'abandoned nothing',[215] that neutrality would be preserved, and that the commitment to 'co-operate more and more closely together' did not 'at any stage . . . conflict with our neutrality', nor did 'neutrality conflict with our participating in this aim to participate in the close union of the countries of Europe'.[216] The reality was the recognition that a 'political union without the capacity and the means to defend that union would be utterly meaningless', since such a union 'necessarily' implied 'the formulation of a common defence policy and the working out of common defence arrangements'. After all, as Haughey asked, 'what is wrong with nations getting together and deciding they are going to have a common bond of defence between them?'[217]

The enduring Irish position has been that the question of any commitment to European defence is dependent upon considerable evolution within the Community, and is highly conditional. It has depended upon whether political unity 'develops far enough', or 'if political development goes to its finality and an institution is created of which we are a

207 Cosgrave, ibid. 230 (1967), 833.
208 FitzGerald, ibid. 241 (1969), 1986.
209 Lynch, ibid. 241 (1969), 969.
210 Hillery, interview with *Irish Press*, 2 Dec. 1970.
211 Hillery, *Dáil Debates*, 255 (1971), 2123.
212 Ibid. 249 (1970), 265.
213 Booth, ibid. 201 (1963), 993.
214 O. J. Flanagan, ibid. 252 (1971), 667.
215 Hillery, ibid. 249 (1970), 1913 ff.
216 Ibid. 255 (1971), 2121 ff.
217 Haughey, ibid. 230 (1967), 1104.

part and defence is discussed in that Community'. The Irish would 'not renege on' their 'duties', if 'in the context of political evolution, the question of the defence of the Community arises'.[218] An additional condition was that commitment depended upon 'enjoying all the benefits of being part of Europe'.[219] It was also emphasized that as of 1971 there was no commitment to defend any Community country which was attacked, even after Ireland became a member. There was 'no guaranteed continuation of the European concept',[220] and the 1972 White Paper emphasized that 'progress towards the achievement of an ever closer union . . . must be pursued with due deliberation . . . joint action in the political sphere must develop gradually but at the same time on a progressive basis'.[221]

Such statements led Keatinge to ask whether the Irish were paying little more 'than the obligatory lip service which any applicant's negotiator must pay'.[222] This misses the point that even in its conditional statements the government was abandoning the principle of, and aspiration to, neutrality. Friend and foe alike knew the Irish position, its distinctiveness from the three neutral countries, and the problems that economic dependence generated for political independence. While Lynch might argue that it was 'not a question of neutrality but of meeting obligations within a complex', he was nearer the mark in admitting that neutrality 'in the context of the EEC would not be the old conception of neutrality at all'.[223]

Pro-European politicians, like FitzGerald, thought that it would be 'dishonest and dishonourable' to join if there were reservations about the 'moral obligations' to 'move towards a common foreign policy'. However, he distinguished foreign policy from defence, arguing that the latter was 'nowhere in the offing at the present time', and would only arise 'if this becomes a full political union'.[224]

Opponents of entry argued that the government was accepting 'a military commitment'[225] and was engaged in a 'shocking' betrayal of

---

[218] Hillery, ibid. 247 (1970), 2011 ff., 2068 ff.

[219] Ibid. 249 (1970), 1917.

[220] Ibid. 255 (1971), 2123.

[221] *The Accession of Ireland to the European Communities*, 57–8.

[222] Patrick Keatinge, 'Odd Man Out? Irish Neutrality and European Security', *International Affairs*, 48/3 (July 1972), 440.

[223] Kavanagh, quoting a statement by Lynch on television, in *Dáil Debates*, 252 (1971), 734.

[224] FitzGerald, ibid. 247 (1970), 1933 ff.

[225] Keating, ibid. 248 (1970), 575, in reference to the 1970 White Paper, *Membership of the European Communities: Implications for Ireland* (Prl. 1110; Dublin, 1970). See also O'Brien, in *Dáil Debates*, 247 (1970), 1875 ff.

traditional policy.[226] Echoing Swedish arguments, they claimed that the Community was 'essentially a NATO European membership' or involved a 'side-door' involvement with NATO.[227] The Community was not 'a philanthropic body' but a 'ruthless capitalist superpower with an empire and a nuclear capability', comprising notorious aggressors.[228] Was 'communism any less atheistic . . . in 1949–50'?[229] Labour resurrected the rationales for neutrality used by de Valera, and compared those with the government sacrifice of Irish identity and sovereignty,[230] as well as its apparent '[willingness] to do anything . . . to be allowed . . . in'.[231]

There was some attempt to reconcile the perceived traditional position and Community membership, in the vision of the Community as 'a Third Force between the Soviet Union and the United States . . . not a third power of the same kind . . . but . . . capable of looking after itself to a large degree and . . . able to take an independent line',[232] being not 'pro-American . . . or . . . pro-anything but . . . independent'.[233] The Irish claimed not to accept that the European ideal 'is a confrontation against the powers of the Warsaw Pact', but rather that it 'was to put an end to war in Europe'. The idealism involved

in the idea of a united Europe is not represented by the North Atlantic Treaty Organisation. When we say that we are prepared to undertake the defence commitments of a European Community we are not pledging our loyalty to NATO. We are saying that the European Community which we wish to join is something worthwhile and therefore worth defending, but it is only worth defending for itself and not defending for any other ideology outside itself.[234]

However, as Tully pointed out, such a Europe would need a 'military force' and would not, therefore, preserve neutrality *per se*.[235] One senior

[226] Browne, *Dáil Debates*, 199 (1963), 679.

[227] O'Brien, ibid. 247 (1970), 1876.

[228] The quotation is from Keating, ibid. 248 (1970), 687. Cf. 575 ff.; Kavanagh, ibid. 252 (1971), 734 ff.; Browne, ibid. 191 (1961), 303–4.

[229] O'Brien, ibid. 247 (1970), 1878. Browne also made a similar point: ibid. 199 (1963), 673 ff.

[230] O'Brien, ibid. 247 (1970), 1884.

[231] Ibid. 1879.

[232] FitzGerald, ibid. 241 (1969), 1992 ff.

[233] Ibid. 247 (1970), 1933 ff.; and see O'Kennedy, later Foreign Minister, ibid. 252 (1971), 770 ff., and O'Leary, ibid. 242 (1969), 78 ff.

[234] Senator Dooge, later Foreign Minister, *Seanad Debates*, 69 (1971), 1345–6.

[235] Tully, *Dáil Debates*, 248 (1970), 68 ff. This was part of a wider debate epitomized by the contrast between Johan Galtung, *The European Community: A Superpower in the Making* (London, 1973), and François Duchene, 'The European Community and the Uncertainties of Interdependence', in M. Kohnstamm and W. Hager, *A Nation Writ Large? Foreign Policy Problems before*

Fine Gael politician, Ryan, was willing to argue for the Community having a neutral role, Irish neutrality being an example and encouragement to others. Ryan believed that the Six wanted Ireland to assert neutrality as a proper doctrine for any member nation of the EEC,[236] partly in order to demonstrate that it itself was 'not a war-like instrument'.[237] The Six did not want a European army, and therefore membership did not involve alliance.[238]

Ireland differed from the three neutrals in finding no insurmountable obstacle to Community membership in neutrality. Unlike Austria, Sweden, and Switzerland, the Irish accepted:

1. the political obligations of membership and the political objectives of the Community, including political unification and a European identity in the world;

2. the Bonn Declaration and the need ultimately to partake in Community defence;

3. the supranational nature of the Community, the possibility of majority voting and of the supranational direction of external trade, and the general constraints on sovereignty;

4. the constraints placed upon 'economic defence' by particular treaty articles, and the general constraints upon the domestic economy, especially with the future prospect of Economic and Monetary Union; and

5. Article 224 and the lack of either provisos for neutrality or provisions for terminating the treaties.

The crucial distinction between the case of the three neutral countries and of Ireland was the degree to which Ireland depended economically upon one state, Britain.

Some of the Irish hypotheses were tested before entry in January 1973. On 18 May 1971 the Ten Foreign Ministers met and the 'subject of European security was . . . amongst those discussed'.[239] This attracted little attention, but a meeting at The Hague on 20–1 November 1972

---

the European Community (London, 1973), and Duchene, 'A New European Defence Community', Foreign Affairs, 50/1 (Oct. 1971), 69–82.

[236] Ryan, Dáil Debates, 260 (1972), 429 ff.; 255 (1971), 679 ff.

[237] Ibid. 257 (1971), 1296 ff. He went on to say that Irish membership would be welcomed by the Six 'to show just how a neutral country can be a member of the EEC without having its right to remain neutral qualified in any way'.

[238] Ibid. 255 (1971), 680.

[239] Ibid. 254 (1971), 2268. Ireland joined the Political Committee of the Community officially only in Apr. 1972.

caused some consternation, since the CSCE, the recent German treaty, and the Middle East were all discussed. The government also announced that it would itself 'take into account the views of its partners', especially West Germany, on the question of the timing of German entry into the UN and the recognition of East Germany. The opposition saw this as 'the first major question' upon which 'the principle of acting in concert with other members' appeared to have operated and, clearly surprised by it, worried that it might be an 'anticipation of future changes in our foreign policy'. The government answered in what became a familiar pattern, namely that the discussion simply involved an attempt to find 'where there is consensus' and that there was 'no pressure on any country to change its individual stand'. Ireland would continue to consult its partners.[240] This was precisely what Aiken had derided in 1961, and it was part of a wider question relating to Irish sovereignty and the ability to pursue an independent foreign policy, particularly at the United Nations.

Much of Irish policy had traditionally been concerned with sovereignty issues, and sovereignty was itself linked to neutrality. Just as neutrality was redefined in the period between 1961 and 1972, so too was sovereignty. The 1972 White Paper, for example, argued that 'no form of co-operation between nations' failed to involve 'limitations on their freedom of action', and that states willingly accepted such limitations if they were perceived to be in the national interest. The Community was to be seen in this light, but any 'limitations on national freedom of action' would be 'more than counter-balanced by the influence' Ireland would be able to bring to bear 'on the formulation of Community policies affecting . . . [Irish] interests'. This was contrasted with the reality of being 'independent but with little or no capacity to influence events abroad that significantly affect us'—in other words, 'the nominal right' to freedom. Real freedom was constrained in an interdependent world but Community membership meant that the powers which Ireland was to share 'would in fact be enhanced rather than diminished by the co-operation involved'.[241] The Community would place Ireland in a much better position than the current pervasive bilateral relationship with the United Kingdom.[242] Notwithstanding

240 Hillery, ibid. 264 (1972), 22.
241 *The Accession of Ireland to the European Communities*, 58–60.
242 FitzGerald, 'Ireland and the EEC', in *Ireland, Britain and Europe*, 37–8, indicated seven possible ways in which the relationship with Britain might change.

complaints from Labour, this view generally prevailed,[243] undermining further the aspiration to neutrality.

It also adversely affected the aspiration to have a genuinely independent foreign policy, although other problems had arisen long before in that connection. These were epitomized by the famous Cosgrave statement in July 1956, outlining the basic principles of Irish policy with particular relevance to Irish policy at the United Nations. The first principle was that Ireland would observe the Charter and insist that others also do so. It was in the interests of the weak that the Charter be upheld, and upholding such principles would also increase Irish influence. Secondly, Ireland would 'try to maintain a position of independence, judging the various questions . . . strictly on their merits, in a just and disinterested way', and therefore 'avoid becoming associated with particular blocs or groups so far as possible'. Finally, there would be a wish to reflect national traditions, objectives, and moral concepts, which meant an obligation to do 'whatever we can as a member of the United Nations to preserve the Christian civilization of which we are a part and with that end in view to support wherever possible those powers principally responsible for the defence of the free world in their resistance to the spread of Communist power and influence'. In terms of general policy, in the 'great ideological conflict . . . our attitude is clear, by geographical position, culture, tradition and national interest. We belong to the great community of states, made up of the United States of America, Canada and Western Europe. Our national destinies are indissolubly bound up with theirs.' Cosgrave did admit that there would be difficulties in applying the principles, specifically given the issue of self-determination.[244]

With the change of government in March 1957, it was Aiken who was responsible for Irish policy at the United Nations for the next twelve years. In 1956 he had supported Cosgrave's first two principles but noted that the third 'departed to some extent from the first and second', and that Cosgrave was 'rather tying himself up' in the third point, since there were 'sins that are common' to communist and non-communist states alike. The crucial point was not to 'become a part of any tied group bound by agreements to support one another, no

[243] See Lemass, *Dáil Debates*, 191 (1961), 2571-80; 230 (1967), 742 ff.; Aiken, ibid. 194 (1962), 1412 ff.; 201 (1963), 1073 ff.; 230 (1967), 887 ff.; Corish, ibid. 230 (1967), 782 ff.; O'Leary, ibid. 260 (1972), 473 ff.

[244] Cosgrave, ibid. 159 (1956), 127-46.

matter what the subject matter up for discussion'.[245] Despite this, Conor Cruise O'Brien has argued that, although the second principle initially held 'relative ascendancy' over the third, as symbolized by the vote on Chinese representation in 1957, this position 'became eroded and eventually collapsed'.[246] The change dated from the 1961 vote on Chinese representation.

Did such a change occur; and if so, to what extent was it motivated by the application in August 1961 to join the Community, and by the concern of some that Ireland's 'economic interests' were not being enhanced by 'fatuous observations which have no effect other than a disturbing one on our friends'?[247] Certainly Declan Costello thought it 'quite obvious that the Government's foreign policy . . . changed radically . . . from the time they took their decision to join the EEC'.[248] Could Ireland be uncommitted at the United Nations, yet blather its support for Europe?[249]

The most detailed analysis of the question of whether there was a change is by Norman MacQueen in a statistical analysis of Irish voting behaviour in the UN General Assembly between 1956 and 1970. It is most interesting that this analysis does not support the charge by Costello and O'Brien, although there was an increase in levels of co-operation with the United States and Britain, except on colonial questions. MacQueen argues that the degree of identity between Irish and Swedish voting (Sweden being regarded as a traditional European neutral) remained 'largely steady', whereas, had a 1961 change 'taken place as a result of domestic political circumstances, voting co-operation with Sweden might be expected to show a discernible decline'. Since there is

no evidence to support the suggestion that any change took place in Swedish foreign policy . . . the changing emphasis throughout the 1960s must be seen to have taken place *within the UN itself* and not as a positive redirection of Irish policy as a result of extraneous influences . . . the transformation was rather in the nature of the Assembly which underwent a general radicalisation during this period. Ireland and Sweden, progressive neutrals in the earlier period, now by standing still, objectively moved to the right.

*

245 Aiken, ibid. 147–8. Cf. de Valera, ibid. 432–40, who saw no fundamental disagreement on policy.
246 O'Brien, 'Ireland in International Affairs', in Owen Dudley Edwards (ed.), *Conor Cruise O'Brien Introduces Ireland* (London, 1969), 130–1.
247 Costello, *Dáil Debates*, 164 (1957), 1231.
248 Ibid. 201 (1963), 951–2.
249 McQuillan, ibid. 191 (1961), 641–52, 551 ff.; see also FitzGerald, ibid. 241 (1969), 1984 ff.

Sweden did not apply for Community membership, yet 'a close affinity is detectable throughout the period' with Irish voting behaviour, and this affinity 'appears to have been little affected by the supposed rightward shift in Irish policy after 1961'. Indeed, MacQueen argues that the 'gradual move towards greater co-operation with the western powers . . . cannot . . . be dated as beginning in 1961 . . . Rather, the process appears to begin in the plenary votes around 1959'.[250]

Aside from the United Nations, there clearly was some change in policy after 1961, as is evident in the attitude to sovereignty and neutrality. There was also a fragmentation in policy-making, whereby problems were 'segmented into constituent elements':[251] this fragmentation had a historical basis, in that the Department of Industry and Commerce had acquired certain responsibilities for trade, and it was the economic departments who determined the need to move away from protectionism and had predominant roles in the early dealings with the EEC. Moreover, finance, trade, and constitutional issues had also traditionally involved the Taoiseach's Office.[252] Lemass was therefore in a strong position to take charge of the Community issue. He was also the inspiration for the post-revolutionary élite which was 'economically oriented with a view to the establishment of . . . sound economic policy for steady economic growth'.[253]

In view of the economic and constitutional implications of the Community, Aiken believed it 'right and natural' for the Taoiseach to play a leading role in the issue,[254] and consequently he himself hardly mentioned it in the Irish parliament, only uttering 58 words on Europe in 20,000 espousing policy in the External Affairs debates in the Dáil during 1963-5.[255] This division of labour allowed Ireland to pursue a number of policies which were 'mutually conflicting . . . [and] contradictory'.[256] One foreign policy was operated by Lemass towards Europe and the creation of 'a viable Irish society',[257] while Aiken continued in

250 All quotations are from MacQueen, 'Neutrality', 177-200 (emphasis in original).

251 Henry Kissinger, 'Domestic Structure and Foreign Policy', in James N. Rosenau, (ed.), *International Politics and Foreign Policy* (New York, 1969), 268.

252 See MacQueen, 'Neutrality', 113, and Keatinge, *Formulation*, 66.

253 A. S. Cohan, *The Irish Political Elite* (Dublin, 1972), 71.

254 Aiken, *Dáil Debates*, 201 (1963), 1075; Keatinge, *A Place*, 209; Farrell, 109.

255 FitzGerald, *Seanad Debates*, 61 (1966), 1833 ff. See also Costello, *Dáil Debates*, 176 (1959), 685 ff., and Aiken, ibid. 191 (1961), 662 ff.; 194 (1962), 1412 ff.

256 FitzGerald, *Dáil Debates*, 241 (1969), 1990; Keatinge, *Formulation*, 87, 93-4; T. Desmond Williams, 'Irish Foreign Policy 1949-1969', in J. J. Lee (ed.), *Ireland 1945-1970* (Dublin, 1979), 144-5.

257 J. J. Lee, 'Sean Lemass', in id., *Ireland*, 22-3.

the de Valera mould, prone to 'the rhetoric of his ideals', in New York.[258]

LACK OF ISOLATIONISM

In his speech of July 1956 setting out the basis of Irish foreign policy, Cosgrave had welcomed admission to the United Nations as a necessary consequence of Irish sovereignty, and argued that to turn their backs upon it would lead to isolation and insignificance in world affairs. That, it was argued, would be contrary to the ideals of those who had worked for freedom, to the principles of Irish policy since 1922, and to Irish national interest. Ireland would rather seek to play an active part in world affairs for both moral and material reasons.[259] Trade followed the flag, and in the contemporary, competitive world Ireland could not, in any case, isolate itself.[260]

It was also in Ireland's interest to participate, since 'the weaker States' benefited from 'the protection and support afforded by the moral influence' of the United Nations, which was 'the protector of weak nations and friend of the poor, and our own best hope for the security and reunification of the Irish nation'.[261] Support for the Charter had been Cosgrave's first principle in July 1956.[262] Aiken believed that support for the United Nations and the Charter were the best hope for small nations, for the evolution of world order based on justice and the rule of law, and that this in turn was the only basis of permanent peace.[263] With this perspective, de Valera argued that, as UN members, it was their 'duty' to make suggestions to resolve conflicts, and that this was the 'only point' of being involved.[264] Not all agreed, since Deputy Sherwin asked why Ireland should concern itself with the rows of others when it had a major unresolved row at home.[265] More generally, it was felt that Ireland could play a particularly valuable role and exert influence because

---

[258] Ibid. 170–1. Lee was actually comparing Lemass and de Valera, but it also applies to the Lemass–Aiken comparison.

[259] Cosgrave, *Dáil Debates*, 159 (1956), 139 ff.

[260] John A. Costello, Taoiseach, ibid. 159 (1956), 610.

[261] Speech by Aiken to General Assembly, 8 Dec. 1964, in *Ireland/UN 1964*, 9.

[262] Cosgrave, *Dáil Debates*, 159 (1956), 142.

[263] Aiken, ibid. 194 (1962), 1315.

[264] De Valera, ibid. 164 (1957), 1290 ff.

[265] Sherwin, ibid. 176 (1959), 568.

it had not been a colonizing power, it had had to struggle for its own freedom, and it had ties of Catholicism with Europe and Latin America and influence in numerous countries through its emigrants.[266] Irish historical experiences were thought to present 'a unique opportunity to stand as an example' to the newly independent, while Ireland had 'throughout the world an influence far beyond any material strength or wealth', in view of the role of Irish missionaries and their contribution to education in many parts of the world.[267] Ireland had a 'special role in certain spheres'.[268]

To maximize this role many, including de Valera and Aiken, thought that the emphasis should be upon Cosgrave's second principle, since it was not in accord with Irish 'interests . . . or . . . traditions . . . to stand silent and not offer our opinion truthfully and honestly'. On the contrary, it was 'valuable to countries that bear the real burden to have an independent nation which is prepared to make proposals and suggestions in the present disastrous world situation'.[269] Some, like MacBride, felt that Ireland could make little material contribution but could contribute to the battle for men's minds, and thus 'carve out a niche' for itself.[270] Others went further, wanting Ireland to 'follow the Indian line',[271] although Fine Gael urged Aiken not to copy the Indian position or try to outdo it in neutralism, but rather sympathize with it.[272] O'Brien has described how, for many younger officials in Iveagh House, 'the ideal of what constituted good international behaviour was exemplified at this time by Sweden', whose actions were 'independent, disinterested and honourable'.[273] A few preferred instead the Swiss model, as they wished to make a contribution while maintaining neutrality.[274]

As already seen, there was some similarity between Irish and Swedish voting. In the first half of Aiken's tenure (1957–69) the Irish also made a number of proposals to ameliorate the world situation, as well as contributing to UN peace-keeping. The attempt to mark out a distinctive position was most sharply demonstrated by the vote on China in 1957,

266 Costello, ibid. 163 (1957), 598 ff.
267 Cosgrave, ibid. 191 (1961), 620 ff.
268 Cosgrave, ibid. 194 (1962), 1361.
269 Aiken, ibid. 164 (1957), 25 ff.
270 MacBride, ibid. 159 (1956), 602.
271 McQuillan, ibid. 221.
272 Costello, ibid. 164 (1957), 1177 ff.
273 O'Brien, Katanga, 24.
274 Booth, Dáil Debates, 167 (1958), 268 ff.

when Aiken voted for a 'full and open discussion of the question of the representation of China'.[275] According to O'Brien, this issue was regarded as an important indicator of a state's alignment, and of how it was likely to vote 'on all other critical issues'.[276] However, the estrangement with the United States did not last. During this period Aiken made a series of proposals to enhance international security. In the 'disengagement' proposal of September 1957 Aiken suggested 'a fair and reasonable drawing back of the non-national forces on both sides from the border of Russian-occupied Europe . . . along latitudinal lines from either side of the border for an equal number of kilometres', supervised by a 'United Nations inspection unit'.[277] This idea was developed into a series of proposals for 'ever-widening areas in which the contest for the adherence of smaller States will be brought to an end'.[278] These would be 'area[s] of law', by which term was meant 'a specific region . . . in which the neighbouring States would agree to limit their arms below blitzkrieg level, to exclude foreign troops from their territories and to accept supervision by the United Nations of the fulfilment of these conditions'.[279] These regions of neutrality would gradually be built up throughout the world, as areas committed to peaceful change and settlement.[280] These proposals were linked by Aiken to other proposals on limitation of nuclear tests, proliferation issues, and disarmament.[281] In 1958, for example, Ireland submitted a resolution calling for 'an *ad hoc* Committee to study the dangers inherent in the further dissemination of nuclear weapons and recommend . . . appropriate measures for averting these dangers',[282] and in 1961 the General Assembly unanimously adopted an Irish resolution on the 'Prevention of the Wider dissemination of nuclear weapons'; it is also possible to argue that Aiken made a significant contribution to the Non-Proliferation Treaty of 1968.[283]

---

[275] Speech by Aiken to General Assembly, 23 Sept. 1957, in *Ireland/UN 1957*, 28.

[276] O'Brien, *Ireland, the United Nations and Southern Africa*, 3.

[277] Speech by Aiken to General Assembly, 10 Sept. 1957, in *Ireland/UN 1957*, 3.

[278] Speech to General Assembly, 19 Sept. 1958, in *Ireland/UN 1958*, 19.

[279] Speech to General Assembly, 6 Oct. 1960, in *Ireland/UN 1960*, 10; and speech, 23 Sept. 1959, in *Ireland/UN 1959*, 9–19.

[280] Speeches to General Assembly, 7 Aug. and 19 Sept. 1958, in *Ireland/UN 1958*, 8 and 19; and 23 Sept. 1959, in *Ireland/UN 1959*, 9–19.

[281] For some of his contributions on these matters see: *Ireland/UN 1957*, 13–17; *Ireland/UN 1958*, 17–25, 29–38, 39–53; *Ireland/UN 1959*, 12–15, 55–77; *Ireland/UN 1960*, 27–34, 40–6, 58–60; *Ireland/UN 1961*, 13–21; *Ireland/UN 1962*, 35–9; *Ireland/UN 1963*, 17–18.

[282] Text of draft resolution submitted by Ireland, 17 Oct. 1958, *Ireland/UN 1958*, 39.

[283] Text of resolution submitted by Ireland and adopted, 4 Dec. 1961, *Ireland/UN 1961*, 37–8; Keatinge, *A Place*, 163.

During this time Aiken also spoke out 'firmly in support of the office of the Secretary-General', since no 'triumvirate or committee' could replace the Secretary-General in his role of providing 'the means of effective implementation of the Organisation's decisions'.[284] Aiken linked attacks on the Secretary-General to other attempts to destroy the organization, such as the non-payment of subscriptions[285] and the failure to meet the cost of implementing the decisions of the Security Council and the General Assembly.[286] In 1965 Ireland co-sponsored a number of draft resolutions of the financing of peace-keeping operations.[287] In addition, it refused initially to be reimbursed from voluntary funds for its peace-keeping endeavours, in case this undermined the principle of collective action or tainted the Irish contribution.[288] By the spring of 1966 this policy changed to accepting money from any fund the Secretary-General might have, but Aiken continued to fret about the situation.[289]

In the period 1956-72 the Irish made a significant contribution to UN peace-keeping, beginning initially with co-sponsorship of the idea of a United Nations Emergency Force (UNEF) for Suez, and following this by contributing to the United Nations Observer Group in Lebanon in 1958 and the United Nations Truce Supervision Organisation (UNTSO) in the Middle East from 1958. Other similar missions followed. More substantial were the contributions to ONUC and UNFICYP, which at times represented one-eighth of the PDF effort.

The Irish contributed partly because of general considerations concerning their view of the international milieu, particularly support for the United Nations and its principles. They also felt that it was in Irish interests to maintain the rule of law, and the United Nations was the only channel for that in international affairs. Ireland could also, perhaps, help to avoid world wars, although it could not of itself stop such wars. However, it could contribute to the prevention of local wars and their escalation. Some saw more local reasons for contributing, such as giving the PDF experience and making it more attractive.[290] The Irish did

---

[284] Speech by Aiken to General Assembly, 6 Oct. 1960, *Ireland/UN 1960*, 21.
[285] Speech, 28 Mar. 1961, *Ireland/UN 1961*, 11.
[286] Speech, 4 Oct. 1962, *Ireland/UN 1962*, 6 ff.
[287] Speeches by Aiken, *Ireland/UN 1965*, 17-71.
[288] Aiken, *Dáil Debates*, 214 (1965), 194 ff.   [289] Ibid. 221 (1966), 2070.
[290] See the debates in 1960 on the Defence (Amendment) Bill: ibid. 183 (1960), 1875-904, and on the Defence (Amendment) (2) Bill, ibid. 185 (1960), 774 ff. This legislation allowed troops to be sent abroad. On peace-keeping see also ibid. 186 (1961), 905 ff.; 159 (1956), 209 ff.; 208 (1964), 1085 ff.; and Con Cremin, 'United Nations Peace-Keeping Operations: An Irish Initiative 1961-1968', *Irish Studies in International Affairs'*, 1/4 (1984). Cremin was Irish Ambassador to the United Nations 1964-74.

baulk at the notion of establishing a special, permanent UN unit on the grounds of expense, especially when the demand for it was uncertain, and also because they did not wish to appear readily available for each and every emergency.[291] None the less, the Irish contribution to peace-keeping has been substantial and reflects a lack of isolationism and a desire to contribute to the maintenance of international peace and security.

On the other hand, the Irish have never been active mediators, a fact which drew particular domestic criticism in the 1960s, especially during the Nigeria–Biafra, Vietnam, and India–Pakistan conflicts. In each case, in marked contrast to earlier behaviour and pronouncements, there was considerable official Irish silence and an emphasis upon the limited influence of small states. Indeed, Aiken's successor talked of the advantages of 'quiet diplomacy', since one could not 'approach problems with an open mouth all the time', without causing 'harm and . . . damage'.[292] A future minister ridiculed suggestions of giving Ireland's 'American friends' advice on Vietnam, since no one welcomed public advice. O'Kennedy went on to bemoan the 'type of thinking that can prevail too widely here—that all we have to do is to express our view as a nation . . . we are limited in scope from the financial point of view and also . . . from the point of view of international reality'.[293]

These limitations were revealed clearly on the Biafran issue, when, despite clamour from the opposition, a review by the new Minister in July 1969 concluded that there was no initiative which Ireland could take 'which could have any real influence in helping to solve the major issues'. Instead, the Organisation for African Unity (OAU) was regarded as 'ideally suited' to mediate.[294] Similarly, with respect to the India–Pakistan conflict, there was a reluctance to become actively involved in mediation because Irish 'usefulness could be diminished considerably if [the mediation] offer is ill-timed' or the proposed solution 'not acceptable' to one side.[295] On Vietnam, there was again 'no initiative' which the government 'could usefully take'.[296] All that a small country could do was 'to hope that good sense will prevail'.[297]

---

[291] Speech by Aiken to General Assembly, 3 Oct. 1963, in *Ireland/UN 1963*, 26–7; *Dáil Debates*, 188 (1961), 144–6; 208 (1964), 114, ibid. 1382; 214 (1965), 1583.

[292] Hillery, ibid. 245 (1970), 281.

[293] O'Kennedy, ibid. 242 (1969), 68 ff.

[294] Hillery, ibid. 241 (1969), 1882; and for Aiken's views, ibid. 235 (1968), 1638; 236, ibid. 502, 1101; 237 (1968), 1302; 238 (1969), 37.   [295] Hillery, ibid. 255 (1971), 1497.

[296] Ibid. 242 (1969), 1491.

[297] Aiken, ibid. 239 (1969), 403.

A further difficulty was that of partiality, and the continuing tension between Cosgrave's second and third principles. Corish suggested a possible way out, in that Ireland should generally ally with the West but 'not be led by the nose', making specific reference to Suez.[298] Furthermore, as O'Brien has pointed out, there was 'a considerable area of common ground' between these principles, 'since Ireland is a Western country' and 'its genuinely independent assessments will often also be "Western" assessments'.[299] Indeed, Aiken's original stance at the United Nations drew charges, in the censure debate on the government's foreign policy there, that the government was not supporting the West enough, and an affirmation that Ireland was 'not uncommitted' in the great struggle of the times.[300]

In the Dáil there was general agreement that Ireland could 'no longer stay on the fence in . . . [an] ideological clash'.[301] Even Fianna Fáil members argued that Ireland should not upset the United States on the issue of China.[302] Greater emphasis came to be focused on the formulation advanced by Costello in 1957, namely that while pursuing 'military neutrality' Ireland was 'not uncommitted in the war of ideas',[303] and this was contrasted with the pronouncement of the Tánaiste, Sean MacEntee, that Aiken was a 'non-committed statesman'.[304] Deputies like Dillon hoped that Irish policy was not to treat the superpowers exactly the same.[305] A further illustration of the ambiguity in Ireland's position was the desire of some that Ireland should use its 'independent and detached' position to lead the 'emergent countries along the paths we believe can strengthen the defence of the free world', in view of the fact that Ireland's own future was 'indissolubly bound up with the West'.[306]

One indicator of Irish partiality or impartiality is voting behaviour at the United Nations. MacQueen examined Irish voting between 1956 and 1970 by means of a statistical analysis of votes in the General Assembly plenary sessions and in the First, Fourth, and Special Political Committees.[307] His general conclusion is that 'Irish neutrality at the

---

[298] Corish, ibid. 164 (1957), 1244.

[299] O'Brien, 'International Affairs', 130.

[300] For censure debate see Dáil Debates, 164 (1957), 1169-304. The censure was defeated 78:38.   [301] Lindsay, ibid. 176 (1959), 570 ff.

[302] Boland, ibid. 601-5.

[303] Costello, ibid. 163 (1957), 598.

[304] Quoted by Costello, ibid. 182 (1960), 770.

[305] Dillon, ibid. 167 (1958), 287; 176 (1959), 543.

[306] Cosgrave, ibid. 191 (1961), 620 ff.; 176 (1959), 500.

[307] MacQueen, 'Neutrality', 177-200.

United Nations did not involve equidistant levels of support for each power bloc . . . Irish voting behaviour was more closely aligned to that of the western powers', although it also demonstrated a 'consistently high degree of similarity with that of Sweden'.[308]

ATTITUDE TO NATIONAL IDENTITY

In 1966 Garret FitzGerald complained that a European minister had recently asked him how he liked his new opposition leader, Mr Heath; the minister 'was not aware that we had a separate Government. It had slipped his mind. So unconscious are people of the realities of our position.'[309] Issues of identity and independence were still, therefore, a major concern. As late as 1969 FitzGerald was drawing attention to the need 'to give effect to our belief in the value of maintaining the national identity of this country—our belief . . . that Irish interests are best served by a separate, individual, Irish presence in the world', in view of the distinctiveness of Irish culture, way of life, and values. The Irish wanted to preserve that difference because it was thought to be of value to them and to the world.[310] Identity was particularly important because of the approach to the European Community, and was given added significance by the 1966 celebrations of the fiftieth anniversary of the 1916 Rising. The eruption of violence in Northern Ireland in 1968-9 also had a crucial importance.

For most of the period Northern Ireland and unity were not major issues. The question was periodically raised at the United Nations, 'particularly whenever the Irish experience of the evils of partition seemed relevant to the specific international problem then under discussion',[311] but there was no return to the 'sore thumb' approach. In the island itself, the period 1956-62 saw an IRA border-campaign. More significantly, Lemass became Taoiseach, and began to intervene on the question. Essentially, he took a functionalist approach, believing that economic co-operation could create a climate conducive to reunification. He also made a number of political gestures, such as visiting the Northern Ireland Prime Minister, O'Neill, on 14 January 1965.[312] A few months earlier Lemass had acknowledged that the government and

[308] Ibid. 198.
[309] FitzGerald, Seanad Debates, 61 (1966), 1871 ff.
[310] FitzGerald, Dáil Debates, 241 (1969), 1993 ff.
[311] Introductory commentary to Ireland/UN 1969, 5.
[312] See Keatinge, A Place, 113-19, 195-6, and Farrell, 114-17.

parliament of Northern Ireland 'exist with the support of the majority' in the area, 'artificial though that area is'.[313] The Dáil established a Committee on the Constitution in 1966, which reported in December 1967. It recommended that Article 3 be replaced 'by an expression of the aspiration that the island be "re-united in harmony and brotherly affection between all Irishmen"', and that the state's jurisdiction was limited to the twenty-six counties "until the achievement of the nation's unity shall otherwise require" '.[314] Nothing came of this, because of opposition within Fianna Fáil, and after O'Neill returned Lemass's visit, followed by further visits between them, this approach was overtaken by events.

This is not the place to detail the events relating to Northern Ireland during and after 1968-9, but some issues are particularly relevant.[315] One such was the question of whether the Irish government would intervene to 'save' the minority population or take the opportunity to use force to secure reunification. In September 1969 the Minister for Foreign Affairs, Patrick Hillery, told the UN General Assembly that the Irish had not had, 'nor do we now have, any wish to achieve [reunification] by force'.[316] The Taoiseach affirmed in the late summer that the government had 'no intention of mounting an armed invasion of the Six Counties . . . [the] use of force would not advance our long-term aim of a united Ireland. Nor will the Government connive at unofficial armed activity.'[317] In the spring of 1971 the Dáil approved an opposition motion, 'That Dáil Éireann formally rejects the use of force as an instrument to secure the unity of Ireland'.[318]

However, at critical moments in August 1969 this message was not so clear, and opposition deputies had some grounds for arguing that the 'Government hinted at armed intervention'.[319] In addition, some backbenchers argued that if the Bogside had been attacked further, there

[313] Quoted in Donald Harman Akenson, *The United States and Ireland* (Cambridge, Mass., 1973), 262.

[314] Keatinge, *A Place*, 114.

[315] For such details see John Darby, *Conflict in Northern Ireland* (Dublin, 1976), esp. 'Bibliography', pp. 198-242, and Richard Rose, *Governing without Consensus* (London, 1971), and their further references.

[316] Speech by Dr Hillery to General Assembly, 26 Sept. 1969, in *Ireland/UN 1969*, 5-46, esp. 40. For Ireland's arguments and a detailed account see Con Cremin, 'Northern Ireland at the United Nations, August/September 1969', *Irish Studies in International Affairs*, 1/2 (1980).

[317] Lynch, *Dáil Debates*, 241 (1969), 1406.

[318] Introduced by Cosgrave, ibid. 252 (1971), 234 ff.

[319] Corish, ibid. 241 (1969), 1425.

'would have been an invasion across the Donegal border to protect people'.[320] The situation was exacerbated by the Taoiseach's television statement that the Irish government would not stand 'idly' by, and by the decisions to establish field-hospitals and refugee centres on the border.[321] The *Evening Press* on 14 August carried the headline 'Irish Troops Are on the Border', reporting that 'Very large forces and convoys are moving near the Border areas.' It went on to say that the people of the Bogside had their 'eyes . . . turned chiefly to the Border only five miles away where they have heard Irish troops are building up', asking 'But why don't they come?'[322]

Five field-hospitals and two refugee centres were immediately established, but the PDF did not cross the Border.[323] What the troops were to do aroused some confusion, since two explanations were given of the PDF's role. Initially, reference was made to the field-hospitals and refugee centres and the need to defend them, but then it was argued that troops had been moved in anticipation of an Anglo–Irish peace-keeping mission, since the British had rejected a UN force.[324] The tension was heightened by the mobilization of about 2,000 First and Second Line Reserves,[325] and by dissension in the Cabinet over what to do, although there is evidence that 'the Government adopted a Contingency Plan for the defence of the threatened population . . . and that this consisted of the disposition of small arms where they could most readily be made available to recognised representatives of those under attack'.[326] This plan was adopted because of army advice that there was no other effective help they could provide. Part of the dilemma was what to do in the so-called 'doomsday situation' of a possible pogrom. A further complication is uncertainty as to whether certain ministers attempted unofficially to smuggle arms and money to the beseiged population, or whether they acted legally and within the terms of the Contingency Plan.

As the immediate crisis passed, this became a major issue, bringing the

---

[320] Harte, ibid. 241 (1969), 1441.

[321] The broadcast is reproduced in *Keesing's Contemporary Archives 1969–70*, 17 (London, 1969–70), 23583A, without 'idly'. On field hospitals and refugee centres see Lynch, *Dáil Debates*, 241 (1969), 1401 ff.

[322] Read out by O'Donnell in *Dáil Debates*, 241 (1969), 1468–9.

[323] Gibbons, ibid. 244 (1970), 1682. A month later a further refugee-centre opened. Peak occupancy (of 720) occurred on 23 Aug. 1969.

[324] FitzGerald, ibid. 241 (1969), 1505 ff.; Lynch, ibid. 1401 ff.

[325] Lynch, ibid. 1401 ff.; Tully, ibid. 246 (1970), 1690.

[326] Kevin Boland, *Up Dev!* (Dublin, n.d.), 44, *passim*.

dismissal, resignation, and trial of some ministers.[327] Clear answers are not possible because of contradictory evidence, but it seems that, although no invasion *per se* was planned, a contingency plan for helping Northern nationalists did exist and that may have involved some incursions, if these were ultimately deemed necessary. The intervention would be to 'save' the nationalist population, not to bring about unity, which the Irish lacked the power to do. Unity remained a long-term aspiration.[328] These questions nearly brought down the Fianna Fáil government and they continue to divide the party. However, it is significant that the army's own assessment stressed the PDF's weakness. Although some politicians wished, in effect, to go to war, a neutral state can hardly voluntarily do so.

The Northern issue has remained on the agenda. After 1968-9 there has been a reaffirmation of the goal of unity, and initially a re-emphasis upon functional co-operation, with suggestions, for example, of a joint economic council.[329] Internment in 1971 and 'Bloody Sunday' on 30 January 1972, when Catholics were killed in Derry by the British army, temporarily halted that process. After 'Bloody Sunday' the Irish ambassador to London was withdrawn and the British embassy in Dublin burnt. Some had fears that the Irish might 'be in a war situation',[330] or have 'to face the reality of the issue of peace or war'.[331] Certainly speeches in 1972 by one of the ministers dismissed in 1970, Neil Blaney, suggested that the 'entire reserves' should be called up, and that the army should be 'on the Border', although the crucial uncertainty as to what the army would do remained.[332] A supporter of Blaney, Brennan, did suggest that, if there were any more Derrys, the army should be sent 'across the border'.[333] This did not happen.

CONCLUSION

In this period there was again no unambiguous, stirring assertion of neutrality, and despite the rhetoric, Ireland maintained a critical attitude towards the non-aligned. Confusion persisted as to Ireland's position, as

[327] Kevin Boland, ibid., *passim*, for a personal view of these events. See also the motion on 'Nomination of Members of the Government', *Dáil Debates*, 246 (1970), 641-1350.
[328] Keatinge, *A Place*, 115.
[329] Ibid. 117-18.
[330] Corish, *Dáil Debates*, 258 (1972), 1164.
[331] Cosgrave, ibid. 827.
[332] Blaney, ibid. 950 ff.
[333] Brennan, ibid. 1120-30.

is illustrated by an exchange between Corish and Lemass in 1963. Corish was criticizing the government for preparing 'to abandon our traditional policy of neutrality'. Lemass interjected: 'Will the Deputy define neutrality for me?' The exchange continued:

CORISH. Non-participation.
LEMASS. In what?
CORISH. In military encounters—non-participation . . . we would not side with anybody . . . Is that not what we mean by neutrality?

Lemass then asked whether this included the struggle of the free world against Communism.

CORISH. Even the Hottentots know we are anti-Communist.
LEMASS. In that case we are on one side and not neutral.[334]

Increasingly it was argued that it was 'owing to an accident of history' that Ireland was 'independent, untied and neutral, in the accepted sense of the term, in the *military* sense of the term'.[335] This redefinition reflected the exigencies of the economic situation and the consequent perceived need to join the European Community. Adherence to neutrality had become conditional and transient, depending upon how the Community developed; any lingering long-term aspiration to it was yielded in the commitment to the future development of the Community. More important than neutrality had become the maximization of material well-being which the Community appeared to promise, while membership also appeared to offer the chance to change the claustrophobic bilateral relationship with Britain. In joining the Community, the Irish finally decided to put aside the austere ideals and aspirations of de Valera, and to seek comfort, at the expense of independence and neutrality. They still remained unprepared to provide the necessary wherewithal, or to pay the necessary costs, for a genuinely independent and neutral stance. They were neither neutral nor members of an alliance; Ireland's policy was again *sui generis*.

[334] Lemass and Corish, ibid. 199 (1963), 1035–6.
[335] Aiken, ibid. 191 (1961), 675 (emphasis added).

8

Independence or Solidarity?
1973–1982

THE start of 1973 saw both entry into the European Community[1] and, a few weeks later, the formation of a new Coalition government after sixteen years of Fianna Fáil rule.[2] In April 1973 the new Minister for Foreign Affairs, Garret FitzGerald, held a 'Conference of Heads of Mission and Other Senior Officials', and told the Dáil in his first major policy speech on 9 May that it had been 'essential . . . to re-examine at this time existing general guidelines and formulate new ones for future foreign policy'. This re-examination was necessary because of the movement 'towards greater interdependence' in the world economy, 'the evolving situation in Northern Ireland', and 'the accession to membership of the European Communities'.[3] That accession had also, as 'a consequence and corollary', already involved Ireland for a year in European Political Co-operation (EPC).[4] A quantitative and qualitative change in the scope of Irish foreign policy had again occurred, and in November 1974 FitzGerald observed that it was 'still perhaps not fully recognised in Ireland . . . the extent to which our membership of the EEC has brought us into a new and direct relationship with countries

---

[1] Ireland signed the Treaty of Accession on 22 Jan. 1972. On 10 May 1972 the decision was overwhelmingly endorsed by a referendum with a vote of 1,041,880 in favour (83% of those voting) in a turnout of 71%. For the background see Trevor C. Salmon, 'Ireland', in Carol and Kenneth J. Twitchett (eds.), *Building Europe: Britain's Partners in the EEC* (London, 1981), esp. pp. 197–202; E. Wistrich, 'Referenda: The Lessons for Britain', *New Europe*, 3/1 (Winter 1974–5); Patrick Keatinge, *The Formulation of Irish Foreign Policy* (Dublin, 1973), 167–8, 257–60; id., *A Place Among the Nations: Issues in Irish Foreign Policy* (Dublin, 1978), 140–4; Tom Garvin and Anthony Parker, 'Party Loyalty and Irish Voters: The EEC Referendum as a Case-Study', *Economic and Social Review*, 4/1 (Oct.1972); Denis Maher, *The Tortuous Path: The Course of Ireland's Entry into the EEC 1948–73* (Dublin, 1986).

[2] Fianna Fáil had been in government from 20 Mar. 1957 to 14 Mar. 1973. Its defeat in 1973 was not related to entry into the European Community.

[3] FitzGerald had been at one time Chairman of the Irish Council of the European Movement. For his speech see *Dáil Debates*, 265(1973), 740–69, esp. 741.

[4] Padraic MacKernan, 'Ireland and European Political Cooperation', *Irish Studies in International Affairs*, 1/4 (1984), 16. MacKernan was in 1984 Political Director of the Dept. of Foreign Affairs, and also believed that entry into EPC had 'entailed the development of a basic political approach—the definition of principles and objectives' for Irish foreign policy (p. 17).

throughout the world between whom and ourselves until last year there was virtually no political or economic contact'.[5]

The decade after January 1973 saw successive Irish governments trying to steer a path for Ireland in the changed and changing environment. It culminated in severe challenges to Irish policy-makers arising out of Anglo-Irish relations and attempts to ameliorate the Northern Ireland crisis, the plans for the development of the European Community and EPC, and the Falklands conflict of 1982.[6] All raised the question of whether, during sixty years of independence and ten of Community membership, the basic principles of Irish security policy had been defined, established, and agreed.

DUE DILIGENCE

Throughout the post-war period the Irish had failed to meet the requirement of due diligence, and in the early 1970s some senior Irish army officers regarded the Irish defence effort as 'criminally inadequate'.[7] However, a notable feature of the period 1973–82 was the increase in the scale of that effort: for example, numbers in the PDF rose to their highest in over twenty years, as is shown in the following list:[8]

Year	Numbers (Officers and Men)
1973	10,618
1974	11,312
1975	12,059
1976	13,996
1977	14,666
1978	14,464
1979	13,425
1980	13,383
1981	14,092
1982	14,982

None the less, there continued to be a shortfall of between 10 and 20 per cent compared to the peacetime Establishment figure during this

---

[5] FitzGerald, Dáil Debates, 275 (1974), 908.
[6] These challenges are discussed fully later in this chapter.
[7] Interview with senior Irish army officer, Dublin, Nov.1983.
[8] The figures are from Ireland: Statistical Abstract, 1978 (Prl. 9034: Dublin, 1981), table 234, p. 251; and ibid., 1982–85 (Pl. 3217; Dublin, 1986), table 272, p. 279.

period, although the relative shortfall was smaller than before and was based on higher figures.[9] The reason for the increased effort was 'the very important task' of 'supporting the State and State institutions and in particular supporting the largely unarmed . . . Garda Síochána in their Border duties.'[10] During the Coalition's period in office (1973-7) a major preoccupation was internal security, and when the Minister for Defence, Donegan, spoke of the government's determination to provide adequate resources for defence, he specifically linked this to ensuring 'not only that our democratic institutions are safeguarded but also that the conditions of security and internal stability . . . are maintained'.[11] The government had to deal with 'subversion', with ' a group of people who are saying that the State must be pulled down'. The army had a role in this struggle; and only it and the police stood 'between anarchy and democracy'.[12] In 1976 the Oireachtas in fact declared that 'arising out of the armed conflict now taking place in Northern Ireland, a national emergency exists affecting the vital interests of the State'.[13]

The burdens which this and the task of aiding the civil power imposed upon the PDF were significant.[14] In the 1970s between two and three thousand members of the PDF were engaged in security duties in the Border area,[15] and by 1982 the PDF was providing 21,032 military parties for checkpoint duties and 11,244 parties for joint patrols with the Garda.[16] They also had other 'non-soldiering duties', which meant assisting in the protection of explosives, vital installations, and VIPs, as well as participating in searches, prison guard duties, and bomb disposal.[17] In addition to aiding the civil power in this area, the PDF was also concerned to 'show the flag' and demonstrate the authority of the government. Evidence of it being stretched is provided by the fact

---

[9] See *Dáil Debates*, 277 (1975), 1073; 289 (1976), 197; 303 (1978), 310; 304 (1978), 648; 313 (1979), 2134. The Establishment figure varied, and was not publicly announced every year. See also Capt. J. Sheehan (ed.), *Defence Forces Handbook* (Dublin, n.d.), 18.

[10] John Kelly, Parliamentary Secretary to the Taoiseach, *Dáil Debates*, 272 (1974), 1667-8.

[11] Donegan, Minister for Defence, ibid. 649-56 (quotation from col. 656).

[12] Ibid. 285 (1975), 1005-6; 273 (1974), 1751.

[13] For the resolution, debate, and vote see ibid. 292 (1976), 3 ff.

[14] For a general discussion of this issue see Trevor C. Salmon, 'The Civil Power and Aiding the Civil Power: The Case of Ireland', in John Roach and Jurgen Thomaneck (eds.), *Police and Public Order in Europe* (Beckenham, 1985).

[15] Liam Cosgrave, Taoiseach, *Dáil Debates*, 273 (1974), 1576.

[16] This compared with 5,500 and 14,000 respectively in the mid-1970s; see Salmon, 'The Civil Power', 83.

[17] Donegan, Minister for Defence, *Dáil Debates*. 275 (1974), 329.

that for most of the period some members both of the First and of the Second Line Reserve, An Fórsa Cosanta Áitiúil (FCA), were on full-time duty.[18] Such was the strain that the government only acceded after very serious consideration to a request to contribute to UNEF II in the Middle East in the autumn of 1973. The Minister for Defence, Donegan, admitted that 'security duties are heavy', that the army was 'under-established', and that the 'removal . . . of 300 officers and men has a much greater effect on us than the proportion of 300 to 11,000 would seem to represent'. Moreover, at the time some members of the PDF were serving 100 hours per week (35 of which were in barracks, waiting for a call-out).[19] The government only agreed, despite their own difficul-ties, because they felt that so few other countries were acceptable, so that there was 'little alternative but to do what we could even if . . . [this] puts our own domestic security under strain'.[20]

The strain became too much after the Dublin and Monaghan bombings on 17 May 1974, which caused the government to seek 'the temporary release of the Irish contingent' from UNEF II.[21] The 'excep-tional strain imposed on the forces at home at present on security duties made this step necessary',[22] and continued to limit the Irish contribution for a further three years.[23] It was only in the spring of 1977 that it was decided 'in principle' that a major contingent could again be made available.[24] In the summer of that year, a new Minister for Foreign Affairs, O'Kennedy, sought permission to allow 300 personnel to be sent to UNFICYP, telling the Dáil that the government was 'satisfied that a contingent can be made available . . . given the increase in . . . strength in recent years' of the PDF, which had increased by over 3,000 between 1974 and 1977.[25]

The strains upon the PDF generated by the problems with Northern Ireland and internal security were so severe in the aftermath of the May 1974 bombings that the Taoiseach, Liam Cosgrave, floated the idea of 'voluntary local security service units' based on Garda stations to patrol local areas. Prevarication later hit the scheme, so that, although plans

---

[18] Barrett, Minister for Defence, ibid. 326 (1981), 1002.
[19] Donegan, Minister for Defence, ibid. 268 (1973), 820-1.
[20] FitzGerald, Minister for Foreign Affairs, ibid. 825.
[21] FitzGerald, Minister for Foreign Affairs, ibid. 273 (1974), 692.
[22] Donegan, Minister for Defence, ibid. 1715.
[23] See ibid. 275 (1974), 1322; 288 (1976), 1345.
[24] FitzGerald, Minister for Foreign Affairs, ibid. 298 (1977), 942.
[25] O'Kennedy, Minister for Foreign Affairs, ibid. 300 (1977), 128.

were drawn up for it, they were not implemented.[26] The PDF, as noted above, was helped by the Reserves, but the numbers in the First Line Reserve never topped 1,000, averaging nearer 600 during this period.[27] The FCA, although officially of the order of 16,000 to 20,000, only had half of that number who did as much as eight to fourteen days' annual training in addition to their weekly sessions.[28] In 1975 the Minister for Defence, Donegan, said he was 'thoroughly dissatisfied with the present situation regarding the FCA', given their drop-out rates and cost, as well as the difficulties in giving them adequate training.[29] This dissatisfaction, together with the problems of the enlarged PDF resulting from the expansion (of nearly 40 per cent) between 1973 and 1977 mentioned above, led to a rethink about the organization and structure of the Irish forces. In September 1979 this produced the first major reorganization since 1959. The PDF and FCA were now to be separated into 'combat and local defence forces respectively', which was in effect a return to the pre-1959 system.[30] Incidentally, despite the strain on the defence forces, the idea of some form of compulsory military service continued to be ruled out as being against the Irish tradition.[31]

As Table 8.1 shows, the period 1973–82 also saw an increase in the financial resources allocated to defence, although it is interesting that its share of total supply services was below that of earlier years.[32] However, these increases were significant and outstripped inflation, so that they were increases in real terms. Between 1975 and 1980, for example, while the Consumer Price Index rose from 100 (at mid-November 1975) to 197.7 (mid-November 1980), defence expenditure rose from £59.2m. to £140.7m., an increase of 138 per cent.[33] One problem was that this extra effort was related to requirements for internal security and Northern Ireland. In 1980 the Minister for Finance calculated that the

---

[26] See Cosgrave, Taoiseach, ibid. 273 (1974), 1580, for the original idea, and 274 (1974), 165; 277 (1975), 1041; 295 (1976), 482, for what happened subsequently.

[27] *Ireland: Statistical Abstract*, 1978 (Prl. 9034; Dublin, 1981), table 234, p. 251.

[28] Ibid.; *Dáil Debates*, 326 (1981), 1002.

[29] Donegan, Minister for Defence, *Dáil Debates*, 282 (1975), 1426–30.

[30] Faulkner, Minister for Defence, ibid. 318 (1980), 659–60, and 320 (1980), 71. On the new structure see also ibid. 322 (1980), 1639–40; Sheehan, 18–38; C. P. D. Dorman-O'Gowan, 'The Irish Defence Forces: Their Role and their Problems', *Royal United Services Institute*, 126/3 (Sept. 1981); and John Keegan and Adrian English, 'Irish Republic', in John Keegan (ed.), *World Armies*, 2nd edn. (London, 1983).

[31] A Labour TD, Coughlan, floated the idea, but both Fine Gael and Fianna Fáil opposed it, as did a majority of Labour: see *Dáil Debates*, 265 (1973), 302, 387; 271 (1974), 1208; 272 (1974), 1742; 274 (1974), 750.

[32] See above, tables 4.3, 5.1, 6.1, and 7.3.

[33] See table 8.2 and *Ireland: Statistical Abstract*, 1980 (Pl. 1618; Dublin, 1983), table 330, p. 338.

cost incurred for the PDF in 1975 for extra security arising out of the problems surrounding Northern Ireland was £20m., in 1979 £40m., and in 1980 about £57m., that is between 33 and 40 per cent of the total expenditure on the PDF.[34] A report to the New Ireland Forum in 1983 put the total extra costs on security arising from Northern Ireland in the period 1973–82 as between 19.7 and 25.6 per cent of the total expenditure on security, including PDF, prisons, and police.[35] If the extra effort is discounted, the remaining effort, as a percentage of GNP, is of the traditional order of magnitude.[36]

Table 8.1. Irish Defence Expenditure 1973–1982

Year ended	Defence exp. (£m.)[a]	Total Supply Services (%)	GNP (%)
31.3.1973	29.735	4.76	1.1
31.3.1974	32.873	4.37	1.1
4.–12.1974[b]	30.006	4.37	1.0
31.12.1975	59.154	4.71	1.6
31.12.1976	71.920	4.77	1.6
31.12.1977	84.229	4.75	1.6
31.12.1978	99.033	4.49	1.6
31.12.1979	110.602	4.17	1.5
31.12.1980	140.676[a]	4.15	1.6
31.12.1981	169.276[a]	3.90	1.6
31.12.1982	201.244[a]	3.93	1.6

[a] For 1980, 1981, and 1982 the figures are in IR £m.
[b] In 1974, the financial year was changed to end on 31 Dec.

Sources: *Ireland: Statistical Abstract*, 1978, table 250, pp. 266–7, table 238, p. 257; 1980, table 258, pp. 286–7, table 246, p. 278; 1982–1985, table 288, p. 295; table 275, p. 285.

The level of commitment continued to attract criticism, most significantly perhaps from Lieutenant-General Carl O'Sullivan in September 1982. O'Sullivan, who had been Chief of Staff of the PDF between July 1976 and June 1981, was scathing about the inadequacies of the period around 1969, when the PDF had even lacked combat uniforms, and

---

[34] O'Kennedy, Minister for Finance, *Dáil Debates*, 322 (1980), 2318–19.
[35] 'The Cost of Violence Arising from the Northern Ireland Crisis since 1969: New Ireland Forum; *Ireland Today* (Bulletin of the Dept. of Foreign Affairs), suppl. 1003 (Nov.–Dec.1983), table 6, p. 5.
[36] See above, tables 4.3, 5.1, 6.1, and 7.3.

claimed that although the defence forces were now strong enough to cope with internal security, they were still in no position to maintain the country's neutrality in the face of external aggression: they could not, for example, counter a Soviet attack from the North Atlantic. In 1979 the PDF compiled a review of what would be required to meet external aggression and maintain neutrality, a review which was influenced by O'Sullivan's trips to Sweden. They concluded that if Ireland wished to adopt a posture of minimum deterrence to preserve its neutrality 'around £500 million even at that time' would need to be spent immediately, 'and even that would not [be] enough to fight . . . [a] protracted war'. The £500m. would only have provided the basics, such as radar and planes, and perhaps six or seven days' ammunition and was regarded merely as a first step. In 1979 defence expenditure was only 22 per cent of this sum. O'Sullivan personally favoured neutrality, 'but [only] if I was in the same position as Sweden'.[37] Throughout the period 1973–82 Ireland was not in such a position, and some officers believed that there was 'no will to militarily defend the Irish stance'.[38] The enhanced resources had been used to confront internal security problems, and much of the effort could not be easily switched to meet external aggression.

The Irish performance led some senior politicians to acknowledge that it was 'scarcely possible to argue' that the purpose of the PDF was 'to provide 100 per cent security against aggression'. John Kelly, when Parliamentary Secretary to the Taoiseach, had gone on to argue that even states with greater resources that Ireland could not 'guarantee to repel invaders . . . without the help of an alliance', an option which the Irish had chosen not to adopt.[39] In opposition, he went somewhat further, arguing that if the rest of the Western world felt the need of, and was 'already taking part in a defensive alliance, then self-respect, if nothing else, should require us to review our supposed policy of neutrality'.[40] This drew an immediate riposte from a Fine Gael colleague, Richie Ryan, who argued that the best contribution the Irish could make to their own defence and to the defence of Europe was to defend the island

[37] Report of O'Sullivan speech to Association of European Journalists in *Irish Times*, 25 Sept. 1982; and other details from interviews in Dublin in Nov. 1983.

[38] Interview with senior Irish army officer, Dublin, Nov. 1983. For a slightly different informed view, but one which also talks of the Soviet threat, see Comdt. P. O'Sullivan, 'Irish Neutrality and Defence', *An Cosantoir*, 41/3 (Mar. 1981).

[39] Kelly, Parliamentary Secretary to the Taoiseach, *Dáil Debates*, 272 (1974), 1667.

[40] In *Irish Times*, 20 Oct. 1978.

against a conventional attack, and that 'Nobody could do it better'.[41] However, Ryan attempted no detailed analysis of the relative strength of Ireland's efforts as against putative belligerents, or as against the European neutrals, and it is difficult to ignore the judgement of the professional, O'Sullivan, on Irish inadequacy.

This judgement is all the more relevant, since 'defending the State against external aggression' was still regarded as the 'primary role' of the PDF, although the Minister for Defence who made that statement, Barrett, admitted in 1981 that the 'primary role often tends to be glossed over'.[42] In the key debate in March 1981 on defence and neutrality, Barrett went on to list the other roles: aiding the civil power; participating in UN peace-keeping missions; fishery protection; aiding civil defence; and general search, rescue, and emergency service duties.[43] It was acknowledged that, although 'a secondary defence objective, Aid to the Civil Power has become a major part of the Defence Forces operational employment throughout the 1970s and the 1980s'.[44] It is noteworthy that while Barrett listed these roles, and spoke of the army as 'the outward and practical manifestation of a nation's sovereignty and of its determination to maintain and protect that sovereignty', he made no explicit reference to the defence and upholding of neutrality. Indeed, in the key debate on neutrality, he preferred the formulation of being determined 'to resist attempts by any party to a conflict to usurp the State's *non-belligerency* status in time of war. It behoves a State such as Ireland, which is not committed to *co-belligerency*, to take in peacetime such defensive measures as will safeguard its security in time of war.'[45] The Irish did not take such measures to a sufficient degree. The equipment issue provides further evidence of this.

Keegan and English have noted that, for example, although a few armoured vehicles 'of original conception' had been developed in Ireland and even produced abroad, and a few Naval Service vessels built, 'Ireland cannot be said to have a defence industry in the accepted sense of the word and almost all items of equipment, including even small arms ammunition, must be imported', the principal suppliers being Britain, Sweden, France, Belgium, and West Germany.[46] As

---

[41] Ryan, Minister for Finance (1973–7), reported in *Irish Times*, 24 Oct. 1978.
[42] Barrett, Minister for Defence, *Dáil Debates*, 327 (1981), 1432–4
[43] Barrett, ibid.; and see Sheehan, 17.
[44] Sheehan, loc. cit.
[45] Barrett, Minister for Defence, *Dáil Debates*, 327 (1981), 1433 (emphasis added).
[46] Keegan and English, 299. See also Dorman-O'Gowan, 54.

a senior Irish officer put it bluntly, 'we do not even make one bullet'.[47]

Irish policy has been to shop around for arms, looking for a combination of quality, price, and service, without any tests of 'political acceptability',[48] but there have been problems in acquiring the weapons desired at the time desired.[49] None the less, increased resources did lead to improvements in mobility and communication, with, for example, the purchase of armoured personnel-carriers.[50] However, the purchase of four tanks could still cause excitement, while only in 1979 did the Artillery Corps move into the missile age.[51] Only in mid-1980 was a 105mm. light gun introduced, an event described in the *Defence Forces Handbook* as a milestone.[52] Despite these improvements, significant equipment problems remained. For example, by the early 1980s the FCA's equipment was largely out of date,[53] and O'Sullivan clearly had reservations.

One arm of the PDF to be transformed was the Naval Service. However, crucial in the transformation was outside help, in the form of a European Community grant to aid the Irish in building up their Naval Service to police the EEC 200-mile fisheries limit and the exclusive economic zone introduced in 1977. As a result the Naval Service had to patrol 136,000 instead of 15,000 square nautical miles as previously. This aid was crucial, since even before that expansion the Coalition government was emphatic that the 'provision of a naval force on a scale sufficient to patrol our length of coastline is beyond the financial capabilities of this country'.[54] The Community eventually agreed to contribute to Irish capital costs in providing for patrols for the extended waters, and in July 1978 agreed to provide 46 million European units of account, or IR£31.2m., for the period from 1 January 1977 to 31 December 1982.[55] The Irish subsequently (in December 1978) submitted a programme totalling IR£60.5m., describing the need for six vessels (four similar to the purpose-built fishery-protection vessel, the *Deirdre*, and two helicopter-bearing vessels) and five maritime aircraft.[56]

[47] Interview with senior Irish army officer, Dublin, Nov. 1983.   [48] Ibid.
[49] Donegan, Minister for Defence, *Dáil Debates*, 272 (1974), 672.
[50] Molloy, Minister for Defence, ibid. 304 (1978), 432.
[51] A down-payment for the tanks was made in 1978 (ibid.), while the Milan Surface-to-Surface Missile was acquired in 1979, and a Surface-to-Air guided missile capability in 1980: Sheehan, 28.
[52] Sheehan, loc. cit.
[53] Dorman-O'Gowan, 53.
[54] Donegan, Minister for Defence, *Dáil Debates*, 265 (1973), 247, 387 ff.
[55] Faulkner, Minister for Defence, ibid. 319 (1980), 707–8.
[56] Faulkner, Minister for Defence, ibid. 320 (1980), 63–4.

If completed, the programme would have added to the three mine-sweepers used for inshore patrols and the training ship *Setanta*. In March 1977 the Minister for Defence, Flanagan, had argued that Ireland needed at least eighteen extra ships.[57] In fact, although four *Deirdre*-class vessels were acquired (*Deirdre* 1972, *Emer* 1977, *Aoife* 1979, and *Aisling* 1979), the helicopter-vessels were delayed, and the second was ultimately shelved, since it had in effect to be paid for by the Irish themselves. The armaments on the vessels—each of the *Deirdre*-class had a Bofors 40mm. gun on a powered mount and two single Oerlikon guns—were of Irish choice and bought at their own expense.[58]

Despite the Community's help with this expansion for fishery protection, the Minister for Defence, Faulkner, was quite emphatic in June 1980 that the vessels were 'available to participate as required in other Naval Service functions'.[59] The provision of Community money led inevitably to questions as to whether 'this agreement might get us involved in a military alliance', to which the reply was that there 'was not the slightest danger of that', since the vessels would be under the Irish flag.[60] None the less, in 1978 Flanagan, in opposition, asked about proposals for an 'EEC navy', only to be told that no such proposals had been put to Ireland, although the Agriculture Committee of the European Parliament had made some recommendations along those lines.[61]

In spite of the increase, the Naval Service remained small for an island-state. It also faced problems of manpower: in 1982, for example, it was 17 per cent short of Establishment,[62] although two years earlier the Minister for Defence, Faulkner, when asked directly whether there were enough men to man all the vessels in an emergency, had replied 'Yes, just about enough.'[63] In addition, the Naval Service had problems in detecting and preventing violations of Irish territorial waters: the Taoiseach, Mr Haughey was amazed to discover that Ireland could not flush out a Soviet submarine,[64] while in 1982 the Minister for Defence, could not say whether any had been detected.[65]

[57] Flanagan, Minister for Defence, *Irish Times*, 29 Mar. 1977.

[58] Dorman-O'Gowan, 54; interviews in Dublin, Nov. 1983, with senior Irish army officer; and in Brussels, May 1980, with Commission officials. The PDF had wanted all the armament it could possibly have on the vessels.

[59] Faulkner, Minister for Defence, *Dáil Debates*, 322 (1980), 1226–7.

[60] Gallagher–Kelly exchange, ibid. 296 (1977), 415–16.

[61] O'Kennedy, Minister for Foreign Affairs, ibid. 307 (1978), 931.

[62] Power, Minister for Defence, ibid. 334 (1982), 780; Sheehan, 18.

[63] Faulkner, Minister for Defence, ibid. 320 (1980), 1864.

[64] Interview with senior Irish army officer, Dublin, Nov. 1983.

[65] Power, Minister for Defence, *Dáil Debates*, 334 (1982), 1306–8.

The Air Corps too benefited from the increased concern with fishery protection,[66] but other improvements were also made. The Vampires were replaced by the Fouga Magister Cm 170 in 1976, and in 1977 ten Siai Marchetti SF 260W Warriors replaced the Chipmunks and Provosts. The Air Corps also possessed nine helicopters, including a small provision for troop-carrying. None the less, its capability was small, with a 'fighter squadron' of six Fouga Magister Cm 170 and perhaps a dozen or so other combat-aircraft.[67]

The Irish, despite the increases, still failed to meet the criteria for 'due diligence'. Indeed, speaking on behalf of Ireland to the First Committee of the UN General Assembly in 1982, Noel Dorr admitted that ' we are small, militarily insignificant . . . and have acknowledged our own vulnerability. Our armed forces are about the same size, and serve the same peacekeeping and other purposes, as those which every country would be allowed to maintain even in a disarmed world.'[68] Such a state is, in the words of Clarke, 'incapable of carrying out its obligations'.[69]

RECOGNITION OF NEUTRAL STATUS

In the full glare of publicity in March 1981 the Dáil rejected the suggestion that it reaffirm 'the principle of the neutrality of Ireland in international affairs and [declares] that . . . foreign and defence policies will continue to be based on this principle'. It similarly rejected the view that, 'in accordance with [the] traditional policy of neutrality', it needed 'to establish without doubt the reality of . . . neutrality', and that it should seek membership of the Non-Aligned Nations of the world' in order to strengthen the forces of peace.[70] The government majority rejected these notions on the ground that 'Political neutrality or non-alignment is incompatible with . . . membership of the European Community, and with our interests and our ideals.'[71] In winding up the debate, the Minister for Foreign Affairs, Brian Lenihan, declared that

---

[66] e.g. in 1977 two Beechcraft S K A 200 Super King Airs were leased, and then purchased.

[67] See Sheehan, 60–3; Keegan and English, 296–7; Dorman-O'Gowan, 54; Dáil Debates, 265 (1973), 240; 272 (1974), 649; 291 (1976), 15; 297 (1977), 1277; 302 (1977), 412; 319 (1980), 1105–12. Although it was claimed that there was no shortage of personnel (Dáil Debates, 297 (1977), 1277), in 1982 it was 30% below Establishment (ibid. 334 (1982), 779–80).

[68] Noel Dorr, quoted in Patrick Keatinge, A Singular Stance: Irish Neutrality in the 1980s, (Dublin, 1984), 73.

[69] John L. Clarke, 'NATO, Neutrals and National Defence', Survival, 24/6 (Nov.–Dec. 1982), 261.

[70] For the debate, motion, and amendments see Dáil Debates, 327 (1981), 1392–490, 1562–9.

[71] Haughey, Taoiseach, ibid. 1399.

'We are neutral in a military sense, but we are not neutral in a political sense. That is the net position.'[72] The Dáil also rejected an amendment confirming 'that a defence pact with the United Kingdom has not been mentioned in the current discussions with the U.K. Government and that it is not part of the joint studies now under way'.[73]

It was doubt on this question that led to the debate. The doubt arose from the meeting on 8 December 1980 between Haughey and Thatcher, when both decided to give 'special consideration' to 'the totality of relationships within these islands. For this purpose they . . . commissioned joint studies covering a range of issues . . . including . . . security matters.'[74] The press in both Britain and Ireland speculated that the issue of defence had been raised by Haughey himself, although in the Dáil he refused at first to state whether joint defence arrangements were under discussion, on the grounds of confidentiality.[75] On the other hand, the British Secretary of State for Northern Ireland, Humphrey Atkins, in February 1981 had said that defence was 'something, no doubt, that can be talked about'.[76] It was only in the March debate that Haughey stated 'unequivocally that the Government are not discussing or negotiating any kind of secret agreeement on defence with Britain or with any other country or group of countries',[77] although the opposition wondered about 'the significance of the word "secret" '.[78]

The furore was significant, since some perceived that Irish neutrality was 'now at an end' that 'there was not a willingness on the part of Ireland to maintain her neutral position in future'.[79] Moreover, a full diplomatic gallery heard the explicit rejection of an affirmation of either neutrality or non-alignment, and witnessed instead the acceptance of an anodyne motion that 'Dáil Éireann confirms the principles which have guided the defence policy of the Government and their predecessors'[80]—despite the fact that (as previous chapters have shown, and the opposition Leader FitzGerald pointed out) 'there is no set of

---

[72] Lenihan, ibid. 1466.
[73] Proposed by Fine Gael, ibid. 1566. The other amendments were proposed by Labour and by Noel Browne.
[74] The official communiqué, in *Ireland Today*, 972 (Dec. 1980–Jan. 1981), p. 3.
[75] Haughey, Taoiseach, *Dáil Debates*, 326 (1981), 1511–12.
[76] Atkins, *The Times*, 27 Feb. 1981.
[77] Haughey, Taoiseach, *Dáil Debates*, 327 (1981), 1392.
[78] Cluskey, the Labour Leader, ibid. 1408, at which the Fine Gael Leader, FitzGerald, interjected 'Hear, hear.'
[79] Ryan, ibid. 1454–5.
[80] Ibid. 1562–8.

common principles that have guided . . . defence policy'.[81] In the early 1980s the Dáil also failed to act on the 1980 Labour Party Conference decision that 'neutrality . . . be affirmed permanently by amendment of the national Constitution', although Labour was in the Coalition government for much of the time.[82]

At this time further doubts were raised about the Irish position and others' perceptions of it, arising out of the Irish response to the proposals of the German and Italian foreign ministers, Genscher and Colombo, for formalizing and expanding EPC.[83] This will be dealt with more fully below, when considering Irish freedom of action,[84] but it should be noted that the Irish stance in mid-1981 caused at least one leading European figure, Piet Dankert, to ask whether Irish policy on neutrality remained the same.[85] Confusion persisted over the summer as to what Ireland had agreed or would accept, and the position was only partially restored by the 'London Report' of October 1981,[86] and Lord Carrington's explanation, as President-in-Office of the Community, that it was of particular interest to Ireland, 'because they are not members of NATO, they are neutral', and that what had been agreed was 'certainly not going to impinge on defence or embarrass the Irish'.[87]

The Irish position was also weakened by the continuing failure to be directly involved in the Non-Aligned Movement (although private consideration was given to attending the New Delhi summit as a 'Guest'),[88] and by the Irish public disavowal of their membership in March 1981. When asked whether the lack of any invitation to attend the Movement's conference meant that most of the non-aligned felt that 'we are not non-aligned', the Minister for Foreign Affairs, Lenihan, did not

[81] FitzGerald, ibid. 1424. On 2 Dec. 1981 Seanad Eireann agreed without division to call 'on the Government to declare unequivocally that Ireland will not join a military pact': Seanad Debates, 96 (1981), 1103 ff.   [82] Quinn, Dáil Debates, 327 (1981), 1440–1.

[83] See speeches by Genscher, Foreign Minister of the Federal Republic of Germany, on 17 Nov. 1980, and by Colombo, Italian Foreign Minister, on 3 Feb. 1981, cited in William Wallace, 'Political Cooperation: Integration through Intergovernmentalism', in Helen Wallace, William Wallace, and Carole Webb (eds.), Policy-Making in the European Community, 2nd edn. (Chichester, 1983), 397, 402.

[84] See below, section on Freedom of Decision and Action.

[85] Dankert was a Dutch Socialist, reported in the Irish Press, 4 June 1981.

[86] 'Report on European Political Cooperation', London, 13 Oct. 1981, published in Bulletin of the European Communities, suppl. 3/81 (Brussels; Commission of the European Communities, 1981), 14–17.

[87] Verbatim report of Lord Carrington's press conference, 13 Oct. 1981: see Keatinge, A Singular Stance, 89, and Irish Times, 14 Oct. 1981.

[88] Interview with senior Dept.of Foreign Affairs official, Dublin, Nov. 1983, The idea was—ironically—partly thwarted by the change to a Coalition government. At least one other Community member also considered going to New Delhi.

answer directly, but argued that there was 'a difference between non-alignment and neutrality', and that Ireland happened to be one of the countries 'genuinely totally committed to neutrality'.[89]

The Irish regarded the Non-Aligned Movement as 'diffuse',[90] and felt that 'many countries within the non-aligned movement . . . perhaps are less non-aligned . . . than we are . . . membership or otherwise of this movement is not in any way a comment on the consistency of the foreign policy being pursued'.[91] Many members of the movement were, in any case, 'very heavy users of . . . military hardware'.[92] The Irish preferred to be 'objective', to avoid 'group membership', so as to avoid 'constraining' themselves,[93] although at times they tried to establish close contacts with states such as Yugoslavia.[94]

Ireland also remained outside the NNA group at CSCE meetings. Indeed, before the Madrid review conference it was made clear that a 'major part of our preparatory work is being carried out jointly with our partners in the European Community', since it was felt that 'a joint approach' was 'likely to carry more weight than proposals with a single sponsor'.[95] While Ireland had 'working contacts with . . . other groups', it did 'not participate in their meetings'.[96] None the less, at times the close Community–NATO relationship created an impression in some third-party minds that Ireland was involved in the NATO caucus.[97] The Irish, on the contrary, have argued that their 'special position' was recognized, for example, by the German Foreign Minister, Genscher, when he asked them to 'make the necessary contacts with other countries outside NATO . . . in an attempt to get talks going'.[98]

---

[89] The question was asked by Quinn: see *Dáil Debates*, 319 (1980), 467–8.

[90] Interviews with Dept. of Foreign Affairs officials, Dublin, Mar. 1981 and Nov. 1983; and with senior Irish politician, Mar. 1981.

[91] O'Kennedy, Minister for Foreign Affairs, *Dáil Debates*, 307 (1978), 1116–18.

[92] Lenihan, Minister for Foreign Affairs, ibid. 327 (1981), 1465.

[93] Interviews with Dept. of Foreign Affairs officials, Dublin, Mar. 1981 and Nov. 1983; and with senior Irish politician, Mar. 1981.

[94] e.g. in 1978–9 there was an exchange of visits between the foreign ministers, during which time the Irish minister, O'Kennedy, stressed Ireland's 'natural sympathy' for other countries not in alliance and spoke of future co-operation between Ireland and the NNA at the CSCE: see text of addresses delivered by O'Kennedy in Belgrade, 12 Apr. 1978, and in Dublin, 9 Apr. 1979.

[95] Lenihan, Minister for Foreign Affairs, *Dáil Debates*, 322 (1980), 725; 319 (1980), 2106–7.

[96] J. Kirwan, Private Secretary, Office of the Minister for Foreign Affairs, *Irish Times*, 12 Oct. 1982.

[97] The author was wrong to say that Ireland attended a formal NATO caucus (in 'Ireland: A Neutral in the Community?', *Journal of Common Market Studies*, 20/3 (Mar. 1982) 223), although he was so informed by an NNA delegation member. On the NATO–Community relationships see Karl E. Birnbaum, 'Alignments in Europe: The CSCE Experience', *World Today*, 37/6 (June 1981). [98] Lenihan, in opposition, *Dáil Debates*, 330 (1981), 131.

None the less, in general the Irish fell foul of the fact that the ties binding a state to some are often barriers separating them from others, that membership in one group implies non-membership in others.[99] It is interesting that a survey on neutrality and non-alignment taken among members of the Arab League and OAU found that 'not a single state which responded regarded Ireland as either "neutral" or "non-aligned" '.[100]

At the United Nations Ireland continued to distance itself from the non-aligned in a number of votes. It refused 'to support guerilla activities'[101] and 'unsubstantiated allegations' against friendly countries, as well as opposing the increasing tendency to introduce matters which they found offensive into resolutions on principles—e.g. the introduction of references to Zionism into resolutions on racism.[102] On the other hand, Ireland was voting with an alternative group, and member states of the Community were 'increasingly viewed by third countries as a coherent force in international relations'; so Ireland was increasingly 'regarded as a Community state' and 'identified with the Community caucus in international conferences'.[103] Keatinge agrees that Community states 'clearly form an important diplomatic "bloc" ',[104] while the biannual reports of *Developments in the European Communities* from the Irish government are replete with references to the Community states adopting 'common positions',[105] achieving 'co-ordination of their position', or having found it 'possible to harmonise successfully the various attitudes', leading to 'an agreed policy',[106] or on occasion 'a common foreign policy'.[107]

Ireland has self-confessedly been 'one of the "Nine" ',[108] as O'Kennedy told the General Assembly, this being perhaps most pro-

---

[99] See Marshall Singer, *Weak States in a World of Powers: The Dynamics of International Relationships* (New York, 1972), 71.

[100] Dennis Driscoll, 'Is Ireland really "Neutral"?', *Irish Studies in International Affairs*, 1/3 (1982), 57—although he gives no details as to the nature of the survey.

[101] John Kelly, Parliamentary Secretary to Minister for Foreign Affairs, *Dáil Debates*, 279 (1975), 354-5.

[102] FitzGerald, Minister for Foreign Affairs, ibid. 294 (1976), 633; 286 (1975), 498.

[103] Brigid Laffan, 'The Consequences for Irish Foreign Policy', in David Coombes (ed.), *Ireland and the European Communities: Ten Years of Membership* (Dublin, 1983), 96, 104.

[104] Patrick Keatinge, 'The Europeanisation of Irish Foreign Policy', in P. J. Drudy and Dermot McAleese (eds.), *Ireland and the European Community* (CUP, 1983), 45.

[105] See *Developments in the European Communities* (hereafter *Developments*), ii (Prl. 3478; Dublin, Nov. 1973), 7-8, and *Developments*, iii (Prl. 3908; June 1974), 12.

[106] *Developments*, iv (Prl. 4319; Dec. 1974), 13.

[107] Ibid. v (Prl. 4663; Aug. 1975), 17.

[108] O'Kennedy, Minister for Foreign Affairs, to 32nd Session of the UN General Assembly, 5 Oct. 1977.

nounced when the Irish held the Presidency of the Community. For example, in 1979 O'Kennedy spoke to the UN General Assembly 'On behalf of the European Community and its nine member States and as Foreign Minister of Ireland', and his speech was full of references to 'we', and 'the Nine'; only towards the end did he say, ' I should now like as Minister for Foreign Affairs of Ireland to touch on a number of issues of particular concern to us in Ireland'.[109] As President, the Irish Minister was responsible for almost daily co-ordination of the Community states' position, for 'negotiating on behalf of the Community with other regional groups . . . speaking on behalf of the Community . . . and . . . delivering explanations of vote'.[110]

Ireland clearly 'does not today act in isolation. We face the world in partnership within the European Community', seeking 'together' to resolve common problems.[111] This perhaps reached its height in the 'concerted action' taken with regard to sanctions against Iran in 1980, and the similar action over Poland, Afghanistan, and the Middle East.[112] Concerning Iran it was made quite clear that it was the foreign ministers of the Community who 'decided to take certain measures', that Ireland 'acted in conjunction with our Community partners', and that 'as one of the nine partners', it 'could not stand apart', although, as will be seen, it did just that in 1982.[113] Irish governments themselves have admitted that the Community 'is increasingly regarded by the external world as a coherent entity in world affairs'.[114]

On the other hand, the record of Community states on EPC is at best 'mixed' and there is no generally agreed foreign policy.[115] While 'a pattern of solidarity has been reached, it is by no means complete or wholly predictable', and there is evidence that the Irish have 'consistently maintained their freedom of manœuvre'.[116] Certainly, on occasion the Irish have deviated from the Community 'norm', and in the period

[109] O'Kennedy, Minister for Foreign Affairs and President-in-Office of the Council of Ministers of the European Communities, to the UN General Assembly, in 'Statements and Speeches, 7/79', *Ireland Today*, 958 (Oct. 1979).

[110] MacKernan, 19.

[111] Lenihan, Minister for Foreign Affairs, *Dáil Debates*, 322 (1980), 1339.

[112] William Wallace, 'European Political Cooperation: A New Form of Diplomacy', *Irish Studies in International Affairs*, 1/4 (1984), 3; although the actual measures against Iran were passed through national parliaments: *Dáil Debates*, 322 (1980), 1811 ff.

[113] Lenihan, Minister for Foreign Affairs, *Dáil Debates*, 322 (1980), 1817, 1829-30; and see below, pp. 268-72.

[114] Lenihan, Minister for Foreign Affairs, ibid. 323 (1980), 1181.

[115] Laffan, 'Consequences', 96.

[116] Keatinge, 'Europeanisation', 47.

1975-7 they were among the minority voting group of Community states most often.[117] Foot, writing in 1979, claimed that her analysis tended 'to reduce the credibility of the claim that the Community has become recognized as a united political force at the U.N.', and noted that the issues they disagreed upon were 'the major ones',[118] although it was increasingly rare for the Community to be split for or against a resolution.[119] The Irish divergences occurred mostly on issues regarded as important before 'involvement in EPC, namely, support for the process of decolonisation and self-determination and advocacy of effective measures of arms control and disarmament',[120] as well as issues concerning Southern Africa and the Third World generally.[121]

Irish officials therefore argue that, while 'aligned', they have not lost 'independence on voting or action' and that third parties, especially the Third World, look at Irish UN behaviour and perceive that it is different from other Community states on these issues.[122] Irish ministers have asserted their continuing ability 'to act in isolation if we so wish'[123] and to speak 'in a reasonably independent and disinterested manner'.[124] Moreover, officials observe that although the Community Presidency may 'heighten the profile of the country . . . "deviant" voting behaviour . . . also serves to heighten Ireland's profile and increase the impact of its vote'.[125] They also point to the election to the Security Council in 1980 as recognition of Ireland's position,[126] and to the continuing acceptability of Ireland for UN peace-keeping missions. The request for Irish participation in UNEF II in 1973, for example, was regarded as 'a recognition of our impartiality and independent and constructive attitude',[127] and more generally it was felt that the 'fact that we are not

---

[117] On 15 occasions in 1975, 17 in 1976, and 11 in 1977: see Rosemary Foot, 'The European Community's Voting Behaviour at the United Nations General Assembly', *Journal of Common Market Studies*, 17/4 (June 1979), 353-6.

[118] Ibid. 359-60. This tends to confirm Beate Lindemann, 'Europe and the Third World: The Nine at the United Nations', *World Today*, 32/7 (July 1976), 260 ff., and her 'European Political Cooperation at the UN: A Challenge for the Nine', in David Allen, Reignhardt Rummel, and Wolfgang Wessels (eds.), *European Political Cooperation* (London, 1982); see also Leon Hurwitz, 'The EEC and Decolonization: The Voting Behaviour of the Nine at the U.N. General Assembly', *Political Studies*, 24/4 (Dec. 1976), 435-47.

[119] R. Foot, 360.

[120] MacKernan, 20-1.

[121] See R. Foot, Lindemann, 'Third World', and Hurwitz, *passim*.

[122] Interviews with Dept. of Foreign Affairs officials, Dublin, Mar. 1981 and Nov. 1983.

[123] O'Kennedy, Minister for Foreign Affairs, *Dáil Debates*, 306 (1978), 367.

[124] Lenihan, Minister for Foreign Affairs, ibid. 323 (1980), 1169.

[125] MacKernan, 19.

[126] Interview with Dept. of Foreign Affairs official, London, Apr. 1985.

[127] FitzGerald, Minister for Foreign Affairs, *Dáil Debates*, 268 (1973), 797 ff.

members of any military alliance certainly enables us to play a role' in peace-keeping,[128] although (as demonstrated in the previous chapter) it did not necessarily represent a recognition of the Irish claims for their position.[129]

Perhaps the most distinctive Irish action in heightening its profile was its refusal to continue to participate in Community sanctions against Argentina after the sinking of the *General Belgrano*. On 2 May 1982 the Irish government announced its anxiety to 're-affirm Ireland's traditional role of neutrality in relation to armed conflicts';[130] as Keatinge has noted, the resort to neutrality made 'Irish neutrality a diplomatic issue, not for some ill-defined future but for the present . . . it exposed the Irish position on avoidance of collective defence to a much greater extent than hitherto'.[131] Ireland also heightened its profile by seeking an 'immediate' meeting of the Security Council on 4 May, and attempting to use its membership of the Security Council to ameliorate the situation —but in a way which, like sanctions, distanced it from Britain.[132]

These actions in 1982 followed earlier self-conscious attempts to distinguish the Irish position from that of Britain. This was partly done by emphasizing Ireland's initial *communautaire* approach to the Community, and also by the distinctive policy in 1974–5 of trying to remain a member, whatever Britain did. The Minister for Foreign Affairs, Fitz-Gerald, was emphatic that this led others 'to see Irish membership in a different light to hitherto', breaking the perceived link in British and Irish membership.[133] This severance was furthered by Irish participation in the European Monetary System (EMS) from 1979 while Britain stayed aloof, and by the consequential breaking of the link with sterling.

The distinctiveness of the Irish position in the Community and EPC was emphasized when the Irish insisted upon distinguishing between defence and security in the discussions following the Genscher–Colombo proposals: ultimately both the 'London Report' of 1981 and Lord Carrington in his press conference recognized Ireland's special position, the former specifically in its reference to 'the different situations of the member states' and the agreement 'to maintain the flexible and pragmatic approach' to EPC, which had allowed discussion of 'the political

---

128 Haughey, Taoiseach, ibid. 327 (1980), 534; and see O'Kennedy, ibid. 268 (1973), 801.

129 See ch. 7.

130 Statement by Govt., 2 May 1982, in *Ireland Today*, 988 (May 1982).

131 Keatinge, 'Europeanisation', 54.

132 Statement issued by Govt., 4 May 1982, *Ireland Today*, 988 (May 1982).

133 FitzGerald, Minister for Foreign Affairs, in a major speech to Royal Irish Academy, 10 Nov. 1975.

aspects of security'.[134] The Taoiseach, FitzGerald, saw this as an explicit recognition of the Irish position in its reference to differing situations among the member states, in maintaining and not expanding EPC, and in limiting discussions to the political aspects of security.[135] It continued to be argued that there was 'no necessity' to make clear to Community partners the Irish intention to stay outside military pacts, since it was not an issue and had never been raised.[136] This in itself is perhaps a comment on the perception by others of Ireland.

Indirect evidence that the Soviets were aware of the Irish position, at least theoretically, may be found in the *Pravda* attacks upon those whom it regarded as trying to undermine Irish neutrality.[137] Soviet–Irish relations were transformed in 1973 by the signing of a joint communiqué in New York on 29 September announcing the decision to exchange diplomatic missions at embassy level. However, it is noteworthy that the communiqué made no reference to Irish neutrality.[138] Although Marcus Wheeler has argued that one of the Soviet motivations was 'the wish to be seen to enjoy normal relations with a small, but increasingly internationally respected neutral state', no evidence is produced to support this.[139] Subsequently, a trade agreement was signed and FitzGerald visited the Soviet Union in 1976.[140] More generally too, in this period the Soviet view of the European Community became a little more relaxed, and while it continued to refuse to establish diplomatic relations with the Community, it did enter into negotiations over fisheries. Between 1977 and 1980 negotiations also took place between the Community and the Council for Mutual Economic Assistance, although no agreement was reached.[141]

---

[134] 'Report on European Political Cooperation', London, 13 Oct. 1981, p. 14.

[135] FitzGerald, Taoiseach, *Dáil Debates*, 330 (1981), 314–15.

[136] O'Kennedy, Minister for Foreign Affairs, ibid. 306 (1978), 423; Lenihan, Minister for Foreign Affairs, 319 (1980), 466.

[137] At least one Dept. of Foreign Affairs official offered this view in an interview in Dublin in Nov. 1983. [138] Text published in *Irish Times*, 1 Oct. 1973.

[139] Marcus Wheeler, 'Soviet Interest in Ireland', *Survey*, 21/3 (1975), 91; see also his 'The Dublin–Moscow Accord', *World Today*, 29/11 (Nov. 1973).

[140] John Kelly, Parliamentary Secretary to Dept. of Foreign Affairs, *Dáil Debates*, 295 (1976), 464.

[141] Individual East European states have negotiated specific trade agreements with the Community. For the general position see John Pinder, 'Integration in Western and Eastern Europe: Relations between the EC and CMEA', *Journal of Common Market Studies*, 18/2 (1979); 'Report on the State of Relations between the EEC and East European State-Trading Countries and Comecon', Working Documents, European Parliament 1978 (doc. 89/78; 11 May 1978); 'Report on Relations between the European Community and the East European State-Trading Countries and the CMEA (Comecon)', ibid. 1981 (doc. 1-424/81; 28 Aug. 1981). See also Michael O'Corcora and Ronald J. Hill, 'The Soviet Union in Irish Foreign Policy', *International Affairs*, 58/2 (Spring 1982).

The development of relations with the Soviet Union was only part of a rapid expansion of Irish diplomatic relations in the period 1973–7. During that time Ireland virtually doubled its diplomatic relations, although, in marked contrast to the period before 1973, many were now non-resident missions.[142] While trade and increasing participation in the world were important, it was the European Community which 'provided the impetus', especially the prospect of holding the Presidency.[143] However, FitzGerald, had recognized in May 1973 that Irish policy could 'be limited by the range of our existing diplomatic representation', which was predominantly orientated towards Western Europe and North America. He recognized that an active Irish role required 'a greater range of contacts'.[144] None the less, ten years later Keatinge still felt that Irish diplomatic relations looked 'thinly spread', and that Ireland trailed behind its Community partners (except Luxemburg).[145] It is interesting that, where no Irish mission existed, Irish citizens in trouble were still advised to contact the British embassy.

In the period 1973–82 third parties found it difficult to determine the real nature of Irish policy.

DISAVOWAL OF EXTERNAL HELP

The inadequacies of the Irish in respect of 'due diligence' had led to a 'conventional external view' that 'implicitly Ireland relies upon the armed forces of the West for its security, and thus maintains armed forces totally inadequate for effective self-defence',[146] that 'Irish neutrality is . . . an illusion and something of a pious fraud indulged in under the implicit security of the NATO umbrella'.[147] While some in Ireland have recognized that 'neutrality was incompatible with the incidental protection of a NATO umbrella',[148] a recent Minister for Defence, Patrick Cooney, argued in 1983 that the Irish could 'confidently rely on [the Western bloc] to protect our territory should any state or

---

[142] See Keatinge, *A Place*, app. 2, pp. 270–1.

[143] *Irish Times*, 28 Jan. 1975. See also Patrick Keatinge, 'Ireland', in Christopher Hill (ed.), *National Foreign Policies and European Political Cooperation* (London, 1983), 147.

[144] FitzGerald, Minister for Foreign Affairs, *Dáil Debates*, 265 (1973), 745.

[145] Keatinge, 'Ireland', 147.

[146] Keatinge, *A Singular Stance*, 74 quoting T. N. Dupuy *et al.*, *The Almanac of World Military Power*, 4th edn. (Navota, Calif., 1980), 186.

[147] Keegan and English, 300. See also Ciaran Farrelly, 'Irish Defence Policy Options', *European Opinion* (Jan. 1977), 2, who describes the present situation as equivalent 'to depending on NATO for protection'.

[148] Keatinge, *A Singular Stance*, 74, summarizing Haughey's position in the Dáil, in *Dáil Debates*, 343 (1983), 2709–10.

combination of states hostile to the Western world threaten it'.[149] More generally, the official position was that Ireland would 'protect and defend' itself,[150] albeit within the limits of its resources,[151] although even some who took this view had to countenance that in certain circumstances 'the best we could hope for would be to defend and hold an area which would allow us to hold out for third party assistance'.[152]

Despite this, at least until 1980, no formal arrangements for joint defence were considered or made, and no proposal was made or received concerning membership of NATO, or any military alliance.[153] In 1980–1 this was called into question by both the Anglo-Irish and the Genscher–Colombo discussions (these will be dealt with when discussing Irish freedom of action),[154] but no concrete arrangements for help emerged. Whatever the position with formal alliances, the Irish continued to maintain close ties with several states on defence matters, and in the period 1974–6, for example, 170 personnel went on 86 courses abroad in Britain, the United States, France, Luxemburg, Holland, Italy, and Sweden,[155] while some senior officers were frequent visitors to Aldershot and the Federal Republic of Germany, as well as Sweden in 1978–9 to examine Swedish defence.[156] A key factor promoting the British link was language.

Other forms of co-operation also took place, most notably in the four-way relationship between the Irish Army, Garda Síochána, Royal Ulster Constabulary, and the British Army. While the PDF, 'restricted as it is to aiding the civil power, was not able to talk directly with the RUC or the British Army', a 'four-way link-up across the border' developed as communications improved, and cross-border co-operation was generally close.[157] This was not formalized in the period 1973–82 and did not amount to an alliance,[158] and neither did the Community contribution to building up the Irish Naval

[149] Cooney, Minister for Defence, Dáil Debates, 343 (1983), 2015; see also William Fitz-Gerald, Irish Unification and NATO (Dublin, 1982), 41, 49, and passim. For an alternative view see Patrick Comerford, Do You Want to Die for NATO? (Dublin, 1984), and Bill McSweeney (ed.), Ireland and the Threat of Nuclear War (Dublin, 1985).

[150] Haughey, Taoiseach, Dáil Debates, 327, (1981), 1396.

[151] Liam Cosgrave, former Taoiseach (1973–7), in interview, Dublin, Mar. 1981.

[152] O'Sullivan, 60.

[153] See Dáil Debates, 265 (1973), 1560; 301 (1977), 3; 306 (1978), 423; 322 (1980), 960; 325 (1980), 820 ff.; 327 (1981), 1392 ff.   [154] See below, pp. 264 ff.

[155] Dáil Debates, 296 (1977), 671; 304 (1978), 427.

[156] Interview with senior Irish army officer, Dublin, Nov. 1983.

[157] Salmon, 'The Civil Power', 84–6.

[158] Neither did the joint patrols of disputed fishery- and territorial waters, such joint patrols being 'in accordance with international practice': FitzGerald, Dáil Debates, 298 (1977), 937.

Service;[159] however, it is clear that certain aspects of the relationship with Britain remained close.

In general, the attitudes and arguments with respect to disavowal of external help in possible conflicts remained the same as in previous years.

FREEDOM OF DECISION AND ACTION

The Irish have appreciated that those who have their eggs in different baskets, or avoid over-dependency upon one other country, have the best prospect of autonomy of action.[160] In the post-1973 period a striking feature of the Irish economy was the 'very marked pattern of export diversification' as the 'trend towards a diminished concentration on the UK market, which had been evident in the decade preceding membership, continued'.[161] The UK share of the Irish export market dropped from 54.7 per cent in 1973 to 38.7 per cent in 1982, as can be seen from Table 8.2, although the import dependence upon the United Kingdom appeared relatively static.

Table 8.2.   Trade by Areas in 1973, 1977, and 1982

	1973	1977	1982
Imports from (%)			
Great Britain/Northern Ireland	50.7	48.2	48.0
Rest of EEC	21.0	19.9	21.8
EFTA	5.9	4.3	4.5
Dollar Countries[a]	8.0	10.1	14.1
Eastern Europe[a]	< 1	2.2	1.3
Exports to (%)			
Great Britain/Northern Ireland	54.7	47.0	38.7
Rest of EEC	21.3	29.2	31.7
EFTA	2.7	3.1	4.2
Dollar Countries[a]	11.2	7.5	8.4
Eastern Europe[a]	< 1	0.7	0.8

[a] Figures for these areas reflect orders of magnitude only.

Sources: *Ireland: Statistical Abstract*, 1972–73, table 121(a), p. 161, tables 114, 115, p. 154; 1978, table 129, p. 170, tables 131, 132, p. 188; 1982–1985, table 134, p. 175, tables 128, 129, p. 171.

[159] See above, pp. 248–9.
[160] Interview with senior Irish Dept. of Foreign Affairs official, Dublin, Nov. 1983.
[161] Dermot McAleese, 'Ireland and the European Community: The Changing Pattern of Trade', in Drudy and McAleese, 154.

However, the import figures conceal a shift from UK manufactured goods to an increased proportion of energy requirements,[162] and ten years after entering the Community, the Irish economy remained heavily trade-dependent, since essential supplies of materials and fuels needed to be imported, and exports and imports constituted 'over 120 per cent of Irish Gross Domestic Product . . . a figure twice the EEC average'.[163] Moreover, the Community states, including Britain, retained a preponderant position in Irish trade, and Irish external trade was conducted within the framework of the Common Commercial Policy (CCP) and the Common External Tariff (CET) of the Community.[164] Despite the diversification, a significant dependence upon the United Kingdom remained. Nevertheless, in December 1974 FitzGerald felt able to speak of the 'new relationship' with Britain in the new 'multilateral context' and of the 'considerable effect' of this and of the reduced economic dependence upon Britain, 'not just economically but politically and psychologically'.[165]

Evidence of this was shown in the broad consensus in 1974–75 that Ireland should seek to stay in the Community, even if Britain withdrew—a stark contrast to the attitudes before entry.[166] It was acknowledged that British withdrawal 'would pose some problems',[167] but the Irish felt that they should stay 'as a matter of principle and economic advantage', as well as because of 'political obligation'.[168] Similarly, in 1978–9 the Irish, albeit hesitantly, agreed to participate in the EMS, although Britain did not. The problems involved the link with sterling, the trade relationship with Britain, the common currency on the island, and the general level of Irish economic development. However, 'the Irish were offered substantial inducements, in the form of so-called "resource transfers", to join the EMS', and those eased the decision, although it was still difficult.[169] Ireland joined the EMS at its commencement, and 'on 30 March 1979 . . . adherence to the EMS

---

[162] Dermot McAleese, 160–1.

[163] Ibid. 145. See also John Blackwell and Eoin O'Malley, 'The Impact of EEC Membership on Irish Industry', in Drudy and McAleese.

[164] Laffan, 'Consequences', 94–5, also mentions the CAP and Common Fisheries Policy as factors.   [165] FitzGerald, Minister for Foreign Affairs, Dáil Debates, 276 (1974), 770–2.

[166] FitzGerald claimed that he was one of the few who would have been prepared for entry, even without Britain: speech to Royal Irish Academy, 10 Nov. 1975.

[167] FitzGerald, Dáil Debates, 275 (1974), 919–20.

[168] O'Kennedy, opposition spokesman, ibid. 275 (1974), 993.

[169] Colm McCarthy, 'EMS and the End of Ireland's Sterling Link', Lloyds Bank Review, 136 (Apr. 1980), 35; see also 30–42 for the background and effect of the decision. In fact, not all of the inducement turned out to be 'resource transfer' per se, since the bulk of the aid was in the

intervention limits forced the Central Bank of Ireland to fix the value of the Irish pound below that of sterling', breaking the link of 150 years.[170] Fundamentally, the Irish preferred multilateral to bilateral constraint.

In 1978 O'Kennedy acknowledged that a series of constraints faced Irish policy-makers, recognizing that they produced a 'framework' which created 'the limits within which we must determine our policies and our attitudes', although he remained adamant that neither the 'present situation nor . . . past choices can wholly determine what our future will be', and that there were still choices to be made.[171] One such was on the question of membership of alliances.

In May 1973 FitzGerald made it clear that the Irish attitude remained 'one of not wishing to become involved in any pre-existing defence organisation such as NATO or WEU', and that the Irish desired 'to make more explicit the distinction . . . between a possible independent European defence body in the more distant future' and existing alliances. Ireland did not wish the Community to become a power bloc or to 'evolve as an element of NATO'. Instead, it should evolve independently.[172] When asked specifically what the difference was between NATO and a future European arrangement, FitzGerald resorted to a reference to the origins of NATO and its 'balancing function' in a divided Europe, and then claimed that 'European defence is quite . . . different', since it would arise out of a European federation, which naturally would wish to defend itself. However, he clearly recognized that this was not likely in the foreseeable future.[173] Irish governments continued to give undertakings not to consider joining NATO, and in February 1981 resurrected the argument 'that we were not able, and are still not able' to join NATO, 'because of its implications for the Six County area situation'.[174]

It also became routine to assert that joining 'the EEC did not entail any military or defence obligations for Ireland. The Community have

form of loans (IR£1,125m. over five years from the Community, and IR£250m. over two years bilaterally), while the grants were to be IR £225m. over five years from the Community, and IR £50m. over two years bilaterally.

[170] Ibid. 31. On the EMS decision see also Brendan M. Walsh, 'Ireland's membership of the European Monetary System: Expectations, Out-Turn and Prospects', in Drudy and McAleese; and C. H. Murray, 'The European Monetary System: Implications for Ireland', *Central Bank of Ireland Annual Review* (1979).

[171] O'Kennedy, Minister for Foreign Affairs, *Dáil Debates*, 306 (1978), 342 ff., 366–7.

[172] FitzGerald, Minister for Foreign Affairs, ibid. 265 (1973), 744.

[173] FitzGerald, interview on 'This Week', RTE radio, 4 July 1975.

[174] Haughey, Taoiseach, *Dáil Debates*, 326 (1981), 1513–14; in his RTE interview on 4 July 1975 FitzGerald had been uncharacteristically vague on this.

not got a common defence policy.'[175] However, this was made somewhat problematic by the continued acceptance by Fianna Fáil governments that, 'in the event of political developments occurring in Europe and in the event of a situation arising . . . [where] the Community of which we were a member were under attack, then obviously we would face our obligations'.[176] However, even Fianna Fáil were conditional in their commitment, predicating it upon 'full political union',[177] in the argument that 'defence arrangements within the Community would have to be consequent upon and following upon the achievement of an acceptable political union',[178] although they occasionally caused trouble for themselves by reiterating Lynch's statement of July 1969, that they were interested in the defence of Community territories, with the doubt as to whether this implied 'at the moment' or 'in the future'.[179] Dooge, as Coalition Foreign Minister, in December 1981 when asked specifically whether Ireland was under any current obligation to defend a Community partner, was emphatic that it was not, and did 'not feel committed to act' in such a way.[180] All were happier talking of the future, and Haughey in 1981 suggested that the question of Ireland and Community defence could be opened, 'when full economic and monetary union has been achieved, and when Ireland's *per capita* income is at least 80 per cent of the Community average and rising, instead of 61 per cent as it is today'.[181]

Not surprisingly, the Irish were somewhat disconcerted in November 1981 to see the proposed British, French, Italian, and Dutch contribution of a peace-keeping force in Sinai described 'as a European, or EEC contingent', and represented as the 'EEC's first-ever military decision'.[182] The Irish were insistent that it was no such thing, but only 'a decision of those four countries', and all that the EPC members had done was to confirm that such a force 'was entirely compatible with the Community policy which had been declared at Venice'.[183] The period 1980–2 also saw other, more substantial, challenges to Irish attitudes.

---

175 Lenihan, Minister for Foreign Affairs, *Dáil Debates*, 327 (1981), 1466.
176 O'Kennedy, Minister for Foreign Affairs, ibid. 309 (1978), 1799. See also 306 (1978), 424.
177 Haughey, Taoiseach, ibid. 327 (1981), 1395–6.
178 Lenihan, Minister for Foreign Affairs, ibid. 1464.
179 Haughey, Taoiseach, ibid. 1396, quoting Lynch, ibid. 241 (1969), 1157.
180 Dooge, Minister for Foreign Affairs, *Seanad Debates*, 96 (1981), 1140.
181 Haughey, *Dáil Debates*, 331 (1981), 922. FitzGerald, in his Royal Irish Academy speech of 10 Nov. 1975, also linked the question to redistribution.
182 *Irish Times*, 13 Dec. 1981. Wallace, 'A New Form of Diplomacy', also refers to it as EPC's 'first military decision' (p. 12).
183 Dooge, Minister for Foreign Affairs, *Seanad Debates*, 96 (1981), 1144.

In May 1980 it was reported by the *Sunday Times* that Mr Haughey was to present Mrs Thatcher with a 'package of proposals aimed at transforming the Northern Ireland problem', and that the package included 'Anglo-Irish cooperation on defence . . . to ease British qualms about Ireland's traditional neutrality'.[184] No such suggestion appeared in the communiqué,[185] but Haughey subsequently refused in the Dáil to reject explicitly the possibility of a deal over defence, although he flatly rejected the suggestion of a return to the Commonwealth.[186] At the end of the year doubts resurfaced, in view of the agreement on 8 December to examine 'the totality of relationships', including 'security matters',[187] and of the statement by the Minister for Foreign Affairs, Lenihan, that 'everything was on the table'.[188] Early in 1981, the *Daily Telegraph* claimed that the Irish were reviewing neutrality and considering a bilateral defence agreement in return for concessions over Northern Ireland, although apparently NATO membership was still ruled out. It claimed that 'Mr Haughey is known to have discussed' these questions, and that he was influenced by the realization 'that sooner or later they will have to abandon the stance of neutrality', because of European developments.[189] Even Síle de Valera (Éamon de Valera's granddaughter) appeared ready to countenance such a deal.[190]

However, in March 1981 Mrs Thatcher ruled out a bilateral defence treaty,[191] and on 11 March 1981 Haughey denied 'unequivocally' that any secret arrangement was being discussed with anyone, although he did say that when 'a satisfactory political solution is arrived at, we would of course have to review what would be the most appropriate defence arrangements for the island as a whole'.[192] The *Irish Times* noted that the eventual possibility of a pact had not been ruled out, and that there was little doubt that the matter had been raised, but Haughey had had second

[184] *Sunday Times*, 18 May 1980.

[185] See *Ireland Today*, 967 (June 1980).

[186] Haughey, Taoiseach, *Dáil Debates*, 321 (1980), 1079–80.

[187] See *Ireland Today*, 972 (Dec. 1980–Jan. 1981).

[188] *Irish Times*, 13 Dec. 1980.

[189] *Daily Telegraph*, 28 Jan. 1981. See also the *Irish Times*, 17 Dec. 1980, and the *Sunday Press*, 21 Dec. 1980.

[190] She stated that 'a united and independent Ireland could well make possible a fresh approach to the consideration of her place within the scheme of western defence'—like her grandfather, she did not give a clear commitment: *Irish Times*, 28 Feb. 1982.

[191] Stating, on a visit to Northern Ireland, that if Ireland wished to discuss defence, it would presumably do so 'with a much wider group of nations': *The Times*, 7 Mar. 1981.

[192] Haughey, Taoiseach, *Dáil Debates*, 327 (1981), 1392–400 (quotation from col. 1394).

thoughts.[193] It is difficult to be definite about what occurred, but it is clear that at least some in Dublin recognized that a deal with Britain over Northern Ireland could not avoid defence.[194]

If the old issue of a deal with Britain could cause difficulty, so too periodically did the new relationship with the Community, although, despite some initial fears that EPC might be 'the thin end of the wedge', Ireland settled into it 'fairly comfortably', finding that it was 'very tolerant' and allowed 'genuine diversity'. Officials claim that Ireland's 'special position' was accepted, and that there was no division of the eight in NATO against Ireland, the division being more likely to be 'big v. small'.[195] Ireland appreciated the 'non-institutionalised, intergovernmental' nature of EPC, and saw that it operated 'pragmatically and by consensus'.[196] It denied that EPC could be equated with a common foreign policy, on the grounds that it lacked instruments and an internal union, as well as being limited by the need for consensus and by the historical divergencies.[197]

None the less, it was the framework within which Irish policy-makers worked and it has occasionally been regarded as exhibiting a tendency towards 'groupthink',[198] as the participants develop a 'European reflex' from the habit of consultation, allowing them to see the 'collective dimension' of issues, and making it 'normal' to search 'for consensus'.[199] It may also be argued that 'the various collective actions of the Ten . . . gradually constitute a policy line from which it is difficult to depart',[200] and that as the 'London Report' of 1981 put it, political co-operation became 'a central element in the foreign policies of all member states'.[201]

The Irish, then, found a certain 'in-built pressure towards con-

---

[193] *Irish Times*, 12 Mar. 1981. On 13 Mar. the *Irish Times* attributed his second thoughts to the furore which the issue had raised.

[194] Interview with senior Irish army officer, Dublin, Nov. 1983.

[195] Interviews with Dept. of Foreign Affairs officials, Dublin, Mar. 1981 and Nov. 1983.

[196] Lenihan gave a description of its operation in 1980, *Dáil Debates*, 322 (1980), 969.

[197] Interviews with Dept. of Foreign Affairs officials, Dublin, Mar. 1981 and Nov. 1983; FitzGerald, Minister for Foreign Affairs, 'European–Arab Cooperation', Cairo, 7 June 1976.

[198] Christopher Hill, 'National Interests: The Insuperable Obstacles?' in Hill, 189, using the term popularized by Irving Janis for the notion that groups tend to close in on themselves, in his *Victims of Groupthink* (Boston, 1972).

[199] MacKernan, 21, cites approvingly Phillippe de Schoutheete, *La Co-operation politique européenne* (Paris, 1980), 118 (MacKernan's translation). Lenihan, Minister for Foreign Affairs, *Dáil Debates*, 322 (1980), 971, also used the word 'reflex'.

[200] MacKernan, 21, quoting Schoutheete.

[201] 'Report on European Political Cooperation', London, 13 Oct. 1981, p. 14.

sensus'[202] and the need for 'give and take'.[203] It was accepted that the question of balancing an independent role and the EPC role was 'difficult', and that there was a 'certain dilution of capacity to act completely independently',[204] since it was necessary to 'accept a compromise on some issues about which we feel concern'. The Irish accepted 'a serious commitment to try and reach a common position', but also argued that the obligation, 'though binding in the sense that we have committed ourselves to co-ordinate our policies, is not absolute since we are not obliged to reach agreement'.[205] However, EPC was regarded as 'not so much a constraint . . . as an opportunity',[206] since a small country could not decisively influence events 'by its own actions',[207] whereas the Community states acting together 'carry much greater weight than anything which a small nation like ours could achieve in isolation'.[208] Indeed, some officials believed that Ireland now had a greater importance than when it was 'free-floating'.[209]

None the less, when 'fundamental interests' were at stake, Ireland managed to pursue an 'independent role',[210] still being 'free to act in isolation if . . . it wish[ed]',[211] and able to speak and act 'in a reasonably independent and disinterested manner'.[212] As has been seen, Ireland was prepared to take a minority view, and even to stand alone, apart from its EPC partners, on a number of issues,[213] although it can be argued that 'its stand on particular issues has altered. Rather than adopting a "yes" or "no" vote, Ireland may now opt to abstain.'[214]

More generally, Ireland adhered 'quite closely'[215] to the predominant EPC view on a range of issues such as CSCE, Poland, Afghanistan, the southern enlargement, the Euro-Arab dialogue, and the Middle East, despite reservations about suggested parallels between the PLO and the IRA. For the most part, Ireland acted as a part of the Community.

[202] Laffan, 'Consequences', 100.
[203] FitzGerald, Minister for Foreign Affairs, Dáil Debates, 275 (1974), 912.
[204] Lenihan, Minister for Foreign Affairs, ibid. 323 (1980), 1169.
[205] O'Kennedy, Minister for Foreign Affairs, ibid. 306 (1978), 365–7.
[206] Ibid.
[207] Lenihan, Minister for Foreign Affairs, ibid. 322 (1980), 1339.
[208] O'Kennedy, Minister for Foreign Affairs, ibid. 306 (1978), 366.
[209] Interview with Dept. of Foreign Affairs official, London, Apr. 1985.
[210] Lenihan, Minister for Foreign Affairs, Dáil Debates, 323 (1980), 1169.
[211] O'Kennedy, Minister for Foreign Affairs, ibid. 306 (1978), 367.
[212] Lenihan, Minister for Foreign Affairs, ibid. 323 (1980), 1169.
[213] See above, p. 256, and R. Foot, 353–6.
[214] Laffan, 'Consequences', 98–100; Keatinge, 'Ireland', in Hill, 144.
[215] Keatinge, 'Ireland', in Hill, 142.

Many of Ireland's policies were, in action, touched upon and constrained by the Community treaties. Under the CCP, for example, Ireland was no longer free to conclude bilateral trade agreements with non-member countries, although like other Community states it had retained 'some independence of action' outside the CCP by the conclusion of co-operation agreements.[216] The two Lomé agreements straddled treaty and non-treaty areas and also constrained Irish policy. Both were concluded under an Irish Presidency, and the Irish claimed a role in their successful conclusion. In addition, both the CAP and Common Fisheries Policy, amongst other policies, had external impacts: Ireland's interactions with the world were, as a result, more heavily influenced by the Community; and this reinforced the notion of Ireland as part of the Community.

Certainly, until 1982 Ireland also showed that it was one of the Community by taking part in sanctions with its partners. Although the sanctions agreed were largely 'minimal and . . . informal',[217] they were evidence of commonality and solidarity. They were imposed against Iran, albeit on 'an almost inter-governmental pattern', although there was some Commission involvement.[218] Moreover, Lenihan, in introducing the measures, was emphatic that they followed a decision of the Nine, and that Ireland was acting 'in conjunction with . . . [its] Community partners', and that, as 'one of the nine partners', it 'could not stand apart'.[219] In addition, collective action was taken against the Soviet Union over Afghanistan and Poland, in the first case utilizing CAP regulations, and in the second invoking CCP. It is interesting that although the Greeks, for political reasons, made an economic case to opt out of the latter sanctions,[220] the Irish did not argue any special case with respect to 'neutrality'. The question of sanctions and Community solidarity took a different turn in 1982.

The Irish condemned at the outset the Argentinian invasion of the Falkland Islands and supported the British-inspired Resolution 502 in the Security Council. The Irish felt that the Argentinians had flouted UN authority by ignoring the Security Council call of 1 April for a peaceful settlement, and they also opposed the use of force and the

[216] FitzGerald, Minister for Foreign Affairs, Royal Irish Academy, 10 Nov. 1975.

[217] Hill, 191.

[218] Pieter Jan Kuyper, 'Community Sanctions against Argentina: Lawfulness under Community and International Law', in D. O'Keefe and H. G. Schermers (eds.), *Essays in European Law and Integration 1983* (Deventer, 1983), 145.

[219] Lenihan, Minister for Foreign Affairs, *Dáil Debates*, 322 (1980), 1811 ff., 1829–30.

[220] Kuyper, 144–7.

general challenge to the rule of law.[221] However, subsequently certain tensions arose between a concern for freedom of action, a concern for neutrality, the desire to utilize their Security Council position, and the British effort to secure Community support and solidarity.[222]

After initial hesitations concerning the efficacy of sanctions,[223] on 10 April the Irish announced that they would support them 'in the interests of EEC solidarity',[224] and subsequently explained that it had been hoped that sanctions would complement other measures, rendering 'unnecessary further military action'.[225] In mid-April, the Department of Foreign Affairs was adamant that the acceptance of sanctions had 'no implications whatsoever for Ireland's neutrality',[226] and on 16 April Ireland supported Council Regulation 877/82, 'suspending imports of all products originating in Argentina' until 17 May 1982.[227]

The Preamble to the Regulation referred to discussions 'in the context of European political cooperation', consultations under Article 224, a proposal from the Commission, and 'in particular Article 113' of the EEC Treaty. It is interesting that both the EPC and Article 224 involve consultations between member-states, and the Irish could not have been compelled to take action, in the form of sanctions, under either. However, Article 113 allows for qualified majority voting, and regulations are, as Regulation 877/82 specifically stated, 'binding in . . . [their] entirety and directly applicable in all Member States'.[228]

On 20 April—the eve of the British attack on South Georgia—the Minister for Foreign Affairs, Collins, warned that neutrality was 'sacred to us' and would be maintained in the event of a formal declaration of war.[229] Indeed, as violence increased, the Irish government grew more anxious about the compatibility of sanctions and neutrality. On 2 May a statement was issued, confirming the 'wish to re-affirm Ireland's traditional role of neutrality in relation to armed conflicts', and after the sinking of the *General Belgrano* a further statement on 4 May expressed

---

221 Interview with Dept. of Foreign Affairs official, London, Apr. 1985. See also Norman MacQueen, 'The Expedience of Tradition: Ireland, International Organization and the Falklands Crisis', *Political Studies* 33/1 (Mar. 1985), 38–55; Haughey, Taoiseach, *Dáil Debates*, 334 (1982), 798 ff.

222 MacQueen, 'Expedience', 43.

223 Haughey, Taoiseach, *Dáil Debates*, 334 (1982), 798 ff., 1424 ff.

224 *Irish Times*, 12 Apr. 1982.

225 Haughey, Taoiseach, *Dáil Debates*, 334 (1982), 800.

226 *Irish Times*, 13 Apr. 1982, echoing a previous statement that 'Ireland's neutrality was in no way watered down by this decision' (ibid., 12 Apr. 1982).

227 *OJ* L102, Council Regulation (EEC) 877/82, of 16 Apr. 1982.

228 Ibid.

229 Collins, Minister for Foreign Affairs, RTE interview, 20 Apr. 1982.

dismay at what amounted to 'open war'. It said that the government would seek an 'immediate meeting of the Security Council' at which Ireland would call for an 'immediate' ceasefire and a negotiated settlement. In a further assertion of an independent stance, the statement concluded that the government 'regard[s] the application of economic sanctions as no longer applicable and will therefore be seeking the withdrawal of these sanctions by the Community', although it did not give neutrality as a reason.[230]

It came to be argued that 'as a neutral nation' Ireland had always 'refrained from military alliance of any kind', and thus had to take 'a very clear view of any action, economic or otherwise, that would appear supportive of military action'. Therefore, 'sanctions complementing military action' were unacceptable, and Ireland had to assert its 'neutral status'.[231] None the less, it was also made clear that Ireland would in the meantime 'act in concert with our EEC partners' and 'would not unilaterally lift the embargo'.[232] In fact, Ireland was constrained until 17 May by Regulation 877/82, especially since at a meeting on 8–9 May they failed to convince others that sanctions should be discontinued.[233]

The Irish do not appear to have led the campaign against renewal as 17 May approached (the Italians were in the forefront), and some observers failed to detect signs 'of a nation resolutely defending its "traditional neutrality" against the depredations of a belligerent neighbour'.[234] None the less, on 18 and 24 May Ireland and Italy opted out of the continuance of further measures, although both Council Regulations 1176/82 and 1254/82 specifically stated that they were binding in their 'entirety and directly applicable in all Member States'.[235] It is not clear, therefore, that the Irish and Italian action can be reconciled with those Regulations and Community law, although the matter was not tested in the courts. The argument turns on the relationship between Articles 113 and 224, and the status of the original Preamble, but doubts exist as to the legality of the Irish position, and whether, if hostilities had been more protracted, they could have been made to comply.[236]

---

[230] For these statements see *Ireland Today*, 988 (May 1982).

[231] Haughey, Taoiseach, in the *Irish Times*, 7 May 1982.

[232] Ibid, 5 May 1982.

[233] Haughey, *Dáil Debates* 334 (1982), 802–4.

[234] MacQueen, 'Expedience', 50.

[235] *OJ* L136, Council Regulation (EEC) 1176/82, of 18 May 1982; L146, Council Regulation (EEC) 1254/82, of 24 May 1982.

[236] For a discussion of the legal question see Kuyper, 147–51. The change of policy over sanctions was against the advice of senior Irish officials: interview with senior Dept. of Foreign

Haughey was emphatic, while not addressing this problem directly, that nothing in Irish obligations to the Community required Ireland 'to back military action',[237] and that Ireland's position had changed when it found itself 'moving into a situation which would seriously endanger . . . [its] traditional policy of neutrality'. Ireland was 'being seen . . . as . . . associated with a serious escalation of military activity', with sanctions operating in a situation of open war.[238] Because of this, Ireland was 'not afraid to stand alone on the issue of peace' or in reasserting its 'neutrality'. It had faced pressure before, and would withstand it again, especially since the people were so 'deeply attached to neutrality'. The government had, claimed Haughey, made it clear 'in principle and in practice' that Irish neutrality would not be eroded. If Community solidarity was threatened, it was only threatened by those seeking to use it for purposes for which it was not designed.[239]

The Community dimension became less significant and the Irish pursued their independent line at the Security Council, which reconvened on 21 May. Having made it clear that they would support a ceasefire, on 24 May the Irish circulated a draft resolution calling for a ceasefire for seventy-two hours and negotiations, although the agreed resolution dropped the reference to a ceasefire. The Irish draft made no explicit reference to Argentinian withdrawal.[240]

A key feature in this episode appears to have been a concern 'to uphold Ireland's independence of action',[241] although at times it degenerated into anti-British sentiment, as when the Minister for Defence referred, after the sinking of the *General Belgrano*, to the British as 'very much the aggressors now',[242] a view disowned by Haughey.[243] However, some in Ireland wondered at the sudden resurrection of the traditional policy of neutrality, in view of the debates of 1980–1, and it has been argued that the government's stance was influenced by concerns of domestic popularity,[244] battles for leadership within Fianna Fáil, and frustration

Affairs official, Dublin, Nov. 1983. On the earlier operation of sanctions, see also the 'Report on the Significance of Economic Sanctions', by Mr Seeler (Working Documents, European Parliament, doc. 1-83/82; Apr. 1982).

[237] Haughey, Taoiseach, *Dáil Debates*, 334 (1982), 802.
[238] Ibid. 1425.
[239] Ibid. 804.
[240] MacQueen, 'Expedience', 50–3: neither did the 4 May statement.
[241] Senator John A. Murphy, *Sunday Press*, 23 May 1982.
[242] Power, Minister for Defence, *Irish Times*, 4 May 1982.
[243] Haughey, Taoiseach, *Dáil Debates*, 334 (1982), 35–8.
[244] FitzGerald, opposition Leader, ibid. 1429.

at the failure of the hoped-for 'historic breakthrough' over Northern Ireland.[245] Moreover, in May 1982 the British had also made life difficult for the Irish by trying to block Community farm-price rises.[246] Certainly, Ireland had previously accepted participation in sanctions after military action, and in this case action started on 2 April, after which the Irish again accepted sanctions.[247] More problematic is that the events of 1982 left somewhat unresolved the compatibility of Ireland's position and Community law, although in the short term they demonstrated that Ireland retained sufficient freedom of action to adopt a neutral stance. It is interesting that, in addressing the UN General Assembly on 30 September 1982, Collins made no reference to neutrality.[248]

The question of the relationship between defence, security, neutrality, and Community membership also caused the Irish some anguish in 1981 in the context of the Genscher–Colombo proposals for a 'Treaty of European Union', consolidating 'the bases of concerted action in foreign affairs' and extending 'coordination in the field of security policy'.[249] For years, at least since Irish entry, EPC had touched on matters such as disarmament and CSCE,[250] and European Councils had touched on NATO issues, which were also discussed *en marge* at Foreign Ministers' meetings.[251] Now the issue was being raised formally, with security as 'a code word', meaning 'as little or as much as its listeners like[d] to understand by it',[252] since it was in any case accepted that there was a 'grey area where defence merges into security policy in a general sense'.[253] Nevertheless, Lenihan argued publicly in November 1980 that there was a 'clear distinction' between EPC, involving foreign policy consultation, 'and defence', which was not discussed. He

---

[245] For a discussion of these aspects see MacQueen, 'Expedience', 53–5.

[246] Haughey, Taoiseach, on RTE, 12 May, said that all issues 'impinged' on each other: *Irish Times*, 14 May 1982.

[247] FitzGerald, opposition Leader, made these points, in *Dáil Debates*, 334 (1982), 1427–30.

[248] Collins, Minister for Foreign Affairs, address to 37th General Assembly of the UN, 30 Sep. 1982, in *Ireland Today*, 993 (Nov.–Dec. 1982); Gerard M. M. MacSweeny, 'Irish Neutrality and International Law', *Irish Law Times* (Aug. 1984), 149.

[249] See Wallace, 'Integration', 397, 402.

[250] Dooge, Minister for Foreign Affairs, *Seanad Debates*, 96 (1981), 1138–9.

[251] Interview with senior Irish politician with experience of these matters, Dublin, Nov. 1983. As it was put in the interview: 'If a Foreign Minister has just returned from spending hours with Gromyko, he naturally wants to report to colleagues. If he strays into certain areas, I would not hold up my hand and say you can't, but rather say nothing, sip my drink deeply, and keep my ears open.'

[252] Wallace, 'A New Form of Diplomacy', 12.

[253] President-in-Office at time of Venlo meeting, Dutch Foreign Minister, Dr van der Klaauw, *The Times*, 11 May 1981.

went on, 'the question of harmonising the national defence policies of the member states simply does not arise'.[254]

In 1981 it did arise, and the issue became whether 'defence is indivisible from security'[255] or whether, as Lenihan reiterated in March 1981, there was 'a very big difference between security, as such, and defence', since security was 'a much wider concept bringing in our whole relations within the United Nations, international relations generally, political relations and all that area other than defence'. There was a difference therefore, between 'security on an international level and military neutrality'.[256]

In May 1981 at Venlo, although the Community ministers agreed that there was no question of the Community becoming involved in 'defence questions proper', some wished for regular exchanges on 'security policy in the broad sense of stabilization and confidence-building'.[257] Four options with regard to EPC were discussed: (1) to maintain the present system as it was; (2) to make minor administrative or procedural modifications to the present system, while retaining its present aims and basic features; (3) to draw up a new report which would change the nature and expand the scope of political co-operation; or (4) to draw up a formal treaty of political co-operation.[258] What the Irish representatives agreed to at this and subsequent meetings became a heavily contested issue.

Lenihan, the Irish minister at Venlo, subsequently claimed that he had favoured the first and second options, but not the third, the drawing-up of a new report.[259] However, the official record showed agreement that 'the political directors . . . should examine options two and three' and this, according to FitzGerald, put Ireland 'on a slippery slope of a highly dangerous kind'. FitzGerald claimed that it was only the subsequent activity by the new minister, Dooge, and his officials which managed 'for the moment' to push shut the door that Lenihan had opened.[260] Dooge had apparently been emphatic that there was to be no

---

[254] In a speech at a Conference on Neutrality organized by the Royal Irish Academy International Affairs Committee, 21 Nov. 1980 (four days after the Genscher speech): see *Dáil Debates*, 325 (1980), 820.

[255] The view of Lt.-Gen. Carl O'Sullivan, reported in the *Irish Times*, 2 Feb., 25 Sept. 1982.

[256] Lenihan, Minister for Foreign Affairs, *Dáil Debates*, 327 (1981), 1466.

[257] e.g. Genscher, *The Times*, 11 May 1981.

[258] Lenihan (who had been at Venlo), speaking in opposition, and FitzGerald, as Taoiseach, in Oct. 1981: *Dáil Debates*, 330 (1981), 125–6, 310–11.

[259] Lenihan, in opposition, ibid. 124–34.

[260] FitzGerald, Taoiseach, ibid. 305–18.

discussion of political-military issues by foreign ministers, and that defence or other officials should not co-ordinate policy on these issues.[261] FitzGerald claimed that Lenihan had left the impression that Ireland 'would be willing' to move, and had thereby encouraged these ideas.[262]

For his part, Lenihan (in opposition by October 1981) claimed that the 'London Report' had 'profound implications' for Irish neutrality, and that for all practical purposes it made Ireland a political member of the Western alliance, there being 'no limit' on the political subjects which could be discussed. He now spoke of 'the artificial distinction between security and defence, which are really synonymous, but which had some value', and of Irish independence of action being eroded.[263] What worried Lenihan was the Report's reference to the agreement 'to maintain the flexible and pragmatic approach which had made it possible to discuss in political cooperation certain important foreign policy questions bearing on the political aspects of security'. He now wondered, 'What does "the political aspect of security" mean?', and claimed that it was a new phrase, that, instead of an 'excellent' ad hoc arrangement within a 'loose framework', there was for the first time a 'formalising of the situation and the first step towards having a treaty on this basis', and that this involved Ireland 'still closer in military matters'. He now felt that the 'political aspects of security' covered 'the whole area of weaponry and military and defence aspects in relation to political security', although the 'ugly word "defence" ' as such did not appear. Dooge had bargained away, or put Ireland 'on the slippery slope to bargaining' away, 'the cornerstone of Irish diplomatic policy', neutrality.[264]

FitzGerald claimed that the 'slippery slope' had started with the agreement at Venlo to study the third option, and that the Coalition had secured the subsequent insertion of the key clause, which had been only partially quoted by Lenihan. FitzGerald referred to the additional initial clause, 'and having regard to the different situations of the member states', arguing that this was 'a reference to our position', while the 'London Report' agreed to 'maintaining and not expanding' the EPC system, and constrained it to the 'political aspects of security'.[265] Moreover, the Coalition believed that a paper on the scope and nature of

[261] Interview with Dept. of Foreign Affairs official, and with senior politician, Dublin, Nov. 1983; Dooge, Seanad Debates, 96 (1981), 1142.

[262] FitzGerald, Taoiseach, Dáil Debates, 330 (1981), 313.

[263] Lenihan, Irish Times, 15 Oct. 1981.

[264] Lenihan, Dáil Debates, 330 (1981), 124-34.

[265] FitzGerald, Taoiseach, ibid. 306-18.

the EPC actually strengthened the Irish position by serving as a benchmark for what was or was not acceptable.[266]

In fact, the 'London Report' was a compromise between the second and third options discussed at Venlo. While it maintained the existing basic features of the system, it also contained some new features. EPC was to be extended, in that, instead of reacting to events, governments might consider taking 'a longer-term approach to certain problems' and instituting 'studies to that end'. In addition, the presidency was in future to be aided by a small team from preceding and succeeding presidencies, in order to strengthen it organizationally and to enhance continuity. It was also made clear that there could be both formal and informal meetings under the aegis of EPC, the latter being confidential. Confidentiality was regarded as a key to success,[267] although it also had the benefit of erecting a smoke-screen around what was discussed.[268]

In general, on this issue of EPC reform the Irish avoided some of their worst fears, since military matters *per se* were to be left to NATO, and it was not only the Irish who were worried by the possible expansion of EPC. On the other hand, no definitive definition of 'the political aspects of security' had been agreed and Irish equivocation did not provide a firm basis upon which to resist slipping further down 'the slippery slope'. Indeed, by November 1981 Genscher was circulating the text of a draft treaty or solemn undertaking on European Union, which called for regular exchanges of view on security questions, leading to harmonization of viewpoints and to strengthening of the Atlantic alliance. It was suggested that to allow for such discussion the Council of Ministers should be able to vary its composition, which was regarded by some 'as diplomatic code for saying that Defence Ministers or experts should attend European Council meetings with the aim of strengthening NATO',[269] something which Dooge in December 1981 claimed was beyond the pale.[270] In October 1981 FitzGerald had warned of further pressure, and had even suggested that it 'could lead to our isolation and to a two-tier political co-operation which would be greatly to our political disadvantage'.[271]

---

[266] Interview with senior Irish politician, Dublin, Nov. 1983.

[267] 'Report on European Political Cooperation', London, 13 Oct. 1981, pp. 15–16; *Irish Times*, 28 Oct. 1981.

[268] See Desmond Dinan, 'Irish Involvement in European Political Cooperation', in McSweeney, *Threat*, 144.

[269] *Irish Times*, 5 Nov. 1981.

[270] Dooge, *Seanad Debates*, 96 (1981), 1142.

[271] FitzGerald, *Dáil Debates*, 330 (1981), 315–16.

With regard to the general development of the Community the Irish 'produced a certain amount of integrationist rhetoric, paying lip-service to the idea of European "togetherness" '[272] and European Union, but the latter was clearly seen as something for 'the distant future'.[273] As well as expressing their continuing acceptance of the political objectives of the Community,[274] the Irish stressed the importance of redistribution,[275] and of inter-governmental progress not out-stripping treaty-based progress, and showed a strong preference for building 'on the Treaty foundations'.[276] Specific proposals to make progress in the direction of European Union often caused embarrassment, as with the Genscher–Colombo initiative and subsequent developments. Irish caution was also shown in the reaction to the reports on European Union in 1975–6. Tindemans, for example, caused alarm by raising the possibility of two-tier development in the Community, and by his calls for exchanges of view on defence, leading to 'a common analysis of defence problems', and for co-operation in armaments manufacture.[277] The Irish were wary of such proposals. They also, on occasion, obstructed smaller steps, such as allowing the incoming Commission President to pick his own team, although, on the other hand, FitzGerald expressed general support for a more democratic, supranational Community, with a stronger voice for the European Parliament.[278]

In terms of the development of the Community, the Irish faced problems in the way in which action taken under the Treaty—for example, the achievement of a customs union—presaged other activity, namely, in this case, pressure for an industrial policy in order to make the single market a reality.[279] This in turn led to defence-related questions being raised, since it was argued that the Community could not 'draw

---

[272] Keatinge, 'Europeanisation', 42.

[273] FitzGerald, Minister for Foreign Affairs, interview on 'This Week', RTE radio, 4 July 1975. See also O'Kennedy as Foreign Minister, *Dáil Debates*, 306 (1978), 421–2; Dooge, *Seanad Debates*, 96 (1981), 1143.

[274] FitzGerald, Minister for Foreign Affairs, *Dáil Debates*, 265 (1973), 756.

[275] Haughey in opposition, ibid. 331 (1981), 922; FitzGerald, Minister for Foreign Affairs, Royal Irish Academy, 10 Nov. 1975.

[276] Dooge, Minister for Foreign Affairs, *Seanad Debates*, 96 (1981), 1141; a point reiterated in interviews with senior Irish politicians and Dept. of Foreign Affairs officials, Dublin, Nov. 1983.

[277] 'Report on European Union' by Mr Leo Tindemans, Dec. 1975, in *Bulletin of the European Communities*, suppl.1/76 (Brussels, 1976), 18–20.

[278] FitzGerald, Minister for Foreign Affairs, *Dáil Debates*, 265 (1973), 756 ff.; and see Salmon, 'Ireland', in C. and K. J. Twitchett, 203–13, for a general review of Irish attitudes on these questions.

[279] See Michael Hodges, 'Industrial Policy: Hard Times or Great Expectations?', in Wallace, Wallace, and Webb, 265–6.

an artificial dividing line between the civilian and defence industry sectors',[280] and that 'without the development of a single organised market for the armaments sector' it was 'hardly possible to imagine how a common industrial policy could be brought into play', especially in ship-building, electronics, and aircraft industries. The Klepsch–Normanton Report of June 1978, which argued in this way, went on to propose that there should be Community representation, through either the Commission or the President-in-Office, in the Independent European Programme Group, a collaborative forum for armaments co-operation.[281] The Irish did not object 'in principle to there being a Community policy for the manufacture or export of arms', but clearly were wary of any blurring of competences or linkage between the Community and defence organizations.[282] Irish difficulties on such issues as the Klepsch–Normanton Report raised were illustrated by the three-way division among Irish Members of the European Parliament (MEPs) when the report was voted on in the European Parliament: Fianna Fáil MEPs abstained on the grounds that it was irrelevant to Ireland; Fine Gael supported it on the grounds of employment; and Kavanagh of Labour voted against on the grounds that it might draw Ireland into NATO involvement.[283] Fortunately for Ireland, subsequent reports tended to be more modest,[284] although in October 1981 the Commission sent to the Council of Ministers a document on industrial innovation which drew attention to the problems caused by nationalistic approaches to defence procurement, and urged closer co-operation over purchases of military equipment as an important element in developing Community policy on industrial innovation.[285]

Another possible aspect of the development of the Community was seen on 18 May 1982, when at the very moment when the Irish were asserting their own freedom of action, in regard to the Falklands

[280] Christopher Tugendhat, Vice-President of the Commission, First Annual Shell Lecture, University of St. Andrews, 14 May 1981.

[281] 'Report on European Armaments Procurement Cooperation', by Mr E. Klepsch, Political Committee, European Parliament, 8 May 1978 (Working Documents, European Parliament 1978–1979, doc. 83/78).

[282] Keatinge, A Singular Stance, 91.

[283] Irish Times, 15 and 14 June 1978.

[284] See e.g. D. Greenwood, 'A Policy for Promoting Defence and Technological Cooperation among West European Countries, report for the Commission of the European Communities (Brussels 1980), and the report by Mr Haagerup, Working Documents, European Parliament, 1982–1983, doc. 1-946/82.

[285] Irish Times, 16 Oct. 1981. The paper also reported that O'Kennedy, the Irish Commissioner, had 'fought . . . a spoiling action . . . to prevent any detailed suggestions emerging'.

conflict, they consented to the overriding of a British veto, and thus placed in potential jeopardy both Irish independence of action and a basis of neutrality. It is most interesting that, while Ireland joined with the majority to vote through farm-price rises, both Greece and Denmark refused to vote on the grounds that this would set a precedent which could be used against them, although the increases would have been to their benefit. Ireland not only voted, but also failed to have recorded at the end of the meeting its belief in the continuing validity of the veto principle, the course adopted by France and Italy. The Irish believed that there was a distinction between using a veto over the implementation of agreed policy and law, and using it over new developments. None the less, as an Irish diplomat admitted, they had put themselves in a position where other people could 'now tell us what our national interest is'.[286]

The Irish, then, faced pressures upon their independence of action and their claim to neutrality emanating from the natural evolution of policies within the Treaty framework, for example, the CCP, fisheries policy, and industrial policy; from the evolution of EPC, as the difficulties of separating defence and security grew; and from the overspill from these two factors. Moreover, in the tenth year of membership FitzGerald felt obliged to point out that had Ireland not joined the Community, the 'level of public and social services would by now have been at a . . . totally unacceptable' level, a point which, he argued, those 'who urge that we would be better to be outside the Community . . . alleging a threat to our neutrality . . . ought to reflect on'.[287]

LACK OF ISOLATIONISM

In 1980 Ireland was elected to the UN Security Council for 1981–2. In December 1980 the Dáil was reminded of the functions of the Security Council and assured that Ireland would play its 'part in efforts to resolve whatever international disputes are considered by the Council', joining in efforts to promote the implementation of solutions and working within the general aims of Irish foreign policy 'for a more peaceful, stable and just international order'.[288] The most conspicuous Irish activity on the Council was their calling for ceasefires during the

[286] Irish Times, 19 May 1982. Lenihan did attempt to stress outside the meeting that he did not regard it as the end of the Luxemburg compromise.

[287] FitzGerald, Leader of the opposition, Irish Times, 12 May 1982.

[288] Lenihan, Minister for Foreign Affairs, Dáil Debates, 325 (1980), 594–6; see also ibid. 322 (1980), 741–2.

Falklands conflict. While it is arguable that this contributed to both the fulfilment of Irish policy and Council responsibilities, some of the Irish activity at this time was badly thought out, in that, for example, their call for an 'immediate' Security Council meeting had to be dropped, and their proposals made no explicit reference to Argentinian withdrawal.[289] On the other hand, the government and Foreign Affairs officials argued that Irish activity reflected the seriousness with which they took their responsibilities as members, their view of the need to bolster the UN role, and their belief that the conflict was precisely the sort of conflict that the United Nations should have been able to handle.[290]

Perhaps of greater long-term significance was the continued Irish contribution to UN peace-keeping, particularly in the Middle East between 1973 and 1982, save for the interruption between July 1974 and May 1978 because of the domestic security situation. Even during 1974–8 small numbers served at times with UNFICYP and UNTSO (of whom some served with the United Nations Disengagement Observer Force).[291] The Irish were flattered by the requests for their contribution, and saw it as a role they could play precisely because they were 'not members of any military alliance'.[292] Their peace-keeping contribution was regarded as 'out of all proportion' to their size, and it was felt it 'might well be compromised if we were to become members of any particular military alliance'.[293] This non-membership, together with Ireland's history, was regarded as enhancing Irish 'acceptability among the Third World countries', and, in addition, placing Ireland in a good position to play a 'prominent role in the various disarmament debates',[294] perhaps even being able to lead 'a movement for peace in the UN', because Ireland was 'one of the nonaligned nations who can speak with independence and confidence about . . . world peace and security'.[295]

According to Lenihan, it also allowed Ireland to play a crucial role in

[289] See Govt. statement, 4 May 1982, in *Ireland Today*, 988 (May 1982); FitzGerald, Leader of the opposition, *Dáil Debates*, 334 (1982), 809.

[290] Haughey, Taoiseach, *Dáil Debates*, 334 (1982), 798–806; Noel Dorr's speech to the Security Council, 25 May, in *Irish Times*, 26 May 1982; interview with senior Foreign Affairs official, London, Apr. 1985.

[291] Usually 6 with UNFICYP and 21 with UNTSO, of whom 6 or 7 served with UNDOF: see *Dáil Debates*, 275 (1974), 1322; 279 (1975), 356; 287 (1976), 1168. For 'Record of Unit Service with United Nations' see Sheehan, app. b, pp. 79–80.

[292] Haughey, Taoiseach, *Dáil Debates*, 327 (1981), 534.

[293] Haughey, Taoiseach, ibid. 327 (1981), 1397.

[294] Dooge, Minister for Foreign Affairs, *Seanad Debates*, 96 (1981), 1136–8.

[295] O'Kennedy in opposition, *Dáil Debates*, 268 (1973), 801 ff.

the Madrid CSCE review conference,[296] as has been seen. More generally, it was felt that Ireland could help push EPC into a 'progressive'
direction,[297] and FitzGerald in 1981 argued that Ireland, in conjunction
with other countries, had influenced British policy on issues like
Zimbabwe, and had made a 'constructive' contribution on Namibia and
the Middle East.[298] This view from 1981 echoed his argument in 1975 on
the influence of the Irish Presidency in the Euro-Arab dialogue and in the
Lomé agreements.[299]

Some (particularly the Labour Party) felt that Ireland should be more
active, and fretted at the constraints of EPC. In Cork in the autumn of
1980, as well as calling for neutrality to be enshrined in the Constitution
and for co-operation with the non-aligned, the party called on the
government to pursue 'active neutrality', which would involve a 'total
commitment to peace, détente and disarmament, together with a
programme of involvement in world affairs', as part of 'the evolution
and implementation of a positive policy of neutrality'.[300] The Labour
Leader, Cluskey, explained that neutrality could no longer simply be 'an
assertion that one wishes to avoid being drawn into war' (sic), but rather
that its value was in 'preventing war not escaping from it', and that this
required 'positive proposals' rather than withdrawal into a 'neutralist
cocoon'.[301] Ryan of Fine Gael continued to see a version of active
neutrality as appropriate for the European Community.[302]

The official view was rather more low-key, acknowledging the limitations imposed by the range of Irish diplomatic representation and the
'lack of resources',[303] which meant that Ireland could not contribute
financially and economically.[304] Indeed, its record on aid was poor,[305]
and while the Irish continued to seek an input into the disarmament
process, and supported, for example, nuclear-free zones, they were

[296] See above, pp. 253-4.
[297] In his 10 Nov. 1975 speech to Royal Irish Academy, FitzGerald, as Minister for Foreign
Affairs, argued that the EPC process inevitably involved 'pressure on the more "conservative"
countries to adopt a more progressive stance' and vice versa, although generally the movement was
in a 'progressive direction'.
[298] FitzGerald, Taoiseach, Dáil Debates, 330 (1981), 307-8.
[299] FitzGerald, Minister for Foreign Affairs, 10 Nov. 1975, Royal Irish Academy.
[300] Quinn, Dáil Debates, 327 (1981), 1440-1.
[301] Cluskey, Labour Leader, ibid. 1405-6.
[302] Ryan, ibid. 306 (1978), 411; Irish Times, 24 Oct. 1978.
[303] FitzGerald, Minister for Foreign Affairs, Dáil Debates, 265 (1973), 745.
[304] FitzGerald, Minister for Foreign Affairs, ibid. 276 (1974), 781.
[305] See Helen O'Neill, 'Irish Aid: Performance and Policies', Development and Peace, 4 (Spring
1983).

limited by a lack of technological expertise.[306] Apart from nudging the policy of others, the government saw Ireland's role as that of being 'imaginative and constructive', which, it was felt, was all the more valuable in view of alleged recognition of Ireland's 'disinterestedness'.[307]

Principally, after 1973 the Irish sought to exert influence within and via EPC, as has been seen. It came to be argued that Ireland no longer acted 'in isolation', but rather now faced 'the world in partnership within the European Community',[308] thus carrying 'much greater weight' in the world.[309] Moreover, it was clear that membership of the Community and involvement in EPC were incompatible with isolationism.

Notwithstanding occasional 'deviant' Irish behaviour within EPC, and the stance during the Falklands conflict, there was also the question of whether involvement in the Community and EPC was incompatible with impartiality, especially in view of the number of other occasions on which the Irish did join their Community partners in sanctions against third parties. As has been seen, Haughey as Taoiseach acknowledged that 'political neutrality or non-alignment' was 'incompatible' with Community membership. More generally, a further difficulty was the continuing and related belief that Ireland's place was 'with the Western democracies', since it shared with them 'common concepts of human rights, freedom under the law, individual liberty and freedom of conscience'. According to Haughey, Irish economic interests also were 'tied in with the Western industrialised world'.[310] Indeed, FitzGerald was quoted in 1980 as going further: 'There really isn't such a thing as neutrality today: we are part of Western Europe and our interests coincide with theirs.'[311]

Ireland was not indifferent to what happened between East and West, or to the issues which divided them. On 'crucial issues', its sympathies were 'clearly . . . with the West', according to FitzGerald, and when asked whether Ireland was neutral between ideologies, he replied 'Who is?'[312] Given such clear commitment to the West and the Community,

---

[306] Interviews with Dept. of Foreign Affairs officials, Dublin, Mar. 1981; and see *Dáil Debates*, 276 (1974), 1180; Lenihan, *Irish Times*, 28 Oct. 1981.

[307] FitzGerald, Minister for Foreign Affairs, *Dáil Debates*, 265 (1973), 743.

[308] Lenihan, Minister for Foreign Affairs, ibid. 322 (1980), 1339.

[309] O'Kennedy, Minister for Foreign Affairs, ibid. 306 (1978), 366.

[310] Haughey, Taoiseach, ibid. 327 (1981), 1392–400 (quotation from col. 1395).

[311] FitzGerald, Leader of the opposition, *Irish Times*, 8 Feb. 1980.

[312] FitzGerald, Minister for Foreign Affairs, interview on 'This Week', RTE radio, 4 July 1975.

some doubted whether the succinct formulation by Lenihan, that 'we are neutral in the military sense, we are neither ideologically neutral nor politically indifferent', was sufficient to gainsay the position,[313] especially if one took into account the Irish performance as examined against other variables. The Labour Party, in particular, raised the issue of impartiality, claiming that the close association with the West meant that it had been lost. To them, Ireland appeared to favour US policy in El Salvador, as it had in Vietnam, British connivance in Rhodesia, and the West's support for apartheid. Querying Irish acquiescence in the decision of the Council of Ministers not to release humanitarian aid to the refugees in El Salvador, Quinn of Labour asserted 'That is some neutrality. That is some independence',[314] while the March 1981 debate led to the Irish Times to ask, 'Whose side are you neutral on?'[315]

ATTITUDE TO NATIONAL IDENTITY

Membership of the European Community, at least within the immediate environment of Europe, served to enhance Ireland's distinctive identity, and especially its distinctiveness from Britain, albeit that in the world more generally, as has been seen, Ireland was increasingly identified as a Community state. Enhancing the separateness of Ireland from Britain appears to have been a deliberate policy of FitzGerald as Foreign Minister in the first years of Community membership,[316] and in 1974 he argued that the Irish communautaire attitude had 'certainly marked us out in contrast' to the United Kingdom.[317] He claimed that nobody was 'in any doubt as to whether Ireland is some kind of British satellite', since on many issues Irish and British views 'diverge markedly'.[318] The Irish Presidency of the Council of the Community in 1975 and the determination to remain as members, even if Britain did not, broke any remaining link which people may have perceived. Four years later, the divergent British and Irish paths over the EMS confirmed the distinction and it is arguable that, subject only to the uncompleted business of unity, this marked the drawing to a close of the independence struggle with Britain.

The issue of unity and the related question of stability on the island remained high on the Irish agenda throughout the period 1973–82. The

---

[313] Lenihan, Minister for Foreign Affairs, Dáil Debates, 327 (1981), 1465.
[314] Quinn, ibid. 1440–8 (quotation from col. 1445).   [315] Irish Times, 9 Mar. 1981.
[316] In the summer of 1974 while on holiday he prepared a memo on planning the Presidency: private information.
[317] FitzGerald, Minister for Foreign Affairs, Dáil Debates, 276 (1974), 798–9.
[318] Ibid. 270 (1974), 1861 ff.

concern for stability was reflected in the increased defence effort and in 1976 by the Oireachtas' decision 'that, arising out of the armed conflict now taking place in Northern Ireland, a national emergency exists affecting the vital interests of the State'. The Taoiseach, in introducing the measures, spoke of the challenge to the 'public safety' and 'the preservation of the State', by 'an illegal organisation dedicated to the overthrow of the institutions of this State'.[319]

In the period after 1969 more than forty-five civilians and nine members of the security forces were killed by terrorist explosions and activity in the Republic. In addition, the Republic paid a severe economic cost, estimated at IR£1,050m. in 1982 prices (UK£850m.) between 1969 and 1982. Within the Republic there were periodic disturbances and riots: for example, over the hunger strikes in 1981, when some 13,000–15,000 people marched on the British embassy. In addition, there was a significant rise in armed robberies, kidnapping, and extortion.[320]

At the beginning of the period, just as the forces of law and order in the Republic were ill-equipped to deal with the situation in the Republic, so too the PDF remained ill-equipped to intervene in the North. In the summer of 1974 two Coalition ministers publicly warned of Dublin's limited ability to help. O'Brien argued that it would be wrong to suppose that there was a 'reassuring contingency plan', since if certain things happened 'neither we nor anyone else can divert dire consequences for many people'.[321] In September 1974 O'Brien caused an outcry when he warned that the Irish army did not possess the capacity to control events in the North and that it could only hope to hold one border town, such as Newry, in the event of civil war.[322] FitzGerald meanwhile suggested that people were asking the wrong question when they asked whether the government had 'the will to protect the minority in Northern Ireland', since 'nobody raised . . . the question of the extent to which we have the power to protect the minority'.[323]

In their general policy on Northern Ireland, for some of the time, Irish governments were reacting to British initiatives, but at both the beginning and the end of the period they engaged in major joint

---

319 *Dáil Debates*, 292 (1976), 3 ff., for the motion, Cosgrave's speech, and the debate.
320 See Salmon, 'The Civil Power', 81–3; 'The Cost of Violence', *Ireland Today*, suppl. 1003, *passim*.
321 O'Brien, Minister for Posts and Telegraphs, *Dáil Debates*, 273 (1974), 1632 ff.
322 O'Brien, reported in *Irish Times*, 25 Sept. 1974.
323 FitzGerald, Minister for Foreign Affairs, *Dáil Debates*, 273 (1974), 1699.

initiatives with Britain. In December 1973 British, Irish, and Northern Irish representatives met together for the first time and agreed to the formation of a Northern Ireland power-sharing Executive, involving representatives from both communities in Northern Ireland. An 'Irish dimension' was also to be catered for by a Council of Ireland, composed of a Council of Ministers and a Consultative Assembly with representation from Belfast and Dublin. In the Sunningdale agreement of December 1973 the Irish recognized that unity required the consent of a majority in Northern Ireland.[324] The power-sharing Executive and the Sunningdale agreement collapsed in May 1974, because of opposition within Northern Ireland, and for nearly five years periodic British initiatives elicited periodic Irish attempts to influence them and to become accepted as a party with a legitimate interest in Northern Ireland.

One feature of this period was the 1975 call by Fianna Fáil for the British government to declare its 'commitment to implement an ordered withdrawal from . . . involvement in the six counties', although it transpired they did not wish a date to be set, being fearful of the consequences, and that by a declaration of 'withdrawal' they meant a declaration of intent regarding a united Ireland.[325] In 1979-80 the Republic began to take the initiative rather more and sought a solution in the wider context of relationships between Ireland and Britain, although the process was disrupted by elections and consequent changes of government in June 1981 and February and November 1982. 8 December 1980 saw the Haughey-Thatcher agreement on studying the 'totality of relationships in these islands'[326] and prompted Haughey's claim that the governments were 'in the middle of an historic breakthrough'.[327] Subsequently, in November 1981 FitzGerald and Thatcher agreed to set up an Intergovernmental Council, which was to give institutional expression to the 'unique character of the relationship between the two countries'. The November 1981 agreement again saw an Irish acknowledgement 'that any change in the constitutional status of Northern Ireland would require the consent of the majority of the people of Northern Ireland',[328] which led to a row between Fine Gael and Fianna Fáil as to whether this involved abandonment of the legitimacy of the Irish claim to unity, especially since FitzGerald had made it clear that he favoured

---

[324] For the agreement see Richard Deutsch and Vivien Magowan, *Northern Ireland: A Chronology of Events 1968-74*, ii: *1972-73* (Belfast, 1974), app. 7.
[325] See Padraig O'Malley, *The Uncivil Wars: Ireland Today* (Belfast, 1983), 95.
[326] See the official communiqué, in *Ireland Today*, 972 (Dec. 1980-Jan. 1981).
[327] Haughey, Taoiseach, *Irish Times*, 9 Dec. 1980.
[328] See the official communiqué, in *Ireland Today*, 983 (Dec. 1981).

deletion of Articles Two and Three of the Irish Constitution. However, in practice it was a question of tactics and strategy rather than of objective, and in any case no substantial progress was made by the end of 1982; indeed in 1982 relations were temporarily strained over the Falklands conflict and other issues.[329]

CONCLUSION

The first ten years of Community membership did not see the dramatic foreclosure of Irish freedom of decision that some had envisaged before 1973. While somewhat constrained by Community membership and EPC, the Irish clearly retained a degree of freedom. They managed to walk this tightrope because the nature of the Community between 1973 and 1982 meant that there was little general inclination among the member-states to engage in measures for vertical integration, which would really have challenged the Irish. None the less, FitzGerald hinted at how dependent upon the Community Ireland was becoming,[330] and this suggests there was some validity in the 'escalator analogy' used before entry, even if the escalator moved rather more slowly between 1973 and 1982 than anticipated.[331]

On the other hand, despite the increased effort, there was still a lack of genuine due diligence in terms of the scale, scope, and orientation of the defence effort; and despite the assertion of neutrality in 1982, in general, the period saw equivocation and confusion as to what Ireland really stood for (most obviously, the convolutions over EPC and the possibility of a defence deal with Britain). No clear or consistent set of principles was enunciated or upheld, except the continued narrow and technical view of neutrality as being equal to non-alliance membership. The key element continued to be an assertion that they were not committed to co-belligerency, which they regarded as the essence of alliance.[332] However, this also continued to be a partial and inadequate view of neutrality, reflecting more a concern with 'non-belligerency status in time of war' than neutrality *per se*.[333] In essence, then, while the Irish refrained from alliance, their policy was neither 'for neutrality', nor of non-alignment, but rather *sui generis*.

---

329 For Irish policy on Northern Ireland, events in Northern Ireland, and the Anglo-Irish process see Padraig O'Malley, *passim*, and James Downey, *Them and Us: Britain, Ireland and Northern Ireland 1969–1982* (Dublin, 1983), *passim*.

330 FitzGerald, *Irish Times*, 12 May 1982.   331 See above, p. 219.

332 A point strongly emphasized by a senior Dept. of Foreign Affairs official in an interview, Dublin, Nov. 1983.

333 Barrett, Minister for Defence, *Dáil Debates*, 327 (1981), 1433.

9

Conclusion:
The 'Unfettered Right to Decide: to say
Yes or No'?

THE quotation in the chapter title comes from Chief Justice Finlay, in a judgment which exposed many of the problems relating to Irish neutrality.[1] Neutrality *per se* involves the fulfilment of specific duties and the support of specific rights. Moreover, it only truly exists in time of war or armed conflict. However, as war itself has been absent from Europe since 1945, several European states have attempted to pursue a policy 'for neutrality', that is, a peacetime policy aiming at the legal status 'of neutrality' in the event of war. Both neutrality *per se* and a policy 'for neutrality' require the fulfilment of certain criteria.[2]

Rather than identify non-alignment with any one particular policy, it is better to understand it as the spirit within which policies are approached, as a frame of mind. This frame of mind has been shaped by socio-economic and political experiences which Austria, Sweden, Switzerland, and—particularly—Ireland have not experienced in the same form or in the same degree. Thus, while these states may, on occasion, seek to act as do the non-aligned, that cannot be equated with non-alignment as such.[3]

A point fundamental to neutrality and non-alignment has been shown to be the degree to which the state can maintain its freedom of decision and action, its sovereignty, its 'unfettered right to decide: to say yes or no'. Ørvik was right to identify sovereignty as a necessary condition of neutrality, since neutrality is 'inseparably connected with and dependent upon the amount of sovereignty which a country enjoys',[4] and a neutral state requires to be 'absolutely sovereign and absolutely independent of

---

[1] Chief Justice Finlay, *The Supreme Court: Crotty v. An Taoiseach and Others* (9 Apr. 1987) (hereafter, *Supreme Court*). For the hearing see *Irish Law Reports Monthly*, 400; John Temple Lang, 'The Irish Court Case which Delayed the Single European Act: Crotty v. An Taoiseach and Others', *Common Market Law Review*, 24/4 (1987); James Casey, *Constitutional Law in Ireland* (London, 1987), 179–85; Michael Forde, *Constitutional Law of Ireland* (Cork, 1987), chs. 9, 10.

[2] See ch. 2.

[3] See ch. 2.

[4] Nils Ørvik, *The Decline of Neutrality*, 2nd edn. (London, 1971), 73.

other states in all matters'.[5] The European neutrals have also propounded the view that the basis of neutrality is the ability to maintain freedom of decision and action in all spheres of national policy, and to be seen to be free and independent.[6] Similarly, a key aspect of the frame of mind underlying non-alignment is the pursuit of independence.

For over sixty years Ireland has had difficulties in fulfilling the requirements of this central criterion in its fullest sense, despite the coming of formal political independence, the declaration of the Republic, and the renunciation of Commonwealth membership. Although in the period before 1939 the pre-eminent Irish concern was the establishment of Irish sovereignty, particularly *vis-à-vis* Britain, that preoccupation was undermined by the lack of adequate unilateral defence and economic self-sufficiency, and by the enormous continuing dependence upon British trade. Similarly, during the war itself, Irish freedom of decision and action was severely constrained by these same defence and economic inadequacies.

While it must be recognized both that the Irish retained sufficient freedom of decision and action to say 'no' regarding the ports and to reject, for example, threats (such as the American Note) and promises (on unity), and that they did not become belligerents, they, like others, did bend with the wind and showed 'a certain consideration for Britain'.[7] Moreover, the evidence suggests that the screw was never really turned on Ireland; for example, in 1942 the British decided to keep Ireland going on a 'minimum basis'.[8] The lack of self-sufficiency did pose difficulties, and Irish freedom of decision and action was relative, as well as conditional upon others, as de Valera admitted.

In the initial post-war period the Irish managed to maintain a basic freedom of decision and action, for example, staying out of the Atlantic Pact and ultimately rejecting the revised American Economic Co-operation Act. However, to some extent the Irish were again allowed this freedom because neither the United States nor Britain considered Irish participation in the new defence arrangements to be crucial. Subsequently, the Irish faced the constraints imposed by their own decision that it was better to be comfortable than independent, as they were on the one hand enticed by the economic opportunities offered by EEC membership, and, on the other, frightened by the consequences of a truly autarkic, independent Irish economy. To some extent, they had no

[5] Ibid. 268.
[6] See ch. 3.
[7] *DGFP*, vii, doc. 484, 'The Minister in Eire to the Foreign Ministry' (31 Aug. 1939), pp. 471-2.
[8] Joseph T. Carroll, *Ireland in the War Years 1939-1945*, (Newton Abbot, 1975), 78-94.

choice, since at the time of the original decision in 1961, 50.8 per cent of Irish imports were from Britain and 74.3 per cent of exports went to Britain. In 1972, the last year before entry into the Community, the figures were still 51 and 60.8 per cent respectively. The decisive preoccupation was by now maximization of welfare and economic growth, although Community membership also offered the benefit of reducing the dependence upon Britain.

In the post-war period there has been a marked decline in the economic and political dependence upon Britain, as a result of both the Irish diversification of trade and the opening up on many fronts of the previously claustrophobic bilateral relationship. This is shown particularly by the policy decision in 1975 to continue as a Community member, even in the event of a British withdrawal, and by the decision in 1979 to enter the EMS, despite British abstention. Moreover, ten years after entering the Community, the Irish retained sufficient freedom to say 'no' on certain questions, for example, on the extension of EPC and in respect of certain actions during the Falklands conflict.

None the less, Community membership has imposed new constraints upon Ireland. For example, in 1982 Garret FitzGerald spoke in terms which implied that there was some foundation to fears before entry that membership would develop its own momentum. In 1986–7 the furore over the Single European Act served to illustrate both the fundamental validity of this 'escalator analogy' and just how fettered the Irish 'right to decide: to say yes or no' had become. While the Supreme Court decided on 9 April 1987 that Community membership and the formalization of EPC by treaty did represent 'a diminution of sovereignty',[9] the Irish people and their political leaders demonstrated in the public debate on the issue and in the result of the 26 May referendum that they accepted such a diminution, the vote being 69.9 per cent in favour of ratifying the Single European Act.[10]

The Supreme Court made two separate judgments on 9 April, one concerning the European Communities Act 1986 (which, for the most part, made the provisions of Title II of the Single European Act part of domestic law), the other concerning Title III of the Single European Act (which dealt with EPC). In the first, it declared 'that it has not been shown to the satisfaction of the Court that any of the provisions of the

---

[9] Chief Justice Finlay, in *Supreme Court*. For the Single European Act, see 'Single European Act', *Bulletin of the European Communities, Suppl. 2/86* (Brussels, 1986).

[10] There was a turnout of 44%. See *Ireland Today* (Bulletin of the Dept. of Foreign Affairs), 1037 (May–June 1987).

European Communities Act 1986 are invalid having regard to the provisions of the Constitution'.[11] In the second, the Court decided that, 'without the appropriate constitutional amendment, the ratification of the Single European Act (insofar as it contains Title III) would be impermissible under the Constitution'.[12]

With regard to the European Communities Act 1986, the Plaintiff, Raymond Crotty, (an inveterate campaigner against Irish Community membership), had argued that it was unconstitutional because it involved: (1) an unauthorized surrender of sovereignty; (2) an unauthorized surrender of judicial power; (3) additional new objectives to the Treaty of Rome, outside the existing constitutional authorization; and (4) a challenge to the existing guarantees of fundamental rights under the Irish Constitution.

Both the Supreme Court and the Irish government's lawyers accepted that ratification of the Single European Act was not, as it was put in the 1972 Constitutional Amendment, 'necessitated by the obligations of membership of the Communities'. However, the government argued that the Amendment envisaged joining Communities which were 'dynamic and developing entities' and could be interpreted as authorizing 'amendments of the Treaties which are within the original scope and objectives of the Treaties'. While the Supreme Court thought that the 1972 wording did not give a blanket authorization for new developments, it accepted that the wording covered these, provided they 'do not alter the essential scope or objectives of the Communities'.[13]

The Court rejected arguments about alleged new objectives and challenges to Irish fundamental rights. While it accepted that the capacity of the Council of Ministers 'to take decisions with legislative effect is a diminution of the sovereignty of Member States', it argued that this diminution had already been accepted by the Amendment to the Constitution in 1972, which covered legislative and judicial powers.[14] By accepting this Amendment, the Irish people had agreed to a diminution in Ireland's right 'to say yes or no'.

With regard to Title III, 'Treaty Provisions on European Co-operation in the Sphere of Foreign Policy', the Court also focused upon the 'unfettered right to decide: to say yes or no', and in doing so raised the

---

[11] Chief Justice Finlay, in *Supreme Court*.
[12] Justice Henchy, ibid.
[13] Chief Justice Finlay, ibid.
[14] Chief Justice Finlay, ibid.

question of the validity of a whole range of other Irish international treaties. The Supreme Court decided by three to two that Title III was unconstitutional. Justice Henchy argued that, with ratification, each member-state would 'immediately cede portion of its sovereignty and freedom of action in matters of foreign policy', and that a 'purely national approach to foreign policy' was 'incompatible with accession' to the Treaty. Each ratifying state was 'bound to surrender part of its sovereignty in the conduct of foreign relations', and there was, therefore, clearly a 'diminution of Ireland's sovereignty'. He felt that the very purpose of the changes involved in Title III was 'to erode national independence . . . in the interests of European political cohesion in foreign relations'. Title III meant that Ireland 'would be bound in international law to engage actively in a programme which would trench progressively on Ireland's independence and sovereignty in the conduct of foreign relations.[15]

Related to this was a complex argument about the powers of the Irish government. In essence, the three majority Justices agreed that it 'would be incompatible with the freedom of action conferred on the Government by the Constitution for the Government to qualify that freedom or inhibit it in any way'.[16] As Justice Hederman put it, the government could not 'contract to exercise in a particular way or by a particular procedure their policy-making roles or in any way to fetter powers bestowed unfettered by the Constitution'.[17] In other words, the apparent restrictions contemplated by Title III were not within the power of the government, under the Constitution, to accept.

The third and related argument was best expressed by Justice Henchy. He argued that 'To be bound by solemn international treaty' to 'take full account of the common position of the other member states'' was 'inconsistent' with the constitutional 'obligation of the Government to conduct its foreign relations in accordance with the common good of the Irish people'. That is, the common good of the Irish people was the superior good, and could not, in terms of the Constitution, be curtailed by a formal treaty in the interests of the common good of the member-states as a whole. While the government could participate in an informal arrangement, the apparent contractual obligation was *ultra vires*. The only remedy was a constitutional amendment, whereby the

---

[15] Justice Henchy, ibid. For the contents of Title III see the Appendix, pp. 312–14.

[16] As paraphrased by Dick Spring, Leader of the Labour Party, in *Dáil Debates*, 371 (1987), 2236.

[17] Justice Hederman, in *Supreme Court*.

Irish people gave their consent to the new arrangement and commitments.[18]

The minority did not accept that there was a contractual obligation. The Chief Justice, Finlay, for example, argued that Title III did 'not impose any obligations to cede any national interest in the sphere of foreign policy'. It did 'not give to other High Contracting Parties any right to override or veto the ultimate decision of the State on any issue of foreign policy' and only imposed 'an obligation to listen and consult and grant a right to be heard and to be consulted'.[19] His colleague, Justice Griffin, agreed, arguing that the language used in Title III 'would appear to have been chosen with extreme care to ensure that the obligations of the Parties under the Treaty would permit the utmost freedom of action to each of the Parties in the sphere of foreign policy and is in stark contrast to that used in Title II'.[20]

The government itself clearly took this view. The Coalition government in its *Explanatory Guide* on the Single European Act, published in mid-November 1986, and the Fianna Fáil Government in its *Information Booklet*, published in May 1987, used identical language on this question: 'The undertakings contained in Title III are notable in their formulations in that they bind the partners only, for example, *"to endeavour"*, *"to take full account of "*, *"to give due consideration to the desirability of "*, *"as far as possible, to refrain from"* . . . A *consensus* continues to be required for a common position to be adopted or common action taken.'[21] The latter document attempted to make it clear that 'No partner is obliged to conform to any proposed position or decision with which it is not in complete agreement.'[22]

These documents refused to accept the notion of any diminution of sovereignty *per se* because of the Single European Act, although the November *Guide* acknowledged that joining the Communities had involved 'accepting the limitations on our national freedom of action'.[23] The preferred tactic in both November and May was to stress the enhancement of Irish influence which followed from 'sharing of sovereignty'.[24] Peter Barry, when Minister for Foreign Affairs, echoed this.

[18] Justice Henchy, ibid.
[19] Chief Justice Finlay, ibid.
[20] Justice Griffin, ibid.
[21] *The Single European Act: An Explanatory Guide* (Dublin, 1986), 29, and *The Single European Act: A Government Information Booklet* (Dublin, 1987), 32 (emphasis in the former but added to the latter).
[22] *Single European Act: Information Booklet*, 32.
[23] *Single European Act: Explanatory Guide*, 33, quoting the 1972 White Paper on Accession.
[24] Ibid., and *Single European Act: Information Booklet*, 36.

In particular, he believed that 'Far from acting as a constraint on our freedom', Irish involvement in EPC had allowed the Irish 'to promote, to a greater extent than we could have done in isolation, our aims and priorities'. In essence, a Community composed of more than 320 million people was bound to be more influential and respected than a small, isolated voice.[25]

Those who supported the Supreme Court minority argued that Ireland had already followed an independent line in EPC on a number of occasions and had been, and remained, free 'to do our own thing'.[26] Particular attention was focused on the 1982 refusal 'to follow the advice of its fellow member states in, for us and for them, an important aspect of foreign policy', namely 'the imposition of sanctions against Argentina'. Ireland had been 'free to refuse. We are still equally free.'[27] It was also commented upon that Title III was specifically excluded from the judicial review powers of the European Court of Justice: 'Strange indeed is the binding contractual obligation in which the parties have excluded all means of adjudication on conflicts concerning its meaning or effect!'[28]

Notwithstanding these arguments, the majority decision of the Supreme Court vindicated the argument that Community membership is incompatible with freedom of action. This is generally accepted with regard to the main Community treaties, but is clearly more contentious in respect of EPC. The basic argument is between those who believe that the requirement of consensus in Title III means that any member-state retains the final ability to say 'no' and those who believe that the solemn international treaty-undertaking involved in Title III encroaches upon that freedom to say 'no', and fetters what was once unfettered. It is clear that there is now a legal, rather than merely political and moral, obligation to take into account the views of others and to be prepared to be influenced by them. It was this obligation which the Swedes, Austrians, and Swiss had found repugnant, even before the arrangement was formalized by treaty, because of their belief that it was important for neutrals 'not to give the rest of the world the impression that . . . actions are dependent upon consultations with a certain group of

---

[25] Peter Barry, Minister for Foreign Affairs, *Dáil Debates*, 370 (1986), 1909.

[26] Barry, in opposition, ibid. 371 (1987), 2208.

[27] Desmond O'Malley, Leader of the Progressive Democrats, paraphrasing an article by Dr Finbar Murphy in the *Irish Times*, 15 Apr. 1987, ibid. 2226–7.

[28] Murphy, in the *Irish Times*, 15 Apr. 1987.

states'.[29] They had argued they could not co-operate in matters of foreign policy in a 'binding' way or in a system 'which aims at the working out of common policies'.[30] They had to be seen to be free.

The Supreme Court itself did not address the neutrality issue *per se*, although in view of the link between sovereignty and neutrality which he himself on other occasions had acknowledged, Haughey went too far in 1987 in suggesting that there was no support in any of the Supreme Court judgments for the notion that Irish neutrality was incompatible with the Single European Act.[31] Both Coalition and Fianna Fáil governments tried to argue that the Act did not impinge upon neutrality: the Coalition *Explanatory Guide* boldly stated that the Act 'in no way affects our neutrality',[32] while the Fianna Fáil *Information Booklet* affirmed that the government was satisfied 'that Title III of the Single Act does not affect Ireland's long established policy of military neutrality'.[33]

Not all were so sanguine; indeed, the Fianna Fáil leadership was not consistent on this question, and there was a volte-face between December 1986, in opposition, and their position in government in April 1987. In December 1986 Fianna Fáil had made much of the fact that the central Article on security, Article 30.6, contained references to security which had no qualifications of the term, and only one reference to co-ordination 'on the political and economic aspects of security'.[34] This point was highlighted by other critics of Title III.[35] In December 1986 Haughey himself argued that the reference in the first part of Article 30.6(a), to 'closer co-operation on security', could be interpreted as committing Ireland 'to a position of closer co-operation on questions of European Security, and that term "Security" is unqualified in any way'. In addition, he linked this to Article 30.6(b) which referred to the determination of the member-states 'to maintain the technological and industrial conditions necessary for their security', security again being unqualified. Article 30.6(b) was particularly felt to be a threat, because of the plethora of reports calling for a common armaments industry for the Community.

[29] Swedish Govt. statement, 31 Mar. 1971, in *DSFP* 1971 (NS 1:C:23; Stockholm, 1971), 31.

[30] Swedish Minister of Commerce, 10 Nov. 1970, in *DSFP* 1970 (Stockholm, 1970), 60.

[31] Haughey, Taoiseach, *Dáil Debates*, 371 (1987) 2199.

[32] *Single European Act: Explanatory Guide*, 29.

[33] *Single European Act: Information Booklet*, 34.

[34] Haughey, Leader of Fianna Fáil, in opposition, *Dáil Debates*, 370 (1986), 1922–9.

[35] See, e.g. the Workers Party, *Ireland and the Single European Act* (Dublin, Aug. 1986), and Irish CND, *Disarm*, 22 (July 1986).

Article 30.6 (c), which said that nothing in Title III was to 'impede closer co-operation in the field of security between certain of the High Contracting Parties within the framework of the Western European Union or the Atlantic Alliance', could, it was argued, be interpreted as ensuring that the co-ordination amongst the Twelve did not cut across the work of the WEU or NATO, and Haughey cited the British Foreign Office as holding that view.[36] Others regarded this Article as significant, especially when linked with the earlier Article 30.2 (d), in which the signatories agreed to 'endeavour to avoid any action or position which impairs their effectiveness as a cohesive force in international relations or within international organisations'. Some suggested this had already affected the behaviour of the Department of Foreign Affairs at the United Nations.[37]

The general tenor of concern was that Title III did not protect Irish neutrality, that the wording on 'security' was ambiguous, and that it was a misrepresentation to claim that the Act specifically or categorically excluded the military aspect of security, since all it did was not specifically include it. In December 1986, in opposition, Haughey expressed concern that in the development of the Community and EPC, there was on

each occasion . . . an inching forward, and the stage reached is used as a springboard to go further. We have reached, perhaps gone beyond, what is strictly compatible with Irish neutrality . . . it will only be a matter of time until some important issue will arise in some troubled spot around the world about which a majority of the members of the Community will wish to take an attitude . . . At that point our position will come very sharply and clearly into focus. We will have no alternative, whatever our feelings may be, our neutrality may suggest or public opinion may favour, but to act upon the decision of the Community acting through the political co-operation machinery.[38]

Why did the Irish government not have inserted, asked Flynn of Fianna Fáil, a simple clause stating that 'This agreement shall not govern military matters', or 'Security . . . shall be taken to mean the political and economic aspects of security only', thus ending ambiguity and uncertainty?[39]

The Coalition government which negotiated the Single European

---

[36] Haughey, in opposition, Dáil Debates, 370 (1986), 1922–9; see also De Rossa, Workers Party, ibid. 370 (1986), 2093.
[37] Irish CND, 17–18.
[38] Haughey, Dáil Debates, 370 (1986), 1925 and 1941–2.
[39] Flynn, ibid. 2223.

Act believed that there was no ambiguity. It argued that Article 30.6 'confirms that the scope of discussions on security in EPC will remain limited to the political and economic aspects of security', and that the reference in Article 30.6 (a) to the 'political and economic aspects of security' governed all other references to security. Furthermore, it was asserted that, contrary to opposition claims, Article 30.6 (c) 'for the first time ever' protected the Irish position, since those who wished to co-operate more closely on security, 'that is on military and defence questions', or on anything 'beyond the political and economic aspects of security',[40] could do so in WEU or NATO. Ireland was 'not a member of either' and had 'no intention of joining them. Ireland will, therefore, neither be involved in nor committed to any co-operation that takes place in those organisations'.

Similarly, the Coalition protested about the misrepresentations concerning Article 30.6 (b), on maintaining the technological and industrial conditions necessary for security, denying that this was shorthand for 'weapon procurement', and claiming rather that it simply reflected 'the growing realisation by Europeans, instanced for example in the EUREKA project in which neutral countries (such as Sweden, Switzerland, Austria and Finland) also participate, that Europe must face up to the technological and industrial challenges it faces internationally'. Such co-operation as there was on such questions would be confined to the political and economic dimensions.[41]

Between December 1986 and April 1987 Fianna Fáil changed its mind on the implications of Title III, and the alleged threat it posed to neutrality. Of crucial importance in this change was that Fianna Fáil entered government on 10 March 1987 and then had to cope with the need to pilot the Single European Act, particularly Title III, through a referendum following the Supreme Court verdict of 9 April. In effect, Fianna Fáil altered course because they realized that if Ireland wished to prosper it needed not only to remain as a full member of the European Community, but also to be in good standing with its partners, for the benefits it had acquired through membership to continue. Consequently in April 1987, as Taoiseach, Haughey told the Dáil that the 'Community has no competence to discuss matters of military policy or to embark on a policy of military procurement. This

---

[40] The phrase is from the *Single European Act: Explanatory Guide*, 32; quotations in the rest of this paragraph are from Barry, Minister for Foreign Affairs, *Dáil Debates*, 370 (1986), 1910–11.
[41] Ibid. 28–30.

is generally acknowledged . . . The Single European Act does not provide for the co-ordination of positions on the military aspects of security',[42] and that the provisions of Article 30.6 were now felt 'in no way' to 'effect Ireland's military neutrality. On the contrary, our partners have fully accommodated our position as a State which is not a member of any military alliance.'[43]

Haughey told the Dáil on 22 April 1987 that 'the basic reality is that we cannot contemplate a satisfactory economic future isolated from the countries that surround us, who are all members of the European Community. We could not maintain present standards, never mind prosper, in such isolation . . . Let no one be under any illusions that we have any real alternative options.' The government was not prepared to put at risk 'the welfare and the livelihood' of the Irish people by allowing a situation to develop which might jeopardize full Irish participation in the Community.[44] As Mr Calleary, Minister of State at the Department of Foreign Affairs put it, 'To leave the Community . . . would be economic suicide.'[45] Because of this perspective, the Irish were hardly free in their choice in 1987, whatever their feelings about neutrality: the escalator had moved too far.

As Table 9.1 shows, the Irish received in the period 1973–86 some IR£5,744.6m. in net receipts from the Community budget by way of grants and subsidies. In 1986 the net budgetary transfers amounted to IR£900.2m., or 13½ per cent of current government revenue and over 4 per cent of Irish Gross Domestic Product.[46] Despite the trade diversification away from Britain, Irish dependence on foreign trade remained. In 1986, 69 per cent of Irish exports were to the Community,[47] and the dependence on the imports and exports of goods and services represented 120 per cent of GNP, twice the Community average.[48] As the Information Booklet summed it up in May 1987: 'Our agriculture is vitally dependent on the price support system of the Common Agricultural Policy and access to the Community market.

[42] Haughey, Taoiseach, Dáil Debates, 371 (1987), 2198–9.

[43] Single European Act: Information Booklet, 30.

[44] Haughey, Taoiseach, Dáil Debates, 371 (1987), 2195. For another assessment see Dermot McAleese and Alan Matthews, 'The Single European Act and Ireland: Implications for a Small Member-State', Journal of Common Market Studies, 26/1 (Sept. 1987).

[45] Calleary, Minister of State at the Dept. of Foreign Affairs, Dáil Debates, 371 (1987), 2297.

[46] Barry, Minister for Foreign Affairs, ibid. 370 (1986), 1892; Single European Act: Information Booklet, 38.

[47] Irish Council of the European Movement, The Single European Act (briefing paper, Dublin, n.d.).

[48] Flynn, Dáil Debates, 370 (1986), 2214.

Irish industry cannot survive without exports and more than two-thirds of our industrial exports go to the Community market.'[49] It was strongly felt that membership had quickened the pace of industrialization; helped in the establishment of new high technology industries all over Ireland; transformed Irish agriculture; helped provide funds for infrastructure investment; raised industrial and environmental standards; and provided opportunities through the EMS. In addition, it was felt to have provided the political advantages of making the Irish more outward looking; generating new relationships; encouraging greater confidence; and, crucially, enhancing Irish influence, while reducing the dependence upon Britain.[50]

Furthermore, it was felt that the Single European Act would enable Ireland to build upon these benefits, particularly with the movement to a proper internal market by 1992. The Irish could see the benefits of free-trade access to a market of 320 million people, believing that liberalization of intra-Community trade would be to their advantage. The removal of the barriers to trade was also regarded as significantly enhancing the attractiveness of Ireland as a location for foreign investment. Also attractive to the Irish was the point that Article 23 of the Single European Act brought into the body of the EC treaty the objective of reducing regional disparities and the means to achieve that objective. There were hopes that the new emphasis upon 'cohesion' would bring new resources to Ireland.[51]

Many were also fearful as to the consequences of a failure to ratify the Single European Act. While it was acknowledged that it could not immediately bring about Irish withdrawal or expulsion from the Community as it stood, there were fears that the other member-states would 'move to establish as between themselves the economic conditions at which the Single Act aims. In that event we would *at best* be confined to second class status in the Community', with a loss of influence over decisions, of equitable access for exports, and of financial support.[52]

---

[49] *Single European Act: Information Booklet*, 37.
[50] Even Haughey, in opposition in Dec. 1986, admitted this: *Dáil Debates*, 370 (1986), 1929–43.
[51] See e.g. Barry, Minister for Foreign Affairs, ibid. 1889–913.
[52] *Single European Act: Information Booklet*, 37.

Table 9.1. Ireland's Receipts by Way of Grants and Subsidies from EEC Budget 1973–1986 (IR£m.)

	1973	1974	1975	1976	1977	1978	1979	1980	1981	1982	1983	1984	1985	1986	TOTAL
FEOGA[a] Guarantee section	37.1	63.8	102.2	102.0	245.1	365.6	396.5	381.1	304.6	344.3	441.7	644.6	836.6	884.0	5,149.2
FEOGA Guidance section	—	—	0.6	2.6	7.4	9.7	18.5	31.8	41.9	59.6	63.7	49.3	55.8	46.6	387.5
Fisheries surveillance	—	—	—	—	—	—	7.8	4.4	5.6	—	12.8	—	1.4	—	32.0
European Social Fund	—	3.6	4.0	4.6	8.2	19.3	28.8	46.7	45.3	73.2	92.7	84.3	141.3	124.5	676.5
European Regional Development Fund	—	—	1.8	8.5	8.5	11.1	25.5	46.4	54.6	66.1	58.2	65.2	76.0	77.1	499.0
Community food aid for Third World countries	—	—	0.2	1.4	2.7	3.7	5.1	2.2	6.1	7.3	12.9	23.0	15.5	9.7	89.8
EMS interest subsidies	—	—	—	—	—	—	44.5	45.5	46.0	50.1	43.6	—	—	—	229.7
Research & development projects[b]	—	—	—	—	—	0.5	0.8	0.3	0.7	0.2	1.1	0.1	0.2	0.2	4.0
Projects in the energy sector	—	—	—	—	—	0.2	1.3	1.5	1.7	1.0	0.5	0.0	0.6	0.6	7.4
Miscellaneous	—	—	0.3	0.4	1.0	0.1	0.3	0.7	0.4	0.3	0.5	0.2	1.3	1.0	6.5

TOTAL RECEIPTS	37.1	67.4	109.1	119.5	272.9	410.2	529.1	560.6	506.9	602.1	727.7	866.7	1,128.7	1,143.7	7,081.7
Ireland's contributions to EEC budget	4.5	5.5	9.8	13.4	22.1	46.1	60.6	88.9	105.4	136.7	184.7	202.5	213.4	243.5	1,337.1
NET RECEIPTS	32.6	61.9	99.3	106.1	250.8	364.2	468.5	471.7	401.5	465.4	543.0	664.2	915.3	900.2	5,744.6

[a] FEOGA: European Agricultural Guidance and Guarantee Fund.

[b] Such projects include ESPRIT (European Strategic Programme for Research and Development in Information Technologies) and BRITE (Basic Research for Industrial Technologies for Europe).

Source: The Single European Act: A Government Information Booklet (Dublin, May 1987), app. III, p. 71.

Not all accepted the foregoing arguments, while even those who did had to admit that there had been disappointments since 1973. One such was the absence of a coherent, comprehensive, and sufficiently funded Regional Fund, and many believed that no progress had been made in closing the gap between the poorer and richer member-states. It was widely felt that previous Irish hopes on the Regional Fund had been disappointed and, that too much significance should therefore not be accorded to Article 23, since even the revised Regional Fund did not amount to a realistic policy for dealing with the economic problems of peripheral areas in the Community, especially Ireland.[53]

Agriculture had not been an unqualified success either, and it was argued that 'agricultural incomes are now between 10 and 15 per cent below the 1973 level and about 100,000 people have left the land since 1973'.[54] That 100,000 represented one-third of the 1973 agricultural workforce. By 1986–7 it was also evident that a major problem facing the Community was how to provide the financial resources necessary for the continued operation and further development of the CAP.[55] This was crucial since, of Ireland's IR£5,744.6m. net receipts during 1973–86 IR£5,149.2m. had come from FEOGA Guarantee section and IR£387.5m. from its Guidance section.[56]

It was not only agriculture which had suffered job losses. Unemployment had increased by a factor of four since 1973, up from 60,000 to 240,000; some of the native industries suffered particularly badly, and 40 per cent of jobs in the textile/footwear sector were lost in the first decade of membership. Ireland had also begun to re-experience the nightmare of emigration on the scale of the 1950s.[57]

Those who emphasized such problems did not regard the Single European Act as a solution. It was feared that the proposed internal market would aggravate the divide between rich and poor, while the monetarist philosophy held to underlie the Act was regarded as not helping with unemployment.[58] In addition, there was a very specific Irish fear that the proposals relating to the harmonization of VAT rates or of excise duties could cost the Exchequer IR£650m., or some 9.7 per cent of its current revenue.[59] This harmonization was dependent

---

[53] See Dáil Debates, 370 (1986), 1893, 1933, 1993.
[54] Collins, ibid. 2342.
[55] Barry, Minister for Foreign Affairs, ibid. 1894.
[56] See table 9.1.
[57] See Dáil Debates, 370 (1986), 1931–2, 2216.
[58] Haughey, in opposition, ibid. 1935–40.
[59] A figure given by FitzGerald, Taoiseach, ibid. 2239.

upon unanimity, but some were not confident about Ireland's ability to resist.[60] There were, in any case, reservations about the widening of the principle of the qualified majority vote, which was to take place mainly in areas which would help to complete the internal market.[61]

Finally, Michael O'Kennedy, in opposition in December 1986, pointed out that they should 'acknowledge that the European countries which stayed outside the EC, Norway, Sweden, Finland and Austria, not to speak of Switzerland, have been more economically successful and have been much more inspiring and invigorating for their people than have the member states of the European Community, particularly the member states on the periphery of the European Community'.[62] This was true; but it was also the case that by the end of 1987 some of the members of EFTA, including Sweden and Austria, were so worried about the threat posed by their potential exclusion from the internal market that they were reconsidering their own attitudes to the Community.

Despite these reservations about disadvantages, most accepted that the advantages were preponderant. Some called for a renegotiation of the Single European Act,[63] but it was generally accepted that this was impossible and undesirable: impossible, because the other member-states had completed their procedures for ratification, and had, a year previously, rejected a Danish request for renegotiation; and undesirable, because it would be regarded as a serious breach of good faith, since Ireland had participated actively in the negotiations, and the Act had to be accepted as a 'carefully negotiated compromise between the different points of view of individual member States'.[64]

Even Fianna Fáil, in opposition, accepted that it could not be renegotiated: in December 1986, Haughey said that the 'Irish people . . . faced . . . a very troublesome and difficult decision', since there were many things in the Act which were not to Ireland's benefit; he continued, 'If we had any great freedom of choice I do not think that we would opt for this particular instrument . . . It weakens our position and it contains inherent dangers . . . The alternative, however, of not

---

[60] De Rossa, ibid. 2091-2.

[61] See ibid. 1905-6, 2198-9, 2204, 2236.

[62] O'Kennedy, former Irish Foreign Minister and member of Commission of European Community, ibid. 2260.

[63] See Workers Party, De Rossa, *Dáil Debates*, 370 (1986), 2086; 371 (1987), 2429; and Blaney, ibid. 371 (1987), 2471. Deputies MacGiolla and De Rossa moved an amendment calling for renegotiation on 10 Dec. 1986, but only four Deputies supported this; ibid. 370 (1986), 2366-7.

[64] *Single European Act: Information Booklet*, 37, 33.

ratifying the treaty . . . would have even more serious implications . . . It is not possible, now that we have arrived at the ratification stage, to reverse what was agreed during the negotiations.'[65] The problem with this attitude was that it revealed the limitations of Irish choice. Even aside from the particular arguments about not renegotiating, it was clear to most by the winter of 1986–7 that they had little real choice but to agree to be fettered. A few recognized and complained about this lack of real choice, noting that in 1972 the Dáil and Irish people had been assured that the Treaty could only be changed with the consent of the member-states, while now they were being told that if the Dáil or people did 'not unconditionally ratify the Single European Act then immediate and terrible things will happen'.[66]

When the Irish government finally deposited the Instrument of Ratification with the Italians on 24 June 1987, it also deposited alongside it a Declaration. The Declaration contained two clauses. The first sought to remind the other member-states of Protocol 30 of the original 1972 Treaty of Accession, which recognized special problems concerning Ireland and the need to even out regional differences. The second clause asserted the Irish view of Title III and of their neutrality. It read:

> The Government of Ireland note that the provisions of Title III do not affect Ireland's long established policy of military neutrality and that coordination of positions on the political and economic aspects of security does not include the military aspects of security or procurement for military purposes and does not affect Ireland's right to act or refrain from acting in any way which might affect Ireland's international status of military neutrality.[67]

It was Fianna Fáil, still regarding the Single European Act with some doubt in 1986, who had formally proposed the Declaration in the Dáil in December 1986.[68] They argued that the all-party Joint Oireachtas Committee on the Secondary Legislation of the European Communities had unanimously called, in its report on the Single European Act, for the government 'to append a formal reiteration of our position of military neutrality to the act of ratification'.[69] The Committee, and Fianna Fáil, felt that such a reiteration or declaration

---

[65] Haughey, in opposition, Dáil Debates, 370 (1986), 1913–14.
[66] De Rossa, ibid. 2096–7.
[67] Ireland Today, 1037 (May–June, 1987); 1039 (Aug. 1987).
[68] Amendment proposed by Vincent Brady, Dáil Debates, 370 (1986), 2367–8.
[69] Haughey, in opposition, ibid. 1925; Collins, ibid. 2339.

would avoid any possible ambiguity or misunderstanding of Ireland's position and prevent any possible erosion of it.[70] Fianna Fáil felt that whatever the arguments about whether Title III implicitly recognized Irish neutrality, 'it is clearly necessary and desirable in view of the fundamental importance of this policy issue from our point of view, to have an explicit reiteration of our long established policy of military neutrality included by way of declaration as other countries have done in regard to matters of special importance to them'. The Danes, for example, had appended a declaration asserting that Title III did not affect their participation in Nordic foreign policy co-operation.[71]

Fianna Fáil believed that the great merit of the Irish Declaration was that it would bring the Irish position 'specifically to the attention of the other signatories'. Ireland 'should avail [itself] of this process of ratification to signal' that it was prepared to make a stand on the matter' and was 'not going to be pushed further and further along the road that leads directly into membership of NATO'. It was felt that the Declaration would 'have our neutral status internationally and clearly acknowledged in the Community'.[72] Fianna Fáil felt that the Declaration should have been inserted before the Single European Act was finalized and signed, since this would have involved the other member-states' acceptance and acknowledgement, just as they had noted declarations by Greece, Portugal, Denmark, the Presidency, and the Commission. By the time the Irish had made their deposition, it did not involve any action or recognition by Ireland's partners, but the Fianna Fáil government felt that 'our declaration will put beyond all doubt the Government's position on this'.[73]

The Coalition government had not supported the Declaration in December 1986. They preferred a motion in the Dáil moved by the Minister for Foreign Affairs, Peter Barry. This motion also had two clauses. The second welcomed Article 23 of the Single European Act on 'Cohesion', as strengthening the commitment to Protocol 30. The former proclaimed:

That Dáil Éireann reaffirms Ireland's position of neutrality outside military alliances, and notes with satisfaction that the provisions in Title III . . . relating to the co-operation . . . on the political and economic aspects of

---

[70] Wilson, ibid. 2062.
[71] Haughey, ibid. 1928–9.
[72] Haughey, ibid. 1926, 1943.
[73] Haughey, Taoiseach, ibid. 371 (1987), 2198–9.

security and closer co-ordination of their positions in this area do not affect Ireland's position of neutrality outside military alliances.[74]

It is particularly noteworthy that in 1986–7 Dáil Éireann was ready to pass this motion, and subsequently the Fianna Fáil Declaration, in complete contrast to its attitude in 1981. The Coalition favoured a motion instead of a Declaration, on the legal advice of their Attorney-General, who had six objections to the Fianna Fáil Declaration. In sum, the objections revolved around the question of whether a Declaration could be regarded as putting in doubt the validity of the Irish ratification, by introducing an element of conditionality or apparent reservation.[75] Moreover, the Coalition and others believed that the Declaration had 'no bearing, it is a piece of paper that will have no legal binding', amounting 'to nothing more than a declaration' by the Irish government. They also argued that their negotiating skill, and the consequent wording of Title III, 'was a more effective defence of Ireland's position than the lodging . . . of a piece of paper', which Barry argued had 'absolutely no bearing as far as Europe is concerned'.[76] Others pointed out that it had 'no legal validity whatsoever',[77] and no 'place in international law', since it was a 'unilateral proposal without consultation or discussion, certainly without agreement from the European partners who will not be in any way bound by it'.[78]

Dick Spring, the Labour Leader, who took this view, proposed instead that the wording of the Constitutional amendment proposed in 1987 should explicitly state that 'ratification shall not diminish the adherence of Ireland to an independent foreign policy outside membership of any military alliance'. Labour believed that this would put before the Irish people, and others, a straightforward clarification of the Irish position on neutrality and, in conformity with Labour policy, 'would give an opportunity to enshrine . . . neutrality in . . . [the] Constitution'.[79] The Fianna Fáil government rejected this proposal, feeling that after the Supreme Court's decision the need to act urgently required a narrow and specific amendment to overcome the specific obstacles which that decision had created. Although acknowledging that

---

[74] Haughey, Taoiseach, ibid. 370 (1986) 1888–913, for the motion and the reasoning of Barry, Minister for Foreign Affairs (quotation from col. 1888).

[75] Barry, ibid. 2356–9.

[76] Barry, in opposition, ibid. 371 (1987), 2204, 2215.

[77] Kennedy, Progressive Democrats, ibid. 2454.

[78] Spring, Leader of Labour Party, in opposition, ibid. 2522.

[79] Spring, ibid. 2520–4.

the Court's decision had wider implications (for example, raising the questions of executive–judiciary relations and the validity of several international treaties which Ireland had signed), they felt that the significance of these wider implications required to be considered calmly over a period of time. To prevent delay, Fianna Fáil preferred to focus on the Single European Act, and to confront the people with a decision on that issue alone.[80]

Although the Declaration is significant, in that for the first time an exposition of the Irish position was attached to an international agreement, and had attention drawn to it, the debate over it, the Single European Act, and Community membership simply illustrated and reiterated the Irish penchant throughout the century for wishing to have the best of both worlds; it demonstrated the illusion associated with rhetoric and inconsistent aspiration, the reality of the constraints imposed upon Irish freedom by Ireland's economic position, and the divide between the two. The 1980s were not the first time when, despite the talk of neutrality, there was a demonstrable failure to maintain in practice a single, unequivocal tradition on neutrality.

While a tradition regarding neutrality can be identified, it is not a consistent tradition, and an alternative tradition of practice has generally been more powerful and enduring, reflecting a basic concern with sovereignty, distinctiveness *vis-à-vis* Britain, and boosting the economy and social welfare. This alternative tradition has seen a high degree of pragmatism and expediency, an awareness of geographical realities, and a recognition of the constraints imposed by a lack of economic resources and by economic dependence. This alternative tradition, for the most part, has been adopted in practice as Ireland's policy framework. It has illustrated the usefulness of Wolfer's observation that 'an aspiration will not be turned into a policy goal unless it is sufficiently cherished by those who make and influence policy to justify the costs that its attainment is expected to require in terms of sacrifices'.[81]

Concerns for sovereignty and prosperity have generally been accorded greater weight and commitment of resources (in the widest sense) than have the pursuits of neutrality, non-alignment, or the European model represented by Austria, Sweden, and Switzerland, despite the fact that the apparent success of Irish neutrality between 1939 and 1945 led to

---

[80] See Haughey, Taoiseach, ibid. 2188–90, and Lenihan, Minister for Foreign Affairs, ibid. 2513–14.

[81] Arnold Wolfers, *Discord and Collaboration* (Baltimore, 1965), 71.

some elevating it to a 'mystery of faith'. Irish neutrality has frequently been a question of faith rather than good works. The alternative tradition has increasingly been preferred to the austere, autarkic, and Arcadian vision of de Valera. There has, therefore, been no enduring commitment to a common set of principles relating to neutrality underlying Irish security policy in the twentieth century.

With all the variables under consideration, there has been a difference between aspiration and policy. There has, for example, been a pervasive failure to fulfil the requirements of 'due diligence'. Even when improvements in the Irish defence effort took place, they were directed towards either the Northern Ireland situation or fishery protection rather than the support of neutrality, with the exception of the period of 'the emergency'. Ireland's own professional defence experts have judged the Irish defence effort to be inadequate, when it was measured against the requirements of a truly neutral stance. The PDF was smaller in the late 1980s than at the beginning of the decade,[82] and the Irish still had to accept border incursions.[83] They had to admit in June 1987 that the 'Air Corps have not the capacity to detect overflights or the equipment to intercept any aircraft violating our airspace',[84] while in December 1986 the Dáil was told that the 'numbers of overflights by military aircraft . . . without specific advance permission' had been 2,300 in 1984, 2,304 in 1985, and 1,210 in 1986.[85] It also had to be admitted in 1987 that the Naval Service was incapable of monitoring submarine activity in Irish waters, since 'the cost of equipping and manning the Naval Service and Air Corps to carry out an adequate level of surveillance . . . would be enormous and beyond our resources'. Not even Sweden, the Dáil was told, could cope.[86] More than sixty years after independence, Ireland still lacked its own munitions factory, was concerned about its ammunition stocks, and remained dependent upon others for supplies of weapons. Irish forces were still those appropriate for a state 'in a disarmed world'.[87]

The record on recognition of Ireland's status has been rather more

---

[82] On 30 Apr. 1987 13,381 personnel were serving with the PDF: Brady, Minister of State, Dept. of Defence, *Dáil Debates*, 373 (1987), 1241. The opposition expressed worries about the size of the PDF.

[83] Ibid. 370 (1986), 1790–3.

[84] Brady, ibid. 373 (1987), 1238.

[85] Barry, Minister for Foreign Affairs, ibid. 370 (1986), 1808.

[86] Brady, ibid. 373 (1987), 1233–4.

[87] Noel Dorr, quoted in Patrick Keatinge, *A Singular Stance: Irish Neutrality in the 1980s* (Dublin, 1984), 73.

mixed. While, for example, the Germans were willing to recognize Irish neutrality during the war, they also violated it, and the British never formally recognized Irish neutrality throughout the war. The lack of a tradition about neutrality in Ireland and the omission of neutrality from the Constitution gave belligerents some grounds for questioning the Irish commitment to it, especially in view of the Irish lack of resources and due diligence. These inadequacies continued to cloud the issue after the war, but even more problematic was the Irish failure to advance neutrality as a reason for non-participation in the Atlantic Pact, when Partition was put forward instead as the 'sole obstacle' to participation.[88] Moreover, there was equivocation regarding possible bilateral defence arrangements. Both Britain and the United States have at times seen Irish neutrality as negotiable, as have members of the European Community.

The continued failure to join the NAM—the lack of any intention of doing so was reiterated in June 1987[89]—and the NNA at the CSCE review conferences, has further clouded the issue. However, the real difficulty is that it is generally accepted that the Irish application to join, and their membership of, the European Community meant that they 'definitely parted company with the European neutrals'.[90] Ireland has become clearly identified as 'one of the Twelve' and, for the reasons adduced above, it is not clear that the Declaration of 1987 has proved sufficient to alter that image. The West Germans, for example, still seem intent on introducing defence into the Community.[91]

There has been no explicit, consistent Irish disavowal of external help. In the 1920s Desmond FitzGerald revealed a willingness to co-operate with Britain, as had Collins and Griffith during the treaty negotiations. In the 1930s de Valera clearly accepted the implicit 'protective umbrella', and was also prepared to discuss possible defence arrangements, and even an agreement, with the British. During the war itself, Anglo-Irish discussions continued. For the whole of the post-war period there has been an implicit reliance upon the British and NATO umbrella, although, as previously, no formal alliance has been agreed. Furthermore, the 1980s have seen an apparent Irish readiness to take the

---

[88] See ch. 6.

[89] Lenihan, Minister for Foreign Affairs, *Dáil Debates*, 373 (1987), 1889.

[90] Hanspeter Neuhold, 'Permanent Neutrality in Contemporary International Relations: A Comparative Perspective', *Irish Studies in International Affairs*, 1/3, 14.

[91] See Herr Genscher's speech, as Council of Ministers' President, to European Parliament, Jan. 1988: European Parliament, *EP News* (Jan. 1988).

initiative in raising the question of defence co-operation with the British. Although the Anglo-Irish Agreement finally signed at Hillsborough on 15 November 1985 avoided any question of an alliance or defence co-operation *per se*, it did envisage 'enhancing cross-border co-operation on security matters' through a programme of work involving the Garda Síochána and the RUC, 'and, where appropriate, groups of officials'. The Anglo-Irish Inter-Governmental Conference was also 'to deal . . . on a regular basis with . . . security and related matters'—by which was understood, but not spelt out, 'anti-terrorist activity'.[92]

Ireland has only briefly exhibited isolationist tendencies, most markedly perhaps in the initial post-war period. Generally speaking, Ireland's attitude has been more typically demonstrated by the endeavours to reform the British Commonwealth and de Valera's active support for the League in the mid-1930s. Membership of the United Nations and, more recently, of the European Community and EPC has involved, as a corollary, participation in world affairs. In that participation Ireland has never been strictly impartial; it was not truly impartial during the war; and in the post-war period its sympathies have lain decisively with the West, albeit that there has been occasional disagreement with some of the specific policies pursued by leading Western states.

Except in the general sense of wishing to help shape the international milieu through the contribution to international organizations, there have been few notable Irish efforts to ameliorate world problems. The initial period of Aiken's activity at the United Nations was clearly the high point of such Irish efforts; but, generally, the Irish have found it difficult to play a substantial role. The curiosity of the Irish stance was shown by FitzGerald in April 1987, when he revealed that, because of Irish views on neutrality, he 'remained silent' during discussions at dinner after European Council meetings when they touched on security questions. He maintained this silence even when views 'deeply distasteful to most people' in Ireland were propounded. In 1987 he at last raised the question whether it was 'in fact necessitated by our military neutrality that we should not utter on such occasions? Are we living up to our own principles', and should not 'as many voices as possible . . . be raised in every possible arena' in favour of reducing nuclear weapons in

---

[92] See *Ireland Today*, special issue (Nov. 1985), and Anthony Kenny, *The Road to Hillsborough: The Shaping of the Anglo-Irish Agreement* (Oxford, 1986).

Europe?[93] FitzGerald's remarks suggest a remarkable quiescence and passivity on Ireland's part, promoted by the perceived need to distinguish the military from the political and economic aspects of security. Again, although the rhetoric has often highlighted 'Ireland's role', the reality has often been very different.

Concern with the national question has been a pervasive element of Irish rhetoric, particularly with de Valera's campaign in the late 1940s, the 'sore thumb' policy in international forums, and the reference to Partition and the lack of national unity as the 'sole obstacle' to participation in the North Atlantic Treaty. However, more generally, other imperatives have been of more immediate concern. Ever since the eruption in Northern Ireland in 1968–9 the predominant concerns have been the restoration of order there and the maintenance of stability in the Republic. It remains to be seen what the long-term significance of the Anglo-Irish Agreement of 1985 will be, especially in view of its recognition of an Irish consultative status on some aspects of life in Northern Ireland. Ireland has undoubtedly enhanced its distinctive identity vis-à-vis Britain over the years, but it must be said that this has only been, to some extent, at the cost of identification with 'the Twelve'. That is no help to an aspirant neutral.

The Irish, then, have consistently and significantly failed to measure up to the principal prerequisites 'of' or 'for' neutrality. There has been 'no set of common principles' underlying their defence policy.[94] Despite the shibboleth of neutrality, and the claims of the Irish themselves, Ireland has never been truly neutral. Neither can it be regarded as non-aligned. In addition, Irish policy has not met the requirements inherent in the Swedish formulation of 'non-participation in alliances in peacetime, aiming at neutrality in the event of war',[95] because of its failure to meet the criteria of a policy 'for neutrality'—most strikingly in the lack of due diligence and in the equivocations surrounding the real nature, foundation, and objectives of Irish policy.

Irish assertions of being 'neutral in a military sense',[96] of 'neutrality outside military alliances',[97] and of a 'long established policy of military neutrality'[98] do not save the concept of Irish neutrality, since (as has been clearly established and demonstrated) genuine neutrality is not to be

---

[93] FitzGerald, in opposition, Dáil Debates, 371 (1987), 2276–8.

[94] FitzGerald, ibid. 327 (1981), 1424.

[95] Fact Sheets on Sweden: The Swedish Defence System (Stockholm, July 1982).

[96] Lenihan, Minister for Foreign Affairs, Dáil Debates, 327 (1987), 1466.

[97] Barry, Minister for Foreign Affairs, in his motion, ibid. 370 (1986), 1888–9.

[98] Ireland Today, 1037 (May–June 1987), 3; 1039 (Aug. 1987), 16.

equated with mere non-belligerency, or non-alliance membership. Thus, despite Keatinge's claim that 'Ireland fulfils two basic conditions to be categorised as neutral: it does not belong to any military alliance, and it continues to make declarations asserting its neutrality',[99] these are not sufficient to affix the term 'neutral' to Ireland. The declarations have not been consistent and, in any case, they have been more than matched by declarations yielding any real claim to neutrality. Moreover, even if the concept of 'military neutrality' were compatible with neutrality as properly understood (which it is not), the equation of 'military neutrality' with neutrality *per se* is singularly inappropriate in the Irish case, because of its totally inadequate, unilateral defensive measures and effort. This is important, because of the persistent Irish tendency recently to regard neutrality as synonymous with non-membership of any military alliance. There clearly is public support for such non-membership, since 64 per cent of respondents in a 1985 poll believed that Ireland should never join a military alliance; but it is not neutrality.[100] It is insufficient in these circumstances to suggest that 'the term neutrality is best qualified in the Irish context', or to refer to 'the limited nature of Irish neutrality'.[101] Such approaches have merely led to confusion over what neutrality is and demands. Indeed, in the 1985 poll, over 30 per cent of those questioned acknowledged that they had no idea at all what neutrality meant, and almost 20 per cent gave answers which showed that their understanding of the policy was either vague or non-existent. The largest number of respondents, 21 per cent, saw neutrality as simply not becoming involved in wars.[102]

This confusion is also reflected in recent suggestions regarding 'active neutrality'. The Irish Labour Party and Bill McSweeney, amongst others, have taken to advocating this policy in the 1980s, calling for a policy based upon the foundation of 'an active political philosophy',[103] leading in turn to an endeavour 'to construct an active involvement in the process of peacemaking'.[104] This is thought to imply 'a total commitment to peace, detente and disarmament, together with a programme of involvement in world affairs in which policy is determined

---

[99] Keatinge, *A Singular Stance*, 55.

[100] The *Irish Times*–M R B I Poll, in *Irish Times*, 29 Apr. 1985.

[101] Keatinge, *A Singular Stance*, 56.

[102] *Irish Times*, 29 Apr. 1985.

[103] Labour Party, *Ireland: A Neutral Nation* (Principles of International Policy, i; Dublin, n.d.), 4, citing 1980 Conference resolution.

[104] Bill McSweeney, 'Postscript: The Case for Active Irish Neutrality', in Bill McSweeney (ed.), *Ireland and the Threat of Nuclear War* (Dublin, 1985), esp. p. 183.

independently in accordance with national needs and on the merits of the individual case'.[105] Such a policy may or may not be appropriate for Ireland, but it is not neutrality, and the notion of 'active neutrality' involves a contradiction in terms and a disregard for the established meaning of the concept.

The concept of neutrality is inappropriate and inapplicable to Ireland. Similarly, it would be wrong to regard Ireland as contributing to the evolution of a *genus* of neutrality that is 'somewhat messy'.[106] It is not a question of messiness; rather, Ireland has over several decades consistently failed to meet the criteria either 'of' or 'for' neutrality. It has been too fettered. No current concept in international relations properly fits the Irish case, which is *sui generis*. Ireland certainly is, and has been, 'unneutral'.

---

[105] Labour Party, 4.

[106] Roderick Ogley, *The Theory and Practice of Neutrality in the Twentieth Century* (London, 1970), 205.

Appendix
Single European Act: Title III
[Source: *Bulletin of the European Communities*, suppl. 2/86]

TREATY PROVISIONS ON EUROPEAN
CO-OPERATION IN THE SPHERE OF FOREIGN POLICY

Article 30

European Co-operation in the sphere of foreign policy shall be governed by the following provisions:

1. The High Contracting Parties, being members of the European Communities, shall endeavour jointly to formulate and implement a European foreign policy.

2. (*a*) The High Contracting Parties undertake to inform and consult each other on any foreign policy matters of general interest so as to ensure that their combined influence is exercised as effectively as possible through co-ordination, the convergence of their positions and the implementation of joint action.

(*b*) Consultations shall take place before the High Contracting Parties decide on their final position.

(*c*) In adopting its positions and in its national measures each High Contracting Party shall take full account of the positions of the other partners and shall give due consideration to the desirability of adopting and implementing common European positions.

In order to increase their capacity for joint action in the foreign policy field, the High Contracting Parties shall ensure that common principles and objectives are gradually developed and defined.

The determination of common positions shall constitute a point of reference for the policies of the High Contracting Parties.

(*d*) The High Contracting Parties shall endeavour to avoid any action or position which impairs their effectiveness as a cohesive force in international relations or within international organisations.

3. (*a*) The Ministers for Foreign Affairs and a member of the Commission shall meet at least four times a year within the framework of European Political Co-operation. They may also discuss foreign policy matters within the framework of Political Co-operation on the occasion of meetings of the Council of the European Communities.

(*b*) The Commission shall be fully associated with the proceedings of Political Co-operation.

(*c*) In order to ensure the swift adoption of common positions and the implementation of joint action, the High Contracting Parties shall, as far as possible, refrain from impeding the formation of a consensus and the joint action which this could produce.

4. The High Contracting Parties shall ensure that the European Parliament is closely associated with European Political Co-operation. To that end the Presidency shall regularly inform the European Parliament of the foreign policy issues which are being examined within the framework of Political Co-operation and shall ensure that the views of the European Parliament are duly taken into consideration.

5. The external policies of the European Community and the policies agreed in European Political Co-operation must be consistent.

The Presidency and the Commission, each within its own sphere of competence, shall have special responsibility for ensuring that such consistency is sought and maintained.

6. (*a*) The High Contracting Parties consider that closer co-operation on questions of European security would contribute in an essential way to the development of a European identity in external policy matters. They are ready to co-ordinate their positions more closely on the political and economic aspects of security.

(*b*) The High Contracting Parties are determined to maintain the technological and industrial conditions necessary for their security. They shall work to that end both at national level and, where appropriate, within the framework of the competent institutions and bodies.

(*c*) Nothing in this Title shall impede closer co-operation in the field of security between certain of the High Contracting Parties within the framework of the Western European Union or the Atlantic Alliance.

7. (*a*) In international institutions and at international conferences which they attend, the High Contracting Parties shall endeavour to adopt common positions on the subjects covered by this Title.

(*b*) In international institutions and at international conferences in which not all the High Contracting Parties participate, those who do participate shall take full account of positions agreed in European Political Co-operation.

8. The High Contracting Parties shall organise a political dialogue with third countries and regional groupings whenever they deem it necessary.

9. The High Contracting Parties and the Commission, through mutual

assistance and information, shall intensify co-operation between their representations accredited to third countries and to international organisations.

10. (a) The Presidency of European Political Co-operation shall be held by the High Contracting Party which holds the Presidency of the Council of the European Communities.

(b) The Presidency shall be responsible for initiating action and co-ordinating and representing the positions of the member States in relations with third countries in respect of European Political Co-operation activities. It shall also be responsible for the management of Political Co-operation and in particular for drawing up the timetable of meetings and for convening and organising meetings.

(c) The Political Directors shall meet regularly in the Political Committee in order to give the necessary impetus, maintain the continuity of European Political Co-operation and prepare Ministers' discussions.

(d) The Political Committee or, if necessary, a ministerial meeting shall convene within forty-eight hours at the request of at least three member States.

(e) The European Correspondents' Group shall be responsible, under the direction of the Political Committee, for monitoring the implementation of European Political Co-operation and for studying general organizational problems.

(f) Working Groups shall meet as directed by the Political Committee.

(g) A Secretariat based in Brussels shall assist the Presidency in preparing and implementing the activities of European Political Co-operation and in administrative matters. It shall carry out its duties under the authority of the Presidency.

11. As regards privileges and immunities, the members of the European Political Co-operation Secretariat shall be treated in the same way as members of the diplomatic missions of the High Contracting Parties based in the same place as the Secretariat.

12. Five years after the entry into force of this Act the High Contracting Parties shall examine whether any revision of Title III is required.

BIBLIOGRAPHY

PRIMARY DOCUMENTATION

IRELAND

State Paper Office, Dublin (SPO)
Cabinet minutes/conclusions (CAB)
Memoranda of the Taoiseach's Department (S).

Eire, Parliamentary Debates: Report of the First Dáil, 11 April 1919.
Eire, Official Report: *Debate on the Treaty between Great Britain and Ireland Signed in London on 6 December 1921* (Dublin, 1922).
Eire, *Parliamentary Debates: Dáil Éireann: Official Report*, vol. 1 (1922) to vol. 373 (1987).
Eire, *Parliamentary Debates: Seanad Éireann: Official Report*, vol. 20 (1935) to vol. 116 (1987).
Ireland, Oireachtas Éireann, League of Nations (Obligations of Membership) Act 1935 (Dublin: Stationery Office, 1936).
Ireland, Oireachtas Éireann, League of Nations (Obligations of Membership) Order 1935 (Dublin: Stationery Office, 1936).
Ireland, Oireachtas Éireann, Executive Authority (External Relations) Act 1936 (Dublin: Stationery Office, 1936).
Bunreacht na hÉireann, 29 December 1937.
Ireland, Oireachtas Éireann, Neutrality (War Damage to Property) Act 1941 (Dublin: Stationery Office, 1941).
Ireland, Oireachtas Éireann, Defence Act 1945 (Dublin: Stationery Office, 1945).
Ireland, Oireachtas Éireann, Defence (Amendment) Act 1960 (Dublin: Stationery Office, 1960).
Ireland, Oireachtas Éireann, Defence (Amendment) Act (No. 2) 1960 (Dublin: Stationery Office, 1960).
Ireland: Statistical Abstract, 1931–85 (Dublin: Stationery Office, 1931–86) [annually].
Ireland, Department of External Affairs, *Texts Concerning Ireland's Position in Relation to the North Atlantic Treaty* (P. 9934: Dublin, Stationery Office, 1950) [presented to both Houses of the Oireachtas by the Minister for External Affairs on 26 April 1950].
Trade Statistics of Ireland (December 1982) (Dublin: Stationery Office, 1983).
Economic Development (Pr. 4803; Dublin: Stationery Office, 1958).
European Economic Community (Pr. 6106; Dublin: Stationery Office, 1961).
European Economic Community: Developments Subsequent to White Paper of 30 June 1961, (Pr. 6613; Dublin: Stationery Office, 1962).

Membership of the European Communities: Implications for Ireland 1970 (Prl. 1110; Dublin: Stationery Office, 1970).

The Accession of Ireland to the European Communities (Prl. 2064; Dublin: Stationery Office, 1972) [laid by the Government before each House of the Oireachtas, January 1972].

Fourth Joint Oireachtas Committee on Secondary Legislation of the European Communities, *European Parliament Draft Treaty Establishing the European Union* (Report 14; Dublin: Stationery Office, 1985).

—— *Completing the Internal Market* (Report 29; Dublin: Stationery Office, 1986).

—— *The Single European Act* (Report 34; Dublin: Stationery Office, 1986).

Development in the European Communities, 1–29 (Dublin: Stationery Office, 1973–87) [biannually].

The Single European Act: An Explanatory Guide (Dublin: Stationery Office, 1986).

The Single European Act: A Government Information Booklet (Dublin: Stationery Office, 1987).

Eire-Ireland (Bulletin of the Department of External Affairs; Dublin, 1948–70).

Ireland Today (Bulletin of the Department of Foreign Affairs; Dublin, 1970–).

Ireland at the United Nations (Dublin: Brun agus Ó Nuilláin Tea, 1957–71) [annually].

Department of Foreign Affairs: Texts of Speeches by Ministers for Foreign Affairs (Dublin: Department of Foreign Affairs, 1973–).

Conference on Security and Cooperation in Europe, Helsinki, 30 July–1 August 1975. Address by An Taoiseach, Mr. Liam Cosgrave, T. D., and Final Act (Dublin: Department of Foreign Affairs, 1975).

Ireland, Department of Defence, *The Irish Army Handbook 1941* (Dublin: Department of Defence, 1941).

Understanding the EEC, viii; *Defence and Neutrality* (Dublin: Irish Council of the European Movement, 1971).

The Single European Act (Dublin: Irish Council of the European Movement, n.d.).

Irish CND, *Disarm* [bi-monthly].

The Workers' Party, *Ireland and the Single European Act* (Dublin: Aug. 1986).

Labour Party, *Ireland: A Neutral Nation* (Principles of International Policy, i; Dublin: Labour Party, n.d.).

Patrick McGilligan Papers, Archives, University College, Dublin.

BRITAIN

The United Kingdom of Great Britain and Ireland *Parliamentary Debates: House of Commons: Official Report*, 5th Ser., 65 (1914), 335 (1938), 356 (1940).

Public Records Office, Kew (PRO)
   Foreign Office (FO)
   Cabinet (CAB)
   Dominions Office (DO)
   Prime Minister's Office (PREM).
Agreement on International Energy Program, 18 November 1974 (Cmnd. 5826; London: HMSO, 1975).

GERMANY

Documents on German Foreign Policy 1918-1945 (Series D (1937-1945), 1-13; London: HMSO, 1949-73).

SWEDEN

Documents on Swedish Foreign Policy (Stockholm: Royal Ministry for Foreign Affairs, 1951-82) [annually].
Sweden's Security Policy and Total Defence: A Summary of the First Report by the 1978 Parliamentary Committee on Defence, June 1979 (Ds Fo 1979: 3, Stockholm: Ministry of Defence, 1979).
Sweden's Total Defence 1982-1987 (Ds Fo 1981: 5; Stockholm: Ministry of Defence, 1981).
Fact Sheets on Sweden: The Swedish Defence System (Stockholm: Swedish Institute, 1982).
Sweden in Brief (Stockholm: Swedish Institute, 1982).

UNITED STATES OF AMERICA

Truman Library (TL)
   Acheson Papers, Box 66
   President's Secretary's Files, Box 209
   Official File 218, Truman Papers.

Washington National Records Center (WNRC)
   Department of State: Ireland, RG84 Box 702 and Box 703.

National Archives Building (NAB)
   Department of State: Decimal File 840.20/2.

EUROPEAN AND INTERNATIONAL ORGANIZATIONS

Treaties Establishing the European Communities (Brussels: Office for Official Publications, 1978).
Official Journal of the European Communities L300 (1972), L102, L136, L146 (1982). (Luxemburg: Office for Official Publications of the European Communities) [daily].

Bulletin of the European Economic Community 1–9 (1958–67) [monthly].

Bulletin of the European Communities 1–15 (1968–82) [monthly].

Single European Act (*Bulletin of the European Communities*, Suppl. 2/86; Brussels, 1986).

European Economic Community, Commission, *Report to the European Parliament on the State of the Negotiations with the United Kingdom* (Brussels: EEC, Feb. 1963).

'Report to the Council and the Commission on the Realisation by Stages of Economic and Monetary Union in the Community–Werner Report' (*Bulletin of the European Communities*, Suppl. 11/70; Brussels, Commission of the European Communities, 1970).

'Report on European Armaments Procurement Cooperation', by Mr E. Kepsch, Political Committee, European Parliament, 8 May 1978 (Working Documents, European Parliament 1978–1979, Doc. 83/78; Strasburg: European Parliament, 1978).

'Report on European Political Cooperation' (London, 13 October 1981) (*Bulletin of the European Communities*, Suppl. 3/81: Brussels, Commission of the European Communities, 1981).

'Report on European Political Cooperation and European Security', by Mr N. Haagerup, Political Committee, European Parliament 3 December 1982 (Working Documents, European Parliament 1982–1983, Document 1-946/82; Strasburg: European Parliament, 1982).

'Report on the Significance of Economic Sanctions', by Mr H. J. Seeler. External Economic Relations Committee, European Parliament 8 April 1982 (Working Documents, European Parliament 1982–1983, Document 1-83/82; Strasburg: European Parliament, 1982).

'Report on the State of Relations between the EEC and East European State-Trading Countries and Comecon', 11 May 1978 (Working Documents, European Parliament 1978, Document 89/78; Strasburg: European Parliament, 1978).

'Report on Relations between the European Community and the East European State-Trading Countries and the CMEA (Comecon)', 28 August 1981 (Working Documents, European Parliament, 1981, Document 1-424/81; Brussels: European Parliament, 1981).

David Greenwood, *A Policy for Promoting Defence and Technological Cooperation among West European Countries for the Commission of the European Communities (1980)* (Brussels: European Communities, 1980).

Documents of the Consultative Assembly, Council of Europe, 1949–1963 (Strasburg: Council of Europe, 1949–63) [sessionally].

Official Report of Debates: Consultative Assembly, Council of Europe, 1948–63 (Strasburg: Council of Europe, 1949–63) [sessionally].

'Memorandum on the Legal Aspects of Neutrality', presented by Mr Struye, Chairman of the Political Committee, Consultative Assembly of the Council of Europe, 9 May 1962 (Consultative Assembly of the Council of

Europe, Doc. 1420, for 1962).

'Memorandum on the Political Aspects of Neutrality', presented by Mr Struye, Chairman of the Political Committee, Consultative Assembly of the Council of Europe, 29 April 1963 (Consultative Assembly of the Council of Europe, Doc. 1581, for 1963).

Convention of Stockholm Establishing The European Free Trade Association, 4 January 1960 (Geneva: European Free Trade Association Secretariat, 1967).

Organisation for Economic Co-operation and Development, *Economic Surveys* Sweden (July 1982), (Mar. 1967)
Austria (Feb. 1983), (July 1976), (Mar. 1967)
Switzerland (May 1983), (Mar. 1976), (Feb. 1972).

OECD Statistical Bulletin: Series A [monthly].

World Bank, *World Development Report 1981* (Oxford: OUP, for World Bank, 1981).

Declaration between Denmark, Finland, Iceland, Norway and Sweden for the Purpose of Establishing Similar Rules of Neutrality, Signed at Stockholm, 27 May 1938 (League of Nations Treaty Series, 188, Doc. 4365 [Geneva, 1938/9?]).

League of Nations, *Official Journal* (Special Suppl., 154; 1936)
League of Nations, *Official Journal* (1938).

GENERAL

The Economist
Irish Independent
Irish Press
Irish Times
New York Herald Tribune
Sunday Press
Sunday Times
The Times
The Military Balance 1982–1983, 1983–1984, 1984–1985, 1985–1986 (London: International Institute for Strategic Studies, 1982, 1983, 1984, 1985).

Keesing's Contemporary Archives, i–xxviii (Keynsham: Keesing's/Longman, 1931–82).

SECONDARY SOURCES

Books

AIKEN, FRANK, *Ireland at the United Nations 1959: Speeches by Mr Frank Aiken* (Dublin: Brun agus Ó Nualláin Tea, 1960).

AKENSON, DONALD HARMAN, *The United States and Ireland* (Cambridge, Mass.: Harvard University Press, 1973).

ALLEN, DAVID, and PIJPERS, ALFRED (eds.), *European Foreign Policy-Making and the Arab-Israeli Conflict* (The Hague: Martinus Nijhoff, 1984).

ALLEN, DAVID, RUMMEL, REIGNHARDT, and WESSELS, WOLFGANG (eds.), *European Political Cooperation* (Butterworths European Series; London: Butterworth, 1982).

ALLISON, R., *Finland's Relations with the Soviet Union 1944-1984* (Oxford: St Anthony's College, 1985).

ALTING VON GESAU, FRANS A. M., *The External Relations of the European Community* (Farnborough: Saxon House, 1974).

ANDREN, NILS, *Power-Balance and Non-Alignment: A Perspective on Swedish Foreign Policy* (Stockholm: Almqvist & Wiksell, 1967).

—— *the Future of the Nordic Balance* (Stockholm: Ministry of Defence, 1977).

BAILEY, RICHARD, *The European Community in the World* (London: Hutchinson, 1973).

BARCROFT, STEPHEN, 'The International Civil Servant: The League of Nations Career of Sean Lester 1929-1947', Ph.D. thesis (Dublin: Trinity College, 1972).

BERGQUIST, MATS, *Sverige och EEC* (Lund Political Studies, 2; Stockholm, 1970).

BIRNBAUM, KARL E., *Arms Control in Europe: Problems and Prospects* (Vienna: Austrian Institute for International Affairs, 1980).

BIRNBAUM, KARL E., and NEUHOLD, HANSPETER (eds.), *Neutrality and Non-alignment in Europe* (Vienna: Austrian Institute for International Affairs, 1981).

BJØL, ERLING, 'The Small State in International Politics', in A. Schou and A. O. Brundtland (eds.), q.v.

BLACK, ROBERT, A., jun., 'Plus ça change, plus c'est la même chose: Nine Governments in Search of a Common Energy Policy', in H. Wallace, W. Wallace, and C. Webb (eds.), *Policy-Making in the European Communities* (London: Wiley, 1977).

BLACKWELL, JOHN, and O'MALLEY, EOIN, 'The Impact of EEC Membership on Irish Industry', in P. J. Drudy and Dermot McAleese (eds.), q.v.

BLAKE, JOHN W., *Northern Ireland in the Second World War* (Belfast: HMSO, 1956).

BLYDEN, EDWARD W. III, 'The Idea of African "Neutralism" and "Nonalignment": An Exploratory Survey', in K. London (ed.), q.v.

BOLAND, KEVIN, *Up Dev!* (Dublin: Boland, n/d).

BOWMAN, JOHN, *De Valera and the Ulster Question 1917-1973* (Oxford: OUP, 1982).

BOYD, ANDREW, *Fifteen Men on a Powder Keg* (London: Methuen, 1971).

BRADLEY, J, FITZGERALD, J. D., and ROSS, M. (eds.), *The Economic Consequences of European Union* (Dublin: Economic and Social Research Institute, 1986).

BROWN SCOTT, JAMES (ed.), *The Hague Conventions and the Declarations of*

1899 and 1907, 2nd edn. (New York: OUP, for Carnegie Endowment for International Peace, 1915).

—— *The Reports to the Hague Conferences of 1899 and 1907* (New York: OUP, for Carnegie Endowment for International Peace, 1917).

BULL, H., *The Anarchical Society* (London: Macmillan, 1977).

BURROWS, B., and EDWARDS, G., *The Defence of Western Europe* (Butterworth's European Series; London: Butterworth, 1982).

BURROWS, B., and IRWIN C., *The Security of Western Europe: Towards a Common Defence Policy* (London: Charles Knight, 1973).

BURTON, J. W. (ed.), *Nonalignment* (London: Deutsch, 1966).

—— *International Relations: A General Theory* (Cambridge: CUP, 1965).

CAMPS, MIRIAM, *Britain and the European Community 1955-1963* (London: OUP, 1965).

CANNING, PAUL, *British Policy Towards Ireland 1921-1941* (Oxford, OUP 1985).

CARROLL, JOSEPH T., *Ireland in the War Years 1939-1945* (Newton Abbot: David & Charles, 1975).

CARTER, CAROLLE J., *The Shamrock and the Swastika: German Espionage in Ireland in World War II* (Palo Alto, Calif.: Pacific Books, 1977).

CASEY, James, *Constitutional Law in Ireland* (London: Sweet & Maxwell, 1987).

CHARLESWORTH, J. C. (ed.), *Is International Communism Winning?* (Annals of the American Academy of Political and Social Science, 336; July 1961).

—— (ed.), *Realignment in the Communist and Western Worlds* (Annals of the American Academy of Political and Social Science, 372; July 1967).

CHUBB, BASIL, *The Government and Politics of Ireland* (London: OUP, 1974).

CHURCHILL, WINSTON, *The Second World War,* iii: *The Grand Alliance* (London: Cassell, 1950).

CLAUDE, INIS L., *Swords into Plowshares: The Problems and Progress of International Organization,* 3rd edn. (London: University of London Press, 1965).

COHAN, A. S., *The Irish Political Elite* (Dublin: Gill & Macmillan, 1972).

COLLINS, MICHAEL, *The Path to Freedom* (Cork: Mercier, 1968).

COLLINS, NEIL, 'Ireland', in Juliet Lodge (ed.), *Direct Elections to the European Parliament 1984* (London: Macmillan, 1986).

COMERFORD, PATRICK, *Do You Want to Die for NATO?* (Cork: Mercier Press, 1984).

COOMBES, DAVID (ed.), *Ireland and the European Communities: Ten Years of Membership* (Dublin: Gill & Macmillan, 1983).

COONEY, JOHN, *EEC in Crisis* (Dublin: Dublin University Press, 1979).

COSTELLO, J. A., *Ireland in International Affairs* (Dublin: Monument Press, 1948).

COUGHLAN, ANTHONY, *The EEC: Ireland and the Making of a Super Power* (Dublin: Irish Sovereignty Movement, 1979).

CRABB, CECIL V., jun., *The Elephants and the Grass* (New York: Praeger, 1965).

CRABB, CECIL V., jun., (ed.), *Nonalignment in Foreign Affairs* (Annals of the American Academy of Political and Social Science, 362; Nov. 1965).

CRONIN, SEAN, *Washington's Irish Policy 1916–1986: Independence, Partition and Neutrality* (Dublin: Anvil Books, 1987).

CROTTY, RAYMOND, *Ireland and the Common Market: An Economic Analysis of the Effects of Membership* (Dublin: Common Market Study Group, 1971).

DARBY, JOHN, *Conflict in Northern Ireland* (Dublin: Gill & Macmillan, 1976).

DEAK, F., and JESSUP, P, *A Collection of Neutrality Laws, Regulations and Treaties of Various Countries* (New York: Carnegie Endowment for International Peace, 1939).

—— *Neutrality: Its History, Economics and Law* (New York: Columbia University Press, 1935).

DEUTSCH, RICHARD, and MAGOWAN, VIVIEN, *Northern Ireland : A Chronology of Events 1968–74*, ii: *1972–73* (Belfast: Blackstaff, 1974).

DE SCHOUTHEETE, PHILLIPPE, *La Co-operation politique européenne* (Paris: Fernand Nathan, 1980).

De VALERA, ÉAMON, *Peace and War: Speeches by Mr de Valera on International Affairs (1932–1938)* (Dublin: N. H. Gill, 1944).

—— *Ireland's Stand: Being a Selection of the Speeches of Éamon de Valera during the War (1939–1945)*, 2nd edn. (Dublin: N. H. Gill, 1946).

—— *Speeches and Statements by Éamon de Valera 1917–73*, ed. Maurice Moynihan (Dublin: Gill & Macmillan, 1980).

DINAN, DESMOND, 'Irish Involvement in European Political Cooperation', in Bill McSweeny (ed.), q.v.

DOORN, J. VAN (ed.), *Armed Forces and Society* (The Hague: Mouton, 1968).

DOWNEY, JAMES, *Them and Us: Britain, Ireland and the Northern Question 1969–1982* (Dublin: Ward River Press, 1983).

DRUDY, P. J., and MCALEESE, DERMOT, *Ireland and the European Community* (Irish Studies, 3; Cambridge: CUP, 1983).

DUCHENE, FRANÇOIS, 'The European Community and the Uncertainties of Interdependence', in M. Kohnstamm and W. Hager, q.v.

DUGGAN, JOHN P., *Neutral Ireland and the Third Reich* (Dublin: Gill & Macmillan, 1985).

DUPUY, T. N., et al., *The Almanac of World Military Power*, 4th edn. (Novato, Calif.: Presidio Press, 1980).

DWYER, T. RYLE, *Irish Neutrality and the USA 1939–47* (Dublin: Gill & Macmillan, 1977).

—— *De Valera's Finest Hour: In Search of National Independence 1932–1959* (Cork: Mercier Press, 1982).

EDWARDS, GEOFFREY, and WALLACE, WILLIAM, *A Wider European Community?* (London: Federal Trust, 1976).

EDWARDS, OWEN DUDLEY (ed.), *Conor Cruise O'Brien Introduces Ireland* (London: Deutsch, 1969).

EKSTRÖM, TORD, MYRDAL, GUNNAR, and PALSSON, ROLAND, *Vi och Västeuropa: Andra ronden* (Stockholm: Raben & Sjogven, 1971).

EVERT, P. P., *The European Community in the World: The External Relations of the Enlarged European Community* (Rotterdam: Rotterdam University Press, 1972).

FABIAN, LARRY L., *Soldiers without Enemies: Preparing the United Nations for Peacekeeping Experience* (Washington DC: Brookings Institute, 1971).

FANNING, RONAN, *Independent Ireland* (Dublin: Helicon, 1983).

FARRELL, BRIAN, *Sean Lemass* (Dublin: Gill & Macmillan, 1983).

FAWCETT, J. E. S., *Law and Power in International Relations* (London: Faber, & Faber, 1982).

FELD, WERNER J., *The European Community in World Affairs: Economic Power and Influence* (Sherman Oaks: Alfred Publishing Co., 1976).

—— *The European Common Market and the World* (Englewood Cliffs: Prentice-Hall, 1967).

FISK, ROBERT, *In Time of War: Ireland, Ulster and the Price of Neutrality 1939–45* (London: Deutsch, 1983).

FITZGERALD, DESMOND, *Memoirs of Desmond FitzGerald 1913–1916* (London: Routledge & Kegan Paul, 1968).

FITZGERALD, GARRET, 'Ireland and the EEC', in *Ireland, Britain and Europe* (Collected Conference Papers; London: Institute of Commonwealth Studies, University of London Press, 1982).

FITZGERALD, WILLIAM, *Irish Unification and NATO* (Dublin: Dublin University Press, 1982).

FOOT, M. R. D., *Men in Uniform: Military Manpower in Modern Industrial Societies* (London: Weidenfeld & Nicolson, 1961).

FORDE, FRANK, *The Long Watch: The History of the Irish Mercantile Marine in World War Two* (Dublin: Gill & Macmillan, 1981).

FORDE, MICHAEL, *Constitutional Law of Ireland* (Cork: Mercier Press, 1987).

FOX, CAROL, and MULVEY, CHRIS, *Irish Neutrality and Peace Movements* (Dublin: Irish Messenger, 1986).

FRANKEL, JOSEPH, *National Interest* (London: Macmillan, 1970).

FRANKLAND, NOBLE, with WOODCOCK, PATRICIA (eds.), *Documents on International Affairs, 1955* (London: OUP, for Royal Institute of International Affairs, 1958).

FREYMOND, JACQUES, 'The European Neutrals and the Atlantic Community', in F. O. Wilcox and H. F. Haviland jun. (eds.), q.v.

—— 'How the Small Countries can contribute to Peace', in A. Schou and A. O. Brundtland (eds.), q.v.

FURSDON, EDWARD, *The European Defence Community: A History* (London: Macmillan, 1980).

GAGEBY, DOUGLAS, 'The Media', in J. J. Lee, (ed.), q.v.

GALLAGHER, TOM, and O'CONNELL, JAMES, *Contemporary Irish Studies* (Manchester: Manchester University Press, 1983).

GALTUNG, JOHAN, *The European Community: A Superpower in the Making* (London: Allen & Unwin, 1973).

GARNETT, JOHN, 'Defence Collaboration in the European Community', in Ieuan John (ed.), q.v.

—— The Defence of Western Europe (London: Macmillan, 1974).

GIBSON, NORMAN J., and SPENCE, JOHN E. (eds.), Economic Activity in Ireland: A Study of Two Open Economies (Dublin: Gill & Macmillan, 1976).

GINSBERG, ROY HOWARD, 'The European Community and the Mediterranean', in Juliet Lodge (ed.), q.v.

GOODRICH, LELAND M., and HAMBRO, EDVARD, Charter of the United Nations: Commentary and Documents, 2nd edn. (London: Stevens, 1949).

GOTT, RICHARD, 'The Decline of Neutralism, the Belgrade Conference and after', in D. C. Watt et al., q.v.

GREAVES, C. DESMOND, The Life and Times of James Connolly (London: Lawrence & Wishart, 1961).

GRENVILLE, J. A. S., The Major International Treaties 1914–1973: A History and a Guide with Texts (London: Methuen, 1974).

GUPTA, S. K., 'Asian Nonalignment', in C. Crabb (ed.), Nonalignment in Foreign Affairs, q.v.

GWYNN, DENIS, The Life and Work of Roger Casement (London: Jonathan Cape, 1930).

—— The Life of John Redmond (London: Harrap, 1932).

HADSEL, FRED L., 'Africa and the World: Nonalignment Reconsidered', in J. C. Charlesworth (ed.), Realignment in the Communist and Western Worlds, q.v.

HAGGLOFF, H. GUNNAR, 'A Test of Neutrality: Sweden in the Second World War', in Roderick Ogley (ed.), q.v.

HAKOVIRTA, HARTO, 'Neutrality in Europe: The International System and Neutrality in Europe', in Yearbook of Finnish Foreign Policy 1980 (Helsinki: Finnish Institute of International Affairs, 1980).

HALPERIN, MORTON H., Limited War in the Nuclear Age (New York: Wiley, 1963).

HANCOCK, W. K., Survey of British Commonwealth Affairs: Problems of Nationality 1918–1936 (London: OUP, 1937).

HARKNESS, D. W., The Restless Dominion: The Irish Free State and the British Commonwealth of Nations 1921–31 (London: Macmillan, 1969).

HARRISON, HENRY, The Neutrality of Ireland: Why it was Inevitable (London: Hale, 1942).

HAYES-MCCOY, G. A., 'Irish Defence Policy 1938–51', in K. B. Nowlan and T. D. Williams, q.v.

HEATH, EDWARD, Old World, New Horizons: Britain, The Common Market and the Atlantic Alliance (The Godkin Lectures at Harvard University, 1967; London: OUP, 1970).

HEDERMAN, MIRIAM, The Road to Europe: Irish Attitudes 1948–61 (Dublin: Institute of Public Administration, 1983).

HENDERSON, NICHOLAS, The Birth of NATO (Boulder, Colo.: Westview Press, 1983).

HENIG, RUTH B. (ed.), *The League of Nations* (Edinburgh: Oliver & Boyd, 1973).

HILL, CHRISTOPHER (ed.), *National Foreign Policies and European Political Cooperation* (London: Allen & Unwin, 1983).

HODGES, MICHAEL, 'Industrial Policy: Hard Times or Great Expectations', in Helen Wallace, William Wallace, and Carole Webb (eds.), *Policy-making in the European Community*, 2nd edn., q.v.

HOGAN, V. P., 'The Neutrality of Ireland in World War II', thesis (University of Notre Dame, 1953).

HOLST, J. J., 'The Changing Structure of Security in Europe', in Ieuan John (ed.), q.v.

—— *Five Roads to Nordic Security* (Oslo: Universitetsforlaget, 1975).

HOLSTI, K. J., *International Politics*, 4th edn. (Englewood Cliffs: Prentice-Hall, 1983).

HOWARD, CONSTANCE, 'Eire', in A. J. Toynbee and V. M. Toynbee (eds.), q.v.

HUFBAUER, GARY C., SCHOTT, JEFFREY J., with ELLIOTT, KIMBERLEY A., *Economic Sanctions Reconsidered: History and Current Policy* (Washington, DC: Institute for International Economics, 1984).

HULL, CORDELL, *The Memoirs of Cordell Hull*, ii (London: Hodder & Stoughton, 1948).

JAKOBSON, M., *Finnish Neutrality* (London: Evelyn, 1968).

JAMES, ALAN, *Sovereign Statehood: The Basis of International Society* (London: Allen & Unwin, 1986).

JANIS, IRVING, *Victims of Groupthink* (Boston: Houghton Mifflin, 1972).

JANKOWITSCH, ODETTE, and SAUVANT, KARL P., *The Third World without Superpowers: The Collected Documents of the Non-Aligned Countries*, i–iv (Dobbs Ferry, New York: Oceana Publications, 1978).

JANSEN, G. H., *Afro-Asia and Nonalignment* (London: Faber & Faber, 1966).

JESSUP, P., 'Neutrality', in *Encyclopaedia Britannica*, xi, 14th edn.

JOHN, I. (ed.), *EEC Policy towards Eastern Europe* (Farnborough: Saxon House, 1975).

JONES, THOMAS (ed. MIDDLEMAS, KEITH), *Whitehall Diary*, ii: *Ireland · 1918–1925* (London: OUP, 1971).

KAVANAGH, Lt.-Col. P. D., *The Irish Army Handbook* (Dublin: Department of Defence, 1968).

—— *The Irish Army Handbook 1973* (Dublin: Department of Defence, 1973).

KEATINGE, PATRICK, *The Formulation of Irish Foreign Policy* (Dublin: Institute of Public Administration, 1973).

—— *A Place Among the Nations: Issues of Irish Foreign Policy* (Dublin: Institute of Public Administration, 1978).

—— *A Singular Stance: Irish Neutrality in the 1980s* (Dublin: Institute of Public Administration, 1984).

—— 'The Europeanisation of Irish Foreign Policy', in P. J. Drudy and D. McAleese, q.v.

KEATINGE, PATRICK, 'Ireland: Neutrality in EPC', in Christopher Hill (ed.), q.v.

—— 'Ireland, Political Cooperation and the Middle East', in David Allen and Alfred Pijpers (eds.), q.v.

KEE, ROBERT, *The Green Flag: A History of Irish Nationalism* (London: Weidenfeld & Nicolson, 1972).

KEEGAN, JOHN, and ENGLISH, ADRIAN, 'Irish Republic', in John Keegan (ed.), *World Armies*, 2nd edn. (London: Macmillan, 1983).

KELSEN, HANS, rev. TUCKER, ROBERT W., *Principles of International Law*, 2nd edn. (New York: Holt, Rinehart & Winston, 1967).

KENNY, ANTHONY, *The Road to Hillsborough: The Shaping of the Anglo-Irish Agreement* (Oxford: Pergamon, 1986).

KEOHANE, ROBERT D., and NYE, JOSEPH S., *Power and Interdependence: World Politics in Transition* (Boston: Little, Brown, 1977).

KISSINGER, HENRY, 'Domestic Structure and Foreign Policy', in James N. Rosenau (ed.), q.v.

KOHNSTAMM, M., and HAGER, W., *A Nation Writ Large? Foreign Policy Problems before the European Community* (London: Macmillan, 1973).

KUYPER, PIETER JAN, 'Community Sanctions against Argentina: Lawfulness under Community and International Law', in D. O'Keeffe and H. G. Schermers (eds.), q.v.

LAFFAN, BRIGID, 'The Consequences for Irish Foreign Policy', in David Coombes (ed.), q.v.

—— *Ireland and South Africa: Irish Government Policy in the 1980s* (Dublin: Trocaire, 1988).

LAUTERPACHT, H., and OPPENHEIM, L., *International Law* ii, 7th edn. (London: Longman, 1952).

LEE, J. J. (ed.), *Ireland 1945–70* (Dublin: Gill & Macmillan, 1979).

—— *Reflections on Ireland in the EEC* (Dublin papers, 5; Dublin: Irish Council of the European Movement, Mar. 1984).

LEGUM, M., 'Africa and Nonalignment', in J. W. Burton (ed.), *Nonalignment* (London: Deutsch, 1966).

LEMASS, SEAN, 'Small States in International Organisations', in A. Schou and A. O. Brundtland (eds.), q.v.

LEVENSON, SAMUEL, *James Connolly: A Biography* (London: Martin Brian & O'Keeffe, 1973).

LINDEMANN, BEATE, 'European Political Cooperation at the U.N.: A Challenge for the Nine', in David Allen, Reignhardt Rummel, and Wolfgang Wessels (eds.), q.v.

LODGE, JULIET (ed.), *Institutions and Policies of the European Community* (London: Frances Pinter, 1983).

LONDON, K. (ed.), *New Nations in a Divided World* (New York: Praeger, 1963).

LONGFORD, LORD, *Peace by Ordeal* (London: Sidgwick & Jackson, 1972).

LONGFORD, LORD, and O'NEILL, THOMAS P., *Eamon de Valera* (London: Hutchinson, 1970).

LYNCH, PATRICK, 'The Irish Economy since the War 1946-51', in K. B. Nowlan and T. D. Williams (eds.), q.v.

LYON, PETER, *Neutralism* (Leicester: Leicester University Press, 1963).

LYONS, F. S. L., *Ireland Since the Famine* (London: Collins and Fontana, 1973).

MACARDLE, DOROTHY, *The Irish Republic* (London: Corgi Books, 1968).

MACGREIL, MICHAEL, *Prejudice and Tolerance in Ireland* (Dublin: College of Industrial Relations, 1977).

MACMANUS, FRANCIS, *The Years of the Great Test 1926-1939* (Cork: Mercier Press, 1967).

MACQUEEN, NORMAN, 'Irish Neutrality: The United Nations and the Peace-keeping Experience, 1945-1969', D.Phil. thesis (New University of Ulster, 1981).

—— 'Ireland's Entry to the United Nations 1946- 1956', in Tom Gallagher and James O'Connell, q.v.

MAGUIRE, MARIA, *A Bibliography of Published Works on Irish Foreign Relations 1921-1978* (Dublin: Royal Irish Academy, 1981).

MAHER, DENIS, *The Tortuous Path: The Course of Ireland's Entry into the EEC 1948-73* (Dublin: Institute of Public Administration, 1986).

MANSERGH, NICHOLAS, *Survey of British Commonwealth Affairs: Problems of External Policy 1931-1939* (London: OUP, 1952).

—— *Survey of British Commonwealth Affairs: Problems of Wartime Co-operation and Post-war Change 1939-1952* (London: OUP, 1958).

—— (ed.) *Documents and Speeches on British Commonwealth Affairs 1931-1952* i (London: OUP, 1953).

—— 'Irish Foreign Policy 1938-51', in K. B. Nowlan and T. D. Williams, (eds.), q.v.

—— 'Ireland: External Relations 1926-1939', in Francis MacManus, q.v.

MARSH, JOHN S., and SWANNEY, PAMELA J., 'The Common Agricultural Policy', in Juliet Lodge (ed.), q.v.

MARSHALL, CHARLES BURTON, *The Exercise of Sovereignty* (Baltimore: Johns Hopkins Press, 1965).

MARTIN, L. W. (ed.), *Neutralism and Non-Alignment* (London: Pall Mall, 1963).

MATES, LEO, *Nonalignment: Theory and Current Policy* (Dobbs Ferry, New York and Belgrade: Institute of International Politics and Economics, Belgrade, and Oceana Publications, 1972).

MAUDE, G., *The Finnish Dilemma* (London: OUP, 1976).

MAYRZEDT, H., and BINSWANGER, H. C., *Die Neutralen in der europäischen Integration: Kontroversen—Konfrontationen—Alternativen* (Vienna and Stuttgart: W. Braumuller, 1970).

MCALEESE, DERMOT, 'The Foreign Sector', in Norman J. Gibson and John E. Spence (eds.), q.v.

—— 'Ireland and the European Community: The Changing Pattern of Trade', in P. J. Drudy and Dermot McAleese (eds.), q.v.

McMahon, Deirdre, *Republicans and Imperialists: Anglo-Irish Relations in the 1930s* (New Haven, Conn.: Yale University Press, 1984). `

McMurtrie, Francis E. (ed.), *Jane's Fighting Ships 1939* (London: Sampson, Low Marston, 1939).

—— *Jane's Fighting Ships 1944–45* (London: Sampson, Low Marston, 1944).

McSweeney, Bill (ed.), *Ireland and the Threat of Nuclear War* (Dublin: Dominican Publications, 1985).

Meehan, James F., 'The Irish Economy during the War', in K. B. Nowlan and T. D. Williams (eds.), q.v.

Mitchell, Mairin, *The Atlantic Battle and the Future of Ireland* (London: Muller, 1941).

Morgan, Roger P., *High Politics, Low Politics: Towards a Foreign Policy for Western Europe* (Center for Strategic and International Studies, Georgetown University, Washington Papers, i.2; London: Sage Publications, 1973).

Morse, Edward C., *Modernization and the Transformation of International Relations* (New York: Free Press, 1976).

Moynihan, Maurice (ed.), *Speeches and Statements by Éamon de Valera 1917–73*: see under DE VALERA, ÉAMON.

Murphy, John A., 'The Irish Party System', in K. B. Nowlan and T. D. Williams (eds.), q.v.

—— *Ireland in the Twentieth Century* (Dublin: Gill & Macmillan, 1975).

Nikezic, M., 'Why Uncommitted Countries hold that they are not "Neutral" ', in J. C. Charlesworth (ed.), *Is International Communism Winning?*, q.v.

Nowlan, Kevin B., and Williams, T. Desmond, *Ireland in the War Years and After, 1939–1951* (Dublin: Gill & Macmillan, 1969).

O'Brien, Conor Cruise, *To Katanga and Back* (London: Four Square Books, 1965).

—— *Ireland, the United Nations and Southern Africa* (Public lecture; Dublin: Anti-Apartheid Movement, 1967).

—— 'Ireland in International Affairs', in Owen Dudley Edwards (ed.), q.v.

O'Ceallaigh, Daltun, *Political and Military Implications of Ireland's EEC Membership* (Dublin: Irish Sovereignty Movement, 1975).

Ogley, Roderick, *The Theory and Practice of Neutrality in the Twentieth Century* (London: Routledge & Kegan Paul, 1970).

O'Keeffe, D., and Schermers, H. G. (eds.), *Essays in European Law and Integration 1983* (Deventer: Kluwer, 1983).

O'Leary, Marian, 'Ireland and its EC membership', in C. O'Nuallain (ed.), *The Presidency of the European Council of Ministers: Impacts and implications for national governments* (London: Croom Helm, 1985).

O'Malley, Padraig, *The Uncivil Wars: Ireland Today* (Belfast: Blackstaff Press, 1983).

O'Malley, Paul Francis, 'The Origins of Irish Neutrality in World War II 1932–1938', Ph.D. thesis (University of Boston, 1980).

ØRVIK, NILS, *The Decline of Neutrality*, 2nd edn. (London: Cass, 1971).

OSGOOD, ROBERT R., *Limited War Revisited* (Boulder Colo.: Westview Press, 1979).

OSGOOD, R., and TUCKER, R. W., *Force, Order and Justice* (Baltimore: Johns Hopkins University Press, 1967).

PAJUNEN, AIMO, 'Some Aspects of Finnish Security Policy', in Karl E. Birnbaum and Hanspeter Neuhold (eds.), q.v.

PALMER, M., and LAMBERT, J., *et al.*, *European Unity* (London: Allen & Unwin, 1968).

PETITPIERRE, MAX, *Switzerland, Present and Future* (n.p.: New Helvetic Society, 1963).

PINDER, JOHN, 'The Community and the State Trading Countries', in K. Twitchett, q.v.

POLITIS, NICOLAS, *Neutrality and Peace* (Carnegie Endowment for International Peace, pam. 55; Washington, 1935).

PRYCE, ROY (ed.), *The Dynamics of European Union* (London: Croom Helm, 1987).

RANSOM, C., *The European Community and Eastern Europe* (London: Butterworth, 1983).

RAYMOND, RAYMOND JAMES, 'The Economics of Neutrality: The United States, Great Britain and Ireland's War Economy: 1937–1945', Ph.D. thesis, 2 vols. (University of Kansas, 1980).

RENWICK, ROBIN, *Economic Sanctions* (Cambridge, Mass.: Harvard University Center for International Affairs, 1981).

ROACH, JOHN, and THOMANECK, JURGEN, *Police and Public Order in Europe* (Beckenham: Croom Helm, 1985).

ROBERTS, ADAM, *Nations in Arms: The Theory and Practice of Territorial Defence* (London: Chatto & Windus, for I I S S, 1976).

—— 'Can Neutrality Be Defended?', in Bill McSweeney (ed.), q.v.

ROBERTSON, A. H., *The Council of Europe*, 2nd edn. (London: Stevens & Sons, 1961).

ROBINSON, MARY, 'Constitutional, Legal, and Administrative Adaptations in Ireland to Membership of the EEC', LL D diss. (Dublin: Trinity College, 1976).

ROSE, RICHARD, *Governing without Consensus* (London: Faber & Faber, 1971).

ROSENAU, JAMES N. (ed.), *International Politics and Foreign Policy* (New York: Free Press. 1969).

ROTHSTEIN, ROBERT L., *Alliances and Small Powers* (New York: Columbia University Press, 1968).

ROXBURGH, R. F. (ed.), *International Law: A Treatise*, 3rd edn. (London: Longman, Green & Co., 1921).

SALMON, TREVOR C., 'Ireland', in Carol and Kenneth Twitchett (eds.), q.v.

—— 'The Civil Power and Aiding the Civil Power: The Case of Ireland', in John Roach and Jurgen Thomaneck (eds.), q.v.

SAYEGH, FAYEZ A. (ed.), *The Dynamics of Neutralism in the Arab World: A Symposium* (San Francisco: Chandler, 1964).

SCHOU, A., and BRUNDTLAND, A. O. (eds.), *Small States in International Relations* (Uppsala: Almqvist & Wiksell, 1971).

SCHWARZENBERGER, GEORGE, 'The Scope for Neutralism', in *The Yearbook of World Affairs*, xv (London: Stevens & Sons, 1961).

SHARE, BERNARD, *The Emergency: Neutral Ireland 1939–45* (Dublin: Gill & Macmillan, 1978).

SHEBAB, H. M., 'Irish Defence Policy 1922–1950', M.Litt. thesis (Dublin: Trinity College, 1975).

SHEEHAN, Capt. J. (ed.), *Defence Forces Handbook* (Dublin: Department of Defence, n.d.).

SHLAIM, A., and YANNOPOULOS, G., *The EEC and Eastern Europe* (Cambridge: CUP, 1978).

SILJ, A., *Europe's Political Puzzle: A Study of the Fouchet Negotiations and the 1963 Veto* (Occasional Papers in International Affairs, 17; Cambridge, Mass.: Harvard Center for International Affairs, 1967).

SINGER, MARSHALL R., *Weak States in a World of Powers: The Dynamics of International Relationships* (New York: Free Press, 1972).

SIOTIS, JEAN, 'The European Economic Community and its Emerging Mediterranean Policy', in Frans A. M. Alting von Gesau, q.v.

SMITH, MICHAEL, *Western Europe and the United States* (London: UACES and Allen & Unwin, 1984).

STEPHAN, ENNO, *Spies in Ireland* (London: Four Square, 1965).

STOURZH, G., 'Some Reflections on Permanent Neutrality', in A. Schou and A. O. Brundtland (eds.), q.v.

SUNDELIUS, BENGT (ed.), *Foreign Policies of Northern Europe* (Boulder, Colo.: Westview Press, 1982).

SWANN, DENNIS, *The Economics of the Common Market*, 5th edn. (Harmondsworth: Penguin, 1984).

TALBOTT, STROBE (ed.), *Khrushchev Remembers: The Last Testament* (London: Deutsch, 1974).

TAYLOR, PHILLIP, *When Europe Speaks With One Voice* (London: Aldwych Press, 1979).

TAYLOR, TREVOR, *European Defence Co-operation* (Royal Institute of International Affairs, Chatham House Papers, 24; London: Routledge & Kegan Paul, 1984).

TINDEMANS, LEO, *Report on European Union* (Bulletin of the European Communities, suppl. 1/76; Brussels, 1976).

TOWNSHEND, CHARLES, *Political Violence in Ireland* (Oxford: OUP, 1983).

TOYNBEE, A. J., and TOYNBEE, V. M. (eds.), *Survey of International Affairs 1939–46: The War and the Neutrals* (London: OUP, 1956).

TURNER, HOWARD, 'Sweden and European Integration: The Significance of the Neutrality Component in Swedish Foreign Policy', M.A. diss. (Leicester University, June 1975).

TWITCHETT, CAROL COSGROVE, *Europe and Africa: From Association to Partnership* (Farnborough: Saxon House, 1978).

—— *A Framework for Development: The EEC and ACP* (London: Allen & Unwin, 1981).

TWITCHETT, CAROL and KENNETH (eds.), *Building Europe: Britain's Partners in the EEC* (London: Europa, 1981).

TWITCHETT, KENNETH, *Europe and the World: The External Relations of the Common Market* (London: Europa, 1976).

VAUGHAN, RICHARD, *Post-War Integration in Europe* (London: Edward Arnold, 1976).

VAYRYNEN, RAIMO, 'The Evolution of Finland's Foreign Policy since the End of the Second World War', in Karl E. Birnbaum and Hanspeter Neuhold, q.v.

VIGOR, P. H., *The Soviet View of War, Peace and Neutrality* (London: Routledge & Kegan Paul, 1975).

VUKADINOVIĆ, R., 'Small States and the Policy of Non-Alignment', in A. Schou and A. O. Brundtland (eds.), q.v.

WALLACE, HELEN, WALLACE, WILLIAM, and WEBB, CAROLE (eds.), *Policy-Making in the European Communities* (London: Wiley, 1977).

—— *Policy-Making in the European Communities*, 2nd edn. (Chichester: Wiley, 1983).

WALLACE, WILLIAM, 'Political Cooperation: Integration through Intergovernmentalism', in Helen Wallace, William Wallace, and Carole Webb (eds.), *Policy-Making in the European Communities*, 2nd edn., q.v.

WALSH, BRENDAN M., 'Ireland's Membership of the European Monetary System: Expectations, Out-Turn and Prospects', in P. J. Drudy and Dermot McAleese, q.v.

WATT, D. C., *et al.*, (ed.) *Survey of International Affairs 1961* (London: OUP, for Royal Institute of International Affairs, 1965).

WEST, NIGEL, *MI5 British Security Service Operations 1909–1945* (London: Bodley Head, 1981).

—— *MI6 British Secret Intelligence Service Operations 1909–1945* (London: Weidenfeld & Nicolson, 1983).

WHYTE, J. H., *Church and State in Modern Ireland 1923–1979*, 2nd edn. (Dublin: Gill & Macmillan, 1980).

WIGHT, M, ed. H. Bull, *Systems of States* (Leicester: Leicester University Press, 1977).

WILCOX, F. O., and HAVILAND, H. F. jun. (eds.), *The Atlantic Community: Progress and Prospects* (New York: Praeger, 1963).

WILLETTS, PETER, *The Nonaligned Movement: The Origins of a Third World Alliance* (London: Frances Pinter, 1978).

—— *The Nonaligned in Havana: Documents of the Sixth Summit Conference and an Analysis of their Significance for the Global Political System* (London:: Frances Pinter, 1981).

WILLIAMS, T. DESMOND, 'Ireland in the War', in K. B. Nowlan and T. D. Williams (eds.), q.v.

—— 'Conclusions', in K. B. Nowlan and T. D. Williams (eds.), q.v.

—— 'Irish Foreign Policy 1949–69', in J. J. Lee, q.v.

WOLFERS, ARNOLD, *Discord and Collaboration* (Baltimore: Johns Hopkins Press, 1965).

ARTICLES

ALLEN, ROSEMARIE, 'Fishing for a Common Policy', *Journal of Common Market Studies*, 19/2 (Dec. 1980).

ANABTAWI, SAMIR N., 'Neutralists and Neutralism', *Journal of Politics*, 27/2 (1965).

ANDREN, NILS, 'Prospects for the Nordic Security Pattern', *Cooperation and Conflict*, 13/4 (1978).

ARMSTRONG, HAMILTON FISH, 'Neutrality: Varying Tunes', *Foreign Affairs*, 35/1 (Oct. 1956).

ARTHUR, PAUL, 'Anglo-Irish relations in the European Community', *Irish Studies in International Affairs*, 2/1 (1985).

BALDWIN, DAVID A., 'Interdependence and Power: A Conceptual Analysis', *International Organisation*, 34/4 (Autumn 1980).

BARCROFT, STEPHEN, 'Irish Foreign Policy at the League of Nations 1929–1936', *Irish Studies in International Affairs*, 1/1 (1979).

BIGGS-DAVIDSON, J., 'Ireland: Necessary to NATO' *Journal of Defence and Diplomacy*, 2/3 (Mar. 1984).

BIRNBAUM, KARL E., 'Alignments in Europe: The CSCE Experience', *World Today*, 37/6 (June 1981).

BJØL, ERLING, 'The Power of the Weak', *Cooperation and Conflict*, 4/3 (1968).

BRUNDTLAND, A. O., 'The Nordic Balance', *Cooperation and Conflict*, 2 (1966).

BURNS, BRIGID, and SALMON, TREVOR C., 'Policy-Making Coordination in Ireland on European Community Issues', *Journal of Common Market Studies*, 15/4 (June 1977).

CAMMAERT, E., 'Neutrality and its Critics', *Contemporary Review*, 157 (Mar. 1940).

CARTER, CAROLLE J., 'Ireland: America's Neutral Ally', *Eire: Ireland*, 12/2 (1977).

CASSIDY, Lt.-Col. M., 'A Short History of the Air Corps', *An Cosantoir* (May 1980).

CHOUCRI, N., 'The Non-alignment of Afro-Asian States: Policy, Perceptions and Behaviour', *Canadian Journal of Political Science*, 2/1 (Mar. 1969).

CLARKE, JOHN L., 'NATO, Neutrals, and National Defence', *Survival*, 24/6 (Nov.–Dec. 1982).

CONNOLLY, MICHAEL, and LOUGHLIN, JOHN, 'Reflections on the Anglo-Irish Agreement', *Government and Opposition*, 21/2 (1986).

COOMBES, DAVID, 'European Union: The Impulse for Change' *Irish Studies in International Affairs*, 2/1 (1985).

COOPER, RICHARD N., 'Economic Interdependence and Foreign Policy in the Seventies', *World Politics*, 24/2 (Jan. 1972).

COX, W. HARVEY, 'The Anglo-Irish Agreement', *Parliamentary Affairs*, 40/1 (1987).

CREMIN, CON, 'Northern Ireland at the United Nations, August/September 1969', *Irish Studies in International Affairs*, 1/2 (1980).

—— 'United Nations Peace-Keeping Operations: An Irish Initiative 1961–1968', *Irish Studies in International Affairs*, 1/4 (1984).

CULLIS, MICHAEL, 'The Austrian Treaty Settlement', *Review of International Studies*, 7/3 (July 1981).

DORMAN-O'GOWAN, C. P. D., 'The Irish Defence Forces: Their Role and their Problems', *Journal of Royal United Services Institute (RUSI)*, 126/3 (Sept. 1981).

DOYLE, Capt. J., 'European Defence: Is Neutrality an Option Today?', *An Cosantoir* (Nov. 1978).

DRISCOLL, DENNIS, 'Is Ireland Really "Neutral"?', *Irish Studies in International Affairs*, 1/3 (1982).

DUCHENE, FRANÇOIS, 'A New European Defence Community', *Foreign Affairs*, 50/1 (Oct. 1971).

EKSTRÖM, TORD, 'Sverige, EEC och jämlikhetspolitiken', *Tiden* 63/7 (1971).

ENGLISH, A. J., 'Republic of Ireland's Defence Forces', *Jane's Defence Review*, 2/4 (1981).

FALOON, BRIAN, 'Aspects of Finnish Neutrality: An Historical Review', *Irish Studies in International Affairs*, 1/3 (1982).

FANNING, RONAN, 'The United States and Irish Participation in NATO: The Debate of 1950', *Irish Studies in International Affairs*, 1/1 (1979).

—— 'London and Belfast's Responses to the Declaration of the Republic of Ireland', *International Affairs*, 58/1 (1981–2).

—— 'Irish Neutrality: An Historical Review', *Irish Studies in International Affairs*, 1/3 (1982).

—— 'Anglo-Irish relations: Partition and the British Dimension in Historical Perspective', *Irish Studies in International Affairs*, 2/1 (1985).

—— 'The Anglo-American Alliance and the Irish Application for Membership of the United Nations', *Irish Studies in International Affairs*, 2/2 (1986).

FARRELLY, CIARAN, 'Irish Defence Policy Options', *European Opinion* (Jan. 1977).

FITZGERALD, G., 'The Political Implications of the European Community', *Studies*, 51 (1962).

FOGARTY, C. P., 'European Union: Implications for Ireland', *Administration*, 3/4 (1986).

FOOT, ROSEMARY, 'The European Community's Voting Behaviour at the United Nations General Assembly', *Journal of Common Market Studies*, 17/4 (June 1979).

FORTE, DAVID F. P., 'The Response of Soviet Foreign Policy to the Common Market 1957-63', *Soviet Studies*, 19/3 (1967-8).

FREI, DANIEL, 'Switzerland and the EEC: Facts and Trends', *Journal of Common Market Studies*, 12/3 (1973-4).

GALLAGHER, EAMON, 'Anglo-Irish Relations in the European Community', *Irish Studies in International Affairs*, 2/1 (1985).

GARVIN, TOM, and PARKER, ANTHONY, 'Party Loyalty and Irish Voters: The EEC Referendum as a Case-Study', *Economic and Social Review*, 4/1 (Oct. 1972).

GELDART, CAROL, and LYON, PETER, 'The Group of 77: A Perspective View', *International Affairs*, 57/1 (Winter 1980-1)

GEORGE, STEPHEN A., 'Letter to the Editor: The Sovereignty of Parliament and Community Law', *International Affairs*, 56/1 (Jan. 1980).

GOODWIN, GEOFFREY, 'The External Relations of the European Community: Shadow and Substance', *British Journal of International Studies*, 3/1 (Apr. 1973).

HAKOVIRTA, HARTO, 'Neutral States in East-West Economic Cooperation', *Co-Existence*, 18/2 (Oct. 1981).

—— 'Effects of Non-Alignment on Neutrality in Europe: An Analysis and Appraisal', *Cooperation and Conflict*, 18 (1983).

—— 'The Soviet Union and the Varieties of Neutrality in Western Europe', *World Politics*, 35/4 (July 1983).

HANCOCK, M. DONALD, 'Sweden, Scandinavia and the EEC', *International Affairs*, 48/3 (July 1972).

HOPPER, BRUCE, 'Sweden: A Case Study in Neutrality', *Foreign Affairs*, 23/3 (Apr. 1945).

HURWITZ, LEON, 'The EEC and Decolonization: The Voting Behaviour of the Nine at the U.N. General Assembly', *Political Studies*, 24/4 (Dec. 1976).

INGLIS, BRIAN, 'Should Ireland Join NATO', *NATO Letter*, 8/10 (1960).

JAMES, ALAN, 'Sovereignty: Ground Rule or Gibberish?', *Review of International Studies*, 10/1 (Jan. 1984).

JAY, PETER, 'Public Expenditure and Administration', *Political Quarterly*, 41 (June 1976).

JOESTEN, JOACHIM, 'Phases in Swedish Neutrality', *Foreign Affairs*, 23/2 (Jan. 1945).

JOHANSON, BENGT A. W., 'Sweden and the EEC: An Approach to the Study of the Political Process', *Cooperation and Conflict*, 1/4 (1970).

KEATINGE, PATRICK, 'Odd Man Out? Irish Neutrality and European Security', *International Affairs*, 48/3 (July 1972).

—— 'The Foreign Policy of the Irish Coalition Government', *World Today*, 29/8 (Aug. 1973).

—— 'Ireland's Foreign Relations in 1984', *Irish Studies in International Affairs*, 2/1 (1985).

—— 'Ireland's Foreign Relations in 1985', *Irish Studies in International Affairs*, 2/2 (1986).

—— 'Ireland's Foreign Relations in 1986', *Irish Studies in International Affairs*, 2/3 (1987).

KENNEDY, DENIS, 'The Neutrality Question', *Community Report*, 3/5 (1983).

KREISKY, BRUNO, 'Austria Draws the Balance', *Foreign Affairs*, 37/2 (Jan. 1959).

LINDEMANN, BEATE, 'Europe and the Third World: The Nine at the United Nations', *World Today*, 32/7 (July 1976).

LOW-BEER, FRANCIS, 'The Concept of Neutralism', *American Political Science Review*, 58/2 (June 1964).

LYON, PETER, 'Neutrality and the Emergence of the Concept of Neutralism', *Review of Politics*, 22/2 (Apr. 1960).

MACDONAGH, MICHAEL. 'Ireland's Attitude to External Affairs', *Studies*, 48 (1959).

MACKERNAN, PADRAIC, 'Ireland and European Political Cooperation', *Irish Studies in International Affairs*, 1/4 (1984).

MACQUEEN, NORMAN, 'The Expedience of Tradition: Ireland, International Organization and the Falklands Crisis', *Political Studies*, 33/1 (Mar. 1985)

MACSWEENEY, GERARD M. M., 'Irish Neutrality and International Law', *Irish Law Times* (Aug. 1984).

MCALEESE, DERMOT, and MATTHEWS, ALAN, 'The Single European Act and Ireland: Implications for a Small Member-State', *Journal of Common Market Studies*, 26/1 (1987).

MCCARTHY, COLM, 'EMS and the End of Ireland's Sterling Link', *Lloyds Bank Review*, 136 (Apr. 1980).

MCCARTHY, DENIS J., 'Armour in the War Years', *An Cosantoir* (Mar. 1975).

MCKENNA, Capt. T., 'Thank God We're Surrounded by Water', *An Cosantoir* (Apr. 1973).

MCMAHON, DEIRDRE, 'Ireland, the Dominions and the Munich Crisis', *Irish Studies in International Affairs*, 1/1 (1979).

MCSWEENEY, BILL, 'Dilemmas of Irish Neutrality', *ADIU Report*, 6/5 (Sept.–Oct. 1984).

—— 'Out of the Ghetto: Irish Foreign Policy since the Fifties', *Studies*, 300.

MANSERGH, NICHOLAS, 'Ireland: The Republic outside the Commonwealth', *International Affairs*, 28/3 (July 1952).

MARCUS, J., 'Irish Defence Policy: Debate on Neutrality', *Jane's Defence Weekly*, 2/4 (Aug. 1984).

MATTHEWS, ALAN, 'European Union: The Economic Implications for Ireland', *Irish Studies in International Affairs*, 2/1 (1985).

MITCHELL, J. D. B., 'The Sovereignty of Parliament and Community Law: The Stumbling-Block that isn't there', *International Affairs*, 55/1 (Jan. 1979).

MOBERG, ERIK, 'The "Nordic Balance" Concept: A Critical Commentary', *Cooperation and Conflict*, 2 (1966).

MURRAY, C. H., 'The European Monetary System: Implications for Ireland', *Central Bank of Ireland Annual Review* (1979).

NAYAR, N. P., 'Nonalignment in World Affairs', *India Quarterly* (1962).

NEUHOLD, HANSPETER, 'Permanent Neutrality in Contemporary International Relations: A Comparative Perspective', *Irish Studies in International Affairs*, 1/3 (1982).

O'CONNELL, Col. J. J., 'The Vulnerability of Ireland in War', *Studies* (Mar. 1938).

O'CORCORA, MICHAEL, and HILL, RONALD J., 'The Soviet Union in Irish Foreign Policy', *International Affairs*, 58/2 (Spring 1982).

O'NEILL, HELEN, 'Irish Aid: Performance and Policies', *Development and Peace*, 4 (Spring 1983).

ÖRVIK, KAREN E., 'The Limits of Security: Defence and Foreign Trade in Finland', *Survey*, 24/2 (Spring 1979).

ØRVIK, NILS, 'Defence Against Help: A Strategy for Small States', *Survival* (Sept.–Oct. 1973).

O'SULLIVAN, Comdt. P. O., 'Irish Neutrality and Defence', *An Cosantoir*, 41/3 (Mar. 1981).

PARKER, JAMES, 'UNIFIL and Peace-keeping: The Defence Forces' Experience', *Irish Studies in International Affairs*, 2/2 (1986).

PINDER, JOHN, 'Integration in Western and Eastern Europe: Relations between the EC and CMEA', *Journal of Common Market Studies*, 18/2 (1979).

RAYMOND, RAYMOND J., 'Ireland's 1949 NATO Decision: A Reassessment', *Eire-Ireland* (Autumn 1985).

—— 'Irish Neutrality: Ideology or Pragmatism?', *International Affairs*, 60/1 (Winter 1983/4).

REYNOLDS, P. A., 'International Studies: Retrospect and Prospect', *British Journal of International Studies*, 1/1 (Apr. 1975).

ROTHSTEIN, ROBERT L., 'Foreign Policy and Development Policy: From Nonalignment to International Class War', *International Affairs*, 52/4 (Autumn 1976).

SALMON, TREVOR C., 'The Changing Nature of Irish Defence Policy', *World Today*, 35/11 (Nov. 1979).

—— 'Ireland: A Neutral in the Community?', *Journal of Common Market Studies*, 20/3 (Mar. 1982).

—— 'Ireland and European Security', *ADIU Report*, 7/1 (Jan.–Feb. 1985).

—— 'Irish Neutrality: A Policy in Course of Evolution?', *NATO Review*, 32/1 (Jan. 1984).

—— 'Neutrality and the Irish Republic: Myth or Reality?', *Round Table*, 290 (1984).

SCHEICH, MANFRED, 'The European Neutrals After Enlargement of the Communities: The Austrian Perspective', *Journal of Common Market Studies*, 12/3 (1973–4).

SHARP, P, 'Small State Foreign Policy and International Regimes: The Case of Ireland and the European Monetary System and the Common Fisheries Policy', *Millenium*, 16/1 (1987).

SHAY, THEODORE L., 'Nonalignment Si, Neutralism No', *Review of Politics*, 30/2 (Apr. 1968).

SMYLLIE, R. M., 'Unneutral Neutral Eire', *Foreign Affairs*, 24/2 (Jan. 1946).

STALVANT, CARL-EINAR, 'Neutrality and European Integration: A Comparison of Finland's and Sweden's EEC Policies', *Scandinavian Studies*, 46/4 (Fall 1974).

TEMPLE LANG, JOHN, 'The Proposed Treaty Setting Up the European Union: Constitutional Implications for Ireland and Comments on Neutrality', *Irish Studies in International Affairs*, 2/1 (1985).

—— 'The Irish Court Case which Delayed the Single European Act: Crotty v. an Taoiseach and Others', *Common Market Law Review*, 24/4 (1987).

'VOCHT, SHAN VAN', 'Ireland, Germany and the Next War', *Irish Review*, (July 1913).

WAITE, JAMES L., 'The Swedish Paradox: EEC and Neutrality', *Journal of Common Market Studies*, 12/3 (1973–4).

WALLACE, WILLIAM, 'European Political Cooperation: A New Form of Diplomacy', *Irish Studies in International Affairs*, 1/4 (1984).

WHEELER, MARCUS, 'The Dublin–Moscow Accord', *World Today*, 29/11 (1973).

—— 'Soviet Interest in Ireland', *Survey*, 21/3 (1975).

WHITAKER, T. K., 'Monetary Integration: Reflections on Irish Experience', *Quarterly Bulletin* (Central Bank of Ireland; Winter 1973).

—— 'From Protection to Free Trade: The Irish Experience', *Administration*, 21/4 (Winter 1973).

WISTRICH, E., 'Referenda: The Lessons for Britain', *New Europe*, 3/1 (Winter 1974–5).

INDEX